D1559311

MEDIEVAL THEOLOGY
AND THE
NATURAL BODY

On March 11 1995, a conference on medieval theology and the natural body, organised by the University of York's Centre for Medieval Studies, was held at King's Manor, York, under the title 'This Body of Death' (echoing Romans 7. 24). This collection includes the papers delivered on that occasion, together with further invited papers on the theme. An introductory essay by Peter Biller on medieval and contemporary concerns with the body is followed by Alcuin Blamires's examination of the paradoxes inherent in the metaphor of man as head, woman as body, in authors ranging from St Augustine to Christine de Pizan. Peter Abelard, a writer who 'dislocated' this image, is the principal figure of the next two papers. David Luscombe's study looks successively at Abelard's view of the role of senses in relation to thought and mind, the problem of body in resurrected beings, and dualities in his correspondence with Heloise. W. G. East then takes up the famous correspondence and love affair, focusing on the putting to death of the body in the religious life, the discussion in the correspondence of the Benedictine rule's appropriateness for women, and Abelard's hymns and his own mutilation. Peter Biller uses a sketch of the history of the discussion of women and Catharism as a preliminary to an examination of Cathar views of material women, while Alastair Minnis traces and analyses the tradition of scholastic theological discussion of female sex as an impediment to ordination and teaching. Dyan Elliott examines views of the physiological basis of various forms of rapture, concentrating in particular on later medieval female mystics. One prominent figure in later medieval female spirituality, Margery Kempe, stars in the following paper, Rosalynn Voaden's study of the way *The Book of Margery Kempe* constructed Margery's very sexual awareness of both female and male bodies.

The volume concludes with the first of the *Annual Quodlibet Lectures* in medieval theology, which was delivered in York by Eamon Duffy on 30 November 1995, on the early iconography and *vitae* of St Francis of Assisi.

YORK MEDIEVAL PRESS

York Medieval Press is published by the University of York's Centre for Medieval Studies in association with Boydell and Brewer Ltd. Our objective is the promotion of innovative scholarship and fresh criticism on medieval culture. We have a special commitment to interdisciplinary study, in line with the Centre's belief that the future of Medieval Studies lies in those areas in which its major constituent disciplines at once inform and challenge each other.

All inquiries of an editorial kind, including suggestions for monographs and essay collections, should be addressed to: The Secretary, University of York, Centre for Medieval Studies, The King's Manor, York YO1 2EP (E-mail: LAH1 @york.ac.uk).

Previous publications of the University of York's Centre for Medieval Studies:

Latin and Vernacular: Studies in Late-Medieval Texts and Manuscripts, ed. A. J. Minnis [Proceedings of the 1987 York Manuscripts Conference]

Regionalism in Late-Medieval Manuscripts and Texts: Essays celebrating the publication of 'A Linguistic Atlas of Late Mediaeval English', ed. Felicity Riddy [Proceedings of the 1989 York Manuscripts Conference]

Late-Medieval Religious Texts and their Transmission: Essays in Honour of A.I. Doyle, ed. A. J. Minnis [Proceedings of the 1991 York Manuscripts Conference]

York Studies in Medieval Theology I

MEDIEVAL THEOLOGY
AND THE
NATURAL BODY

Edited by
PETER BILLER and A. J. MINNIS

THE UNIVERSITY *of York*

YORK MEDIEVAL PRESS

First published 1997

A York Medieval Press publication
in association with The Boydell Press
an imprint of Boydell & Brewer Ltd
PO Box 9 Woodbridge Suffolk IP12 3DF UK
and of Boydell & Brewer Inc.
PO Box 41026 Rochester NY 14604–4126 USA
and with the
Centre for Medieval Studies, University of York

ISBN 0 9529734 0 5

ISSN 1366–9656

A catalogue record for this book is available
from the British Library

Library of Congress Cataloging-in-Publication Data
Medieval theology and the natural body / edited by Peter Biller and
A. J. Minnis.
    p. cm. – (York studies in medieval theology : 1)
  Papers delivered at a conference on medieval theology and the
natural body, organized by the University of York's Centre for
Medieval Studies, and held at Kings' Manor, York, under the title
'This Body of Death,' along with other invited papers on the same
theme.
  Includes bibliographical references and index.
  ISBN 0–9529734–0–5 (hardback : alk. paper)
  1. Body, Human – Religious aspects – Christianity – History of
doctrines – Middle Ages, 600–1500 – Congresses. I. Biller, Peter.
II. Minnis, A. J. (Alastair J.) III. Series.
BT741.2.M43 1997
233'.5 – dc21   97–1032

This book is printed on acid-free paper

Printed in Great Britain by
St Edmundsbury Press Ltd, Bury St Edmunds, Suffolk

CONTENTS

LIST OF PLATES

Plate 1: Bonaventure Berlinghieri, *St Francis and Six Miracles* (1234); Church of San Francesco, Pescia

Plate 2: Anonymous, *St Francis with Four Post-Mortem Miracles* (*c.*1260); Assisi, Museo del Tesoro del Sacro Convento

Plate 3: Anonymous, *St Francis with Twenty Scenes from his Life and Miracles* (post 1263); Capella Bardi, Santa Croce, Florence

ABBREVIATIONS

AA SS	*Acta Sanctorum*, ed. J. Bollandus (Antwerp, 1643–)
Abelard	
'Letter of Consolation'	J. T. Muckle, ed., 'Abelard's Letter of Consolation to a Friend (*Historia Calamitatum*)', *MS* 12 (1950), 163–213
'Letter of Heloise'	J. T. Muckle, ed., 'The Letter of Heloise on Religious Life and Abelard's First Reply', *MS* 17 (1955), 240–81
'Personal Letters'	J. T. Muckle, ed., 'The Personal Letters Between Abelard and Heloise: Introduction, Authenticity and Text', *MS* 15 (1953), 47–94
Radice, *Letters*	*The Letters of Abelard and Heloise*, trans. B. Radice (Harmondsworth, 1974)
'Rule'	T. P. McLaughlin, ed., 'Abelard's Rule for Religious Women', *MS* 18 (1956), 241–92
AESC	*Annales. Économies. Sociétés. Civilisations* (Paris, 1929–)
AF	*Analecta Franciscana, sive Chronica aliaque varia documenta ad historiam Fratrum minorum spectantia* (Quaracchi, 1885–)
AFP	*Archivum Fratrum Praedicatorum* (Rome, 1931–)
AHDLMA	*Archives d'histoire littéraire et doctrinale du moyen âge* (Paris, 1926–)
Biller and Hudson, *Heresy and Literacy*	*Heresy and Literacy in the Middle Ages, 1000–1530*, ed. P. Biller and A. Hudson (Cambridge, 1994, reprinted with corrections 1996)
Blamires, 'Women and Preaching'	A. Blamires, 'Women and Preaching in Medieval Orthodoxy, Heresy, and Saints' Lives', *Viator* 26 (1995), 135–52.
Blamires, *Woman Defamed*	A. Blamires, ed., *Woman defamed and woman defended: an anthology of medieval texts* (Oxford, 1992)
BMK	*The Book of Margery Kempe*, ed. S. B. Meech and H. E. Allen, EETS OS 212 (London, 1939)
Bonaventure, *Opera*	Bonaventure, *Opera omnia*, 11 vols. (Quaracchi, 1882–1902)

Brown, *Body and Society*	P. Brown, *The Body and Society. Men, Women and Sexual Renunciation in Early Christianity* (New York, 1988)
Bynum *Fragmentation*	C. W. Bynum, *Fragmentation and Redemption: Essays on Gender and the Human Body in Medieval Religion* (New York, 1991)
Holy Feast	C. W. Bynum, *Holy Feast and Holy Fast: The Religious Significance of Food to Medieval Women* (Berkeley and Los Angeles, 1987)
Resurrection	C. W. Bynum, *The Resurrection of the Body in Western Christianity, 200–1336* (New York, 1991)
Cadden, *Meanings of Sex Difference*	J. Cadden, *The Meanings of Sex Difference in the Middle Ages: Medicine, Science and Culture* (Cambridge, 1993)
CaF	*Cahiers de Fanjeaux* (Toulouse, 1966–)
CCCM	*Corpus Christianorum*, Continuatio Medievalis (Turnhout, 1966–)
CSEL	*Corpus scriptorum ecclesiasticorum Latinorum* (Vienna, 1866–)
Douay	Douay-Rheims translation, *The Holy Bible Translated from the Latin Vulgate* (1582–1609, revised edn, Belfast, 1852)
Dunbabin, *Hound of God*	J. Dunbabin, *A Hound of God. Pierre de la Palud and the Fourteenth-Century Church* (Oxford, 1991)
DR	*Downside Review: A Quarterly on Catholic Thought and of Monastic History* (Bath, London, 1880–)
DSP	*Dictionnaire de spiritualité, ascétique et mystique*, ed. M. Villier, 16 vols. (Paris, 1937–94)
EETS	Early English Text Society (London, 1864–)
Elliott, *Spiritual Marriage*	D. Elliott, *Spiritual Marriage: Sexual Abstinence in Medieval Wedlock* (Princeton 1993)
Framing Medieval Bodies	*Framing Medieval Bodies*, ed. S. Kay and M. Rubin (Manchester, New York, 1994)
Friedberg	*Corpus iuris canonici*, ed. E. Friedberg, 2 vols. (Leipzig, 1879)
FS	*Franciscan Studies* (New York, 1924–)
Jacquart and Thomasset	D. Jacquart and C. Thomasset, *Sexuality and Medicine in the Middle Ages*, trans. M. Adamson (Cambridge, 1988)

JMRS	*Journal of Medieval and Renaissance Studies* (1971–)
Lewis and Short	C. T. Lewis and C. Short, *A Latin Dictionary* (Oxford, 1879)
Lochrie, *Margery Kempe*	K. Lochrie, *Margery Kempe and Translations of the Flesh* (Philadephia, 1991)
Lomperis and Stanbury, *Feminist Approaches*	*Feminist Approaches to the Body in Medieval Literature*, ed. L. Lomperis and S. Stanbury (Philadelphia, 1993)
Martin, 'Ordination of Women'	J. H. Martin, 'The Ordination of Women and Theologians in the Middle Ages', *Escritos del Vedat* 16 (1986), 115–77
Minnis, '*Accessus* in Henry of Ghent'	A. J. Minnis, 'The *Accessus* Extended: Henry of Ghent on the Transmission and Reception of Theology', *Ad litteram: Authoritative Texts and their Medieval Readers*, ed. M. D. Jordan and K. Emery, Jr (Notre Dame, 1992)
Margery Kempe:	see *BMK*
MS	*Mediaeval Studies* (Toronto, 1939–)
Newman, *Virile Woman*	B. Newman, *From Virile Woman to Woman Christ: Studies in Medieval Religion and Literature* (Philadelphia, 1995)
Petroff, *Body and Soul*	E. A. Petroff, *Body and Soul: Essays on Medieval Women and Mysticism* (New York and Oxford, 1994)
PG	*Patrologia Graeca*, ed. J. P. Migne, 161 vols. (Paris, 1857–66)
PL	*Patrologia Latina*, ed. J. P. Migne, 217 + 4 index vols. (Paris, 1841–61)
OMT	Oxford Medieval Texts (Oxford, 1971–)
Radice, *Letters*:	see Abelard above
SCH	*Studies in Church History* (London and Oxford, 1964–)
Schriften der MGH	*Schriften der Monumenta Germaniae historica* (Stuttgart, 1938–)
Southern, *Medieval Humanism*	R. W. Southern, *Medieval Humanism and Other Studies* (Oxford, 1970)
SOPMA	T. Kaeppeli and E. Panella, *Scriptores Ordinis Praedicatorum medii aevi*, 4 vols. (Rome, 1970–93)
ST	Thomas Aquinas, *Summa theologiae*, Blackfriars edn, 61 vols. (London, New York, 1964–81)

Thomas of Chobham, *Summa confessorum*	Thomas of Chobham, *Summa confessorum*, ed. F. Broomfield, Analecta Medievalia Namurcensia 25 (Louvain and Paris, 1968)
Vincent, *Speculum naturale*	Vincent of Beauvais, *Speculum naturale*, in *Speculum quadruplex, sive Speculum Maius*, 4 vols. (Douai, 1624), I
Wack, *Lovesickness*	M. F. Wack, *Lovesickness in the Middle Ages: the 'Viaticum' and its Commentaries* (Philadelphia, 1990)

Medieval Theology and
the Natural Body

John of Naples, Quodlibets and Medieval Theological Concern with the Body

Peter Biller

This volume prints papers delivered at a conference held by the University of York's Centre for Medieval Studies at King's Manor, York, on 11 March 1995, under the title 'This Body of Death' (echoing Romans 7. 24), together with further invited papers on this theme, written by Alcuin Blamires, W. G. East and Dyan Elliott. It concludes with the first of the *Annual Quodlibet Lectures* in medieval theology, which was delivered by Eamon Duffy on November 30 1995.[1]

The title of the annual lecture derives from the *quaestiones quodlibetales* (quodlibetal questions) of medieval theology faculties, as does also the spirit of the *York Studies in Medieval Theology* series, which is inaugurated with this volume. Quodlibetal questions, further, provide a proud precedent for a miscellany – a miscellany which in this volume focuses on medieval theology and the body. In its classic form, a quodlibet was one of a series of questions raised during Advent or Lent.[2] A question was initiated during one session and responded to at another, perhaps several days later. It was oral. Like a disputed question it had four parts: a formally raised question, arguments both pro and con, a central determining response, and finally replies to particular objections. Unlike a *quaestio disputata* (disputed question) it was *de quolibet*, about any theme, and raised *a quolibet*, by anyone in the audience: medieval theologians' 'Question-time'. After emerging in the Paris theology faculty by about 1230, the quodlibet achieved its classic form by the 1250s and 1260s, flourished till the 1320s, and declined sharply about 1330. It spread elsewhere, for example to the Oxford theology faculty by about 1280, and also to other

---

[1] The second Annual Quodlibet Lecture, 'From the Ordeal to Confession: In Search of Lay Religion in Early Thirteenth-Century France', was delivered by J. W. Baldwin on June 5 1996, and will be published in the second volume in the *York Studies in Medieval Theology* series, *Handling Sin. Confession in the Middle Ages*, ed. P. Biller and A. J. Minnis.

[2] The up-to-date survey is J. F. Wippel, 'Quodlibetal Questions, Chiefly in Theological Faculties', in *Les questions disputées et les questions quodlibétiques dans les facultés de théologie, de droit et de médecine*, ed. B. C. Bazan, G. Fransen, D. Jacquart, and J. W. Wippel, Typologie des sources du moyen âge occidental 44–5 (Turnhout, 1985), pp. 153–222.

faculties. Quodlibets represent the mature rather than the early thought of masters,[3] and the form could accommodate responses to the moment, the most obvious examples of which are quodlibetic questions generated in 1291 and 1294 by the fall of Acre and Pope Celestine's resignation respectively, and the Cistercian Jacques de Thérines' quodlibet in 1306, the year of Philip the Fair's expulsion of Jews, on the licitness of expelling Jews who have already been expelled from another region.[4] These two features, then, provide the particular interest of quodlibets, whose very miscellaneousness makes them such good mirrors of the current preoccupations of a theologian and his audience.

The fundamental study of quodlibets, by Palémon Glorieux, listed authors of quodlibets, titles and (where possible) dates of the questions, and manuscripts and editions.[5] Let us pick out one of his authors, the Dominican John of Naples. John was a student in the convent of St Dominic in Bologna (1298–1300), taught in the Dominican *studium* at Naples and then at Paris, where he was a regent master in theology (1315–17), and then he was back again in Naples as regent master from 1317 onwards. Papal chaplain in 1347, he is assumed to have died around 1350. There is a reference to a no-longer extant commentary on Peter Lombard's *Libri Sententiarum*, and to *Quaestiones variae*, quodlibetic questions, and sermons.[6] Surviving manuscripts described by Glorieux preserve thirteen sets of quodlibetic questions, containing altogether 299 questions to which John responded at various stages in his career after he had become a master – the dates are not clear, though some were responded to in Paris and must, therefore, belong to 1315–17. Let us look, then, at the interest in the body displayed in the quodlibetic questions of one theologian who was active in the first half of the fourteenth century.

Christ's body was the subject of many. Representative is one dealing with his humanity: 'Whether Christ is called man only on account of the union between them of body and sou''[7] The blood shed from his body attracted attention, 'Whether the whole of Christ's blood shed in his passion was in him after [his] resurrection', and 'Whether in the three days [after] Christ's death his blood could have been consecrated in such a way that it warranted the display of adoration by worship',[8] as did also the physical capacity of his resurrected body in the question 'Whether in Christ after [his] resurrection

---

3   Wippel, 'Quodlibetal Questions', p. 221.
4   Wippel, 'Quodlibetal Questions', p. 193.
5   P. Glorieux, *La littérature quodlibétique*, 2 vols. (Paris, 1925 and 1935).
6   On John see Glorieux, II, 159 (later references to Glorieux are all to this second volume), and *SOPMA* II, 495–8.
7   Qu. xiii.20: 'Utrum Christus dicatur homo propter solam unionem animae et corporis inter se'.
8   Qu. xiii.5–6, Glorieux, pp. 171–2: 'Utrum totus sanguis Christi effusus in passione fuerit in eo post resurrectionem'; 'Utrum in triduo mortis Christi potuerit sanguis ejus consecrari sic quod tali sanguini esset adoratio latriae exhibendae'.

there was the power to convert food'.[9] As one would expect, Christ's body in the consecrated host attracted most attention, theological and also biological, with questions such as 'Whether the consecrated host can be so divided or ground up that it ceases to be the body of Christ', and 'Whether a consecrated host, [when] eaten, can nourish'.[10]

Human bodies on this earth attracted a great deal of attention, beginning with the formation of the embryo and concluding with their natural death, and questions were raised about them from the point of view of natural philosophy and medicine. There is the issue of gender and the embryo: 'Whether a male is more quickly formed in the womb than a woman'.[11] There is concern with the elements, with complexional make-up, and with the radical humidity that was essential to the body's life – 'Whether [the elements of] earth and water abound more in the body of man than air and fire',[12] 'Whether a man can naturally be changed from one complexion to another',[13] 'Whether the operation of a member of the human body is from the soul or the complexion of the member',[14] and 'Whether radical humidity can be restored'.[15] There are also questions on sensation ('Whether the sense of touch is one sense'), the body and food ('Whether food is converted into the strength of the [one who is] fed, and specially [into the strength] of man'), the body's local presence ('Whether God can make the same body be locally in different locations'), and, finally, the body's death ('Whether any death is natural').[16]

---

[9] Qu. i.16, Glorieux, p. 160: 'Utrum in Christo post resurrectionem fuerit virtus conversiva alimenti'.

[10] Qu. xi.10, Glorieux, p. 170: 'Utrum hostia consecrata possit dividi seu teri quod desinat esse corpus Christi'; Qu. x.16, Glorieux, p. 169: 'Utrum hostia consecrata comesta possit nutrire'.

[11] Qu. x.13, Glorieux, p. 169: 'Utrum masculus citius formetur in utero quam mulier'. Compare the question raised by the Italian physician and medical professor, Mondino de' Liuzzi, 'Utrum masculus citius informetur in utero quam femella', N. Siraisi, *Taddeo Alderotti and His Pupils. Two Generations of Italian Medical Learning* (Princeton, NJ, 1981), p. 338. On Mondino (*c.*1270–1326), see the introduction to Mondino de' Liuzzi, *Expositio super capitulum de generatione embrionis Canonis Avicenna cum quibusdam quaestionibus*, ed. R. M. Vico, Istituto Storico Italiano per il Medio Evo, Fonti per la Storia d'Italia 118 (Rome, 1993), pp. x–xiii.

[12] Qu. xii.9, Glorieux, p. 171: 'Utrum in corpore hominis magis habundet terra et aqua quam aer et ignis'.

[13] Qu. ix.16, Glorieux, p. 168: 'Utrum homo possit naturaliter mutari de una complexione ad alia'. Compare early fourteenth-century Italian doctors' questions in Siraisi, *Taddeo Alderotti*, p. 321: 'Utrum complexio innata possit permutari' and 'Utrum complexio naturalis possit permutari' ('whether innate *or* natural complexion can be changed'); there is another example on p. 324.

[14] Qu. xii.10, Glorieux, p. 171: 'Utrum operatio membri corporis humani sit ab anima vel a membri complexione'.

[15] Qu. v.10, Glorieux, p. 163: 'Utrum humidum radicale possit restaurari'. See M. McVaugh, 'The "humidum radicale" in Thirteenth-Century Medicine', *Traditio* 30 (1974), 259–83.

[16] Qu. i.10, Glorieux, p. 160: 'Utrum sensus tactus sit unus sensus' – compare the

Questions deal with virgin bodies and married bodies. Virginity's accept-
ability to God is compared to marriage, its virtue raised as a question, and
vows of continence and fasting on bread and water are discussed.[17] Married
bodies appear mainly in relation to tricky problems arising from the canon
law of marriage, for example 'Whether a serf married with [his] Lord's licence
is bound at the same time rather to obey his Lord [when his Lord] is ordering
[him to do something] than to satisfy his wife [when she] is seeking [the
payment of the marriage] debt', and 'Whether there is marriage between a
boy and a seven-year old girl betrothed to him and [then] carnally known by
him'.[18] Bodies in marriages and family are also present in moral-theological
questions of the sort which might interest those in John's audience who were
trainee confessors, 'Whether a wife is bound to reveal that a child born by her
[was born] illegitimately', 'Whether it is licit for parents to beat their children',
and a question which may perhaps have interested more pastors dealing with
the codes of men living near Naples rather than Paris, 'Whether one who kills
a daughter killed in adultery, and the adulterous man, is punished by God, or
[whether] he sins'.[19]

Physical medicine of the body is as strongly present as its moral medicine.
There is a question comparing the spiritual profitability of the study of
medicine to law,[20] but principally the questions are deontological, that is to
say, medical-ethical. In what follows *medicus* (medical doctor or physician) is
left untranslated to preserve medieval vocabulary's nuances in choosing
medicus or *physicus*. 'Whether a man should have phlebotomy [blood-letting]
by an astrologer-*medicus*, when the judgement by astrology is that if he is

---

medical question in Siraisi, *Taddeo Alderotti*, p. 336, 'utrum sensus tactus sit plures
sensus' ('whether the sense of touch is several senses'); Qu. ii.13, Glorieux, p. 161:
'Utrum alimentum convertatur in virtutem nutriti viventis et specialiter hominis';
Qu. v.1, Glorieux, p. 163: 'Utrum Deus possit facere idem corpus esse localiter in
diversis locis'; Qu. iv.7, Glorieux, p. 7: 'Utrum mors aliqua sit naturalis'.

17 Qu. viii.37, xiii.13, xii.13 and xi.16, Glorieux, pp. 167, 172, 171 and 170.

18 Qu. v.17 and xi.11, Glorieux, pp. 163 and 170: 'Utrum servus uxoratus de licentia
Domini pro eodem tempore teneatur plus obedire domino praecipienti quam satis-
facere uxori debitum petenti, vel e contrario'; 'Utrum sit matrimonium inter
puerum et puellam septennem ei desponsatam et ab eo carnaliter cognitam'. See
other canon-legal cases in Qu. iii.20, viii.28, ix.21, x.22, 23, xi.11 and xiii.19, Glorieux,
pp. 162, 167, 168, 169, 170, 172.

19 Qu. x.28, x.21 and ii.19, Glorieux, pp. 170, 169 and 161: 'Utrum mulier teneatur
revelare viro filium ex se illegitime natum'; 'Utrum parentibus liceat verberare
filios'; 'Utrum puniatur a Deo seu peccet ille qui occidit filiam in adulterio depre-
hensam et adulterum [*perhaps mistake for* adulteram]'. See L. E. Boyle, 'The Quodlibets of St Thomas and Pastoral Care', *The Thomist* 38 (1974), 232–56, for comment
on the pastoral content of quodlibets. For comment on contrasts between attitudes
to adultery between north-western Europe and Italy, see P. Biller, 'Marriage Patterns
and Women's Lives: A Sketch of a Pastoral Geography', in *Woman is a Worthy Wight.
Women in English Society c.1200–1500*, ed. P. J. P. Goldberg (Gloucester, 1992), pp.
60–107 (pp. 84–5).

20 Qu. viii.38, Glorieux, p. 167.

phlebotomised he dies and [the judgement] by medicine is that if he is not phlebotomised he dies'; 'Whether a *medicus* ought to help an ill man of [the Christian] faith sooner than an infidel'; 'Whether a *medicus* ought to give to a pregnant woman medicine from which would follow the death of [her] child, and if he did not give it the death of both would follow'; 'Whether a *medicus* who foresees the death of an ill man in his care ought to reveal it to him'.[21]

Finally, considerable attention was paid to the qualities of the bodies of the resurrected. John turned twice to consider their impassibility, incapacity to suffer ('Whether the impassibility of the glorified body is through some immanent quality or only through the help of divine strength', and 'Whether impassibility comes to glorified bodies through some form inhering in them or only through divine strength aiding them, impeding the action of any harmful agent'),[22] and twice to their *claritas*, that is to say, their splendour or beauty: one of the questions was 'Whether glorified bodies have splendour'.[23] Agility was questioned ('Whether the agility of the glorified body is only through the lack of weight'), and finally the problem arising when one body has consumed part of another: 'Whether the matter of [a man who has been] fed from human flesh resurrects under the soul of [the man who as been] fed or under the soul of the man whose flesh it was'.[24]

I have picked John out of Glorieux's lists, and fanned out these questions

---

21 Qu. viii.31–2, x.27 and xi.14, Glorieux, pp. 167 and 170 : 'Utrum sit flebotomandus a medico astrologo ille de quo judicatur per astrologiam quod si flebotomatur moritur, et per medicinam quod si non flebotomatur moritur'; 'Utrum medicus debeat citius subvenire infirmo fideli quam infideli'; 'Utrum medicus debeat dare medicinam mulieri praegnanti ex qua sequeretur mors filii, et si non daret eam sequeretur mors utriusque'; 'Utrum medicus praecognoscens mortem infirmi cujus habet curam, debeat eam sibi revelare'. On phlebotomy, see P. Gil-Sotres, 'La flebotomia en la terapeutica medieval', in Arnau de Vilanova, *Opera medica omnia* (Barcelona, 1975–), IV, 9–47. On medical astrology in early fourteenth-century Aragon, see M. R. McVaugh, *Medicine Before the Plague. Practitioners and Their Patients in the Crown of Aragon 1285–1345* (Cambridge, 1993), pp. 164–5, and in early fourteenth-century Italy (a closer context for John) Siraisi, *Taddeo Alderotti*, pp. 139–45 (see p. 143 and note 62 on astrology and phlebotomy). On medieval medical ethics in general, see the three medieval articles in *Doctors and Ethics: the earlier historical setting of professional ethics*, ed. A. Wear *et al.* (Amsterdam, 1993), pp. 10–97, and on abortion see discussion below and notes 28 and 31.

22 Qu. viii.22 and xiii.22, Glorieux, pp. 166 and 172: 'Utrum impassibilitas corporis glorificati sit per aliquam qualitatem immanentem vel per solam divinam virtutem assistentem'; 'Utrum impassibilitas conveniat corporibus gloriosis per aliquam formam eis inhaerentem vel per solam virtutem divinam eis assistentem, impedientem actionem cuiuscumque agentis nocivi'. On all these topics see Bynum, *Resurrection*, and in particular on *impassibilitas*, *agilitas* and *claritas* see the discussions referred to under the index-entry '*dotes*' on p. 349.

23 Qu. viii.24, Glorieux, p. 166: 'Utrum corpora glorificata habeant claritatem'; xiii.21, Glorieux, p. 172, is on the same topic.

24 Qu. viii.23 and ix.15, Glorieux, pp. 166 and 168: 'Utrum agilitas corporis glorificati sit sola carentia gravitas'; 'Utrum materia nutriti de carnibus humanis resurgat sub anima hominis nutriti vel sub anima illius cuius tales carnes fuerint'. There is

like a deck of cards, as samples for the reader to look at and consider, under
several guises. Firstly, we can look at these as the raw material for a study, *The
Body in the Quodlibeta of John of Naples*. The texts are clearly there, as are also
the researcher's obvious first moves: the ordering of microfilms of the principally unprinted questions, and listing questions and headings for research
into John's intellectual context. These questions could begin with, 'Who were
John's fellow-Dominicans in Paris, at St Jacques at the same time?' One important figure was Peter of la Palud, a fellow-bachelor in 1313 and collaborating
with John in a commission of enquiry into Durandus of St Pourçain's commentary on the *Sentences*.[25] The researcher is immediately plunged into the
thicket of the important names of the period (Peter and Durandus figure in
Alastair Minnis's study of *Sentences* commentaries in chapter 6 below). There
is the tangle of the relations between these figures, and a question to be asked
about the significance in John's life and writings of his acquaintance with
Peter of la Palud. Another early area of investigation would be John's *other*
questions, his *Quaestiones disputatae*, which were, fortunately for the researcher, printed in the seventeenth century by Neapolitan Dominicans who
proudly preserved John's name and some of his manuscripts. A preliminary
look at its forty-two questions shows *corpus* in the titles of only two, in only
one of which *body* is clearly one of the central themes ('Whether the soul is
whole in the whole body, and whole in each of its parts'), and in general an
apparently much narrower range of interest in the body.[26] 'Why the contrast?'
could be logged as a research question, as the enquiry moves to other lines.
The strong pastoral element in John's quodlibetic questions suggests comparison with the strong pastoral interests of Peter of La Palud. Just as much of the
pastoral theology in Peter of la Palud's commentary was eagerly followed and
copied by St Antoninus, archbishop of Florence, in the mid-fifteenth century,[27]
so also was John's famous quodlibet on the ethics of abortion.[28] A series of
more defined contexts then suggest themselves for further investigation.
These are the parallels and possible connections between Peter and John, and
the combination of sharply concrete pastoral-theological as well as abstract
theological questions at St Jacques in Paris in the early fourteenth century.
There are the interests of both men in medicine, borders between theology

comment on weightlessness in the passages in Bynum's *Resurrection* on *dotes*; see the
index-entry in the same monograph, p. 348,'cannibalism'.

[25] Dunbabin, *Hound of God*, pp. 38–9; see further on John, pp. 29, 83–5 and 182.

[26] John of Naples, *Quaestiones variae Parisiis disputatae* xxviii, ed. D. Gravina (Naples,
1618), pp. 237–46: 'Utrum anima sit tota in toto corpore, et tota in qualibet eius
parte'. Qu. xxii, 'utrum Deus sit in omnibus rebus' ('whether God is in all things'),
contains some discussion of the relation between the existence of a body and the
necessity that it be spatially located, pp. 194 and 196.

[27] Dunbabin, *Hound of God*, pp. 43 and 195.

[28] St Antoninus of Florence, *Theologia moralis* iii, ed. P. Ballerini, 4 vols. (Verona, 1740),
III, 283. The work was written between 1440 and 1454.

and medicine, and the 'medicalisation' of areas of action and thought which has been suggested as a feature of the early fourteenth century.[29] And there is, perhaps, a particular Italian context for John, where commentary on Avicenna's *Liber canonis medicinae* was advancing noticeably in these years, and Avicenna's recommendation of therapeutic abortion[30] was generating ethical discussion of the issue, perhaps beginning with Dino del Garbo in Bologna.[31]

Let us leave this vignette of the opening-up of research, which, as it develops, *particularises* John ever more and more, and think again about the fanned out cards. This time, however, let us think about them as *generally representative* of the theology of the period. There is intense interest in the body in John's questions, in the body seen from many angles, and this is what we would expect from an academic theologian of his time. There is the body in such fundamental theological themes as the incarnation, the Eucharist and the resurrection. There is attention to the constitution of the body as it had been presented to theologians in natural philosophy, in Aristotle's *De animalibus* treatises (and Avicenna's epitome of these, his *De animalibus*), in Aristotle's *parva naturalia*, and in the principal works of learned medicine that had been translated from arabic, in the first place Avicenna's *Liber canonis medicinae*. There is the spiritual status of the virgin body, and also the moral theology and canon law of the married body. In varying proportions we would find these in many theologians of the later thirteenth and early fourteenth centuries.

Let us then look again, but this time at these cards as they appear in modern scholarship. If the importance and variety of the body in academic theology in John's time is the point that his quodlibets have exemplified strikingly so far, the next obvious point concerns today. It is the wealth and variety of the attention which is now being paid in modern scholarship and debate to the themes in John's questions. Here are just a few examples of it: a monograph on Corpus Christi;[32] a monograph soon to appear on the relics of

---

29 This is the term and theme of chapter seven in McVaugh's *Medicine Before the Plague*. The claim deserves special attention, therefore, coming as the conclusion to the fullest picture which has ever been given of the presence of medicine in any medieval kingdom.

30 Avicenna, *Liber canonis medicinae*, lib. III, fen 21, tract. 2, cap. 12 (Venice, 1527), fol. 291va.

31 The question by the physician and medical professor Gentile da Foligno (d. 1348), 'an sit licitum provocare aborsum' ('whether it is licit to provoke abortion') was edited by R. J. Schaefer in his 'Gentile da Foligno über die Zulässigkeit des artifiziellen Abortes (ca. 1340)', *Archiv für die Geschichte der Naturwissenschaften und der Technik* 6 (1913), 321–8 (pp. 325–6). It begins by referring to a response by Dino del Garbo (d. 1327) to the same question; on Dino, see Siraisi, *Taddeo Alderotti*, pp. 55–64, and see also in the same work, pp. 282–3 (and note 61) and 336 further evidence of early fourteenth-century Italian doctors' discussion of abortion.

32 M. Rubin, *Corpus Christi: the Eucharist in Late Medieval Culture* (Cambridge, 1991).

monograph on Corpus Christi;[32] a monograph soon to appear on the relics of
Christ's blood; [33] several monographs in which ideas about the formation of
the embryo and the origin of sex difference constitute the principal or major
issue; [34] monographs on sexual abstinence,[35] ascetic renunciation of the body,
body in female spirituality and the physical nature of the resurrected body; [36]
work on the borders of medical and theological discourses, and preachers'
use, around 1300, of medicine and the body.[37] To this selection we should add
work on a theme which interested John's contemporaries, but perhaps not
John in particular, the female body in relation to the questions of preaching
and ministry.[38]

This work has not only been coming thick and fast, but it is also attracting
comment as a phenomenon itself, in particular in Sarah Kay's and Miri Rubin's introduction to the collection of essays entitled *Framing Medieval Bodies*[39]
and in Caroline Walker Bynum's 'Why All the Fuss about the Body? A Medi-
evalist's Perspective'.[40] Given the existence of these searching discussions, all
that is needed in this introduction is an acknowledgement of this volume's
indebtedness, through a recapitulation of three large sources of modern concern with medieval theology and the natural body. First, the spin-off in medieval studies from modern feminism included stimulus to study medieval
notions of the female body and, more recently, under the banner of gender, the
medieval construction of both female and male. Secondly, the great expansion
in the study of medieval medicine over the same period has applied a steady
pressure.[41] This introduction's footnotes have already supplied the names of
several of its important figures, Nancy Siraisi, Danielle Jacquart, Joan Cadden
and Michael McVaugh, to which must be added that of Monica Green. Exemplified in Green's fundamental and brilliant work on medieval women's
medicine and women's bodies is a seamless integration of a modern critical

---

[33] The relics of Christ's blood are the subject of N. Vincent's *Henry III and the Holy
       Blood: The Blood Relics of Westminster and Hales* (Cambridge, forthcoming).
[34] M.A. Hewson, *Giles of Rome and the Medieval Theory of Conception. A Study of the 'De
       formatione corporis humani in utero'* (London, 1975); Jacquart and Thomasset; Cadden,
       Meanings of Sex Difference.
[35] Elliott, *Spiritual Marriage.*
[36] Bynum, *Holy Feast* and *Resurrection.*
[37] J. Ziegler, 'Medical Similes in Religious Discourse. The Case of Giovanni di San
       Gimignano OP (ca. 1260-ca. 1333)', *Science in Context* 8 (1995), 103–31.
[38] Relevant studies from contributors to this volume include Blamires's *Woman De-
       famed* and 'Women and Preaching', and Minnis's '*Accessus* in Henry of Ghent'.
[39] *Framing Medieval Bodies*, 'Introduction', pp. 1–9.
[40] *Critical Inquiry* 22 (1995), 1–33. Comment not confined to study of the medieval
       period will be found in M. Jenner and B. Taithe, 'The Historiographical Body', in the
       forthcoming second volume of *Medicine in the Twentieth Century*, ed. J. V. Pickstone
       and R. Cooter.
[41] The state of the subject is best seen in *Histoire de la pensée médicale en occident. 1.
       Antiquité et Moyen Age*, ed. M. D. Grmek (Paris, 1995), and its longer historiography
       is sketched by Grmek in the 'Introduction', pp. 7–24.

scholarship on medieval medicine.[42] Thirdly, and bearing more directly on our theme, there are the works of two other great scholars. Peter Brown's *The Body and Society. Men, Women and Sexual Renunciation in Early Christianity* has inspired, stimulated and influenced, as have also Caroline Walker Bynum's studies of gender in mysticism, the role of food in female aseticism, resurrected bodies, and the usefulness for the study of such themes of the ideas of cultural anthropologists.[43] It is Brown and Bynum who have put medieval theology and the body on the map.

Medieval Theology and the Natural Body's contribution begins with Alcuin Blamires's examination of the paradoxes inherent in the metaphor of man as head, woman as body, in authors ranging from St Augustine to Christine de Pizan, who upturned the metaphor with her view of Mary as *head* of the female sex. Peter Abelard, who appears as a writer who 'dislocated' this image, is the principal figure of the next two papers. David Luscombe's punningly titled 'Carnal Thoughts' looks successively at Abelard's view of the role of senses in relation to thought and mind, the problem of body in resurrected beings, and dualities in the correspondence with Heloise – dualities of soul/body, and moral or thought world/physical world. W. G. East then takes up the famous correspondence and love affair, focusing on the putting to death of the body in the religious life, the discussion in the correspondence of the Benedictine rule's appropriateness for women, and Abelard's hymns and his own mutilation. Peter Biller uses a sketch of the history of the discussion of women and Catharism as a preliminary to an examination of Cathar views of material women, while Alastair Minnis traces and analyses the tradition of scholastic theological discussion of female sex as an impediment to ordination and teaching. Dyan Elliott examines views of the physiological basis of various forms of rapture, concentrating in particular on later medieval female mystics. One prominent figure in later medieval female spirituality, Margery Kempe, stars in the concluding paper of the strictly *Body* part of the volume, in Rosalynn Voaden's study of the way *The Book of Margery Kempe* constructed Margery's very sexual awareness of both female and male bodies.

Sex, gender and body in women's spirituality are prominent here, as they

---

[42] Forthcoming are two major works, the monograph *Women and Literate Medicine in Medieval Europe: Trota and the 'Trotula'*, and the translation *'The Diseases of Women According to Trotula': A Medieval Compendium of Women's Medicine*. There is a summary of Green's arguments about Trota in M. H. Green and M. Schleissner, 'Trotula (Trota), "Trotula"', *Die deutsche Literatur des Mittelalters: Verfasserlexikon*, ed. K. Ruh (Berlin and New York, 1978–), IX (1996), 1083–8. A recent example of her social history is 'Documenting medieval women's medical practice', in *Practical Medicine from Salerno to the Black Death*, ed. L. Garcia-Ballester *et al.* (Cambridge, 1994), 322–52, and of her research in medical texts 'The re-creation of *Pantegni, Practica*, book VIII', in *Constantine the African and 'ALĪ IBN AL-'ABBĀS AL-MAǦŪSĪ. The Pantegni and Related Texts*, ed. C. Burnett and D. Jacquart, Studies in Ancient Medicine 10 (Leiden, New York and Cologne, 1994), pp. 121–60.

[43] Brown, *Body and Society*; Bynum, *Feast, Resurrection* and *Fragmentation*.

are in much modern study of the body.[44] But our collection is a miscellany: the themes and arguments of its contributors would only be diluted by any attempt in this introduction to reduce to one editorial formulation of what mattered in medieval theological concern with the natural body. Rather, let us take one final glance at John's cards. Richly coloured, mainly court cards, their main point is, of course, that they are quodlibets, 'what you will' questions on the body: a medieval miscellany. As such their display is an appropriate introduction to a modern miscellany on medieval theology and the natural body, which is constituted by the papers contained within this first volume in the series *York Studies in Medieval Theology*.

---

[44] See Bynum, 'Why the Fuss', p. 5.

Paradox in the Medieval Gender
Doctrine of Head and Body

Alcuin Blamires

On the basis of what they thought they found in some passages in the Epistles to the Ephesians and the Corinthians, the Church fathers formalized and routinely repeated a hierarchical gender doctrine designating man as 'head' and woman as 'body'. They invoked the doctrine in all sorts of contexts to sustain male primacy and exclude women from authoritative functions whether in the public domain (the right to teach, baptize, etc.) or in the private domain (the power to make autonomous decisions or autonomous vows). The head and body analogy was therefore no sooner in circulation than it became a convenient, uninspected and propagandist slogan. And like many patristic slogans it had an extended shelf-life, continuing to support claims about male precedence among scholastic writers such as Bonaventure and Aquinas.

During the Middle Ages, nevertheless, the doctrine did not go unchallenged. One challenge, which Abelard mounted by using gospel evidence to re-gender the hierarchy, remained idiosyncratic and thereby in effect attested the dominance and survival-power of the topos which it attempted to vary. Another challenge focused on the difficulty of aligning the inherited hierarchy with 'known' patterns of behaviour. Already mooted by the fathers themselves, this challenge envisaged the paradox that the 'body' or woman was often morally 'ahead' (so to speak) of her metaphorical marital 'head'. In other words, life was felt to reverse the doctrine in important respects, particularly in the realms of sexual mores and active charity. This problem called for scrutiny in the medieval era when emphasis on confession produced elaborate moral analysis of behaviour and intention. Confessors, and certain women (Christine de Pizan, at least), showed their distrust of the analogy by beginning to drop it, though the underlying hierarchy was not easily disturbed and people still inclined to the solution endorsed by St Augustine, namely that if a woman's 'head' (husband) is corrupt she should transfer her moral allegiance to a higher 'head' (God). The object of the present discussion is to engage with some of the paradoxes and challenges, as well as continuities associated with the doctrine; but such an engagement is best founded on prior investigation of what the fathers understood by the metaphor they so eagerly adopted from the Pauline epistles.

The gendered language of headship seems to derive particularly from two New Testament passages. One is Ephesians 5. 22–33:

Mulieres viris suis subditae sint, sicut Domino: quoniam vir caput est mulieris: sicut Christus caput est Ecclesiae: ipse, salvator corporis eius. Sed sicut Ecclesia subiecta est Christo, ita et mulieres viris suis in omnibus. Viri diligite uxores vestras, sicut et Christus dilexit Ecclesiam, et seipsum tradidit pro ea. . . . Ita et viri debent diligere uxores suas ut corpora sua. Qui suam uxorem diligit, seipsum diligit. Nemo enim unquam carnem suam odio habuit: sed nutrit et fovet eam, sicut et Christus Ecclesiam: quia membra sumus corporis eius, de carne eius et de ossibus eius.

(Let women be subject to their husbands, as to the Lord. Because the husband is the head of the wife: as Christ is the head of the church. He is the saviour of his body. Therefore as the church is subject to Christ, so also let the wives be to their husbands in all things. Husbands, love your wives, as Christ also loved the church, and delivered himself up for it. . . . So also ought men to love their wives as their own bodies. He that loveth his wife loveth himself. For no man ever hated his own flesh: but nourisheth and cherisheth it, as also Christ doth the church. Because we are members of his body, of his flesh, and of his bones.)[1]

Interpretation of the passage is quite difficult, but what can confidently be stated is that simply to extract a hierarchized, gendered 'head/body' metaphor from it is to do violence to a complex system of analogies within analogies. Christ, designated as head of the Church, is then imagined in a spousal relation to the Church which is by extension 'his body' (v. 23) and which he saves through self-sacrifice (vv. 25–7). Husbands are by analogy 'heads' of their wives, and are urged to follow Christ's example in loving wives who are by extension 'their own bodies' and 'their own flesh' (vv. 28–9, linking with v. 23). But husbands and wives are at the same time subsumed into 'we' who are all 'members' of Christ's/the Church's 'body'.

It is reductive to collapse the text's configurations of *sicut* and *ita*, 'just as' and 'so', into a formal hierarchy such as: Christ, head; Church, body; (in turn comprising) husband, head; wife, body. Admittedly one will readily imagine that 'at first it would appear that Paul has a rather degrading view of the wife – she is merely the husband's "body" '.[2] But where the text likens wives to men's bodies (*ut corpora sua*, v. 28) or flesh (*carnem suam*, v. 29), it has in mind not denigration but the lyrical suggestion of mutuality in Genesis 2. 24 (quoted in v. 31) that man and wife are two in one flesh, just as all Christians should be members of Christ's flesh (v. 30).[3] Even the signal of outright wifely 'subjection' in v. 24 is qualified by the implication of universal self-subjection

---

1 Here and throughout this article the English translation of the Vulgate is from the Douay version.

2 B. Witherington III, *Women in the Earliest Churches* (Cambridge, 1988), p. 59.

3 It is reasonable to suppose, with Chrysostom, that Adam's reference to Eve as 'caro de carne mea' ('flesh of my flesh') in Genesis 2. 23 is also implicit in this statement; see *Hom. xx Eph.*, 3, in *PG* 62, 139 (on v. 29); trans. in *Saint Chrysostom: Homilies on Galatians, Ephesians, Philippians, Colossians, Thessalonians, Timothy, Titus, and*

in the verse that precedes the whole extract, where the Ephesians are exhorted to be 'subject one to another in the fear of Christ', as it is also qualified by the emphasis on the altruism of Christ's self-denying 'headship'.

The complementary passage is I Corinthians 11. 3–15:

> Volo autem vos scire quod omnis viri caput, Christus est: caput autem mulieris, vir: caput vero Christi, Deus. Omnis vir orans, aut prophetans velato capite, deturpat caput suum. Omnis autem mulier orans, aut prophetans non velato capite, deturpat caput suum: unum enim est ac si decalvetur.

> (But I would have you know, that the head of every man is Christ: and the head of the woman is the man: and the head of Christ is God. Every man praying or prophesying with his head covered, disgraceth his head. But every woman praying or prophesying with her head not covered, disgraceth her head: for it is all one as if she were shaven.)

In this instance the text speaks of 'head' without speaking at all of 'body'. The 'head' metaphor can be unpacked into a sequence: God is head of Christ who is head of man who is head of woman (*perhaps* of 'wife'; but unlike the Ephesians passage, Corinthians does not move to identify *mulier* as *uxor*). The reader is likely to infer here a chain of rank or command with 'head' in its transferred sense of 'summit' or 'principal', but then arguably God does not 'outrank' Christ,[4] and an alternative meaning of 'source' or 'origin' would be possible both for Greek *kephale* and its Vulgate equivalent *caput* ('head'), especially given the way the text subsequently concentrates on relations of the sexes in creation and procreation.[5]

The sequel, indeed, counters gender asymmetry by dwelling on parity, for although 'the man was not created for the woman, but the woman for the man' (v. 9), 'yet neither is the man without the woman, nor the woman without the man, in the Lord', and 'as the woman is of the man, so also is the man by the woman' (vv. 11–12). The structuring of ideas is fascinating and enigmatic. St Paul develops a difficult symbolism of male and female dignity linked with creation lore and appropriate to solemn religious contexts. But he tantalizes us with the possibility of puns in verses 4–5. Are the heads which man and woman might 'disgrace' literal, or do they punningly allude also to the metaphorical 'head' of each? In the woman's case, the emphasis seems decisively literal.[6] Yet the temptation to resolve it metaphorically, as though

---

Philemon, Select Library of Nicene and Post-Nicene Fathers, ed. P. Schaff, 13 (Grand Rapids, MN, 1969), p. 146.

4 An interpretative problem which Chrysostom tries to deal with in *Hom. xxvi I Cor.*, 2–3, in *PG* 61, 214–16.

5 Witherington summarizes scholarship on *kephale* in *Women in the Earliest Churches*, pp. 58–61 and 84–7. See also G. E. Howard, 'The Head/Body Metaphors of Ephesians', *New Testament Studies* 20 (1974), 350–6.

6 Witherington, *Women in the Earliest Churches*, pp. 85–6, but with the qualification at

her 'uncovered' activity *insults men,* is already painfully apparent when, for instance, the passage is deployed by the fourth-century Alexandrian theologian Didymus the Blind to oppose female preaching. Where St Paul speaks of a woman with uncovered head disgracing her head, says Didymus, 'he means that he does not permit a woman to write books impudently, on her own authority, nor to teach in the assemblies, because, by doing so, she offends her head, man: for "the head of woman is man" '.[7] The nuance of the epistle shrinks to crude slogan – and one can see why; for whatever is reconstructionist about the Pauline statements is in the finessing of the analogies. Their residual impact (especially in Ephesians) is heavily hierarchical:

> Patriarchal domination is . . . radically questioned with reference to the paradigmatic love relationship of Christ to the church. Nevertheless, it must be recognized that this christological modification of the husband's patriarchal position and duties does not have the power, theologically, to transform the patriarchal pattern of the household code. . . . Instead, Ephesians christologically cements the inferior position of the wife in the marriage relationship.[8]

However, before we go on to investigate this 'cemented' pattern, an excursion into semantics seems timely. Head and body after all form a deceptively 'obvious' polarity (or continuum?) whose relational implication, on reflection, lacks clear specificity. How did the Church fathers actually envisage this favourite model?

The first answer is that they themselves often took the terms of the relation for granted. St John Chrysostom introduces the Ephesians passage by confidently proposing that a man holds the rank (*ordo*) and position (*locus*) of head and a woman that of body,[9] but his exegesis expounds the metaphor (which

p. 256, note 45 that there 'could be a *double entendre* if we are talking about wives here; but would it make sense to say the head or source of a woman is man in general (or is Adam the head of all women?)'.

7 'quod significat, non licere mulieri ex propria compositione libros fidenter conscribere, et in Ecclesia docere, atque hac ratione injuriam capiti inferre, id est, viro: "Caput" enim "mulieris est vir: caput autem viri, Christus" ', *De Trinitate* III.xli.3, in *PG* 39, 989–90; trans. E. S. Fiorenza, *In Memory of Her: A Feminist Theological Reconstruction of Christian Origins* (London, 1983), p. 309. Didymus doubtless seeks to undermine a public instructional role for women by manipulating precisely the verse which seemed to proponents to support it (because it implied that in the Pauline communities women *did* prophesy in public).

8 Fiorenza, *In Memory of Her*, pp. 269–70. Witherington also concludes that 'this is Paul's deliberate attempt to reform the patriarchal structure of his day, a structure he inherited, adopted, and adapted. Paradoxically, however, the effect was also to ground that revised patriarchal structure involving the husband's headship in the eternal relationship between Christ and Church. This serves to give an ongoing and permanent theological rationale for the husband's headship and the wife's submission'; *Women in the Earliest Churches*, p. 55.

9 'Ponamus ergo virum quidem ordinem et locum tenere capitis, mulierem autem corporis', *Hom. xx Eph.*, 1, in *PG* 62, 136.

was by no means commonplace in antiquity)[10] only briefly and vaguely as a two-way physiological system in which various limbs serve the head while the head in return 'provides for' or watches over the body.[11] This gives us one model, where the body is that part of the organism which functions to serve under the benign direction of the head. The other two main options appear to have been a calibrated 'top-to-bottom' model in which *caput* is summit, head in the sense 'head of department', and the body (more or less abstractly) is lower, inferior; or a sequential 'lead-and-follow' model in which the head is what leads the way out front while the body, like an animal's, falls into place behind.

Clearly the metaphor attempts to bridge two potentially – though not necessarily – divergent conceptions. It expresses on the one hand a relationship in which organic reciprocity is the primary emphasis; and on the other, a relationship characterized by rigid hierarchy. Chrysostom touches on the potential inconsistency with reference to I Corinthians when he acknowledges that there are certain implications at the 'human' level of the analogy which become 'absurd' if they are predicated of Christ as head of the Church. One has to exclude from *this* headship the inapplicable fact that human bodies and heads are 'liable to identical passions', and extract from the metaphor only the more abstract principles of union (*unio*) and origination (*principium*).[12] Pre-

---

10 As Witherington indicates, patriarchal discourse in antiquity did not customarily talk in terms of the 'headship' of husband over wife; *Women in the Earliest Churches*, pp. 44–7 and 58. Indeed, when Aquinas argues that woman was appropriately formed from man 'as her origin and chief', it is misleading of him to add the 'head' metaphor to a quotation from Aristotle in *Summa theologiae*, Ia, qu. 92, art. 3, concerning the joining of male and female '*to establish a home life, in which man and woman work together at some things, and in which the man is head of the woman*'; trans. E. Hill in *ST* XIII, 40–1 (Hill's continuous use of italics here reinforces the implication that '. . . in qua vir est caput mulieris' is part of the quotation from *Ethica* viii.12, 1162a.) In any case, Aquinas thought that an element of masculine 'headship' was inaugurated at creation: 'even before the Fall the man was the head and governor (*caput . . . et gubernator*) of the woman'; *Summa theologiae*, 2a 2ae, qu. 164, art. 2, in *ST* XLIV, 177.

11 'Mulier est secundus principatus. Neque igitur ipsa exigat aequalitatem honoris; est enim sub capite: neque ille eam despiciat tamquam subjectam; est enim corpus: si caput corpus despiciat, ipsum quoque peribit: sed afferat dilectionem quae tamquam in aequilibrio respondeat obedientiae. Sicut caput, ita et corpus: hoc illi ad ministerium praebeat manus, pedes, et reliqua omnia membra; illud autem huic invigilet omni instructum intelligentia', *Hom. xx Eph.*, 4), in *PG* 62, 140–1; 'The wife is a second authority; let not her then demand equality, for she is under the head; nor let him despise her as being in subjection, for she is the body; and if the head despise the body, it will itself also perish. But let him bring in love on his part as a counterpoise to obedience on her part. For example, let the hands and the feet, and all the rest of the members be given up for service to the head, but let the head provide for the body, seeing it contains every sense in itself'; Chrysostom, *Homilies*, ed. Schaff, p. 146.

12 '. . .si omnia humana accepero, multa consequetur absurditas: nam iisdem est pas-

sumably the fact that men and women *are* 'liable to identical passions' is erroneously taken to imply that the metaphor of male headship requires less selective interpretation: but at least Chrysostom glimpses that the metaphor cannot be pinned down without difficulty.

In practice writers often wobbled erratically between the various models identified above. Chrysostom himself shuffles notions of compliance, sinking, and following, when he articulates Adam's acceptance of the apple from Eve as a scandalous inversion of head-body discipline. Whereas the rest of the body ought to follow or comply with (the medieval Latin rendering is *obsequi*) the head, things here turned out quite otherwise – the head complying with (or following) the rest of the body, and what was at the top (*sursum*) ending up at the bottom.[13] Later when expounding the postlapsarian punishments, he characterizes Eve's subjection to Adam in terms of the body's need to follow (*sequi*) the head, which denotes the proper line-management of husband over wife. The husband has been declared master (*dominus*) so that the wife should obey, not so that head should follow feet. Chrysostom concedes that the contrary often happens, and expresses this through a personnel adaptation of top-to-bottom calibrations: the one who should be head serves in the office of feet, and she who is a member of the foot department becomes head. What is interesting about this is that Chrysostom then recollects that the Bible *does not rule out* such staff redeployment, in that St Paul implies that wives may or may not save husbands, just as husbands may or may not save wives (I Corinthians 7. 16).[14] The commentary hastens away from that disconcerting thought, which entails recognition that women as much as men take moral initiatives – a recognition which the head/body doctrine had always to evade.

Augustine's visualization of the metaphor is as indeterminate as Chrysostom's. In his most influential articulation of it, he combines the 'top-to-bottom' model – emotively nuanced through the suggestion that the household (*domus*) itself 'hangs down its head' where a husband is morally inferior – with the 'lead-and-follow' model, whose failure is sardonically projected in terms of the body's progress towards God in front of the regressive head:

sionibus obnoxium caput, quibus corpus, iisdemque erit obnoxium. Quid ergo relinquendum, et quid accipiendum? . . .accipienda autem est perfecta unio et causa et primum principium'; *Hom. xxvi I Cor.*, 3, in *PG* 61, 216.

[13] 'Ac cum oporteret corpus reliquum capiti obsequi, diverso modo res evenit, corporique reliquo caput obsequutum est, et quae sursum erant, in infimum locum venerunt'; *Hom. xii Gen.*, 4, in *PG* 53, 139 (my translation).

[14] 'Ea enim de causa sub tua potestate facta est, et dominus ejus pronuntiatus es, ut illa tibi pareat, et non caput pedes sequatur. Verum non raro videmus contrarium usu evenire, ut is qui suo ordine caput esse deberet, neque pedum ordinem servet: et ea quae in pedum loco est, in caput constituatur. Idcirco et beatus Paulus magister orbis haec omnia praevidens, clamabat: "Unde namque scis mulier, an virum sis salvatura? aut qui scis vir, an uxorem sis salvaturus?" '; *Hom. xii Gen.*, 9, in *PG* 53, 145.

Et cum tu caput sis uxoris tuae, praecedit te ad deum, cuius caput es. . . .
Vbi autem melius uiuit mulier quam uir, capite deorsum pendet domus.
Si caput est uir, melius debet uiuere uir et praecedere in omnibus bonis
factis uxorem suam, ut illa imitetur uirum, sequatur caput suum. Quomodo caput ecclesiae Christus est, et hoc iubetur ecclesiae ut sequatur
caput suum et ut per uestigia ambulet capitis sui, sic uniuscuiusque
domus habet caput uirum et tamquam carnem feminam. Quo caput
ducit, illuc debet corpus sequi.[15]

There is a vigorous rendering of this in a Middle English treatise on the Ten
Commandments called *Dives and Pauper*, which further sharpens the inversion of the 'lead-and-follow' model by imagining the head actually falling
back in the direction of hell:

And noutwithstondyng þat þu art hefd of þin wyf ʒet þin wyf goth
aforn þe to God & þu þat art hefd of þin wif gost bakward to helle. . . . in
what houshold þe woman lyuyth betere þan þe man in þat houshold
hongyth þe hefd donward, for sith man is hefd of woman he owith to
lyuyn betere þan woman & gon aforn his wif in alle goode dedys þat
she mon suhyn here housebounde & folwyn hyr hefd. The hefd of iche
houshold is þe housebonde & þe wyf is þe body. Be cours of kende,
þedir þat þe hefd ledyth þedir schulde þe body folwyn.[16]

What is less often spelled out, probably because it was considered to be
self-evident, is the equation between head and *government*, or *control*. Nevertheless there are contexts in which that equation is made absolutely clear,
whether by patristic writers such as St Gregory of Nyssa or by later medieval
commentators.[17] That the head 'controls' the rest of the body can also of

---

[15] *Sermo* ix (alternatively known as *De decem chordis*), from the edition in *CSEL* 41
(1961), pp. 100–51 (p. 112). About 150 manuscript copies of this sermon on the Ten
Commandments are extant – more than for any of Augustine's other sermons (p.
100). Most of the passage quoted attracted particular notice in the Middle Ages
because it was quoted in Gratian's discussion of adultery; *Decretum*, C. 32 q. 6 c. 5, in
Friedberg I, 1140. Augustine's contention in the passage that if the husband is 'head'
he should behave better was also given a high profile by Aquinas, who quoted it as
a possible reason for arguing that Adam's sin was greater than Eve's: *Summa theologiae*, 2a 2ae, qu. 163, art. 4; *ST* XLIV, 161.

[16] *Dives and Pauper*, ed. P. Barnum, I, pt 2, EETS 280 (Oxford, 1980), p. 68. The author
has omitted Augustine's 'Quomodo. . .' clause. This English treatise, dating from
between 1405 and 1410, naturally borrows from Augustine's famous sermon on the
Commandments. Parts of the treatise are modernized in Blamires, *Woman Defamed*,
pp. 260–70.

[17] 'Since, according to the divine plan, the wife does not govern herself, but has her
place of refuge in the one who has power over her through marriage, if she is
separated from him for even a short time, it is as if she has been deprived of her
head'; *De virginitate* iii, in *Saint Gregory of Nyssa, Ascetical Works*, trans. V. W. Calla-
han (Washington, DC, 1967), p. 17. The gloss to Eph. 5. 22 in the medieval commentary attributed to Hugh of St Cher states categorically that 'head' signifies rulership:

course logically be claimed as true *of* a woman. Thus it is said of the Virgin Mary that her head 'signifies her mind', because 'just as the head controls the body's members, so the mind rules and controls the feelings of the soul'. However, it is instructive to see how naturally the medieval author (in this case Amadeus of Lausanne) can slip from envisaging this to the more congenial gradations of the traditional metaphor, proposing that in another sense Mary herself signifies the penultimate summit of the body; she is the 'neck' of the Christian body:

> In the neck, which towers over the other members and supplies to the limbs vital power, is expressed her loftiness, by which, presiding over the members of the Church, she unites the head to its body, for she unites Christ with the Church and the life which in the first place she received she pours forth on her other members. . .[18]

Here the conventional status and function of the Virgin Mary is ingeniously contained. 'Presiding' over the rest of the body of the Church, she is yet no more than neck, main distributor or conduit of the life which she 'receives' from Christ as head.

To summarize the implications so far: the Middle Ages inherited from patristic writings in the instance of the metaphor of head and body a simple, memorable and consequently powerful reinforcement of gender hierarchy. This was so despite a certain definitional vagueness, because the hierarchical implication was assumed to inhere (to a greater or lesser extent) in whichever model was operative in a given instance. The metaphor could override challenge – even from the Virgin Mary;[19] in fact, it is interesting to discover how much its use was characteristically reserved precisely for dealing with points of strain, with the prospect of threats to the gender system. In any situation where the possibility or prospect of a female claim to authority was recognized, masculine headship was routinely brandished. We have seen Didymus brandish it against public teaching by women (he was thinking of the Montanists); this can be paralleled in a riposte to the Waldensian sect by Bernard of

---

'. . .vir caput est mulieris: id est rector'; *Postillae domini Hugonis Cardinalis*, 6 vols. (Basle, 1503–4), VI, fol. 161v.

[18] Amadeus of Lausanne, *On the Praises of the Blessed Mary*, Hom. ii, in *Magnificat: Homilies in Praise of the Blessed Virgin Mary by Bernard of Clairvaux and Amadeus of Lausanne*, trans. M.-B. Said and G. Perigo, Cistercian Fathers Series 18 (Kalamazoo, MN, 1979), pp. 73–4.

[19] Albert the Great tempers Mariolatry by limiting what veneration is owed to the Virgin and by emphasizing that in redemption she was 'member' not 'head'; *III Sent.* iii.3, cited by H. Graef, *Mary: A History of Doctrine and Devotion*, 2 vols. (New York, 1963), I, 275. There remained a strong tradition identifying the Virgin as 'hedde and quene of the apostelis' after Christ's ascension, as asserted in the Brigittine *Rule of St Saviour*; see *Women's Writing in Middle English*, ed. A. Barratt (Harlow, 1992), p. 93.

Fontcaude at the end of the twelfth century.[20] Again, where canon law conceded that a woman who had vowed sexual continence with the consent of her husband could persist in her vow despite his subsequent change of mind, elaborate precautions were simultaneously taken to reaffirm the husband's absolute 'headship' where her continuing fulfilment of all other sorts of vow was concerned.[21]

What happened when it was a matter of explaining portions of biblical narrative which seemed in danger of vesting authority in women, can be demonstrated through contrasting responses by Augustine and Abelard. Augustine turns to the hierarchical model in order to explain what Jesus might have meant when in the course of his conversation with the woman of Samaria at the well, he bade her 'call her husband' (John 4. 1–42). Augustine first broaches the notion that Jesus might have wished to 'teach her through her husband' on the Pauline basis that wives who want to ask questions are to learn through their husbands at home. This theory is dismissed; but not before it has made the reader feel that there might be something irregular about the Samaritan woman's lone colloquy with Jesus, in which she gradually comes to recognize him as the Messiah. Augustine then proposes that the 'husband' is to the woman as understanding is to the 'carnal sense': by calling her husband, metaphorically she would be transcending the 'carnal' perception which she has initially shown in the conversation, taking literally Christ's 'thirst' at the well. It would also regularize a situation in which the 'head of man' (Christ) is talking to woman without the presence of the 'husband' or intermediary 'head'. Jesus can only fully enlighten the Samaritan woman when the process of summoning her understanding ('husband') is complete.[22]

---

[20] '. . .si caput mulieris est vir, qua fronte audeat docere virum, scilicet caput suum?' ('if man is head of woman, how dare she teach man, namely her head?'); *Contra Vallenses et Contra Arrianos*, in *PL* 204, 826 (my translation).

[21] 'Si quilibet eorum alterum a suo iure absoluerit, ad preteritam seruitutem ipsum reuocare non poterit. Quia uero in ceteris uir est caput mulieris, et mulier corpus uiri, ita uota abstinentiae uiro permittente mulier potest promittere, ut tamen eodem prohibente repromissa non ualeat inplere': ('if either one of them shall release the other from the marriage right, he or she is not then able to recall the other to the former servitude. But, since in other respects the man is head of the woman and the woman is the body of the man, a woman is able to make vows of abstinence [i.e. fasting] with the man's permission; but if he prohibits her, she may not fulfil her promises'); Gratian, *Decretum*, C. 33 q. 5 c. 11, ed. Friedberg, I, 1253–4; trans. in Blamires, *Woman Defamed*, p. 84.

[22] *In Joannis evangelium*, tract. xv, 18–19; especially, ' "*Voca*, inquit, *virum tuum*: adhibe intellectum per quem docearis, quo regaris". Ergo constitue animam excepto intellectu tanquam feminam: intellectum autem habere, tanquam virum. . . . Loquebatur caput viri cum femina, et non aderat vir' (' "Call your husband", says Jesus: "bring here understanding, through which you can be taught and by which you can be ruled". Read the soul which is without understanding as the woman, and possession of understanding as having a husband. . . . The "head" of man was speaking to the woman; but no "husband" was present'). *PL* 35, 1517.

By this sleight of hand Augustine contrives, first to excuse the obscurity of Jesus's bidding (given that the woman currently has no husband); second, to transpose the literal/metaphorical referents of the head and body topos (in order to retain a metaphorical husband where a literal one is not available); and consequently, third, to undermine the woman's authority, just before on her own initiative she draws hundreds of townspeople out to hear Jesus, by insinuating that what enables her to do so is the access of a masculine *intellectus* without which as woman she would never have penetrated beyond 'carnal' perception of Christ.

Augustine therefore infiltrates the 'absent husband' into the episode (albeit metaphorically) so as to reinstate the lapsed line-management from Christ to male to female. The biblical woman's initially literal reactions are construed as female rather than as simply human. A strategic deployment of the head/body model underminingly suggests that the woman responds to Christ fully only when she is immasculated: for otherwise, 'illa mulier carnem sapit' ('the woman thinks materially').[23]

When Abelard writes of the same episode, he totally ignores the Augustinian reading with its associated head-and-body discourse, and produces an enthusiastic and even sublime interpretation of the Samaritan woman's role.[24] We can turn to Abelard's analysis of a different episode, the anointing of Christ, to see how he, too, adopts the head/body gendering – but in order to enhance women's authority rather than to depress it.

For Abelard, seeking out biblical authorizations for women's religious life, there was an awesome and originary sign of female religious power in the moment when a woman (usually identified as Mary Magdalene in the Middle Ages) poured oil from an alabaster container on Christ's head and/or feet while he was at Simon the leper's table.[25] Commentators were agreed on the emphatic devotion signified by her action. Abelard goes much further, to discover an august sacramental efficacy here. His underlying premise is that the Greek word 'Christ' means 'the anointed'. This woman's action is therefore performative: it consecrates Jesus – not consecrates him 'as it were', but *actually* consecrates him – into Christ. It is like a naming action,[26] and Abelard envisages it as the culminating fulfilment of Daniel's prophecy of a time when

---

23 *PL* 35, 1515.
24 Abelard's interpretation is in Letter 7 of the Abelard-Heloise correspondence (numbering the *Historia calamitatum* as Letter 1); see 'Letter of Heloise', p. 273, and *The Letters of Abelard and Heloise*, trans. K. Scott Moncrieff (New York, 1974), pp. 163–4. For comparison of Abelard's interpretation with Chrysostom's as well as with Augustine's, see A. Blamires, '*Caput a femina, membra a viris*: Gender Polemic in Abelard's Letter "On the Origin of Nuns"', forthcoming in *The Tongue of the Fathers*, ed. A. Taylor and D. Townsend.
25 Matthew 26. 6–7, and Mark 14. 3. In Luke 7. 37–8 she anoints his feet, not head; and in John 12. 3, it is Mary (Martha's sister) who anoints his feet.
26 Abelard refers, in fact, to Canticles 1. 2, 'Oleum effusum nomen tuum' ('Thy name is as oil poured out'). 'Letter of Heloise', p. 255; trans. Scott Moncrieff, p. 133.

sin will end 'et impleatur visio et prophetia, et ungatur Sanctus sanctorum' ('and vision and prophecy may be fulfilled, and the saint of saints may be anointed'; Daniel 9. 24). It is this woman who anoints the saint of saints to be Christ.[27]

Abelard highlights the implications. Christ allowed a woman to anoint him as king, when he refused the offer of kingship from men. He was anointed by women while alive, but by men only when dead.[28] Christ specifically defended the woman's action against the disciples' murmurings, and expressly asked them to include it in their evangelizing.[29] But above all, there is the extraordinary pointed contrast which Abelard draws between the anointing of Christians who are the body or *membra* ('members') of the Church, performed down the ages since Jacob's time symbolically and by men only; and the anointing of Christ the 'head', performed in the full literal sense by a woman: 'Christus ipse a muliere, Christiani a viris inunguntur; caput ipsum, scilicet, a femina, membra a viris'.[30] As I have suggested elsewhere, this is a stunning dislocation of the conventional gendering of body as feminine and head as masculine.[31] Abelard defines a crucial moment when woman and not man is linked with Christ's headship, indeed institutes him *as* 'Christ'.

Of course, it is only stunning because centuries of Augustine-dominated exegesis have contrived to make Augustine's outrageous gloss on the Samaritan woman's 'husband' seem almost plausible, and have correspondingly made Abelard's more logical use of intertextuality to gloss the anointing seem daring.[32] Abelard himself was unable to take the step of applying the hierarchical innovation he had discovered here to other contexts.[33] He probably

---

27 What is woman's prerogative, Abelard asks, 'ut summum Christum omnibus Sancti Spiritus unguentis ab ipsa eius conceptione delibutum mulier quoque inungeret, et quasi corporalibus sacramentis eum in regem et sacerdotem consecrans, Christum, id est, unctum corporaliter ipsum efficeret?' ('that the supreme Christ, anointed from his very conception with all the unguents of the Holy Spirit, a woman also should anoint and, as though with bodily sacraments consecrating him to be king and priest, make him in body the Christ, that is to say the anointed?'). 'Letter of Heloise', p. 254; trans. Scott Moncrieff, p. 133.

28 'Letter of Heloise', p. 255; trans. Scott Moncrieff, p. 134.

29 'Letter of Heloise', p. 256; trans. Scott Moncrieff, p. 135.

30 'Letter of Heloise', p. 255; trans. Scott Moncrieff, p. 133.

31 Blamires, *'Caput a femina, membra a viris'* (forthcoming).

32 Augustine's gloss on the woman's husband circulated *via* the *Glossa ordinaria* on John 4. 16; *PL* 114, 372. Exegesis of the anointing in Abelard's period makes connections with the Canticles, but expresses no sacramental significance: see Honorius Augustodunensis, *PL* 172, 981, and the anonymous *Vita* of Mary Magdalene, *PL* 112, 1457–8.

33 Where practical religious authority was concerned, he instinctively asserted gender hierarchy in the traditional way. In the *Historia calamitatum* he expressed surprise at the custom of allowing abbesses to take charge of convents, since 'the Apostle lays down that the man must always be over the woman, as her head'. Abelard, 'Letter of Consolation', pp. 208–9; trans. Radice, *Letters*, p. 101. For further comment on paradoxes in Abelard's views on women, see M. M. McLaughlin, 'Peter Abelard

thought of it as a special dispensation. He was, however, one of those who felt that where the moral hierarchy of sexual behaviour was concerned, women set a better example than men.[34] This takes us back to the metaphor of heads which 'lag behind', and to some associated paradoxes with which this paper concludes.

In the late twelfth century Bernard of Fontcaude challenged the Waldensians: how dare a woman presume to teach a man, who is designated as her head?[35] Yet the problem was that the very insurrection which was anathema in some contexts, it seemed positively necessary to encourage in others. A celebrated instance in Chrysostom concerns voyeuristic husbands who attend theatres to watch women swimming naked in water tanks, and who are admonished by the homilist to take lessons in chaste behaviour from their wives. He acknowledges that this inverts propriety, 'but since the order is overturned by sin and the body is above while the head is below, let us take even this other route'.[36]

Chrysostom's objective, of course, is to shame males into regaining their ordained headships. But a sense of the entanglement of the situation is that they appear to have lost through (their) sin the seniority which commentators always claimed had come to them through woman's/Eve's sin. Worse, the 'body' – that is woman, who, according to Augustine's gloss on the Samaritan, was liable to 'think carnally' – has to undertake the moral instruction of a depraved husband blatantly obsessed with flesh who ought, by the same Augustinian reasoning, to be not only 'head' but also *intellectus*.

Such paradoxes were not confined to moral analysis of the peep-show culture of Chrysostom's city of Antioch,[37] but were also apparent, as we have seen, to Augustine himself in his sermon on the Commandments. Like Chrysostom, he finds himself conceding that in areas of bodily self-control it may be that the alleged 'body' (woman) leads the way as if she were the head. Husbands who claim a customary right to have sex with maidservants, he points out, would be incensed to hear their wives assert the same right with manservants.[38] Wives must certainly not follow or imitate the example of their 'heads' in this regard. Exhorting husbands to learn from wives was one thing, but Augustine pressed the issue further and asked: how can the head/body model function at all so far as the wife is concerned, if the husband remains

---

and the Dignity of Women: Twelfth-Century "Feminism" in Theory and Practice', in *Pierre Abelard – Pierre le Vénérable: Les courants philosophiques*, Colloques internationaux de Centre National du Recherche Scientifique (Paris, 1975), pp. 287–333.

[34] He suggested that chastity was rarer in men ('Letter of Heloise', p. 275; trans. Scott Moncrieff, p. 166); and was struck by the strength of Heloise's sexual continence as against his own incontinence (Radice, *Letters*, p. 154).

[35] See note 20 above.

[36] *Hom. vii Matt.*, 6, in *PG* 57, 79–80; trans. E. Clark, *Women in the Early Church* (Wilmington, DE, 1983), p. 160.

[37] On which see Brown, *Body and Society*, p. 316.

[38] *Sermo* ix; *CSEL* 41, 128.

promiscuous and society condones such a double standard of sexual behaviour?

Christ whispers the answer in women's hearts where their unworthy husbands cannot hear it, says Augustine, and the Middle English writer follows him in *Dives and Pauper*. A wife should be patient and grieve for her husband's sin; but

> 'in þat he doth omys leet hym nout ben þin hefd to ledyn þe but let þin God ben þin hefd. For ȝif þu folwe hym as hefd in his schrewydnesse boþin hefd & body schul gon doun to helle'; and þerfor mote nout þe body þat is þe wif folwyn þe wyckyd hefd but mote she heldyn hyr to þe hefd of holy chirche þat is Crist. To hym þe wyf owith hyr chaste; to hym principaly she must don worchepe, for he is principal housebond.[39]

In a sense the solution looks deceptively simple and elegant. In a case where one's immediate 'head' offers a model only of obdurate debauchery, accelerate past him and, as it were, go higher to Christ the 'head of the head', to follow his lead instead. Yet, that is not quite how it works, and the problems are perhaps signalled by the furtiveness of the communication between Christ and the wife. It has to be furtive because the husband has been found bodylike instead of headlike: but, according to the hierarchy, there is no-one else to counsel the wife about this except the husband himself – whose advice she is now being urged to ignore. The 'body' has to model herself on *some* 'head', and cannot be allowed to take autonomous decisions about herself or her husband as if she were herself head. So Christ whispers in a role of supra-husband (unbeknown to the wife's normal head): for otherwise, how will she know what to do, and to whom shall she 'owe' her chastity?

Dives and Pauper and Augustine are forced towards this curious concept of chaste adultery or secretive collusion between Christ and wife, against the obdurately errant husband, by the wholesale suppression of female autonomy within the head/body paradigm. By the time of *Dives and Pauper*, however, the clergy were customarily bringing great sophistication to bear on situations where a husband seemed to impede the moral welfare of a wife. It has been observed, for instance, that the right to perform penitential vows constituted an area 'in which the clergy would be most inclined to curtail the husband's authority for the sake of the wife's well-being'.[40] Some canonists were prepared to argue that wives who made harmless vows independent of a husband's will must fulfill them, because there was a duty to please God

---

39 *Dives and Pauper*, I, pt 2, ed. Barnum, p. 70. Cf. 'Christus enim loquitur in cordibus bonarum feminarum, loquitur intus ubi non audit uir . . . "in eo quod male facit, noli eum putare caput tuum, sed me". Nam si et in eo quod male facit caput est, secuturum est corpus caput suum, eunt ambo per praeceps. Vt autem non sequatur malum caput suum, teneat se ad caput ecclesiae Christum': *Sermo* ix; *CSEL* 41, 128–9.
40 Elliott, *Spiritual Marriage*, p. 185.

over their husbands.[41] To an extent, confessors began to get involved in 'furtive coalitions' with women, when it was a matter of sustaining moral objectives against the will of husbands.[42] The argument that a woman obeys God in obeying her husband was seen to be in uneasy conflict with wives' spiritual aspirations. In the sphere of almsgiving particularly, penitential theory constructed intricate justifications whereby a wife might go to the very limit in transgressing a husband's disapproval of her charity, making distinctions between what husbands might ostensibly say and what they might intuitively accept.[43] A husband's authority was still the bottom line, but the line was neither so clear as it had been when Augustine criticized the wealthy matron Ecdicia for undertaking charitable and ascetic activities against her husband's will, nor was it expressed so emphatically in the language of head and body.[44]

How did some of these sophistications and paradoxes appear to women? From a section of Christine de Pizan's *Treasure of the City of Ladies*, a text written in 1405 and hence contemporary with *Dives and Pauper*, we can deduce one segment of female opinion which held that the doctrine was claptrap; another segment of female opinion which was prepared to go along with the kind of solution to the debauched-husband problem which was still upheld in *Dives and Pauper*; and a tacit vote of no confidence in the archaic 'head' metaphor itself.

The first teaching of Prudence for noble ladies in Christine's *Treasure* is that the 'rule of honour' requires them to be humble and obedient towards their lords, and perpetually solicitous about their well-being. It is the lady's role to show joy in the presence of her husband, and to say only what may please him.[45] Christine exposes this model, however, to the crossfire of 'some' who

---

41 Elliott, *Spiritual Marriage*, pp. 185–6, citing Huguccio. Some support for this could be gleaned from biblical reference to women who were wives of (presumed) non-believers, yet who assisted Jesus during his ministry (Luke 8. 2–3). According to the Franciscan author of the thirteenth-century *Miroir des bonnes femmes*, this showed that a woman should do good works even if her husband is an evil man: for although she should obey him in everything when he is with God, she should not herself leave God if the husband becomes dissevered from God. See J. l. Grigsby, 'Miroir des bonnes femmes, pt ii', *Romania* 83 (1962), 30–51 (pp. 49–50). Such exception-clauses had been uneasily acknowledged from as early as the second century, when Clement of Alexandria advised that a wife should 'aim at virtue, gaining her husband's consent in everything, so as never to do anything against his will, with exception of what is reckoned as contributing to virtue and salvation': *Miscellanies*, in *The Writings of Clement of Alexandria*, trans. A. C. Coxe, Ante-Nicene Christian Library II (Grand Rapids, MN, 1977), p. 196.

42 Elliott, *Spiritual Marriage*, p. 187.

43 Elliott, *Spiritual Marriage*, pp. 189–90, citing Raymond of Peñafort and successors.

44 For St Augustine's Epistle to Ecdicia, see *PL* 33, 1078–80 (esp. chs. 7–8, invoking the husband's headship). The letter was kept in the limelight by its mention in Gratian, *Decretum* C. 33 q. 5 c. 4; Friedberg, I, 1251–2.

45 Christine de Pizan, *Le Livre des Trois vertus* i.13, ed. C. C. Willard and E. Hicks (Paris, 1989), pp. 52–4; *The Treasure of the City of Ladies or The Book of the Three Virtues*, trans.

might think that 'we are not taking into account certain defects and that we are talking utter nonsense': what about unloving husbands who do not deserve this solicitude? Prudence's answer is twofold. First, her teaching is not addressed to such husbands (though 'some of them need it'); and second, she is setting out the most honourable – and prudential – behaviour for women. Love, obedience and dignified discretion remain the best course, even in the face of a husband's infidelities. A wife may try tactful dissuasions and the use of a confessor as intermediary, but she will discourage any gossip against her husband, and will put up with his errancy as long as possible; ultimately, if he 'does not want to change his ways', she will 'take refuge in God'.[46]

'Taking refuge in God' is Christine's equivalent to the Augustinian language of turning to God as 'head'. That she does not use that language in the passage, might be construed as a tacit vote of no confidence in it,[47] even though the hierarchy of authority is itself broadly accepted: for Prudence commends undeviating obedience to degenerate husbands and can see no way of tackling them except the third-party route via God. But a body of opinion which is also recognized, and acknowledged to have a point, is that this is 'nonsense'. The 'honorable' course is therefore an ideal *knowingly* upheld as a statement of altruism against the undeserving boorishness of men and against the logical protests of many women.

The *caput/corpus* paradigm had been consolidated with harsh rigour in some patristic contexts. St Jerome argued at one point that a wife not 'subject to her head' or husband commits a crime or blasphemy as great as that committed by a man who fails to be 'subject to Christ'.[48] The paradigm's ostensibly unchallenged status enabled later writers to use it as if it constituted definitive proof of male *auctoritas in praesidendo*. (Thus, Bonaventure thought it explained why Christ did not take female form, since in 'correct order' men 'oversee' women as head oversees body.[49]) The interrelated conclusions emerging from this study, however, indicate that serious inadequa-

---

S. Lawson (Harmondsworth, 1985), pp. 62–3 (in the translation this section is designated i.12)

[46] *Livre des Trois vertus* i.13, ed. Willard and Hicks, p. 55; *Treasure*, trans. Lawson, p. 64.

[47] It is difficult to be sure, because the Augustinian formulae may have reached her in modified form, as exemplified in the sermon on marriage by Jacobus de Voragine quoted by A. Galloway, 'Marriage Sermons, Polemical Sermons, and *The Wife of Bath's Prologue*: A Generic Excursus', *Studies in the Age of Chaucer* 14 (1992), 3–30 (pp. 11–12).

[48] '. . . quaecumque uxor non subjicitur viro suo, hoc est capiti suo, ejusdem criminis rea est, cujus et vir si non subjiciatur Christo capiti suo'; *In Titum*, on 2. 3 and following, in *PL* 26, 582. An influential passage, it is quoted in Gratian, *Decretum* C. 33 q. 5 c. 15, trans. in Blamires, *Woman Defamed*, p. 85.

[49] 'Nam secundum rectum ordinem non mulier viro, sed vir praeficitur mulieri tanquam caput corpori'; *III Sent.*, dist. 12, art. 3, qu. 1 ('Utrum decuerit Deum assumere sexum mulierem'), quoted by Martin, 'Ordination of Women', p. 158.

cies were perceived in the doctrine even by those who most subscribed to it; that its implicit demotion of women to the realm of 'body' was seen as a fiction; and that it was scarcely able to deal with the problems raised by its own intractability.

The doctrine, we saw, is characterized by definitional vagueness. Its apparently palpable metaphor blurs into abstractness ('above and below', 'lead and follow') as often as it is imagined in terms of real heads and bodies. Even when the latter is the case, the significance often remains relatively abstract rather than articulating woman as 'body' in the sense of being 'enmeshed in bodily function'.[50] Certainly, Augustine gave precedent for harping on woman's 'fleshly' status in relation to a masculine 'head', in his exegesis of the Samaritan woman. Certainly, again, the *Glossa ordinaria* encouraged this kind of Augustinian reading by interpreting the concept of the husband (*vir*) who is head of a wife to mean the 'human spirit' which governs human 'animality' as husband governs wife.[51] But it is also Augustine who enables us to see why there was some *reluctance* to fix woman's role within the paradigm in those terms. After all, it is his own sermon *De decem chordis* which most memorably offers a construction of wives as typically chaste, and men as typically bodily creatures, creatures of libido. The popular definition of 'man', he suggested, was 'a person overcome by lust'.[52] The Middle Ages inherited this sermon together with its ingenious mechanism for retrieving masculine headship even amidst the head's obsessive bodiliness. The doctrine continued to put wives in a paradoxical position, however, caught between recalcitrant husbands whose *fiat* they were exhorted to obey on the one hand, and the imperatives of piety on the other. The doctrine only complicated the problems for which it was partly responsible, when it tried to negotiate them by commending various forms of what we might now call 'passive resistance'. It is not surprising that when a woman writer confronted the issues it raised, she dropped its demeaning terminology and flagged its doctrine as being, in some degree, nonsense. (She further subverted it by heralding the Virgin Mary as 'head' of the female sex – a woman as 'head' of women – in the triumphant

---

50 This is quite surprising, given the link that could be forged between the doctrine and Eve's creation out of 'body', e.g. in the fourth-century (probably Syrian) list of church laws, the *Apostolic Constitutions* iii.9, against women baptizing: 'if "the man is the head of the woman", he was chosen for priesthood; it is not right to set aside the order of creation and leave what is chief to descend to the lowest part of the body. For woman is the body of the man, being from his side and subjected to him' (trans. Clark, *Women in the Early Church*, p. 180).

51 'Potest nomine viri intelligi . . . spiritus humanis, qui quasi animae maritus, animalem affectionem tanquam conjugem regit', glossing I Cor. 11. 3; *PL* 114, 537.

52 'Ad hoc delapsa est humana peruersitas, ut uir habeatur uinctus a libidine', *Sermo* ix, *CSEL* 41, p. 131. Compare *Dives and Pauper* (ed. Barnum, p. 72): 'manys schrewydnesse is now so gret þat þer is no man holdyn a man but he be ouercomyn with lecherie'.

conclusion of the *Cité des Dames*.[53]) Before Christine, Abelard offered his own kind of challenge but it was destined to remain idiosyncratic and undeveloped, with less power to disturb dominant medieval principles of gender hierarchy than, perhaps, was possessed by the nagging paradoxes which lurked within the doctrine itself.

---

[53] The Virgin announces, 'tres voulentiers je habiteray et demeureray entre mes suers et amies, les femmes, . . . sy suys et seray a toujours chief du sexe femenin' ('I will live and abide most happily among my sisters and friends . . . for I am and will always be the head of the feminine sex'); M. C. Curnow, 'The *Livre de la Cité des Dames* of Christine de Pisan: A Critical Edition' (unpublished Ph.D. thesis, Vanderbilt, 1975), pp. 976–7, trans. E. J. Richards, *The Book of the City of Ladies* (London, 1983), p. 218.

Peter Abelard's Carnal Thoughts

David Luscombe

The twelfth century generated much new thought about cosmogony and this has been excitingly considered in some excellent recent studies, especially those by Peter Dronke in his *Fabula*[1] and by Tullio Gregory in *Anima mundi*.[2] Abelard was one of several twelfth-century writers, others being William of Conches and Hugh of Amiens, who wrote a commentary on the *Hexaemeron* in which they attempted to provide both a literal and a moral interpretation of the creation. Abelard drew a clear distinction between the process of creation for man on the one hand and for all other living beings on the other. Living beings other than man were created out of the elements with their bodies being produced at the same time as their souls. Their life comes, like their bodies, from the elements. We can speak of the elements providing life or animation; for example if we think of the air which blows as wind, we sometimes speak of this as if it is alive, as when we speak of a breath of wind or a breath of fresh air.[3] And, of course, all living beings would be dead without water. Properly speaking, although other living beings were created, man was not. Man's body was formed out of mud and slime ('homo de humo; de limo terrae; de terra humida'); later a soul was added or infused into this body and at this stage we have the whole man. Form was added to matter, so the process should be called one of formation, not creation.[4] This is a staged process and strictly speaking – Abelard writes – the author of the Book of Genesis was incorrect in stating, 'creavit Deus hominem de limo terrae', because it is not the whole *homo*, body and soul, the inner and the outer man, which is created out of slime, but only the body which in Hebrew is called Adam and in Latin *homo*.[5] Woman on the other hand was not made in the same way as man. Woman was not created *per se* because she was taken from the side of man (*vir*).[6] Moreover, man was created outside of paradise, in the slime of the earth. Woman, on the other hand, was created in paradise after

1 *Fabula. Explorations into the Uses of Myth in Medieval Platonism* (Leiden and Cologne, 1974).
2 *Anima mundi. La filosofia di Guglielmo di Conches e la Scuola di Chartres* (Florence, 1955).
3 *Expositio in Hexaemeron*, PL 178, 774D.
4 *Expositio in Hexaemeron*, PL 178, 774B-D.
5 *Expositio in Hexaemeron*, PL 178, 775A.
6 *Expositio in Hexaemeron*, PL 178, 774C.

man had been brought into the Garden of Eden. However, although woman
was created in the more desirable place, she behaved more badly than man in
getting both of them evicted.[7]

The relationship between soul and body is clearly one of the fundamental
issues in medieval thought. There was (as we have just seen) the problem of
understanding the process of creation with the aid of the theory of the four
elements and also with the idea of the *vis* or power of nature.[8] There was also
a problem of personal identity. If man is defined as a rational animal and if an
animal always has corporeality, then man would appear to cease to be man if
soul and body were to separate, as they do separate at the moment of death,
according to Christian theology. Then there is the problem of the definition of
a person. Boethius provided the most influential definition: a person is an
individual substance of a rational nature.[9] There is no hint of a body in this
definition or of a link with the animal kingdom. By rational nature Boethius
meant to exclude the animal world but also to include the divine persons in
the Trinity. And if Boethius did not bother much about the angels, his definition – individual substances with a rational nature – fitted them perfectly:
substances without bodies – substances without matter – may be persons. But
this leads straight into the problem of the resurrection of the body. Why
defend the resurrection of the human body at the end of time if going to
heaven means being with God, who is pure, incorporeal being? And of what
kind of seeing do we speak when we describe the supreme good for man as
the *visio Dei*, the beatific vision? Man's first entry into Paradise, in the Garden
of Eden, involved both body and soul.

Further problems were presented by the Arab philosophers. They stoked
up the debates that ran through the thirteenth century about the relationship
between form and matter. Our matter, as a human being, is our body which
exists in space and undergoes change. To be a body is to have the form of a
body: a body is a body whether it is dead or alive. When it is alive, however, is
the soul another form? How many forms – one or more – are needed to define
a rational animal?

There is also the question of the relationship between the mind and the
senses. This takes us to the heart of the problem of knowledge. Is the human
intellect truly individual? Or is it networked into some huge information
system that downloads into the individual intellect and enables it (by and

---

7 *Expositio in Hexaemeron*, PL 178, 776BC.
8 Cf. T. Gregory, 'L'idea di natura nella filosofia medievale prima dell'ingresso della
   fisica di Aristotele – il secolo XII', J. Jolivet, 'Éléments du concept de nature chez
   Abélard', and D. E. Luscombe, 'Nature in the Thought of Peter Abelard', all in *La
   filosofia della natura nel medioevo*, Atti del Terzo Congresso Internazionale di Filosofia
   Medioevale, Passo della Mendola (Trento), 31 agosto–5 settembre 1964 (Milan,
   1966), pp. 27–65, 297–304, 314–19.
9 Boethius, *Liber de persona et duabus naturis contra Eutichen et Nestorium*, cap. ii, in *PL*
   64, 1342–3. Cf. H. Chadwick, *Boethius. The Consolations of Music, Logic, Theology, and
   Philosophy* (Oxford, 1981), pp. 192–3.

large) to recognise things in roughly the same way as other people do? Is any of our knowledge implanted in the mind directly by God? Augustine believed that it was, that God impressed divine ideas into the human mind, like seeds pressed into the soil. And this doctrine of the divine illumination of the human mind, the doctrine of seminal reasons, found favour especially with the Franciscan masters of theology in the thirteenth century. The doctrine owed something ultimately to Plato's image, largely unknown in the Middle Ages, of the cave, that vision in which Plato suggested that the knowledge that came to man, through his physical senses, amounted to no more than a sight of the flickering shadows and reflections of light playing upon the darkened wall of a cave, not the light itself which was outside the cave, that is, beyond the world in which human beings experience mortality.

Pitted against this in the Middle Ages was, of course, Aristotle's theory of abstraction: knowledge enters the human mind through the senses. Is it really the case that the human mind can only develop knowledge if the senses present the mind with sensible evidence? Are there no innate ideas? What about intuition as a source of knowledge? Is intuition reliable? What about imagination as a source of knowledge? Can we imagine anything that is completely free of knowledge coming via the senses? Can we dream anything that is not in some way derived from our senses? For an Aristotelian, the mind is active but also passive; it receives data which it then acts upon, by classifying it, abstracting from it, forming ideas and making connections between them, and inventing intelligible means of communicating thought through the senses such as speech. It follows from this that the mind can only build knowledge on what the body, as it were, bumps into. The mind can construct a concept of truth or love or beauty by determining what is true about things or lovable about them or beautiful. But the body, being placed in this material world, cannot know absolute Truth or enjoy pure Love or see the perfection of Beauty. In the thirteenth century these matters were clarified through the identification of the transcendentals such as Being, One, Truth and Beauty. But man who sees only through a glass darkly cannot comprehend them.

Abelard lived before many of these problems and issues became extensively known and discussed in the West, unlike Islam. What Abelard knew about the mind he largely gained from the translations and commentaries of Boethius. In general, we may say that Peter Abelard, through the works of Boethius, followed Aristotle on the problem of knowledge. He distinguished between things, words and thoughts, and wrote that the human mind attaches words like labels to the physical objects that the body encounters, having first generated concepts. It can then communicate those words in physical speech or writing to others, but there can be no communication between the communicator and the person being communicated with except through the senses.[10]

---

[10] See D. Luscombe, 'Peter Abelard', in *A History of Twelfth-Century Western Philosophy*, ed. P. Dronke (Cambridge, 1988), pp. 279–307.

The relationship between mind and body also presented problems to moral philosophers and theologians. Fallen man, as Augustine had shown, had contracted the universal virus of original sin. As a result the human free will was unable to control the disorders of human passion and desire. Everyone was gripped by concupiscence; no one could get rid of it. There was nothing that could be done, at least in an ultimate sense of obtaining a complete recovery. Baptism could remove the stain of original sin, but not its consequence or penalty. Divine grace could wash away further sins as they occur and divine providence could predestine some to eternal happiness, but no one, not even the elect, was emancipated from sin before death. Throughout the Middle Ages tribunals and confessors, in trying to curb crime and sin, reached conclusions on the basis of evidence of what people had done, that is, with the help largely of material facts. The Penitentials of the early Middle Ages laid down the penalties for wrongdoing. Physical offense was punished by physical correction. Peter Abelard tried to break out of the trap that was presented by definitions of acts that are wrong.[11] It is undoubtedly his best known contribution to moral philosophy. But, before attempting to explain it, we should note the close link with what he thought as a logician about the relationship between mind and body. When it comes to forming concepts and finding words and propositions to communicate them, the mind, as it were, scans the sense data first. The primary evidence is out there, in the external world, not here in the mind. This distinction is crucial to Abelard's ethical theories.

Abelard agrees with Augustine that men fall foul of temptation which arrives through the bodily senses even when the imagination is hard at work. People are unavoidably in the grip of desires and suggestions; the devil is always at work like a magician. Good habits can only be formed by hard practice and even the most virtuous of men are far from confirmed in all their good habits or free from concupiscence. But, Abelard insisted, we make a mistake if we confuse our appetites and even our will with sin. The body inclines the will to all sorts of pleasures. But to want to have sex or to have power over others is not to commit sin; it is part of fallen nature. From the moral point of view, the fact that our will is disordered is not basically a fact of our own choice. What matters in personal morality is the response of the mind to suggestions or desires represented through the body by the will to the brain. If the mind decides to follow human desire and have, say, illicit sex, most medieval theologians would say that that is sin. But not Abelard – who complained that the mind-body distinction has not been rightly understood. He would dispute the use of phrases such as morally good or bad acts. Acts are acts, full stop; they are neither morally right nor wrong because they are physical events. What are right or wrong, and never morally neutral, are the

---

11 See especially his *Ethics*, ed. D. Luscombe with an English translation, *Peter Abelard's Ethics*, OMT (Oxford, 1971).

decisions taken by the mind e.g. to have sex licitly or to have it illicitly. The point is made effectively in Abelard's discussion of the killing of one person by another. This too is purely a physical act, and as such it is one hundred per cent morally neutral. The blade of a sword goes into a body and death follows; what has happened is neither right nor wrong. What is right or wrong is the decision taken by the person wielding the sword. He may have swung the sword accidentally; he may have been acting under orders; he may have failed to understand properly what his orders really meant; he may have acted in self-defence; he may invincibly have mistaken his victim's identity; he may have surrendered to the desire to murder someone he loathes. What matters finally, at least in the sight of God, is why he did it, not what is done.[12]

But even after making this correction Abelard went further and argued that even this is not a fair interpretation of what creates morality or immorality. 'Why he did it' is not the final test. It is not the reason for the killing that takes place that makes for right or wrong; the killing does not have to be carried out for the motive to be confirmed. There are many circumstances in which we may consent to act wrongly without being able to fulfill this consent in deed, and there are many situations in which we may intend to do something good but are thwarted in fulfilling our intention. What matters is what is in the mind, not what the body then does about it, at least in the sight of God. The final test is not why one does something, but why one decides to do it.

In one sense Heloise in her correspondence with Abelard turned all this on its head and made it look nonsensical. When she wrote, she was fully installed as the abbess of the convent of the Paraclete; she was properly veiled and professed; she was protected and recognised by charters and privileges; she was highly respected by other religious leaders such as Bernard of Clairvaux and Peter the Venerable. But, even so, she wrote that she was not a nun. She had not consented to be one; it had been forced upon her. She called herself a hypocrite.[13] We shall return to Heloise, but there is another issue to do with mind and body that needs to be brought in. One of the best known debates in Augustine's *De civitate Dei* (xix, 1; viii, 8) is about the definition of supreme goodness and of supreme evil. Augustine turns to the now-lost *liber de philosophia* written by Marcus Varro and to his identification of 288 possible sects offering as many different definitions of supreme goodness and supreme evil given by earlier pagan philosophers. Some of these thought that supreme happiness comes through physical well-being, others through happiness of mind, and others found it in a mixture of mental and physical well-being. Augustine, of course, throws out all these approaches, and all their derivatives and variants, because none could provide one essential factor: perma-

---

[12] 'Non enim homines de occultis, sed de manifestis iudicant, nec tam culpae reatum quam operis pensant effectum. Deus uero solus qui non tam quae fiunt, quam quo animo fiant adtendit, ueraciter in intentione nostra reatum pensat et uero iudicio culpam examinat' (*Ethics*, ed. Luscombe, p. 40).

[13] Letter 3; 'Personal Letters', p. 81.

nence. A man can be perfectly fit, supremely intelligent and entirely virtuous, but he might in the next few minutes suffer a stroke or have a mental breakdown. Supreme happiness or supreme misery are only attained when there is no possibility of either being taken away. Having established this, Augustine moves on to his vision of the two loves which establish the two everlasting cities, on the one hand the supreme love of God which creates the city of God, and on the other hand the supreme love of self which creates the city of the earth, the former providing everlasting peace and beatitude, the latter eternal wretchedness.

Abelard, for whatever reason, was not interested in the idea of the two cities, but he was intensely interested in Augustine's *De civitate Dei* and especially in the investigations made by Socrates and the Platonists into the *summum bonum*. Book ii of his *Theologia christiana* manifests this interest,[14] but nowhere is it more in evidence than in the *Dialogus* that he wrote in which a Philosopher and a Christian debate between themselves the nature of supreme goodness and of supreme evil. It is the Philosopher who turns to the *De civitate Dei* where in Book viii Augustine records that some pagan philosophers call the supreme goodness virtue and others pleasure or *voluptas*.[15] The latter view is that of the Epicureans, although the Philosopher is quick to point out that it is a mistake to think, as many do, that by pleasure the Epicureans meant physical pleasure. The Epicurean definition of *voluptas* is an inner peace in the soul which enables it to be untroubled by any external bodily suffering or by any internal sense of sin or vice, so that the soul can achieve what it wills to achieve and so that the will is not frustrated or contested.[16] Pleasure understood in this sense is really another name for virtue, because excellence in virtue brings peace and pleasure to the soul.[17]

---

14 *Theologia christiana* ii.32–9. At ii.34 Abelard writes: 'Vbi quidem et de Platonica disciplina quam diligenter Deum inuestigauerit et ipsum summum bonum esse definierit, in quo tota beatitudinis summa consistit, et quam recte philosophari determinauerit amare Deum, ut omnium quoque bonorum finem amorem Dei constituat, placet nunc subinferre ex eodem, scilicet VIII *De ciuitate Dei*. . .'. *Petri Abaelardi Opera theologica*, II, ed. E. M. Buytaert, *CCCM* 12 (Turnhout, 1969), pp. 145–6.

15 *Petrus Abaelardus. Dialogus inter Philosophum, Judaeum et Christianum*, ed. R. Thomas (Stuttgart and Bad Cannstatt, 1970), l. 1525. There exists an English translation by P. J. Payer, *Peter Abelard. A Dialogue of a Philosopher with a Jew and a Christian*, Medieval Sources in Translation 20 (Toronto, 1979).

16 'Non ut plerique estimant carnalium illecebrarum inhonestam et turpem oblectationem, sed quandam interiorem anime tranquilitatem, qua inter adversa et prospera manet quieta et propriis bonis contenta, dum nulla eam peccati mordeat conscientia'; *Dialogus*, ed. Thomas, ll. 1528–32. Cf. the Philosopher at ll. 1647–63: 'Et fortassis hoc fuit Epicuri sententia summum bonum voluptatem dicentis, quoniam videlicet tanta est anime tranquillitas, ut nec exterius eam corporalis afflictio nec interius mentem aliqua peccati conscientia inquietet vel vitium obstet, ut optima eius voluntas omnino compleatur. Quamdiu autem voluntati nostre aliquid obsistit vel deest, vera beatitudo nequaquam est'.

17 *Dialogus*, ed. Thomas, ll. 1542–50.

As the debate between the Philosopher and the Christian reaches its climax, the Philosopher states his agreement with the Christian that, properly and absolutely speaking, the supreme good is God and the supreme good for man is the vision of God which makes man truly happy. But the Philosopher asks why, if this vision of God is enjoyed through the eyes of the mind and is not a physical sight, Christians proclaim the doctrine of the resurrection of the bodies of the saints in heaven? What is the point of the souls of the just in paradise having their bodies restored to them when the lack of bodies does nothing to lessen the happiness of the angels? To this the Christian replies that everything God does is done not to increase our happiness but his glory. The resurrection of our bodies does not increase the happiness of the saints but it is not without purpose since God is glorified when what were once weak instruments beset by passion become indissoluble and immune to passion.[18] However, after the resurrection, bodies are, in a certain way – *quodammodo* – subtle, spiritual things, just as Christ's body became an immortal and impassible body after his resurrection.[19] There is no activity left for the senses since all desires are satisfied by the vision of God.[20]

So, through the person of the Christian in the *Dialogus*, Abelard gives a spiritual interpretation to the doctrine of the resurrection of the body, and likewise to the descent of souls into hell. We talk loosely of heaven and hell as places when we speak of heaven being up in the sky or of hell being somewhere below the earth. Some people do think of heaven and hell in terms of physical place, but others (more rightly) understand these expressions as ways of indicating the immense gulf that separates the spiritual height and summit of happiness from the spiritual depths of misery and abjection.[21] As for the fate of the damned, there is much in both the Old and the New Testament that cannot be taken literally, including the famous verse in Isaiah (66. 24), 'vermis eorum non morietur, et ignis eorum non extinguetur' ('their worm shall not die and their fire shall not be quenched'), and Luke's account (16. 19) of the story of Dives and Lazarus with its depiction of the breast of Abraham, the parched tongue of the rich man, the finger of Lazarus, the drop of water and the inextinguishable fire. All this can only be interpreted mystically or spiritually, not literally or physically. The souls in hell have no bodies. The wicked angels likewise have no bodies; as demons they molest us and we call them powers of the air but the sense of the word is the same as when we talk of earthly princes, meaning not princes who are made of earth but men who rule over the world. Airy demons do not actually fly in the air but they are as invisible as air.[22]

In the correspondence between Heloise and Abelard, a sharp distinction

---

18 *Dialogus*, ed. Thomas, ll. 2584–621.
19 *Dialogus*, ed. Thomas, ll. 2667–76.
20 *Dialogus*, ed. Thomas, ll. 2906–47.
21 *Dialogus*, ed. Thomas, ll. 2956–67.
22 *Dialogus*, ed. Thomas, ll. 2967–3014.

between interiority and exteriority, between soul and body, between the moral/conceptual world and the physical world is repeatedly made. Their correspondence concludes with three letters (5, 6, 7 with Abelard's Rule for Heloise and her nuns at the Paraclete) which are almost entirely concerned with problems to do with female monasticism. Sir Richard Southern once described these letters as 'by no means readable' and 'seldom read'.[23] He was right to say that they are seldom read; in the Penguin Classics translation of Letter 6, the late Betty Radice merely summarised in three pages what takes up more than thirty columns in the *Patrologia latina*. In Letters 2 and 4 Heloise delivered her complaints and in Letters 3 and 5 Abelard's response was always to ask Heloise to consider the power of prayer and of contemplation. With this in mind in Letter 5, Abelard turned to the opening of the Song of Songs, to the words *Nigra sum sed formosa*, 'I am black but beautiful . . . therefore the king has loved me'. The point of the text is that it illustrates the beauty of a contemplative soul, such as Abelard wanted Heloise to become. The Ethiopian woman, Abelard writes, looks less lovely than a white woman as regards her exterior appearance; she is discoloured and disfigured by sunlight, and worn down by bodily tribulation and by lack of prosperity. But within she is lovelier. She has softer skin, better bones and her teeth are whiter than milk; in humility she is a lily of the valley.[24] Of his past relationship Abelard writes (in strong contrast to Heloise) that he is glad to be rid of the aspect of carnal desire. The Lord prefers eunuchs in his house (Isaiah 56. 4–5). By his castration (he writes in Letter 4) he is now cut off from filth and more fit to approach the holy altar. He has not been so much deprived of the 'parts of shame' as cleansed and purified. Unlike Origen who misguidedly castrated himself, someone else, through God's compassion, castrated Abelard. I deserved death, he adds, but gain life.[25]

He also expresses a certain disdain for biological motherhood and child-rearing, and writes that it would have been a hateful waste if Heloise had clung to carnal pleasure and had in suffering given birth to a few children for the world. Now as a spiritual mother she is able to deliver numerous progeny for heaven. She has turned the curse of Eve into the blessing of Mary.[26] Finally, in Letter 5 Heloise calmed down and asked Abelard for advice. The advice he gave is full of reflection on the distinction between the inner and the outer self, between mind and body. The abbess has the care of bodies as well as of

---

23 *Medieval Humanism*, p. 101.
24 Letter 4, 'Personal Letters', pp. 83–95. See the English translation by Radice, *Letters*, pp. 138–41. I have followed the numbering of the letters found in the editions which are cited here; if one were to number the *Historia calamitatum* (with which the correspondence began) as Letter 1, then all other numbers would be increased by one.
25 Letter 4, 'Personal Letters', pp. 89–90. Cf. the English translation in Radice, *Letters*, pp. 148–9.
26 Letter 4, 'Personal Letters', p. 90; Radice, *Letters*, p. 150.

souls.[27] No death is more more grievous than that of the soul, but sin enters the soul by means of the five senses. A lying tongue, for example, is death to the soul (Wisdom 1. 11).[28]

One of the most important *topoi* in monastic thought and writing in the Middle Ages is the theme of the desert, and one of Abelard's most striking illustrations of this is the image of the wild ass which loves the freedom of the wilderness.[29] The wild ass, as it appears in the Book of Job 39. 5–8, disdains the noise of the city and roams the hills as its pasture. The wild ass stands for the monk and for the solitary, celibate life. It lives in the saltings of the lands, that is, its members are parched and dry through abstinence. Solitude is a means of protecting human frailty from three kinds of assaults on the flesh, those which come through the senses of hearing, speech and sight. This leaves only the heart to fight against.[30]

Letters 5 and 6, as well as the Rule which follows Letter 7, show a great concern to sort out the chaos and to dispel the vagueness of traditional rules and guidance for running convents of nuns. As Heloise writes in Letter 5, in the Latin church women as well as men try to follow the Rule of St Benedict. But Benedict's Rule was written for men alone and what his Rule says about work, clothing, strong drink and hospitality cannot be observed in detail by women without danger.[31] The yoke that is suitable for the neck of a bull is unsuitable for that of a heifer; those whom nature has created unequal cannot properly be given equal work.[32] Benedict adopted the principle of moderation and allowed for adjustments to be made to suit changing requirements and circumstances, but with men only in mind.[33] This gave Heloise her cue: if Benedict had adopted as one of his principles the principle of adjustability, could not Abelard advise her how to adjust the Rule to suit the needs of her own sisters?

There is a particular focus in Heloise's request to Abelard to review the Rule of Benedict on four issues – work, clothing, food and wine. First, Heloise asks Abelard for guidance on women and work. She wants the nuns to be free for the work of praising God and only to have to do other work if necessary. They should be supported from church funds as they would be supported by their husbands if they were married. They should not have to work to earn a living. St Benedict prescribed manual labour for monks but Heloise appears to think that her nuns should not have to do it.[34] In his Rule Abelard gives his

27 'Rule', p. 255; trans. Radice, *Letters*, p. 204.
28 'Rule', p. 255; Radice, *Letters*, p. 205.
29 Sermon 33, on St John the Baptist, *PL* 178, 582–607, especially cols. 582–5. See also 'Rule', p. 247; Radice, *Letters*, pp. 191–2.
30 'Rule', p. 250; Radice, *Letters*, p. 196.
31 Letter 5, 'Letter of Heloise', pp. 242–3; cf. Radice, *Letters*, pp. 160–1.
32 'Letter of Heloise', pp. 243–4; Radice, *Letters*, p. 162.
33 'Letter of Heloise', pp. 243–4; Radice, *Letters*, pp. 162–3.
34 'Letter of Heloise', p. 252; Radice, *Letters*, pp. 176–8.

guidance on this matter: there should be attached to the monastery a community of brothers who support the nuns and do men's work as necessary
outside the nuns' buildings. The sisters should confine themselves to indoor
work such as making clothes, cooking and washing, as well as light farmyard
tasks such as looking after the hens and the geese.[35]

On clothes Abelard warns against vanity and excessive cost but insists on
cleanliness.[36] He accepts, without going into detail, that the garments
Benedict prescribes for men are unsuitable for women.

On food Heloise is most concerned with the question of meat. Her argument is that meat is not good or evil in itself, but indifferent. Her point is
exactly the same as Abelard's about the morality of physical acts: there is no
morality attaching to material things. It is not in the spirit of the Gospel to
create compulsory dietary observances nor did Christ lay down for the Apostles any dietary restrictions.[37] In his Rule Abelard agreed: no foods are forbidden; only excess must be avoided.[38] Meat may be allowed.

The discussion of wine is perhaps a little humorous. Heloise cites two
passages from Macrobius's *Saturnalia* (vii.6, 16–17 and 18): 'Aristotle says that
women are rarely intoxicated, but old men often. Woman has an extremely
humid body, as can be known from her smooth and glossy skin, and especially from her regular purgations which rid the body of superfluous moisture. So when wine is drunk and merged with so general a humidity, it loses
its power and does not easily strike the seat of the brain when its strength is
extinguished'. And then: 'A woman's body which is destined for frequent
purgations is pierced with several holes, so that it opens into channels and
provides outlets for the moisture draining away to be dispersed. Through
these holes the fumes of wine are quickly released. By contrast, in old men the
body is dry, as is shown by their rough and wrinkled skin'. From this Heloise
concludes that women can drink more safely than men.[39] Nonetheless, wine
presents risks and Heloise gives several texts to illustrate the view that it
should be forbidden to priests and monks. But St Benedict had allowed it to
monks, so what should nuns do?[40] Biblical texts warning against liquor are
also assembled, and in greater number, by Abelard when he gives his guidance in his Rule. He opts again for moderation, not prohibition. Abelard takes
his cue from Heloise and Macrobius: wine has less power over women than
over men, therefore what is allowed to monks should be allowed to women.
Moderation is preferable to total abstinence and for the purposes of the sick
total prohibition is inadvisable anyway. Drinking wine is not in itself wrong;
what is wrong is excess. Nonetheless, wine is a turbulent thing and can

[35] 'Rule', p. 259; Radice, *Letters*, p. 213.
[36] 'Rule', pp. 280–2; Radice, *Letters*, pp. 248–51.
[37] Letter 5, 'Letter of Heloise', pp. 248–9; cf. Radice, *Letters*, pp. 170–2.
[38] 'Rule', pp. 278–80; Radice, *Letters*, pp. 244–8.
[39] Letter 5, 'Letter of Heloise', p. 246; cf. Radice, *Letters*, p. 166.
[40] Letter 5, 'Letter of Heloise', pp. 247–8; cf. Radice, *Letters*, pp. 168–70.

present risks to both continence and silence. So, if total abstinence is not adopted, wine should be taken mixed with water.[41]

Abelard also offers advice on silence. One of the parts of the body over which control is difficult to maintain is the tongue. 'At all times', wrote St Benedict (Rule, Ch. 42), 'monks ought to practise silence'. To which Abelard adds that practising silence means more than keeping silent.[42] He assembles a few texts including James the Apostle (3. 2), 'If any man offend not in word, the same is a perfect man', and then concludes: 'Words impart understanding to the soul, so that it may direct itself towards what it understands and adhere to this by thinking. By thinking we speak to God as we do in words to men. Although we tend towards the words of men, we need to be led away from there, for we cannot tend towards God and man at the same time'.[43] There is much in this passage on the link between words, concepts and understanding, on the human level of speech or writing – the level of language – and also on the level of God and of thought about God which takes place beyond ordinary language. The two levels are respectively body-orientated and God-orientated. The tongue, Abelard writes, is one of the most mobile parts of the body, although smaller and more sensitive than other parts of the body. It forms words. And it is more flexible and sensitive in soft bodies, that is, in women than in men. Paul writing to Timothy absolutely forbade women to speak in church. Woman must be a learner, not a teacher (I Timothy 2. 11–12).[44] In the light of this, and of Paul's view that women are gossips, Abelard imposes perpetual silence on the nuns of the Paraclete at prayer, in the cloister, in the dormitory, in the refectory, and during meals and cooking. Only signs, not words, may be used in these places and at these times.[45]

---

[41] 'Rule', p. 277 and cf. p. 278; Radice, *Letters*, pp. 242–3 and cf. p. 245.

[42] 'Rule', p. 245; Radice, *Letters*, p. 187.

[43] 'Verba quippe intellectum animae immittunt, ut ei quod intelligit intendat et per cogitationem haereat. Cogitatione vero Deo loquimur sicut verbis hominibus. Dumque huc verbis hominum intendimus, necesse est ut inde ducamur, nec Deo simul et hominibus intendere valemus'. 'Rule', p. 245; cf. Radice, *Letters*, p. 188.

[44] 'Rule', pp. 245–6; Radice, *Letters*, pp. 188–9.

[45] 'Rule', p. 246; Radice, *Letters*, p. 189.

This Body of Death:
Abelard, Heloise and the Religious Life[1]

W. G. East

For in that sleep of death what dreams may come,
When we have shuffled off this mortal coil
Must give us pause.
William Shakespeare, *Hamlet*

R. W. Southern has issued a warning against the supposition that Abelard and Heloise held a romantic view of love. He writes, 'The minds of both Abelard and Heloise seem to be untouched by the ideals of romantic love which emerged in the next generation.'[2] But for this warning, one might be excused for supposing, as so many have supposed, that both the 'star-crossed lovers' had a strong romantic streak.

The story of their brief affair and its disastrous conclusion is too well known to need more than the shortest of summaries. In about 1117 Abelard took lodgings in the house of Fulbert, a canon of Notre-Dame in Paris. As part of the agreement he became tutor to Fulbert's niece Heloise. They became lovers, Heloise became pregnant, and Abelard abducted her to his native land of Brittany, where she gave birth to a son. Abelard married her, but this was not enough to appease Fulbert, who had Abelard castrated.

Had the lovers been of a romantic disposition, as they might have been had they lived later in the century, in the age of Marie de France, they could have made a suicide pact, drunk poison from the same cup, and no doubt been buried in the same grave. Marie does in fact tell, in *Les Deus Amanz*, the story of the tragic death of two young lovers, who are buried in the same tomb. She also tells, in *Eliduc*, of a married man who falls in love with a girl. His wife obligingly takes the veil, vacating the marriage-bed. At a later stage Eliduc and his new wife also turn to religion, Eliduc entering a monastery and his second wife entering the same convent as the first, all perfectly amicably.[3]

---

1   This title echoes Romans 7. 24, 'Who will deliver me from this body of death?' (Revised Standard Version), the theme of the York conference in which this collection originated. Cf. above, p. 3, and below, pp. 125 and 190. In the following article the Douay translation of the Bible is used.
2   R. W. Southern, 'The Letters of Abelard and Heloise', in his *Medieval Humanism*, pp. 86–104 (p. 91).
3   Marie de France, *Lais*, ed. A. Ewert (Oxford, 1965).

Conversion to the religious life was clearly seen both as a way out of an impossible amorous entanglement, and as a possible option for a married couple. In fact, Abelard had a close personal precedent for considering the religious life as an honourable option for married people: both his parents had entered the monastic life.[4] Rather than taking the romantic way out, Abelard and Heloise therefore turned to religion. He took the monastic habit at Saint Denis in Paris; she took the veil at Argenteuil.

And yet the religious life is also a form of death. Indeed theologians from St Paul onwards have seen the Christian life itself, even in the secular state, as a form of death. The Christian rite of initiation, baptism, is regarded as a ritual drowning through which the Christian participates in the death of Christ, in order also to share in his resurrection. This is stated most clearly in Saint Paul's letter to the Romans:

> Know you not that all we who are baptized in Christ Jesus are baptized in his death? For we are buried together with him by baptism into death: that, as Christ is risen from the dead by the glory of the Father, so we also may walk in newness of life. For if we have been planted together in the likeness of his death, we shall be also in the likeness of his resurrection. Knowing this, that our old man is crucified with him, that the body of sin may be destroyed, to the end that we may serve sin no longer (Romans 6. 3–6; Douay version).

The religious life witnesses in a particular way to the mortification, the putting to death of the body, which is an essential feature of any form of Christian life. The rite of religious profession has been interpreted as a kind of death. The Rule of Saint Benedict says that at his profession, the novice

> . . . begins the verse: *Receive me*, Lord, *as you have promised, and I shall live; do not disappoint me in my hope* (Ps. 118[119]. 116). The whole community repeats the verse three times, and adds 'Glory be to the Father'. Then the novice prostrates himself at the feet of each monk to ask his prayers, and from that very day he is to be counted as one of the community.[5]

This is straightforward enough; there is no suggestion that the profession is in any sense a funeral ritual. In particular the prostration is no more than a humble attitude of body assumed to ask the prayers of the community. But from the time of Theodore of Tarsus, Archbishop of Canterbury (602–90), we find the profession rite being interpreted in terms of baptism, death and resurrection:

4 'Letter of Consolation', pp. 163–213. Abelard briefly mentions his parents' conversion, without specifying where or why they entered the religious life (p. 179). For a translation of the *Historia calamitatum* see Radice, *Letters*, pp. 57–106.
5 *RB 1980: The Rule of St. Benedict, in Latin and English*, ed. T. Fry (Collegeville, MN, 1981), p. 269.

Theodore prescribes that the abbot shall celebrate Mass (it is supposed that he is a priest) and pronounce 'the three orations' over the monk's head. For seven days the monk shall keep his head covered with the *cuculla* [cowl], in imitation of the neophytes after baptism.[6]

A considerable development of this interpretation is found in the exposition of the Rule of St Benedict by Hildemar, who is thought to have been a monk of Corbie about the middle of the ninth century:

> After the *Suscipe*, the novice prostrates and the others kneel. Then three *Kyries* and five psalms are sung, followed by a number of versicles and an oration. After the investiture the novice receives the kiss of peace from all the monks (Hild. *exp.reg.* p. 547); then he wears his *cuculla* for three days.

The Rule's modern editor comments:

> Besides the Gallican predilection for multiplication of psalms and versicles, this rite shows the influence of baptismal symbolism: the prostration accompanied by the *Miserere* and *De Profundis* symbolises death to sin. A later medieval development that lasted until modern times had the prostrate monk covered with a funeral pall and surrounded by lighted candles.[7]

Saint Bernard of Clairvaux, referring specifically to monastic profession, writes:

> We are, as it were, baptised a second time, when, through mortifying our members here on earth, we once again put on Christ, being formed afresh in the likeness of his death.[8]

There is also a remarkable reference to the religious life as a form of death in the letter of Peter the Venerable to Heloise on the occasion of Abelard's death. He describes the situation of the nuns in the convent of Marcigny:

> You would rejoice to see them in the flower of their angelic virginity united with chaste widows, all alike awaiting the glory of that great and blessed Resurrection, their bodies confined within the narrow walls of their house as if buried in a tomb of blessed hope.[9]

---

6   *Rule of St. Benedict*, ed. Fry, p. 455.
7   *Rule of St. Benedict*, ed. Fry, p. 455. Fry refers to R. Millermüller, *Expositio Regulae ab Hildemaro tradita et nunc primum typis mandata* (Regensburg, 1880), and, for a study of this commentary, to A. Schroll, *Benedictine Monasticism as reflected in the Warnefrid-Hildemar commentaries on the Rule* (New York, 1941).
8   St Bernard, *De Praecepto et dispensatione* xvii.54, in *S. Bernardi opera*, ed. J. Leclercq, H. Rochais and C. H. Talbot, 7 vols. (Rome, 1963), III, 289. Cf. R. Yeo, *The Structure and Content of Monastic Profession*, Studia Anselmiana 83 (Rome, 1982), pp. 209–10.
9   Radice, *Letters*, p. 281.

It is to be noted that the symbolism of baptism and death is contained not only in the act of prostration, but in the wearing of the *cuculla*, the cowl, a garment rather like an academic gown with a hood. Rupert of Deutz (*c*.1075–*c*.1130), an almost exact contemporary of Abelard, writes:

> The monk in a certain way dies with Christ and is buried with him, namely in the three days silence, with the head covered, becoming a witness to his mortification and the penance which he undertook, and becoming a spectacle to angels and to men; then on the third day he is unveiled by the abbot, who gives him the kiss of peace. This is like the resurrection of the Lord, who appeared restored to his disciples after three days of sadness, and said to them, *Pax Vobis*.[10]

This symbolism perhaps gives particular point to Heloise's taking of the veil. She certainly saw this as an offering of herself to death, according to Abelard's vivid account of her profession:

> There were many people, I remember, who in pity for her youth tried to dissuade her from submitting to the yoke of monastic rule as a penance too hard to bear, but all in vain; she broke out as best she could through her tears and sobs into Cornelia's famous lament:
>
> > O noble husband,
> > Too great for me to wed, was it my fate
> > To bend that lofty head? What prompted me
> > To marry you and bring about your fall?
> > Now claim your due, and see me gladly pay . . .
>
> So saying she hurried to the altar, quickly took up the veil blessed by the bishop, and publicly bound herself to the religious life.[11]

The verses which Heloise recited are from Lucan, *Pharsalia* viii.94–8. Southern is illuminating as to their significance here:

> The words are those with which Pompey's wife Cornelia greeted her husband after his defeat at Pharsala. Cornelia offered herself as a sacrifice to placate the angry gods. 'Slay me,' she said; 'cast my ashes on the waves; perhaps then your way will be smoother, your enemies less strong, as a result of this sacrifice.' Just so, Heloise at the moment of her profession offered herself to death that Abelard might live. Long before Abelard had seen himself as the modern Jerome, Heloise had seen herself as the modern Cornelia. Indeed, she was more than Cornelia; for Pompey did not after all slay Cornelia and scatter her ashes on the waves; but Abelard killed Heloise and she willingly made the sacrifice of her life.[12]

10 Rupert of Deutz, *De operibus spiritus* viii.8, in *De Sancta trinitate et operibus suis*, ed. H. Haake, CCCM 24 (Turnhout, 1972), pp. 2082–3. Quoted by Yeo, *Monastic Profession*, pp. 206–7.

11 Radice, *Letters*, pp. 76–7.

12 Southern, *Medieval Humanism*, pp. 93–4.

The religious life may be a form of death, but for Heloise it proved a most unsatisfactory one. Though she was dead, she found that she could not lie down. Her life in the convent was a nightmare, a living death. She was unable to do what every religious needs to do, to follow the counsel of St Paul (Colossians 3. 5): 'Mortificate ergo membra vestra, quae sunt super terram: fornicationem, immunditiam, libidinem . . .' ('Mortify therefore your members which are upon the earth: fornication, uncleanness, lust. . .'). Paul lists many more vices which were not Heloise's failings, but impurity and libido continued to give her great trouble. About fifteen years later, she wrote to Abelard describing in graphic detail the miseries of her monastic existence. She begins with what may seem a pedantic correction of Abelard's epistolary etiquette; he had placed her name before his own in the greeting. She goes on to complain that he had added to her grief by raising the possibility of his own death. Then she proceeds to the main business of the letter, her own state of mind, during which she utters this moving exclamation against her 'body of death':

> . . . the pleasures of lovers which we have shared have been too sweet – they can never displease me, and can scarcely be banished from my thoughts. Wherever I turn they are always there before my eyes, bringing with them awakened longings and fantasies which will not even let me sleep. Even during the celebration of the Mass, when our prayers should be purer, lewd visions of those pleasures take such a hold upon my unhappy soul that my thoughts are on their wantonness instead of on my prayers. I should be groaning over the sins I have committed, but I can only sigh for what I have lost. Everything we did and also the times and places are stamped on my heart along with your image, so that I live through it all again with you. Even in sleep I know no respite. Sometimes my thoughts are betrayed in a movement of my body, or they break out in an unguarded word. In my utter wretchedness, that cry from a suffering soul could well be mine: 'Miserable creature that I am, who is there to rescue me out of the body doomed to this death?'[13]

Finally she begs him not to praise her. She is only too aware of her own imperfections, having expressed them so vividly in one of the most memorable passages of medieval literature, and knows that praise of her monastic virtues would be empty and hypocritical flattery.

Before going on to consider Abelard's response, we may ask why Heloise saw St Paul's words as expressing her own situation. 'That cry from a suffering soul could well be mine' – why? From what was Paul suffering, and how did it relate to Heloise's sufferings? In his second letter to the Corinthians, Paul tells how, to keep him from being too elated by the abundance of the revelations he had received, he was given a thorn in the flesh (σϰόλοψ τῇ

---

[13] Radice, *Letters*, p. 113. 'Infelix ego homo, quis me liberabit de corpore mortis huius' (Romans 7. 24); cf. note 1 above.

σαϱϰι) a messenger of Satan, to harass him – literally, 'to give him a box on the ear' (ϰολαφιζη). Paul does not go into details as to what this thorn in the flesh was. Many of the Fathers (e.g. Tertullian, Jerome, Primasius, Gregory of Naz-ianzus)[14] regarded it as a painful physical affliction, perhaps, in view of ϰο-λαφιζη, a persistent headache or earache. However, in the Vulgate σϰολοφ is rendered as *stimulus*, and this has rather different connotations. Alfred Plum-mer made an interesting study of the resultant tradition of exegesis:

> When the original Greek ceased to be familiar in the West, S. Paul's words were known chiefly or entirely through the Latin. The ambiguous rendering in the Latin version of Irenaeus and in Cyprian, *stimulus carnis*, was diffused through the influence of the Vulgate; and it pro-duced an interpretation which in time prevailed over all others, and which for centuries held the field. It was maintained that the Apostle's great trouble was frequent temptations to sins of the flesh ... Primasius, who preserves the tradition of pains in the head, gives as a secondary interpretation, *alii dicunt titillatione carnis stimulatum*.[15] Gregory the Great (*Mor.* VIII. 29) says that Paul, after being caught up to paradise, *contra carnis bellum laborat*, which perhaps implies this interpretation. Thomas Aquinas says of the *stimulus; quia ad literam dicitur, quod fuit vehementer afflictus dolore iliaco*.[16] But afterwards he quotes the opinion, *quod inerant ei motus concupiscentiae, quos tamen divina gratia refrenebat*.[17] Hugo of St Cher suggests that Thekla was a source of danger to the Apostle . . . Lyra, Bellarmine and Estius all take this view of it; and Cornelius a Lapide says that it is *communis fidelium sensus*.[18]

The *Glossa ordinaria* on II Corinthians 12. 7 interprets *stimulus pungens carnem* as 'angelus malignus missus a Satana, ut colaphizet, id est reprimat omnem motum superbiæ incutiendo tribulationes, vel tentando (ut quidem aiunt) per libidinem' ('an evil angel sent by Satan, to buffet him; that is, to check every feeling of pride by inflicting him with tribulations, or by tempting him (as some say) by lust').[19] There was, then, a strong exegetical tradition that St Paul's affliction was a persistent temptation to lust. Heloise recognised a fellow-sufferer, or rather saw in her own affliction something that had been dignified by troubling in equal measure the greatest of Christian saints. Hers was no common lust; she was possessed by a diviner lust, a Pauline lust, an Apostolic lust.

---

[14] *The Second Epistle of Paul the Apostle to the Corinthians*, ed. A. Plummer (Cambridge, 1912), p. 239.

[15] 'others say, "pricked on by titillation of the flesh" '.

[16] 'because on the literal level, it is said that he was vehemently afflicted by a severe colic'.

[17] 'that there dwelt in him the passions of concupiscence, which however he re-strained by divine grace'.

[18] *Second Epistle of Paul to the Corinthians*, ed. Plummer, pp. 240–1.

[19] *PL* 114, 568.

II

. . . how can I make a cowardly amends
For what she has said to me?
                    T. S. Eliot, *Portrait of a Lady*

How could Abelard reply adequately to Heloise's letter? His reply is quite cool and formal.[20] His editor remarks that 'It is noteworthy that in Abelard's reply . . . he makes no reference to some of her most impassioned statements.'[21] Abelard's greeting is impersonal: 'Sponsae Christi servus eiusdem' ('To the bride of Christ, his servant').[22] The beginning reads like a scholastic response to a disputed thesis. He notes that she has complained on four counts, and he replies to each in turn. First, she has questioned the propriety of putting her name before his in the greeting of his previous letter; secondly, she has chastised him for mentioning the possibility of his own death; thirdly, she has raised what Abelard calls 'veterem illam et assiduam querelam' ('that old and unremitting complaint') about their manner of entry into the religious life – thus he dismisses the heartbreaking revelation of her utter distress – and finally she has complained about being flattered. Had this letter been Abelard's only response to Heloise's situation, we should put him down as a very cold fish indeed.

Heloise did not let the matter rest there. She replied with a more subdued letter,[23] bridling her grief in accordance with Abelard's injunctions. This letter contains what Southern describes as 'a long, sharp-witted criticism of the Benedictine Rule as it appeared to an intelligent and learned woman who for fifteen years had lived under it with a divided mind'.[24] A striking feature of this criticism, however, is that it is concerned solely with what one might call the externals of the Rule. She complains that the regulations for monastic garb are inappropriate for women: 'quid ad feminas quod de cucullis, femoralibus, et scapularibus ibi scriptum est?' ('what has what is written there about cowls, drawers and scapulars to do with women?').[25] How can they wear certain prescribed materials which are to be avoided when having monthly periods? The whole tenor of her letter is that women are weaker than men, and should not be subjected to the same bodily rigours. Bull and heifer should not be yoked together (and the word Heloise uses is *bull* – Radice's translation 'bullock' is perhaps the unkindest cut of all).[26] It is a well-known fact, she says,

---

20 Abelard, 'Personal Letters', pp. 47–94.
21 'Personal Letters', p. 59.
22 'Personal Letters', p. 82.
23 'Letter of Heloise'; Radice, *Letters*, p. 159.
24 Southern, *Medieval Humanism*, p. 101.
25 'Letter of Heloise', p. 242.
26 Heloise's word is *taurus*, 'bull' ('Letter of Heloise', p. 243).

that women are not so easily intoxicated as men – and she cites Aristotle and Macrobius as authorities for this surprising statement.[27] Their bodies, having more holes than men's, cope more easily with a draught of wine, which in women 'loses its force' ('vim suam perdit). This being so, could women not be given a more generous allowance of wine? She also asks for meat in the diet,[28] and would like to wear linen like the Augustinian Canons.[29] Her concern is always for the comfort of the body, for food and drink and clothing. Mortifica- tion of the body is not at all to her taste. She ends the letter by asking Abelard for two things: a history of female monasticism, and a detailed rule of life for her community.

As Southern remarks, Abelard did what she asked, and much more. He sent her the desired Rule and History of the Order, long treatises that must have cost him much time and labour. 'To get the full record of what Abelard did for Heloise, we must add about a hundred hymns, thirty-five sermons, and a substantial series of solutions of Heloise's theological problems.'[30] One should not forget either the half-dozen *Planctus* which Abelard wrote, and which touch very closely on the state of mind of Heloise and himself.[31]

The hymns which Abelard wrote for Heloise's community are among the glories of Latin literature. F. J. E. Raby comments, 'Abélard, the prince of dialecticians, the master intellect of his age, wrote a volume of hymns of which the least that can be said is that it is worthy of his genius.'[32] Their editor describes them as 'a major monument of twelfth-century hymnody and po- etry in general'. He goes on to say that, more than this, they are also 'a work of personal significance . . . a labor of love.'[33] They are a collection of hymns for the daily monastic office. They could be used, as some of them are used, in other churches and monastic houses, without reference to or any necessary knowledge of the story of Abelard and Heloise. But if one does know their story, the poems gain a considerable resonance. Abelard had found an accept- able medium in which to express his love for Heloise. He had written in his *Historia calamitatum* of composing love-songs for Heloise, some of which were still being sung as he wrote.[34] This channel for the expression of his love had now been cut off, but another had opened up. He could now express a love for her, as ardent as before, but now refined, sublimated, subsumed in their

---

27 'Letter of Heloise', p. 246.
28 'Letter of Heloise', p. 248.
29 'Letter of Heloise', p. 245.
30 Southern, *Medieval Humanism*, p. 101.
31 They have been edited by G. Vecchi in *Pietro Abelardo, I 'Planctus', Introduzione, testo critico, trascrizioni musicali*, Istituto di filologia romanza della Università di Roma, Collana Testi e Manuali 35 (Modena, 1951).
32 F. J. E. Raby, *A History of Christian-Latin Poetry from the beginnings to the close of the Middle Age* (Oxford, 1953), p. 290.
33 *Peter Abelard's Hymnarius Paraclitensis*, ed. J. Szövérffy, 2 vols. (Albany, NY, and Brookline, Mass., 1975), I, 7.
34 'Letter of Consolation', p. 184; Radice, *Letters*, p. 68.

common love for Christ. His greeting to her in the epistle dedicatory to the hymnal is certainly warmer than anything he had said in letters i and iv: 'soror mihi Heloisa, in saeculo quondam cara, nunc in Christo carissima' – 'my sister Heloise, once dear to me in the world, now most dear in Christ'.[35] Here at last he had found an appropriate, acceptable and safe mode of discourse. It was to be reflected after Abelard's death in Peter the Venerable's letter of consolation to Heloise: 'Hunc ergo uenerabilis et carissima in domino soror, cui post carnalem copulam tanto ualidore, quanto meliore diuinae caritatis uinculis adhesisti . . .' ('Him, therefore, venerable and dearest sister in the Lord, him to whom after your union in the flesh you are joined by the better, and therefore stronger, bond of divine love').[36]

Abelard was highly sensitive to criticism of his relationship with Heloise, and indeed regarded himself as vulnerable to criticism of any kind. He complains in the *Historia calamitatum*:

> God is my witness that I never heard that an assembly of ecclesiastics had met without thinking this was convened to condemn me. I waited like one in terror of being struck by lightning to be brought before a council or synod and charged with heresy or profanity.[37]

With particular reference to his continuing relationship with Heloise, he had found by bitter experience that he could not win:

> But then all the people in the neighbourhood began attacking me violently for doing less than I could and should to minister to the needs of the women, as (they said) I was certainly well able to do, if only through my preaching; so I started to visit them more often to see how I could help them. This provoked malicious insinuations, and my detractors, with their usual perverseness, had the effrontery to accuse me of doing what genuine charity prompted because I was still a slave to the pleasures of carnal desire and could rarely or never bear the absence of the woman I had once loved.[38]

It was necessary for Abelard to choose his words very carefully. Furthermore, the relationship between Heloise and Abelard had become very complicated. Their correspondence is between a man and his wife, a woman and her husband; between an abbot and an abbess; between master and pupil; between two of the leading scholars of the twelfth century. Heloise herself remarks on the complexity of the relationship in her complaint that Abelard has set her name before his own:

---

35 *Hymnarius Paraclitensis*, ed. Szövérffy, II, 9.
36 *The Letters of Peter the Venerable*, ed. G. Constable, 2 vols. (Cambridge, Mass., 1967), I, 308; *Radice, Letters*, p. 284.
37 Radice, *Letters*, p. 93.
38 Radice, *Letters*, pp. 97–8.

I am surprised, my only love, that contrary to custom in latter-writing and, indeed, to the natural order, you have thought fit to put my name before yours in the greeting which heads your letter, so that we have woman before man, wife before husband, handmaid before master, nun before monk, deaconess before priest and abbess before abbot.[39]

Abelard has reversed not just one accepted order, but a whole cluster of ordered relationships: 'feminam videlicet viro, uxorem marito, ancillam domino, monialem monacho et sacerdoti diaconissam, abbati abbatissam'.[40] The apparent coldness and formality of Abelard's earlier letters to Heloise seems to me to hide both an apprehension of attracting criticism and a genuine uncertainty as to what was now his relationship with her, and consequently what was the appropriate mode of discourse to address to her. In the hymnal he at last hit the right note, and the effect was striking. He no longer had to apologise for his relationship with Helose, or to dismiss it as an aberration, as I think he does in the *Historia calamitatum*.[41]

It has long been noticed that there are frequent personal references in Abelard's six *Planctus*.[42] A common thread running through them is of betrayal to death by someone in whom the victim had a right to trust. The first reference is to the lament of Dinah, daughter of Jacob, for her dead lover. Genesis 34 relates that Shechem the son of Hamor the Hivite took Dinah the daughter of Jacob, and lay with her, and defiled her. It is not said that Dinah was unwilling, or that Shechem used force. On the contrary, he is said to have been an honourable man, to have loved her, and to have made an offer to marry her. Dinah's brothers pretended to agree to the arrangement in order to entrap Shechem. They insisted that they could not agree to the marriage unless Shechem and all the men of his city were circumcised. This was done, and while the Hivites were sore following the operation, Dinah's brothers Simeon and Levi slew all the men of the city, and brought Dinah out of Shechem's house.

Even from the bare outline of the story it is easy to see parallels in the misfortunes of Abelard and Heloise. Abelard had lain with Heloise, and defiled her; he had offered marriage, and Heloise's kinsman Fulbert had agreed to the proposal, but evidently with treachery in his heart. In the circumcision and soreness of Shechem and his people one may see an allusion to the mutilation of Abelard.

Nothing is said in the Genesis story of Dinah's feelings in the matter. Abelard supplies this want. She complains of the cruelty of Simeon and Levi, who had punished the innocent with the guilty, the young with the old,

---

[39] Radice, *Letters*, p. 127.
[40] 'Personal Letters', p. 77.
[41] 'Letter of Consolation', p. 183; Radice, *Letters*, p. 66.
[42] Charles de Rémusat, *Abélard*, 2 vols. (Paris, 1845), I, 124; Raby, *Christian-Latin Poetry*, pp. 325–6.

making no allowance for *amoris impulsio, culpae sanctificatio*, the impulse of love, the sanctification of guilt by marriage. She concludes

> Ve mihi, Ve tibi,
> miserande iuvenis,
> in stragem communem
> gentis tantae concidis.[43]

> (Woe to me, woe to you, pitiable youth;
> you fell in the common slaughter of so many people.)

The last word here, *concidis*, may bear, as Abelard's words so often bear, a *double entendre*. *Concīdo* means to fall in combat, and that is undoubtedly the meaning here, especially as it is linked with *strages*, an overthrow, slaughter, massacre. But *concīdo*, a near homonym, means to cut away or dismember, or, in another sense, to lie with someone.[44] There is a precedent in Cicero for a *double entendre* on the two senses of this verb, in an address to gladiators. *Concīdo* cannot be the verb intended, for it is transitive and there is no direct object, but a *double entendre* does not always take a strict account of grammar. We may see here a particularly pointed reference to Abelard's situation.

Abelard put two *planctus* into the mouth of David, King of Israel, the reputed author of the psalms. Abelard, himself a poet and musician, author of a volume of sacred songs designed to accompany and complement the psalms in the daily office, may well have seen something of himself in the figure of David. His *Planctus David super Saul et Jonatha* begins:

> Dolorum solatium
> laborum remedium
> mea michi cithara . . .[45]

> (Solace of sorrows, relief to me from labours, my lute . . .)

No doubt Abelard, as well as David, found comfort in expressing his feelings in verse. His own feelings would hardly be for Jonathan, and we may again see a particular reference to his feelings for Heloise in the lines

---

[43] *Planctus*, ed. Vecchi, p. 43.

[44] See the entries on both words in Lewis and Short, p. 398. See further *Oxford Latin Dictionary*, ed. P. G. W. Glare, 2 vols. (Oxford, 1982), I, 386; *Dictionary of Medieval Latin from British Sources*, ed. R. E. Latham, D. R. Howlett *et al.*, 4 fascs. so far (1975–89), II, 419. Hereafter referred to as *OLD*, and *DMLBS*. The ambiguity of the two forms here described was fully recognised in medieval grammatical tradition. To take but one (later) example, in the *Catholicon* which Giovanni de' Balbi of Genoa completed in 1286, two Biblical texts are cited, one being Genesis 4. 5 ('concidit vultus eius' – describing how Cain was angry and his 'countenance fell') and the other, Job 16. 15 ('Concidit me vulnere super vulnus', 'He hath torn me with wound upon wound'). *Catholicon* (Mainz, 1460; rpt. Farnborough, 1971), unfol. (s.v. *concido*).

[45] *Planctus*, ed. Vecchi, p. 66.

> Vel confossus pariter
> morerer feliciter . . .[46]

(Would that, wounded in like manner, I had died happily . . .)

The word *confossus* is the past participle of *confodio*, to pierce through, to stab; but actually this is a transferred meaning, *con-fodio* meaning literally to dig thoroughly;[47] *fodio* is to dig, and its past participle *fossa* means something dug, a ditch, a grave.[48] I suggest that Abelard may have intended another *double entendre* here, and that he is expressing his wish not only to have died with Heloise, but to be buried with her. That he did so wish, is evident from his letter to her in which he says,

> But if the Lord shall deliver me into the hands of my enemies so that they overcome or kill me, or by whatever chance I enter upon the way of all flesh while absent from you, wherever my body may lie, buried or unburied, I beg you to have it brought to your burial-ground, where our daughters, or rather, our sisters in Christ may see my tomb more often and thereby be encouraged to pour out their prayers more fully to the Lord on my behalf.[49]

In the same letter, Abelard alludes to Jephtha, a character from the Book of Judges, chapter 11. This Jephtha made a vow to God that, if he were given victory over the Ammonites, he would sacrifice whoever came to meet him on his return home. It happened that his daughter, his only child, came out to meet him, and Jephtha was obliged by his vow to sacrifice her. Abelard's allusion to Jephtha in this letter is in a comparison with men who apply stern justice without mercy. Abelard's point is that God is not like this, and can be turned aside by prayer from his declared intention, just as David in his mercy broke an oath to put to death Nabal the Carmelite, on the entreaty of Nabal's wife.[50] Abelard does not quite make a comparison between Heloise and Jephtha's daughter; rather, the comparison is with Nabal's wife, for Abelard wished Heloise to intercede with God on his behalf:

> Here you have an example, sister, and an assurance how much your prayers for me may prevail on God, if this woman's did so much for her husband, seeing that God who is our father loves his children more than David did a suppliant woman.[51]

Still, Abelard did mention Jephtha's daughter in the context of biblical antecedents of Heloise; and there are obvious parallels between the two. Both were

---

[46] *Planctus*, ed.Vecchi, p. 69.
[47] Cf. Lewis and Short, p. 416; *OLD* I, 402; *DMLBS* II, 435.
[48] Cf. Lewis and Short, p. 774; *OLD* I, 728; *DMLBS* IV, 993–4.
[49] Radice, *Letters*, p. 125; cf. 'Personal Letters', pp. 76–7.
[50] 'Personal Letters', p. 74.
[51] Radice, *Letters*, p. 121; cf. 'Personal Letters', p. 74.

brought to an untimely end as the result of a vow, taken not by themselves but by someone else on their behalf. A foolish vow, no doubt, but in each case the woman concurred with the vow and permitted it to be carried out. Jephtha's daughter had said, 'My father, if thou hast opened thy mouth unto the Lord, do to me according to that which hath proceeded out of thy mouth' (Judges 11. 36). Likewise Heloise had gone to what she clearly regarded as death, in obedience to Abelard's wishes.

Abelard had Jephtha's daughter a good deal in mind, for he mentions her in another letter, and two of his hymns and one of his *planctus* concern her. The epistolary reference is in his history of the order of religious women, a sort of *Legend of Good Women*, written at the request of Heloise:

> Quis in laudem virginum unicam illam Iephthe filiam non censeat; quae ne voti licet improvidi reus pater haberetur et divinae gratiae beneficium promissa fraudaretur hostia, victorem patrem in iugulum proprium animavit.[52]

> (Who would not value – in the praise of virgins – that only daughter of Jephtha, who, lest her father might be held guilty of a vow, albeit rash, and the benefit of divine grace be defrauded of the promised sacrifice, urged her victorious father to [cut] her own throat.)

The last clause, 'she urged her victorious father to [cut] her own throat', must have pleased Abelard, for he versified it in the hymn for the second nocturn of feasts of holy women:

> Iephte nata
> victoris in proprium
> Patris dextram
> animavit iugulum.[53]

> (Jephtha's daughter urged her victorious father's right hand [to cut] her own throat.)

Jephtha's daughter also figures in the hymn for the third nocturn:

> Si cum viris
> feminas contendere
> De virtute
> liceat constantiae,
> Quis virorum
> mentis fortitudine
> Adaequari
> possit Iephte filiae
> Quae ne voti
> pater reus sit,

---

[52] 'Letters of Heloise', p. 270.
[53] Hymn 125; *Hymnarius Paraclitensis*, ed. Szövérffy, II, 259.

> Se victimam
> patri praebuit?[54]

> (If it is permissible for women to contend with men in the
> virtue of constancy, which of men could equal in fortitude of
> mind the daughter of Jephtha, who, lest her father should be
> guilty of breaking a vow, offered herself as a victim to her
> father?)

The idea of the girl urging her father on to cut her throat is recycled again
in the *planctus* for Jephtha's daughter:

> Ne votum sit patris irritum
> promissoque fraudet dominum,
> qui per hunc salvavit populum,
> in suum hunc urget jugulum.

> (Lest the vow of her father should be invalid, and that he should
> defraud the Lord, through whom he had saved the people, of
> what was promised, she urges him [to cut] her own throat.)

Actually there is nothing said in the Book of Genesis about *how* Jephtha killed
his daughter. The frequent mention of cutting her throat is perhaps intended
to reinforce the image of sacrifice, the girl being put to death like a sacrificial
lamb. This image would have been presented to both Abelard and Heloise
frequently in a text which they were committed to read, or hear read, every
day: the Rule of Saint Benedict. In a passage which might seem to have been
written with their situation in mind, the Rule says:

> The fourth step of humility is that in this obedience under difficult,
> unfavorable, or even unjust conditions, his heart quietly embraces suf-
> fering and endures it without weakening or seeking escape. For Scrip-
> ture has it: *Anyone who perseveres to the end will be saved* (Matt. 10. 22), and
> again, *Be brave of heart and rely on the Lord* (Ps. 26[27].14). Another pas-
> sage shows how the faithful must endure everything, even contradic-
> tion, for the Lord's sake, saying in the person of those who suffer, *For
> your sake we are put to death continually; we are regarded as sheep marked for
> slaughter.*[55]

Another influence on the poem may have been some lines from the story of
the sacrifice of Iphigenia by her father Agamemnon, told by Boethius in the
De consolatione philosophiae:

> Exuit patrem miserumque tristis
> Foederat *natae iugulum* sacerdos.[56]

---

[54] Hymn 126; *Hymnarius Paraclitensis*, ed. Szövérffy, II, 259–60.

[55] *Rule of St Benedict*, ed. Fry, p. 197.

[56] Boethius, *De consolatione philosophiae*, Book iv, metre 7. I am grateful to Prof. A. J.
Minnis for this reference.

(He put off the role of a father and, as a sorrowful priest, cut the wretched throat of his daughter.)

Here there is an identical theme – sacrifice of a girl by her father – and an interesting correspondence of vocabulary. The passage may have been in Abelard's mind.

The *planctus* for Jephtha's daughter has been studied in some detail by Margaret Alexiou and Peter Dronke, who suggest that Abelard may have been influenced by the Latin translation of a lament composed in Greek in the first century AD by an author known today as pseudo-Philo, wherein Jephtha's daughter is given the name Seila.[57] Their comparison of texts brings out the distinctive qualities of Abelard's version, wherein the girl's preparation for her death – she bathes and is clothed by her 'bridesmaids' – is seen as a counterpart to the preparations for a wedding:

> Abelard's principal debt to pseudo-Philo is in his conception of the wedding-mime: in the whole notion, quite foreign to the Bible, of seeing Seila's sacrificial death in terms of a marriage-ceremony – in Abelard's words, *ut . . . tanquam nuptiis morti se preparent.*[58] In both authors, the sense of her death as a grim parody of her wedding is evident, and decisive for the poetic structure. Yet Abelard's transformation of pseudo-Philo is also remarkable: threnody becomes drama. Instead of a girl lamenting, dreaming of every aspect of the wedding on earth she will never know, we have a girl who is heroically silent while all her attendants weep, while they give her every aspect of a bride's preparation, every moment of which deepens her ordeal, intensifies for her the contrast between the pretence of wedding and the reality of dying.[59]

Alexiou and Dronke proceed to point out the influence of the Song of Songs:

> . . . in this part of the *planctus* many words carry associations of the Song of Songs: the girl's body is *languidum* – overtly because of her weariness after her homeward journey, yet it cannot help suggesting also the bride's voluptuous expectation of her mystic marriage. The *unguenti*

---

[57] M. Alexiou and P. Dronke, 'The Lament of Jephtha's Daughter', *Studi medievali*, 3rd ser. 12.2 (1971), 819–863.

[58] 'to prepare themselves for death as if for a wedding'.

[59] Alexiou and Dronke, 'Lament of Jephtha's Daughter', p. 856. In support of their assertion that 'Abelard's direct knowledge of pseudo-Philo' is 'highly probable', they cite parallels between Abelard's *planctus* of David over Saul and Jonathan and a passage in pseudo-Philo, while admitting that they 'cannot wholly rule out the possibility that Abelard knew, not pseudo-Philo himself, but some intermediate source as yet untraced' (p. 853, note 49). I myself regard the case for the influence of pseudo-Philo on Abelard's *planctus* for Jephtha's daughter as unconvincing, given the considerable differences between the two texts; the influence of the Song of Songs is, in my view, at once uncontestable and crucial.

species, pixides, monilia[60] of the victim are also the gifts the divine lover of the Song of Songs lavishes on his bride.[61]

The reference is to the luxurious bath which Jephtha's daughter takes before offering herself in sacrifice:

> Varias unguenti species
> aurate continent pixides
> quas flentes afferunt virgines.
> His illam condiunt alie
> capillos componunt relique
> vel vestes praeparent domino.[62]

> (The gilded vessels which the weeping virgins bring contain various sorts of ointment. With these some anoint her, the rest arrange her hair, prepare her garments for the Lord.)

Holy oils have various uses in the Christian Church: at baptism, at an ordination, at a coronation, at the moment of death. The theme uniting these various events is of a setting-apart, a consecration to God. The linking of weeping and anointing suggests the anointing of Christ by the woman of John 12. 3: 'Maria ergo accepit libram unguenti nardi pistici, pretiosi, et unxit pedes Iesu, et extersit pedes eius capillis suis: et domus impleta est ex odore unguenti' ('Mary therefore took a pound of ointment of right spikenard, of great price, and anointed the feet of Jesus and wiped his feet with her hair. And the house was filled with the odour of the ointment'). If the connexion seems tenuous, one should consider St Bernard's Sermon no. 10 on the Song of Songs. He is addressing the text 'Dum esset rex in accubitu suo, nardus mea dedit odorem suum' ('While the king was at his repose, my spikenard sent forth the odour thereof'; Song of Songs 1. 11). He relates this to the woman in the gospel story:

> However, if we say that this visible and spiritual ointment was symbolized by the visible ointment with which the sinful woman, as the Gospel describes, visibly anointed the corporeal feet of God, we cannot regard it as entirely worthless. For what do we read in the Gospel? 'The house', it says, 'was full of the scent of the ointment'.[63]

In Bernard's mind the typological connexion between the Song of Songs passage and the gospel incident was so strong and so obvious as to be readily

---

[60] 'varieties of unction, ointment-boxes, necklaces'.

[61] Alexiou and Dronke, 'Lament of Jephtha's Daughter', p. 857. Their footnote is worth reproducing: 'Cf. especially *Cant.*, I, 1–3, 9–10; II, 5; III, 6: IV, 10; VII, 1. (The closest verbal correspondences are sometimes with Patristic renderings and paraphrases of these verses rather than with the Vulgate text)'.

[62] *Planctus*, ed. Vecchi, p. 52.

[63] *The Works of Bernard of Clairvaux*, vol. 2, trans. K. Walsh, Cistercian Fathers Series 4 (Kalamazoo, MN, 1971), p. 64.

accepted by his hearers. It is not too fanciful therefore to see in Abelard's *planctus* the hint of a comparison between the Jephtha's daughter/Heloise figure and Christ, being prepared by a tearful anointing for his sacrificial death.

Alexiou and Dronke clearly see the relevance of the poem to the situation of Abelard and Heloise:

> ... that he could see the plangent Seila as a creature of fire and air must be in part because he had known such a gesture of reckless heroism in his own beloved Héloise: as he tells us in the *Historia Calamitatum*, she accepted being immured as a nun, at his command, explicitly as a sacrifice and a voluntary dying for his sake.[64]

The ideas of death and sacrifice, marriage and religious profession were all linked together in Abelard's mind. His bride, Heloise, had become the bride of Christ; her marriage had been transposed into religious profession, which is both a death of the body and a spiritual marriage to the heavenly bridegroom. Southern rightly says that the material Abelard wrote for Heloise 'gives him his greatest claim – not to fame, for that is his due on quite other grounds – but to our personal regard'.[65] One could go further, and say that the poetry which Abelard wrote for Heloise lays claim not only to our personal regard, but to our recognition of his status as the greatest poet of his century.

Acknowledgement

I am grateful to Prof. David Luscombe for his valuable comments on an earlier version of this paper.

---

[64] Alexiou and Dronke, 'Lament of Jephtha's Daughter', p. 859.
[65] *Medieval Humanism*, p. 101.

Cathars and Material Women[1]

Peter Biller

In January, 1246,

> Aimersent, the wife of Guilhem the Viguier of Cambiac, swore [to tell the truth] as a witness. She said that a good twenty-three years have passed since her the witness's paternal aunt, Gérauda of Cabuet, took her the witness to Auriac, to the house of Lady Esquiva, the wife of the knight Guilhem Aldric. And she saw two heretics [female] in the said house. And she saw there together with them the said Esquiva, and the said Guilhem Aldric, and their son Guilhem Aldric, and the said Gérauda. And all of them and she the witness, [who was] instructed by the said Esquiva, adored the said heretics [female], genuflecting three times while saying, 'Bless, Good Ladies, pray God for these sinners'. She also said that afterwards, on the same day, R[aimon] of Auriac came to the said heretics [female], in the said house. All of them and she the witness heard the preaching of the said heretics [female] for a long time, and they adored them, as was said above. And in front of everyone the said heretics [female] said to her the witness, because she was a pregnant adolescent girl, that she was carrying the devil in her belly; and everyone began to laugh at this.

After detailing another episode where named individuals came to see male heretics in the same house, Aimersent returned to her own position in all this. 'She also said that her husband, Gilhem the Viguier, often urged her the witness to love the heretics as he and all the others of the place [Cambiac] did. But she the witness did not want to love them, after the heretics [female] had told her that she was pregnant by the devil. And for this reason her aforesaid husband often beat her the witness, and made her many reproaches for not loving the heretics.'[2]

---

[1] I owe thanks to Mary Heimann and Susie Biller for ideas and comment, and to audiences to whom earlier versions of the first part were delivered, the History Society of St Catherine's College, Oxford in November 1990, and the Social and Cultural History Seminar at All Souls College, Oxford, in February 1993. The second part was earlier sketched in P. Biller, 'The Common Woman in the Western Church in the Thirteenth and Early Fourteenth Centuries', in *Women in the Church*, ed. W. J. Sheils and D. Wood, *SCH* 27 (Oxford, 1990), pp. 127–57 (pp. 147–57).
[2] Toulouse, Bibliothèque municipale, MS 609, fol. 239v: 'Aimerssens, uxor Wllmi. Vicarii de Cambiac, dixit quod bene sunt .xxiij. anni quod Geralda de Cabuer, amitta

This deposition confronts us immediately with one level, the text produced by inquisitors' scribes, the language and legal procedure recorded in that, and the line of inquisitor's questions, mainly implied but not spelled out. At this time and when dealing with thousands, inquisitors were (sensibly from their point of view) usually confining themselves to the police questions which they had developed from the earlier *circumstantiae* (circumstances) of sin, 'When?', 'Where?', 'Who?', 'How many?', and so on. Through the grille of this text we see Aimersent bearing witness, doubtless in her eyes with a mixture of truth and lies, but the lies will have to have been very plausible, because these inquisitors were very attentive to the implausible and to inconsistencies. We are then plunged by her evidence into a world of Catharism around 1223. 'Heretics', called 'perfects' by inquisitors (as they will be here) but 'Good Women' or 'Good Men' by their adherents, come to the houses of strong adherents. In some places, for example Cambiac, virtually everyone is a follower. Once the perfects are present in a house, people gather. The perfects preach, and after the sermon those who share their faith, called 'believers', engage in a rite called 'melioramentum', which we will call 'adoration'. Telling of the first time she or he attended such a meeting, a deponent often says who took them along – if the deponent was a girl, this will often be an older woman in the family. So far this is commonplace and found in countless depositions. However, although women perfects were often seen, they were very rarely described as preaching, and at this stage glimpses of the content of preaching by perfects of either gender were also very rare. The picture in this particular deposition not only crackles with the life of its named and dated particulars, but also with the vividness of the apparent paradox which is at its centre. On the one hand women perfects do something they could not do in

ipsius testis, duxit isam testem apud Auriacum, ad domum N'Esquiva, uxoris Wllmi. Aldrici, militis, et vidit in dicta domo duas hereticas, et vidit ibi cum eis dictam Esquivam et dictum Wllm. Aldrici et Wllm. Aldrici, filium eorum, et dictam Geraldam. Et omnes et ipsa testis, edocta a dicta Esquiva, adoraverunt dictas hereticas, ter flexis genibus, dicendo, "Benedicite, Bone Domine, orate Deum pro istis peccatoribus". Dixit etiam quod postea, eadem die, venerunt ad dictas hereticas, in dicta domo, R. de Auriaco [some names missing at this point?], qui omnes et ipsa testis audierunt predicationem dictarum hereticarum diu, et adoraverunt eas, sicut superius dictum est. Et dicte heretice dixerunt ipsi testi, coram omnibus, quia erat adolescentula pregnans, quod demonium portabat in ventre, et alii ceperunt ridere inde . . . Dixit etiam quod Guillmus. Vicarius, vir suus, monuit ipsm testem multociens quod diligeret hereticos, sicut ipse faciebat et alii de villa, sed ipsa testis noluit diligere, postquam dixerunt sibi heretice quod pregnans erat de demonio; et idcirco vir suus supradictus verberavit multociens ipsam testem, et dixit multa convicia, quia non diligebat hereticos'. On the MS see below and note 49, and, on the pressures exerted on Aimersent as a witness, see Y. Dossat, *Les crises de l'inquisition toulousaine au XIIIe siècle (1233–1273)* (Bordeaux, 1959), p. 242. Here and below the forms of Occitan first-names follow those listed in A. Brenon, *Le petit livre aventureux des prénoms occitans au temps du catharisme* (Toulouse, 1992).

the Church, preach, and they take this opportunity to preach lengthily, among other things talking about the pregnancy of one of their listeners. On the other hand it is another woman, then a girl, who rejects Catharism, precisely because of what these Cathar women said on that point. And the girl does this despite a man, her husband, who tried to cajole and beat her into Cathar belief. Not surprisingly, the passage was noticed and used polemically quite early on in modern historical accounts of medieval Catharism.

Here, in a nutshell, are the main themes of this paper – Catharism and women, earlier historians' presentation of this topic, and the role of Cathar doctrines about the female body in it. Particularised in Auriac around 1223, these themes relate, in the modern world, to a very broad and general problem about the medieval Church, medieval heresy, and medieval women. Very widespread in earlier accounts of medieval women is something which, although now long surpassed by sophisticated modern feminist scholarship, still persists as a belief. This is a simple picture of women and medieval 'religion'. 'Women' are thought of as a bloc, repelled by or drawn to the Church or heresy. For women medieval heresy was attractive, set against the misogynist medieval Church. Unsurprisingly, women were specially drawn to heresy. As far as the Church is concerned, absent from the picture is the evidence which makes the study of the relations of ordinary women with the Church more interesting and complex: evidence about ordinary women's greater assiduity than men's in Church-going, prayer, and other pious acts.[3] As far as central-medieval heresy is concerned, the attractive picture downplays or even ignores one group of heretics, the Waldensians. This is odd, because a lot of evidence straightforwardly makes Waldensianism a very good candidate for attractiveness to women. Rather, the picture concentrates on the Catharism. This again is odd, because the evidence for the latter's attractiveness to women is not straightforward, and some of it is adverse. However, Catharism's appeal to women is a modern belief which is 'religious' in the pejorative sense: to some it is an article of faith, to be maintained regardless of the evidence.

It is for this reason that the first part of this paper looks at the origins of this belief. The second part's leitmotif is the presence of a pregnant body in what we have seen women perfects preaching and a girl rejecting in a house in Auriac in the early thirteenth century: it takes the theme of Cathars and female bodies in order to approach the very varied past reality of 'Cathars and women'.

---

[3] Biller, 'Common Woman', 139–41.

1. Historiography: the Origins of the Myth

In 1953, at the age of thirty-eight, the German historian Arno Borst published his first book, *Die Katharer*.[4] In its long first part Borst wrote a history of the history of the subject, ranging from *c*.1000 to *c*.1950.[5] This begins with medieval chroniclers and inquisitors writing about Cathars, and it then goes on to the early great Protestant and Catholic *eruditi*, the men who founded Protestant and Catholic polemical historiography, Matthias Flacius Illyricus and Jakob Gretser, writing about Cathars, and then it goes further, through the romantic historians of the nineteenth century, ending in Borst's own day. Borst showed the various faces the Cathars have presented to writers, or rather the various masks that writers have imposed on them. These have been sometimes masks conceived by writers as opposites of themselves – emissaries of the Devil to medieval Catholic writers – but the masks have been more often cast in the likeness of the writers themselves, who have seen Cathars as their forerunners. Thus Cathars have played Protestant forerunners to Protestant historians, and later different roles: forerunners to Languedocian separatists, to proletarian revolutionaries, and to Nazis. Borst summarised this succession of masks, while at the same time providing a history of scholarship on the Cathars, which was generally progressive, though also not devoid of distorting masks.

Borst's approach and some of his conclusions are adopted here, but for the narrower theme: not Catharism in general, but Catharism and women. And the story is carried on for the forty years after Borst's book. The question is not the philosophically simple, 'What was the past "reality" of Catharism and women?' Rather it is, 'What masks has this theme worn between the middle ages and now, and how have developments in scholarship affected it?' What follows is a sketch of an answer to this question, done in the style of Borst.

i. The Middle Ages

First we turn to medieval writers. Between the early eleventh and mid-twelfth centuries most Catholic writers had patchy knowledge of the heresies they confronted. Patristic writings and scriptural texts on heresy tended to fill the gaps. A passage applied to heretics from II Timothy 3. 6 was one such, 'penetrant domos, et captivas ducunt mulierculas oneratas peccatis' (in the Douay translation, 'they creep into houses and lead captive silly women laden with sins'). It was one source both of the tendency of authors to underline women among adherents of heresy and also of the precise words they used when

---

4   *Schriften der MGH* 12 (Stuttgart); French translation, *Les cathares* (Paris, 1974).
5   'Die Katharer im Spiegel von Quellen und Forschungen', pp. 1–58; in *Les cathares*, pp. 9–53.

making this point.[6] From the mid-1160s knowledge increased, as well as the capacity of observers to describe and analyse 'religious' phenomena.[7] As discrimination came in, blanket use of scriptural texts diminished. From *c*.1190 to the mid-thirteenth century a very interesting pattern is found. A row of French authors, such as Bernard of Fontcaude, Alain de Lille and Stephen of Bourbon, sharply attack one set of heretics, Waldensians, for allowing women to preach.[8] While comparison is not to be looked for in Bernard, since he concentrates on Waldensians, both Alain and Etienne also wrote about Cathars. In both cases the contrast with Waldensians is stark: women do not constitute a theme in their accounts of Cathars.

The theme of heresy and women is also important for two other texts, the first probably and the second certainly from southern Germany, the *De inquisitione hereticorum* and the compilation against heretics, Jews and Antichrist of the Anonymous of Passau (*c*.1266). The author of the first makes the points about Waldensians, that 'non autem solum viri sed et femine apud eos docent' ('not only men but also women teach among them'), and also that 'student diligenter attrahere sibi aliquas potentes et nobiles feminas' ('they diligently apply themselves to attracting some powerful and noble women').[9] The second makes a general claim about heresy's strength among women and the weak, counterposed to the Church: 'omne genus hominum habet fidem nostram, philosophorum, litteratorum, principum, sed hereticorum pauci et hoc tantum pauperes et opifices, mulieres et ydiote' ('every kind of men has our faith, philosophers, the literate and princes, but only a few [have the faith] of heretics, and this [kind is composed] only of the poor, and workmen, and women, and the illiterate'.[10] His work is a compilation, including material on the Cathars, principally through the incorporation of Rainier Sacconi's treatise against Cathars and Waldensians – of which more in a moment – but the heresy which looms largest in his anthology is Waldensianism. The specific points made in it about heresy and women, which are behind this general claim, concern Waldensians. Prominent is the shift of the point about women teaching into a description of a 'model' conversion dialogue, where it be-

---

6   One example is in the first canon of the Council of Rheims (1157), J. D. Mansi, 31 vols. (Florence, Venice, 1757–98), XXI, 843.

7   P. Biller, 'Words and the medieval notion of "religion" ', *Journal of Ecclesiastical History* 36 (1985), 353–69.

8   See G. G. Merlo, *Identità valdesi nella storia e nella storiografia* (Turin, 1991), part 4 'Sulle "misere donnicciuole" che predicavano', pp. 93–112 (pp. 100–105), and P. Biller, 'Women and Texts in Languedocian Catharism', in *Women, the Book and the Godly*, ed. L. Smith and J. H. M. Taylor (Cambridge, 1995), pp. 171–82 (p. 177 and notes 25–8).

9   *De inquisitione hereticorum* vi and xxiv, ed. W. Preger, 'Der Tractat des David von Augsburg über die Waldesier', *Abhandlungen der bayerischen Akademie der Wissenschaften*, Philosophisch-historische Klasse 13.i (1875), pp. 204–35 (pp. 209 and 218).

10 A. Patschovsky, *Der Passauer Anonymus. Ein Sammelwerk über Ketzer, Juden, Antichrist aus der Mitte des XIII. Jahrhunderts*, Schriften der MGH 22 (Stuttgart, 1968), p. 109.

comes a selling-point as a Waldensian attempts to persuade someone. 'Post hereticus facit comparationem status ecclesie Romane ad statum ipsorum, sic dicens . . . Apud nos vero tam viri quam femine docent' ('Afterwards, the heretic makes a comparison of the Roman Church's state with their state, speaking thus . . . Among us however both men and women teach').[11]

The basic Cathar/Waldensian contrast also characterises treatises against heresy written in Italy. In his very long treatise against Cathars and Waldensians, written around 1241, the Dominican Moneta of Cremona made a polemical point about the Waldensians, that 'mulieres . . . eorum praedicant' ('their women preach'), but made no point about any teaching or ministerial role for women in Catharism.[12] In his short treatise on Cathars and Waldensians, written in 1250, the Dominican and former Cathar Rainier Sacconi does briefly refer to the possibility of the Cathar *consolamentum* being administered by 'Cathar women, in case of need'.[13] Dealing with something he is describing as a Cathar 'baptism' Rainier will not have regarded this as unusual or a polemical point – it paralleled lay people, including women, baptising in case of need. Rainier draws no further attention to this, therefore, and does not build it up into a general point about Cathars and women. He is about to describe an entirely male Cathar hierarchy, set over the 'ceteri qui sunt inter eos sine ordinibus' who 'uocantur christiani et christiane' ('others among who are among them, without Orders, [who] are called Christian men and women'):[14] in other words, an ecclesial body cut through by gender in the same way as the Catholic Church was. Given that, any polemical point about women would have looked very odd. But when he turns to the Waldensians he turns a spotlight on the theme. Rainier presents himself as having asked Waldensians, as an inquisitor, about women's ministerial powers. 'Credo etiam quod idem dicant de mulieribus, quia hoc non negaverunt michi' ('I believe that they say the same thing about women [that a simple layman can consecrate the body of the Lord], since they have not denied it to me').[15] Another Dominican, who had worked under Rainier as an inquisitor, Anselm of Alessandria, wrote on both heresies in a compilation which he started

---

11 *Quellen zur Geschichte der Waldenser*, ed. A. Patschovsky and K.-V. Selge, Texte zur Kirchen- und Theologiegeschichte 18 (Gütersloh, 1973), p. 70.

12 Moneta of Cremona, *Adversus Catharos et Valdenses Libri Quinque* V.v.8; ed. T. A. Ricchini O.P. (Rome, 1743; unaltered reprint, New Jersey, 1964), p. 442; henceforth cited as Moneta. See G. Schmitz-Valckenberg, *Grundlehren katharischer Sekten des 13. Jahrhunderts. Eine theologische Untersuchung mit besonderer Berücksichtigung von AD-VERSUS CATHAROS ET VALDENSES des Moneta von Cremona*, Veröffentlichungen des Grabmann-Instituts n.s. 11 (Munich, Paderborn and Vienna, 1971), pp. 4–6 on Moneta and this edition. On Moneta and manuscripts of this work, see further *SOPMA*, III, 137–9, and IV, 200–201.

13 Rainier Sacconi, *Summa de Catharis et Pauperibus de Lugduno*, ed. F. Sanjek, *AFP* 44 (1974), 31–60 (p. 44): 'in necessitate, a Catharabus'.

14 Rainier, *Summa*, p. 48.

15 Rainier, *Summa*, p. 60.

1266/7 and continued for about ten years. He presents the same contrast, but with more nuance. He (a) is silent on the Cathars, (b) raises the theme with Waldensians, and (c) restricts the Waldensian theme, noting that Waldensian women preached, but that they did not consecrate or administer penance.[16]

Let us stand back from the trees, leaving the many cases of individual women (like individual men), who are presented in depositions before inquisitors, and on occasion in a chronicle, as Cathars or Cathar sympathisers, and let us look at two woods. The first and smaller one is composed of heresies, as seen by Catholic writers. The Catholic writers on Cathars do not make a polemical point about Cathar women preaching. They do not make generalising statements about the special appeal of Catharism to women. They do not point to the prominent role of women in Catharism.[17] They *do* make these points about Waldensians.

The second and larger wood is the Church, and the presence of the theme of women and ministry in its Latin theological literature in the central middle ages. Take a student of theology around 1300. Where would he have seen this theme? Not, probably, as he looked at the world around him.[18] But he would have found it presented in texts. In his principal text-book, Peter Lombard's *Libri IV Sententiarum*, the treatment on bars to ordination had attracted and was continuing to attract commentaries which looked at women. Such discussions – which are analysed in Alastair Minnis's article – must have been commonplace in theology faculties. References in such standard works as Eusebius's *Historia Ecclesiastica*[19] and Gratian's *Decretum*,[20] together with the common genre of short lists of names and principal doctrines of heresies, based on St Augustine's *De haeresibus* and Isidore's *Etymologiae*,[21] would pro-

16 Anselm of Alessandria, *Tractatus de hereticis* 11–12, ed. A. Dondaine, *AFP* 20 (1950), 308–24 (pp. 318–19): 'Item mulieres eorum predicant . . . Nec mulieres eorum ordinantur, sed predicant; penitentiam tamen non dant' ('Item, their women preach . . . Nor are the women ordained, but they preach; however, they do not give penance').
17 There is a famous account of a sister of the Count of Foix, protector of the Cathars, being told by a Catholic religious to keep out of a theological disputation (*disputatio*) in Guillaume de Puylaurens, *Chronique* viii, ed. J. Duvernoy (Paris, 1976), p. 48. There is also a vernacular text which describes a Cathar community of five perfects, in which three women perhaps predominate: 'Le débat d'Izarn et de Sicard de Figueiras', ed. P. Meyer, *Annuaire-Bulletin de la Société de l'Histoire de France* (1879), 232–92 (p. 247, lines 60–4). However, neither of these constitute *generalisations* about the theme.
18 Although the Guglielmites clearly advocated salvation through women, the important point here is that they, and this feature, were not well-known. See S. E. Wessley, 'The thirteenth-century Guglielmites: salvation through women', in *Medieval Women*, ed. D. Baker, *SCH* Subsidia 1 (Oxford, 1978), 289–303 (pp. 290–1).
19 See Montanus and women in *Historia Ecclesiastica* v.16, in the convenient translation of G. A. Williamson (Harmondsworth, 1965), at pp. 217–21.
20 *Presbyterae* in D.32 c.19 and *diaconissae* in C.27 q.1 c.23 and c.30; Friedberg, I, 122, 1055, 1057.
21 In the list of heresies in the *Etymologiae* viii.5 the Cataphrygians are given three 'originators', one male and two female, Montanus, Prisca and Maximilla; this is

vide the student with a quite remote historical setting for the theme. There was the vocabulary of 'deaconess', 'priestess', 'prophetess' (*diaconissa, presbytera, prophetissa*), the early Church, and early heresy. There were women prominent as two of the three 'authors' (*auctores*) of the heresy of the Cataphrygians, and acting as 'prophetesses' in it. But texts would also establish a more recent historical setting. The third abbess of the Cistercian house of Las Huelgas in Spain, doña Sanchia Garcia (1207–30), had blessed novices, heard nuns' confessions and preached in public.[22] These activities had attracted a repressive bull from Innocent III on 11 December 1210, and through entry into one of the 'old compilations' of canons and thence into Gregory IX's *Decretalium Libri V* (1234),[23] they became and remained well-known. While entering canon law, doña Sanchia's name and that of her abbey had got lost, but the reader would still find the activities detailed and attributed to Cistercian abbesses in the dioceses of Palencia and Burgos. If asked to think of a near-contemporary example of women's ministry, our theology student would most probably have talked about Spanish Cistercian abbesses.

Well-known to him, though less well-known to modern scholarship, was the easy availability of this material in *summae* and manuals of confession. Here continuing awareness of the theme of sex and order had eventually joined with the growth of questions to be put to particular groups to produce a confessional question for women. Robert of Flamborough's penitential treatise (1215) had contained a section 'On sex' in the treatment of Holy Orders, while Thomas of Chobham's (*c.*1216) had reminded the reader that women do not receive Orders, but that canon law shows some women as deaconesses, reading the Gospel in a nuns' convent.[24] Raymond of Peñafort's penitential *summa* (first recension 1224–6, second 1234) assembled material under the heading 'impediment of sex', referring briefly to the Cataphrygians, that 'dicunt diaconissam debere ordinari' ('they say that a deaconess should be ordained'), while William of Renne's gloss on this work (*c.*1241) extended the reference to the actions of abbesses,[25] and John of Freiburg incorporated both

---

copied in Gratian's *Decretum* C.24 q.3 c.39; Friedberg, I, 1002. In St Augustine's *De haeresibus* 26–7 (*PL* 42, 30–1) Prisca and Maximilla are referred to as *prophetissae* and *auctores* of the sect. On such lists of heresies, see M. A. E. Nickson, 'The "Pseudo-Reinerius" treatise, the final stage of a thirteenth-century work from the diocese of Passau', *AHDLMA* 34 (1967), 255–314 (pp. 284–5), and Patschovsky, *Passauer Anonymus*, pp. 98–100. See the discussion of Cataphrygians in A. Minnis's paper, p. 135.

22 M. de Fontette, *Les religieuses à l'âge classique du droit canon. Recherches sur les structures juridiques des branches féminines des ordres* (Paris, 1967), p. 47 and note 27.

23 4 Comp. 5.14.1, in *Quinque compilationes antiquae*, ed. E. Friedberg (Leipzig, 1882), p. 149; X 5.38.10 (Friedberg, II, 886–7).

24 Robert of Flamborough, *Liber poenitentialis* iii.2, ed. J. J. F. Firth (Toronto, 1971), p. 101; Thomas of Chobham, *Summa confessorum* I.ii.5.3 (p. 117).

25 Raymond of Peñafort, *Summa de poenitentia et matrimonio* iii.23: De impedimento sexus (Rome, 1603), pp. 316–17; William's gloss is printed in the margins of this.

in his *Summa confessorum* (1297).[26] Fusion with interrogatories for different estates was achieved, then, in John of Freiburg's *Confessionale*, whose second part was organised around such questions. Under the heading 'On the abbess' and the 'Sins about which one [should] enquire concerning abbesses', there is a remarkable instruction: 'Item, [enquire] specially if she has put herself into preaching, excommunication or absolution, or [into] the office of any of the Orders, because she cannot do these things'.[27]

This was written around 1300 – it refers to and therefore comes after the *Summa confessorum* – and the theme was soon to be taken further by Alvarus Pelagius. Alvarus, in his *De planctu ecclesiae*, which he drafted first in 1330–2, constructed this material into some general statements in his long list of the sins of women. '59th, they teach in the pulpit, preaching and reading like masters. . . . 61st, some of them receive Orders, although they cannot. . . . 71st, some stupid abbesses veil with the veil of consecration . . . 72nd, some excommunicate, and suspend from office, and bring into [office], and hear confessions. . . . 74th, they bless with solemn and episcopal benediction . . . Some abbesses read [the Bible aloud] in public'.[28] I say 'constructed', because although these sentences purport to be descriptive and are in the present tense, they are probably rooted not in contemporary reality but in Alvarus's reading of confessors' literature, allied perhaps to an Iberian's penchant for a point which had arisen in Spain, with the Cistercians of Las Huelgas. Significant to us is what is suggested about this earlier material – so widespread and prominent in men's minds as to make possible such a remarkable construction of statements about women and Orders. While there is no need to demonstrate the ubiquity of manuscripts of the principal patristic texts and collections of canon law which are being discussed, it is perhaps useful to remember just how widely diffused was the penitential material. Thomas Kaeppeli has listed one hundred and thirty-seven manuscripts of William of Rennes' gloss, and one hundred and seventy-one and one hundred and fifty-eight, respectively, of John of Freiburg's *Summa confessorum* and *Confessionale*.[29]

Finally, what of heresy? Our student would have found fewer copies of

---

[26] John of Freiburg, *Summa confessorum* iii.23: De impedimento sexus (Augsburg, 1476), unfol.

[27] Oxford, Bodleian Library, MS Laud Misc. 278, fol. 360va: 'De abbatissa. De hiis inquirere ab abbatissis. Item, specialiter si intromiserit se de predicacione, excommunicacione, vel absolucione aut officio aliquorum ordinum, quia hec facere non potest'.

[28] *De planctu ecclesiae* ii.45 (Venice, 1560), fol. 149r: '59° Docent in pulpito predicando vel legendo sicut magistre. . . . 61° Alique recipiunt ordinem, quum non possint. . . . 71° Quedam fatue abbatisse velant velo consecrationis . . . 72° Quedam excommunicant et ab officio suspendunt et introducunt et confessiones audiunt. . . . 74° Benedicunt benedictione solemni et episcopali . . . Quedam abbatisse legunt in publicum. On Alvarus, see N. Iung, *Un Franciscain, théologien du Pouvoir pontifical au XIVe siècle. Alvaro Pelayo, évèque et pénitencier de Jean XXII* (Paris, 1931).

[29] SOPMA, II, pp. 156–9, and IV, p. 107 (William), II, pp. 430–6, and IV, pp. 151–2 (John of Freiburg). No distinction is made here or below between complete and part manuscripts.

works on heresy, and some of those which have been discussed were probably very rare. We should therefore put to one side Anselm of Alessandria's treatise, for example, which survives in only one copy,[30] and also Moneta of Cremona. Although Moneta's text was once extant in at least twenty-one copies,[31] it would have been a rare reader who would have picked up the brief reference to Waldensians in this enormous text while at the same time confidently asserting that there was nothing in it about women's ministry among the Cathars. However, there are some shorter texts which were widely diffused, in which the point was more accessible. From France, there was Alain de Lille's *De fide catholica*, still extant in thirty-five manuscripts;[32] from Italy Sacconi's treatise, still extant in over fifty manuscripts; and from Germany both the treatise of the Anonymous of Passau, still extant in this and its later recensions in fifty-four manuscripts,[33] and also the much-copied *De inquisitione hereticorum*.[34] These popular works diffused quite widely the positive point about Waldensian women, and silence on Cathars. We could also reverse the order of the enquiry, beginning by asking, 'What relevant work achieved the largest diffusion?', and then asking, 'What did it contain about heresy and women?' A good candidate in the competition for the prize for mass diffusion would be one of the products of the Dominican convent at Lyons, Guillaume Peyraut's treatise on vices and virtues, which was written between 1236 and 1249.[35] Its contents? Women's ministry crops up neither in the brief comments on Waldensians[36] nor the longer account of Cathars. How-

30 *SOPMA*, I, p. 79.
31 *SOPMA*, II, pp. 138–9.
32 N. M. Häring, 'Alain of Lille's *De fide catholica* or *Contra haereticos*', *Analecta Cisterciensia* 32 (1976), 216–327.
33 See on this Nickson, ' "Pseudo-Reinerius" treatise', Patschovsky, *Passauer Anonymus*, and P. Biller, 'Medieval Waldensian abhorrence of killing pre-*c*.1400 ', in *The Church and War*, ed. W. J. Sheils, SCH 20 (Oxford, 1983), pp. 129–46 (pp. 143–4 and note 79).
34 On its manuscripts, see A. Dondaine, 'Le manuel de l'inquisiteur', *AFP* 17 (1947), 85–194 (pp. 180–3), T. Kaeppeli, 'Traités anti-vaudois dans le manuscrit 30 de la Bibliothèque des Dominicains de Dubrovnik-Raguse', *AFP* 24 (1954), 297–325 (p. 304), and P. Biller, 'Aspects of the Waldenses in the Fourteenth Century' (unpublished D.Phil. thesis, Oxford, 1974), pp. 364–5. On female ministry among the Waldensians in the Dominican Nicholas Eymeric's *Directorium officii inquisitorum*, see G. Gonnet, *Le confessioni di fede valdesi prima della riforma* (Turin, 1967), pp. 116–17; on its date (part 1 written in 1376) and manuscripts, see *SOPMA*, III, pp. 158–9.
35 The edition used here is *Summa virtutum et vitiorum*, 2 vols. (Antwerp, 1571). On the setting of productivity in the Lyons convent, see D. L. d'Avray, *The Preaching of the Friars. Sermons diffused from Paris before 1300* (Oxford, 1985), pp. 147–9 and 158–9, and A. Murray, 'Confession as a historical source in the thirteenth century', in *The Writing of History in the Middle Ages. Essays presented to Richard William Southern*, ed. R. H. C. Davis and J. M. Wallace-Hadrill (Oxford, 1981), pp. 275–322 (pp. 309–12). One of Guillaume's fellows in the convent was another who had written on heresy and women, Stephen of Bourbon.
36 *Summa virtutum* ii.28; I, fol. 90v.

ever, a reader looking for 'women and heresy' would have found something, under Cathars: their teaching that a man should avoid touching a woman, and the point that 'dicunt mulierem damnari si praegnans decedat vel in partu' ('they say that a woman is damned if she dies [when] pregnant or in childbirth').[37] There are still extant over seven hundred of the manuscripts which once conveyed *that* message.[38]

This, then would have been the broad picture available at this time. From the remote past, there would have been some early Church and heresy examples; in the world of a century ago perhaps heresy, and if so, Waldensian, not Cathar. But the centre would have been occupied by the contemporary Church, and, inside it, discussions of sex as a bar to becoming a priest, and the ministerial actions of powerful abbesses. It is unlikely that the Cathars would have had the slightest appearance in the picture, and if a student had pursued the theme 'Cathars and women' the most likely topic to be found was damnation of the pregnant woman who died, or, possibly, post-resurrection change of sex. This last point would depend on a reader of Aquinas's *Summa contra gentiles* identifying as Cathars those heretics who were attacked by Aquinas in chapter 88 for maintaining 'quod in corporibus resurgentium desit sexus femineus' ('that female sex ceases in the bodies of the resurrected').[39] Cathars might have edged into the picture, then, but not as proponents of women's ministry or preaching.

ii. Protestant and Catholic polemic

Next in the story comes the foundation in the sixteenth and early seventeenth centuries of Protestant and Catholic polemical history. This history, which was to dominate until the nineteenth century and is still a living though now sometimes covert force, produced the Protestant portrayal of medieval heretics as medieval protestants and the Catholic portrayal of them as heirs of older heresies. Its founding fathers, Flacius Illyricus and Jakob Gretser, were also remarkable editors of medieval texts. Bossuet's polemical history of medieval heresy in book 11 of his *Histoire des variations des églises protestantes*, published in Paris in 1688, is an example of the effects of their labours – a work written by someone who already has at his disposal a very high proportion of the literary material which a modern historian of heresy uses.[40] This means half of the genres of texts used by the modern historian, because a Bossuet makes little use of trial evidence. Bossuet's fierce intelligence distinguished sects very clearly, but few were like Bossuet. In the minds and texts of

37 *Summa virtutum* iii.14; I, fols. 177v, 178r.
38 *SOPMA*, II, pp. 134–42, and IV, p. 106. My count is 735.
39 See comment in Biller, 'Common Woman', 153 note 109.
40 On Bossuet's account of medieval heresy, see R. Darricau, 'De l'histoire théologien à la grande érudition: Bossuet (XVIᵉ – XVIIIᵉ)', in *Historiographie du Catharisme, CaF* 14 (Toulouse, 1979), pp. 85–117.

many, now, there occurred a confusion and merging of Cathars with Waldensians and of later heretics with earlier ones. The wide publication of many medieval Catholic texts on medieval heresies had made some texts on Waldensians and women very widespread. For example, the Anonymous of Passau had been given a prominent place in Gretser's edition of texts which showed the medieval heretics in the long 'catalogue of witnesses to the truth' between Christ and Luther, and centuries of Protestant historians were to quote it from this edition (or from others quoting it). Combined with this, the blurring of identities now laid open one obvious possibility. This was the wider and indiscriminate application of the texts which *did* bear on women, and then the birth of the myth that medieval Catholic writers commented on the special role of women in Catharism. Silence helped this development: silence about medieval Waldensian 'Sisters' (or nuns),[41] among Protestant historians who were more broadly embarrassed by the celibacy of those (from this point of view) typical medieval religious, the Waldensian 'Brothers' (or friars).

The story now moves to the nineteenth century, which saw the next fundamental developments both within and outside scholarship. In the academic sphere, leading on one religious side was Charles Schmidt. He was from a prosperous Lutheran Strasbourgeois family, and taught history to students who were mainly future evangelical pastors, as Professor in the Theology Faculty and later Professor of Ecclesiastical History at the University of Strasbourg.[42] Later came one of the Molinier brothers, Charles Molinier,[43] and to be added to this camp is Dmitrevsky. On the other side was a succession of scholars associated with the Institut Catholique in Toulouse. Most important were Célestin Douais, who was later Bishop of Beauvais; his pupil Jean-Marie Vidal, later a Monsignor and working in the Vatican Library; and another of Douais's pupils, this time a layman, Jean Guiraud.[44] The Protestants usually published their articles in the *Revue historique*, the Catholics in the *Revue des questions historiques*.

These scholars wrought a revolution in the use of evidence. While sixteenth- and seventeenth-century editors had made available principally literary material, such as inquisitors' and polemical theologians' treatises – and

---

[41] See on them P. Biller, '*Multum ieiunantes et se castigantes*: medieval Waldensian Asceticism', in *Monks, Hermits and the Ascetic Tradition*, ed. W. J. Sheils, SCH 22 (1985), pp. 215–28 (pp. 219–20).

[42] On him see Y. Dossat, 'Un initiateur: Charles Schmidt', in *Historiographie du catharisme*, pp. 163–84.

[43] On him, see C.-O. Carbonell, 'Les historiens protestants libéraux ou les illusions d'une histoire scientifique (1870–1914)', in *Historiographie du catharisme*, pp. 185–203 (pp. 193–4, 197–8, 200–1).

[44] See P. Amargier and A. Ramière de Fortanier, 'La contribution catholique à l'histoire de l'albigéisme (1866–1916)', in *Historiographie du catharisme*, pp. 205–26 (pp. 205–15 on Douais, 215–16 on Vidal and 216–25 on Guiraud).

subsequent histories, such as Bossuet's, were mainly wrought out of such materials – in our times histories are made out of virtually double this evidence: trial material as well as literary evidence. The revolution did not happen overnight, and it was not without foreshadowings: one, for example, was Philip van Limborch's edition of the sentences of the inquisitor Bernard Gui, the *Liber sententiarum inquisitionis tholosanae*, published as a massive appendix to his *Historia inquisitionis* (Amsterdam, 1692).[45] However, *most* of the move towards records of trials, virtually all of which were unprinted, occurred between 1848–9 (Schmidt)[46] and 1906–9 (Vidal).[47] Schmidt used the large collection of later copies of mainly thirteenth-century Toulouse depositions which are kept in the Bibliothèque nationale under the name of 'Doat', the seventeenth-century royal official who was in charge of the copying. Schmidt largely restricts himself to these, however, a point for which he was criticised by Molinier in his thesis, *L'inquisition dans le midi de la France au XIIIe et au XIVe siècle. Études sur les sources de son histoire*, which was published in Paris in 1880.[48] Molinier's work was devoted to an analysis of a much wider range of trial records, largely unprinted – they cover most of those known today. While exploiting the same range of sources, the Institut Catholique scholars, in particular Douais and Guiraud, made particularly heavy use of an immensely rich and in part difficult to decipher manuscript in the Bibliothèque municipale in Toulouse, number 609, which contains depositions of 5471 people from 1245/6.[49] Vidal, in Rome, went further, using the Vatican manuscript of depositions in front of Jacques Fournier in Pamiers (1318–25), which was later to be

45 See M. A. E. Nickson on the refinding of the manuscript of this work, 'Locke and the inquisition of Toulouse', *British Museum Quarterly* 36 (1972), 83–92. A. Pales-Gobilliard has announced the preparation of a new edition, 'Pénalités inquisitoriales au XIVe siècle' in *Crises et réformes dans l'Église de la réforme grégorienne à la préréforme*, Actes du 11e congrès national des sociétés savantes (Paris, 1991), pp. 143–54 (p. 142, note 4). Gui's sentences found a wider audience with the publication of S. R. Maitland's *Facts and Documents Illustrative of the History, Doctrine and Rites of the Ancient Albigenses and Waldenses* (London, 1832), which translated a selection in its section x, pp. 271–341.

46 C. Schmidt, *Histoire et doctrine de la secte des cathares ou albigeois*, 2 vols. (Paris and Geneva, 1848–9). A modern reprint (Bayonne, 1983) contains comment on Schmidt and his work in a preface by J. Duvernoy.

47 J.-M. Vidal, 'Les derniers ministres de l'albigéisme en Languedoc. Leurs doctrines', *Revue des questions historiques* n.s. 35 (1906), 57–107, and 'Doctrine et morale des derniers ministres albigeois', *Revue des questions historiques* n.s. 41 (1909), 357–409, and n.s. 42 (1909), 5–48.

48 Molinier, *Inquisition*, p. viii. Further discoveries of sources, including the manuscript of the hearings in front of Jacques Fournier in the 1320s, were reported by Molinier in his 'Rapport à M. Le Ministre de l'instruction publique sur une mission exécutée en Italie de février à avril 1885', *Archives des missions scientifiques et littéraires* 3rd série 14 (1888), 133–336.

49 The manuscript is described and analysed in Dossat, *Crises de l'inquisition*, pp. 56–70.

published by Jean Duvernoy in 1965[50] and acquire supermarket fame through Emmanuel Le Roy Ladurie's *Montaillou* in 1975.[51]

For the theme of women and heresy this scholarly revolution had some clear and some diffuse results. Although available since 1692, Bernard Gui's sentences, containing only one female perfect,[52] would have done little on their own to encourage what happens now: the appearance of accounts of women in Catharism based on depositions. Into the pages of history books come identifiable individual women, with names and histories which make them seem more real. Though not yet counted, these women now appear to be numerous: the several women who appear on a printed page are clearly selected from an unspecified but much greater number of women, the majority of whom remain unpublicised in the depositions, which contain large numbers of both sexes. The first to appear are the female perfects, given two pages by Schmidt in 1852.[53] With Molinier (1880) there appears a brief deposition-based account of women as a distinct group among the *credentes*, supporters or 'believers' in the Cathars.[54] Douais' analysis of Toulouse MS 609 in 1891 included two densely-packed and fairly objective pages on women as perfects – blessing bread, teaching followers the rite of adoration, instructing children, preaching, and being adored.[55] This implicitly contradicted Schmidt's earlier claim that women perfects had not preached, a point upon which Schmidt was explicitly attacked by Molinier in 1907.[56] With Dmitrevsky (1923–4) the general theme at last has the autonomy conferred by a title and separate treatment, 'Les femmes dans la secte cathare'. This was followed by 'La famille dans la secte cathare', which spelled out the role of families in transmitting Catharism from one generation to another.[57] A polemic had already developed, on the Catholic side, about the family. The Catholic scholars detailed the exemplification in the depositions of Cathar condemnation of

---

50 *Le registre d'inquisition de Jacques Fournier évêque de Pamiers (1318–1325)*, ed. J. Duvernoy, 3 vols. (Toulouse, 1965), henceforth cited as *Fournier*. It has become the fashion for scholars to decry this edition while failing to use the corrections to errata in J. Duvernoy, *Le registre . . . Corrections* (Toulouse, 1972). Duvernoy sketches the history of earlier attention to the text, going back to Döllinger's publication of extracts in 1890, in *Fournier*, I, 8, note 9.

51 J. H. Mundy, 'Village, Town and Society in the region of Toulouse', in *Pathways to Medieval Peasants*, ed. J. A. Raftis (Toronto, 1981), pp. 141–90 (p. 141).

52 Jacmeta – see, e.g., Limborch, *Liber sententiarum*, p. 70.

53 Schmidt, *Cathares*, II, 95–6.

54 Molinier, *Inquisition*, pp. 117–18, and the long note 1 on pp. 118–19.

55 C. Douais, 'Les hérétiques du comté de Toulouse dans la première moitié du XIIIe siècle d'après l'enquête de 1245', *Compte rendu du congrès scientifique internationale des Catholiques tenu à Paris du 1er au 6 Avril 1891*, 5e section (Paris, 1891), pp. 148–62 (157–8).

56 Schmidt, *Cathares*, II, 95; C. Molinier, 'L'Église et la société cathares, *Revue historique* 94 (1907), 225–48 (p. 242 and note 2).

57 M. Dmitrevsky, 'Notes sur le catharisme et l'inquisition dans le midi de la France. I', *Annales du Midi* 35–6 (1923–4), 294–311 (women, pp. 294–303; family, pp. 303–11).

marriage, and in passing paraded some anti-woman passages. Thus Guiraud dug up Aimersent's deposition in Toulouse MS 609, which was quoted at the beginning of this paper, while Vidal paraphrased a late Cathar sermon which included the good God swearing that no woman would enter his heaven.[58] However, Catholic emphasis was more on Cathars as anti-social than anti-woman. 'The Perfects' work aimed at the suppression of the family . . . and from this point of view this heresy seems to us anarchist and revolutionary', in Guiraud's words,[59] while according to Vidal 'it was with the ruin of society that such theories would have ended'.[60]

Protestant scholars tended not to take this up directly – they were not always tender to the Cathars – but the theme of the special appeal of Cathars to women did appear. When noting the women perfects, Schmidt had drawn a contrast with the Waldensians, who left women 'in their natural sphere',[61] while Molinier and Dmitrevsky paraded many examples of women becoming Cathar believers. Both these scholars set women's participation in Catharism in terms of the frivolity and vanity of women, the daughters of Eve, while attributing to them 'passion' for heresy and its ministers, and the display in their service of great self-sacrifice and courage perhaps greater than men's.[62]

iii. Liberty

Just as important for the future of the presentation of women and Catharism were powerful currents from outside academic scholarship. First, from romantic literature and in particular from German literature in the 1840s, there emerged the idea of an association between medieval heresy and struggles for political liberty. Later manifestations of this idea were to be the conception of medieval heretics as forerunners of proletarian revolutionaries, in Friedrich Engels' *Peasant War in Germany* (1850),[63] and medieval heretics as Aryans revolting againt a mediterranean priesthood, in the work of the National Socialist ideologue Alfred Rosenberg in 1932.[64] The general association of

---

[58] J. Guiraud, *Questions d'histoire et d'archéologie chrétienne* (Paris, 1906), pp. 75–6 and note 1 – though correctly transcribing *heretice*, he treated the preaching perfects as male; Vidal, 'Doctrine et morale', p. 375 and note 2.

[59] Guiraud, *Inquisition*, I, 99: 'L'action des Parfaits poursuivait ainsi la destruction de la famille . . . À ce point de vue, cette hérésie nous apparaît comme révolutionnaire et anarchiste'. Chapter 2 in his earlier *Questions d'histoire*, entitled 'La morale des Albigeois' (pp. 49–92), is a prime text for Guiraud's polemic against Catharism as leading to the destruction of society. Guiraud did provide a very restricted picture of female perfects' activities, *Inquisition*, I, 227–8.

[60] Vidal, 'Doctrine et morale', p. 403: 'C'était à la ruine de la societé qu'aboutissaient de pareilles théories'.

[61] Schmidt, *Cathares*, II, 95.

[62] Molinier, *Inquisition*, p. 118, note 1, and Dmitrevsky, pp. 294–303 – the latter's points and words are very close to Molinier's.

[63] *Der deutsche Bauernkrieg*, in K. Marx and F. Engels, *Werke* (Berlin, 1961–), vol. 7.

[64] The point was made by Borst, pp. 48–9 and 49 note 4; J.-L. Biget, 'Mythographie du

heresy, and in particular Catharism, with the spirit of freedom became very pervasive, and the idea eventually found very sharp expression in the mid-twentieth century when Marxism-Leninism was implanted as an orthodoxy in university faculties in the German Democratic Republic.[65] The Karl-Marx University of Leipzig began to specialise in heresy as a medieval theme of special importance because of Engels' argument that, because the Church provided the ideology of the feudal social and political order, social movements of protest against this order had to take on a religious garb. Strip a medieval heresy of its religious veil, and underneath you find a movement of social and political protest. Among Leipzig's prolific output was one work, published in East Berlin in 1962, which married this scripture according to Engels with a tradition of older German history of the so-called *Frauenfrage* (Women-question). This was Gottfried Koch's monograph on heresy and this 'women-question' in the Middle Ages, which presented medieval oppression of women as an outcrop of more general feudal oppression, and heresy as the vehicle of opposition to this – especially the heresy of Languedocian Catharism. Here the notion of a surplus of women in southern cities echoed older German preoccupation with the 'question' or 'problem' of women.[66] Usefully crude expression of what the general thesis really meant is found in a later East German coffee-table book devoted to medieval women: 'heretical movements and the fight for women's rights went hand in hand'.[67]

There had also been emerging, in the 1830s, an association between Catharism and courtly love. In Languedoc there was *Amour courtois*, with exaltation of the Beloved and refinement of Love, and in Languedoc at the same time there was Catharism, with an abhorrence of sex and procreation which could be presented as idealisation of non-carnal love. Surely, it came to be urged, these were intimately connected? Was not courtly love either a 'vehicle for Catharist doctrines or . . . an indirect expression of Cathar sentiments'? These phrases come from Roger Boase's critical history of post-medieval ideas about courtly love.[68] Boase disentangles and briefly summarises the many and often bizarre theories which have been put forward

catharisme (1870–1960)', in *Historiographie du catharisme*, pp. 271–342 (pp. 314–6), argues that Rosenberg's use of heretics has been exaggerated.

[65] See A. Dorpalen, *German History in Marxist Perspective. The East German Approach* (London, 1985), pp. 74–6, 91–2, and W. Malecsek, 'Le ricerche eresiologiche in area germanica', in G. G. Merlo, ed., *Eretici ed eresie medievali nella storiografia contemporanea* (Torre Pellice, 1994), pp. 64–93 (pp. 68–75).

[66] *Frauenfrage und Ketzertum im Mittelalter. Die Frauenbewegung im Rahmen des Katharismus und des Waldensertums und ihre sozialen Wurzeln*, Forschungen zur mittelalterlichen Geschichte 9. Comment in Malecsek, 'Ricerche eresiologiche', pp. 74–5. Lyndal Roper first pointed out to me the misogyny of the term *Frauenfrage*.

[67] S. Harksen, *Women in the Middle Ages*, trans. M. Herzfeld (New York, 1975), p. 38.

[68] R. Boase, *The Origin and Meaning of Courtly Love. A critical study of European scholarship* (Manchester, 1977), p. 77; the account of Cathars and courtly love is given on pp. 77–81.

about the supposed connection between Catharism and courtly love. His excellent account does not need to be repeated here, but we need to take note of the sheer size of the body of literature which these theories have generated, and this literature's role in maintaining widespread belief in and preoccupation with the connection. There has been one by-product of this belief when combined with the chronology of scholarship devoted to urban and rural Catharism. Not until 1948 did there appear an edition of a large body of trials in which what predominated was urban Catharism, in particular Catharism found in an urban elite of merchants, doctors, royal officials, notaries, lawyers and professors of law.[69] Not until the last two decades has good secondary work on urban Catharism begun to hold centre-stage.[70] By contrast, rural nobility loomed large in the earliest depositions to be used, leaving a bias in modern historians' accounts of Catharism. Swarming with knights and ladies, these accounts have therefore provided fertile ground for those whose imaginations swarm like bees with courtly love.

Behind and also linked with belief in this connection with courtly love has been the long growth of Languedocian cultural separatism. Medieval Occitan civilisation and its superior culture and love of liberty was crushed by the brutal north and its gothic civilisation. This found classic expression in the *Histoire des Albigeois* of the reformed Ariègeois pastor Napoléon Peyrat, published 1870–2.[71] Peyrat presented an extraordinary romanticisation of an Occitan, Cathar, and troubadour past. A leading role was played by noble women, high in Occitan civilisation, put over in colourful impressionist prose. Noble ladies in Languedoc spend their girlhoods frisking like lambs gathering flowers on Languedocian hillsides, their beautiful young womanhood presiding over courts of love, and their old age as powerful matriarchal Cathar perfects, 'high priestesses of the Paraclete', hiding in grottos in times of persecution.

In the later and wider history of modern Languedocian cultural separatism we only need to take account of the special place within it played by a martyrised and suppressed past, in which women and Catharism play a central role.[72] It is currently very widely put about, especially outside scholar-

[69] G. W. Davis, *The Inquisition at Albi 1299–1300. Text of Register and Analysis* (New York, 1948).

[70] J.-L. Biget, 'Un procès d'inquisition à Albi en 1300', in *Le Credo, la Morale et l'Inquisition*, CaF 6 (Toulouse, 1971), and 'L'extinction du catharisme urbain: les points chauds de la répression', in *Effacement du Catharisme? (XIIIᵉ – XIVᵉs.)*, CaF 20 (Toulouse, 1985), pp. 305–40, and J. H. Mundy, *The Repression of Catharism at Tououse. The Royal Diploma of 1279* (Toronto, 1985). There is a summary of Biget's achievement in A. Vauchez, 'Les recherches françaises sur les hérésies médiévales au cours des trentes dernières années (1962–1992)', in Merlo, *Eretici ed eresie*, pp. 94–108 (pp. 101–2).

[71] See C.-O. Carbonell, 'D'Augustin Thierry à Napoléon Peyrat: Un demi-siècle d'occultation (1820–1870)', in *Historiographie du catharisme*, pp. 143–62 (pp. 158–62), and also the index entry for Peyrat, *Historiographie du catharisme*, p. 430.

[72] See F. Abel, *Le mouvement occitaniste contemporain*, Tübinger Beiträge zur Linguistik

ship. While tourist guides, popular books and novels diffuse the romanticised Occitan past in words,[73] several theatre companies re-enact Cathar dramas in the open air in the summertime, in villages and small towns of Languedoc, with brutal popes and inquisitors and heroic Cathars, female perfects and noble women. Contemporary Languedoc also contains an academic centre devoted to Catharism, which is discussed below.

Away from Languedoc, what other points are there on a map of this theme in the second half of the twentieth century? Although the Germany Democratic Republic is now dead, the book which its ideology produced in 1962 has been very influential in western democracies, in particular during the mushrooming of women's history in the USA and Great Britain from the 1960s onwards. By the 1970s and in the anglophone world general accounts of medieval women were coming to have a chapter on heresy, just as general accounts of medieval religious movements were beginning to have their chapters on women. Discernible, in varying proportions in these chapters, are Koch and a feminist tradition, going back to around 1900, of interest in the religious woman, especially the nun and even more the abbess, as a woman escaping from a man's world. Most emphasis tended to be on perfects, as equivalents of nuns, rather than believers. This sailed against the general trend in modern historiography away from 'ecclesiastical' history (the clergy and structures) to 'religious' history (the 'lived religion' of the lay person): against this, women's history kept attention focused on the Cathar 'nun'. As this earlier 'presentism' has come under later feminist historical criticism, attention is now swinging towards the more ordinary women in Catharism.[74]

Elsewhere on the world map the two strongest areas of heresy scholarship have been in the former West Germany and the USA. In Germany there was the Catholic Arno Borst. In a recent autobiographical sketch he has written about the late 1940s, when the Lutheranism of his girlfriend encouraged him 'to think about the nervous asceticism of my mother and her historical religious motives. I seized the opportunity when, in 1948, Hans Heinrich Schaeder suggested the investigation of the largest sect in the Middle Ages, the world-rejecting Cathars in southern France and northern Italy.'[75] Certainly, the theme of Cathars and women attracted some characteristically sharp and condensed attention – the best is in the footnotes – in his *Die Katharer*.[76] Like Vidal and Guiraud before him, he was struck by the misogyny of Cathar doctrine and its presentation, and he found new examples of hatred of female

---

377 (Tübingen, 1973) in general and pp. 15–16 on Catharism, and Biget, 'Mythographie du catharisme'.

[73] C.-O. Carbonell, 'Vulgarisation et récupération: le catharisme à travers les mass-media', in *Historiographie du catharisme*, pp. 361–80.

[74] Biller, 'Common Woman', pp. 128–30.

[75] Borst, 'My Life', in his *Medieval Worlds. Barbarians, Heretics and Artists in the Middle Ages*, trans. E. Hansen (Cambridge, 1991), pp. 244–50 (p. 245).

[76] See pp. 180–3, and the index-entries under 'Ehe' (p. 348) and 'Frau' (p. 349).

flesh – 'something as vile as a woman's womb' – which are discussed in the second part of this article. This 'radical woman-hatred' (radikale Frauen-haß),[77] as he called it, Borst found difficult to reconcile with a datum which he accepted, the strength and numbers of women among Cathar perfects and believers. He left this as a problem.

This problem and, at last, the theme of precise numbers stimulated the most important of the contributions from the USA, an article published by Richard Abels and Ellen Harrison in 1979, 'The Participation of Women in Languedocian Catharism'.[78] Discernible in the background were the vogue for quantitative history, and the research materials and scholarly example of the 'Columbia School' of medieval heresiology. Predating the second world war and ideologically various, this school was partly united by the spirit of its founding father, Austin P. Evans, and Walter Wakefield, and partly by its members' use of a range of archival material from Languedoc, in particular Toulouse MS 609; a complete transcript of the latter had been produced.[79] Abels and Harrison began with a sceptical restatement of the thesis of women's special role. They then counted, especially in the Toulouse manuscript. They counted, for example, numbers of male and female perfects and numbers of their sightings by believers, and they broke down numbers chronologically, according to ups and downs in persecution. These and other numbers allowed the two American scholars to say 'No' to the special role thesis.

There were drawbacks. The polemic shifted attention away from the interesting gender patterns which the figures did reveal. The authors ignored one glaring possibility: that their numbers, varying but always showing fewer women, might still reveal a significant 'gender' pattern – women being repelled. Finally, 'women' were still being treated as a bloc.[80] However, there was so much fundamental and precise research that the article rapidly and rightly became regarded as fundamental by other scholars, *the* point of departure for further enquiry. Let us now turn to Languedoc, and conclude with one scholar who did not take this view.

In Languedoc modern academic work on medieval Catharism has been located in two institutes. One, the 'Centre de Fanjeaux', was founded in 1965,

---

[77] Borst, *Katharer*, p. 182.
[78] *MS* 41 (1979), 215–51. There had been brief use of statistics in Koch, *Frauenfrage*, p. 86.
[79] P. Biller, 'La storiografia intorno all'eresia medievale negli Stati Uniti e in Gran Bretagna (1945–1992)', in Merlo, *Eretici ed eresie*, pp. 39–63 (pp. 44–9) describes the Columbia school.
[80] Biller, 'Common Woman', pp. 156–7. An earlier contribution in English was M. C. Barber's attractive statement of the positive case in his 'Women and catharism', *Reading Medieval Studies* 3 (1977), 45–62. The Israeli scholar S. Shahar (in her *The Fourth Estate. A History of Women in the Middle Ages* (London, 1983), pp. 256, 259–67) gave a short but rich account which was remarkable for its balance of negative and positive points.

under the auspices of the Institut d'études mériodionales of the university of Toulouse and the Institut catholique. From its annual colloquium on the religious history of medieval Languedoc, there has appeared each year, since 1966, a volume of papers on a particular theme – including heresy and inquisition.[81] Regional money has gone into the foundation in 1981 and subsequent support of another institute, the Centre Nationale des Études Cathares/Centre René Nelli', located at Villegly, which is now (since 1995) called the Centre d'Études Cathares and is in Toulouse. It has conferences, encourages scholarship and, produces (since 1983) a journal, *Heresis*.[82] Through Jean Duvernoy's participation in its conferences and journal the Centre is associated with one noted sceptic about Cathars and women,[83] but it is led by a believer.

The *directrice* of the Centre is Anne Brenon, who is well-known to heresiologists throughout the academic world as a scholar, the figure of great charm and hospitality who hosts annual conferences on medieval heretical and religious themes, and as a friend. Brenon began her research on medieval heresy on the Occitan dialect books of the Waldensians, a field in which she still publishes, but her recent books are on the Cathars. The first of these, *Le vrai visage de catharisme* (Portet-sur-Garonne, 1988) already contained two chapters on Cathar women,[84] while the second, *Les femmes cathares* (Paris, 1992), was entirely devoted to them.[85] Like Abels and Harrison, Brenon is steeped in the sources, but there the resemblance stops. In her earlier general account of Catharism she briefly used statistics about women in Catharism based on inquisitors' registers, without mentioning Abels and Harrison,[86] but in her second account she side-stepped. Abels and Harrison's reduction of women's role, running counter to a tradition of emphasising it, was alluded to as a clash of arms in a university tournament, and arguments about numbers as vain debates over a false problem. She had nothing to prove, and so, turning away from these arguments, Brenon tried 'simply to open a window'.[87] Brenon knows and presents large numbers of individual women, their life-histories and families, and she shows women varying through their lives, and individual women varying: this is one of the book's great achievements. Brenon has an essentialist view of medieval mentality and medieval Catholicism, and an apologist's view of her 'good Christians', the Cathars. Central for her, here following in Koch's tracks, was the Cathars' extraordinary notion of equality

---

[81] The series is discussed by Vauchez, 'Recherches françaises', pp. 104–5.

[82] See Vauchez, 'Recherches françaises', p. 105.

[83] See J. Duvernoy, *La religion des cathares* (Toulouse, 1976), ch. VII.33, 'La femme', pp. 264–5.

[84] Chapters 13–14 (pp. 166–91); see also pp. 87 and 290–1.

[85] See also Brenon's 'L'hérésie en Languedoc au XIIe–XIIIe siècles: une religion pour les femmes?', in *La femme dans l'histoire et la société méridionales*, 66e Congrès Féd. Hist. Lang.-Rouss. (Narbonne, 1994), 103–16. Her study of Occitan forenames, *Prénoms occitans*, is also evidence for her views on Cathar women.

[86] Brenon, *Vrai visage*, pp. 182–6.

[87] Brenon, *Femmes cathares*, pp. 59–61.

between men and women, based on their view, recalled by one deponent, that 'anime hominum et mulierum inter se differenciam non habenant' ('the souls of men and women had no difference between them') .[88] Bodies come second, but are treated with energetic polemic. The Catholic Church had an opprobrious view of female flesh, and when Cathars express this horror of the flesh they are simply transmitting ideas of the dominant culture – in other words, blame Catholicism not Catharism. 'Cathar hatred of the flesh . . . was not hatred specifically of the flesh of woman'.[89] Brenon's vision of medieval Languedoc encompasses everything from high vernacular culture to sense of place, and it is put over in a prose at once confidingly informal and charged with poetry. Her book on women and Catharism is both the noblest of all expressions of the belief in the theme and the most recent: as such, it fittingly concludes this sketch of the history of this belief.

2. Material Women

What follows is a sketch of one aspect only of the theme, female body and/or flesh in Cathar belief and ritual, which I am pursuing in the hope of breaking free from the succession of masks sketched above. My readers, who should see this as yet another mask, have the right to some clues: the mask is being shaped and imposed on the theme by a feminist (but male) historian, a lapsed Catholic, and an academic who is frustrated by orthodoxies: here the orthodoxy of a belief. The sketch in this part 2 is itself subdivided into two sections, the evidence (a) of an Italian Catholic polemicist, and (b) of depositions in Languedoc.

i. Moneta of Cremona

Used here is one representative of high written theology which has already been cited, the treatise written against Cathars and Waldensians by Moneta of Cremona, around 1241.[90] Moneta's treatise has one great advantage. It was based on heretics' statements and writings. Moneta is emphatic on this. 'Where however, [readers] have seen me stating some arguments against the

---

[88] Fournier, III, 201; Koch, *Frauenfrage*, p. 103; Brenon, *Femmes cathares*, pp. 99–101. Compare Bonaventure's notion that as far as the soul is concerned there is not distinction of sex (*quantum ad animam non est distinctio sexus*) and Aquinas's notion of sex not being in the soul (*sexus non est in anima*), which are discussed in A. Minnis's paper, pp. 117–18. The great diffusion of these theologians' works through the preachers of their Orders combines with the extraordinary presence and ventilation of both Catholic and Cathar theological ideas, in Languedoc around 1300, to suggest the possibility of orthodox influence on the formulation found in this one late Cathar's sermon.

[89] Brenon, *Vrai visage*, p. 87; *Femmes cathares*, p. 102: 'Le mépris cathare de la chair . . . n'était pas mépris spécifique de la chair de femme'.

[90] See above, note 12.

Church or replies [made] on behalf of heretics, they should not attack me, saying that these [statements] did not originate with the heretics but that I have made up out of my own ingenuity these sorts of things, which can nourish and further heretical wickedness. For I have had [= I have heard and taken] these things from their mouth[s] and their writings'.[91] Since Moneta's treatise is massive (about 450,000 words) and many of these words constitute such propositions and arguments attributed to Cathars, we are quite simply provided with a very large number of words which were once Cathar. There is the disadvantage of any polemicist's work, in that it reduces what were once independent and coherent treatises to a series of discrete statements and arguments – and we can do nothing about this beyond remaining on our guard. However, Moneta was a precise scholar and a man of sober outlook. An Arts professor in that city of lawyers, Bologna, before he came a Dominican, he seems in modern terms a journalist for a quality newspaper rather than a tabloid, a dry *Wissenschaftler* rather than a populist. His bias in reporting may be principally this, that he drains some of his material of its original colouring and precise literary quality.[92]

The academic and written Cathar theology known by Moneta was part of a wider body of Cathar Latin literature,[93] whose relation to various sorts of Cathars needs an introductory sketch.[94] The Cathars had a hierarchy, which can be envisaged as a rough equivalent to that of the Catholic secular clergy. Its ranks' members were called 'bishop', 'older son', 'younger son', and 'deacon'. All of these were pastorally active, and all were exclusively male. All had received the *consolamentum*, a Cathar 'sacrament' which has been envisaged as a rough equivalent to baptism. This was conferred on both men and women, who thus became 'perfects', 'Good Men' and 'Good Women'. The *consolamentum* could be passed on, in cases of necessity, by female perfects. These latter led a life more like that of Catholic female religious, i.e. nuns, though at some stages with more freedom and higher prerogatives than in the Catholic Church. As we saw in the example from Auriac, they moved around, entered followers' houses, exhorted, even sometimes, though rarely, preached. Now,

---

91 Moneta, *Praefatio* (p. 2): 'Ubi etiam viderint me ponere argumenta aliqua contra Ecclesiam aut responsiones pro Haereticis, non me lacerent dicentes ea non ab Haereticis duxisse originem, sed me proprio ingenio adinvenisse hujusmodi, quae possent nutrire, et augere haereticam pravitatem, quia vel ex ore eorum, vel ex scripturis suis illa habui'. See further on Moneta's sources L. Paolini, 'Italian Catharism and written culture', in Biller and Hudson, *Heresy and Literacy in the Middle Ages*, pp. 83–103 (p. 101).
92 Slightly less emphatic is the judgement of Duvernoy, *Religion des cathares*, p. 59: 'l'exposé de Moneta, basé sur des écrits ou des souvenirs des polémiques, est relativement sobre'.
93 The most convenient guide to the Latin literature of the Cathars is now provided in Biller and Hudson, *Heresy and Literacy*, pp. 38–103.
94 A sketch of this brevity inevitably brushes over nuances and difficulties. See Borst's *Katharer* and Duvernoy's *Religion des cathares* for fuller accounts.

Cathar texts, including their New Testament, their additional canonical books which they called their *Secrets,* and their learned Aristotle-quoting theological treatises were all read by male Cathars, not, as far as we can see from depositions, by female perfects or their female adherents.[95] It seems further that in Cathar eyes as well as inquisitors' expectations the existence and dissemination of these were part of a descending model. That is to say, male Cathar perfects had these books and this knowledge, sometimes secret, and they preached to others, who understood and believed according to their capacity.

Now, in a now old and famous article Jean-Claude Schmitt criticised the prevalence of such a descending model in studies of medieval Catholic christianity, priests and friars passing down to a purer form of Catholic doctrine and morals to a laity which passively received and distorted according to capacity.[96] To this can be added a point about gender. Accepting Schmitt's criticism and applying it to the study of Catharism means trying to counter what is implied by concentration on a purer Cathar theology, the higher written theology reported by Moneta. This is done here in section (b), which looks at Cathar theology as it was articulated and lived out – *théologie vécue* – by Cathar adherents, as seen in their thousands of depositions: and in particular by women. Higher theology is presented here first, then, not through a notion of higher and lower but because it is easier to begin with that which is more schematic. Finally, an exclusion: there is no room here, as there would be in a monograph, to discuss similarities and dissimilarities between geographically widespread Cathars, in order to qualify the choice made in this article, of theology from northern Italy and depositions from Languedoc.

Moneta delineates for his readers several sorts of Cathars, who fall mainly into two groups: those who believed in two eternal principles of good and evil, and those who believed ultimately in only one principle but had Lucifer shaping the elements and appearances of things in this world and ruling it. In both cases one thing was fundamental. Material bodies in this world were 'vessels' (*vasa*), 'earthenware vessels' (*vasa testea*), 'prisons' (*carceres*),[97] utterly alien to the 'souls' (*animae*) which were shut up in them; 'spirits' (*spiritus*) were outside the body, each the guardian or ruler of a soul, though the two words, 'soul' and 'spirit', were sometimes used indiscriminately.

Starting from this core and looking for the female body, we notice an absence and a presence: absence in the other world and order of existence, presence in this evil and material world.[98] We begin with the absence. The

---

[95] Biller, 'Women and texts in Languedocian Catharism'.

[96] J.-Cl. Schmitt, ' "Religion populaire" et culture folklorique. À propos d'une réédition: "La piété populaire d'Etienne Delaruelle" ', *AESC* 31 (1976), 941–53.

[97] *Carceres,* Moneta, *Descriptio fidei haereticorum* (p. 2); *vasa* (from Romans 9. 22) and *vasa testea,* Moneta I.i and I.iv.1 (pp. 19 and 52).

[98] Schmitz-Valckenberg, *Grundlehren katharischer Sekten,* pp. 256–61, attempts a comparison of woman in Catharism and in the Church. The analysis of Moneta is inadequate, and the choice of St Bonaventure to represent the Church is unfortu-

other world, the other heaven, the other order of existence contained angels, the people of the good God, each composed of celestial body, soul and spirit. A story tells of the devil's seduction of these, a third of whose souls fell and were imprisoned by the devil in evil fleshly envelopes, and then went from body to body until falling into the hands of the perfects. Receiving the *consolamentum* from the perfects, these souls quitted their material fleshly vessels, when these died, and were then reunited with the spirits and celestial bodies which had been left behind in the good principle's or good God's world. Two things should retain our attention in Moneta's presentation of this. One concerns the devil's trickery of the angels. Although, as we shall see later, the story of this could be presented in a coarsely gendered fashion, in Moneta's lunar and strangely beautiful version no part is played by a woman.[99] The other is identification by gender. Moneta's angels are grammatically male, but they inhabit a sexless world. There is one passing reference, however, where the Cathars do not apply a particular passage to the celestial Jerusalem, for 'alioquin ibi sunt et mulieres et viri' ('otherwise there are [would be] both women and men there'). There is the reflexive implication for that world of what is said about this, that the devil or evil principle created distinction in bodies according to sex. Both indicate the sexlessness of the celestial bodies or identities of those who inhabited and were to be resurrected into that other world. This is not explored by Moneta, probably both because his opponents did not and because of its elementary obviousness, although, as we shall see later, other Cathars propounded starkly gendered views of this.

When we turn to 'vasa testea, quae sunt opus manuum figuli hujus Mundi' ('the earthenware-vessels which are the handiwork of the potter of this world'), as the Cathars put it,[100] we turn from absence to presence of the female body. We need to remember the Cathars' elementary positions. Material bodies were evil. Christ did not take on flesh. The devil had created distinction of bodies by sex. The first sin of Adam and Eve was sexual intercourse, not disobedience, and of the two it was Eve who was identified with this. As Moneta's counter-arguments indicate, Cathars presented Eve herself as the forbidden tree.[101] To procreate was to co-operate in the devil's work, and sexual intercourse, marriage and procreation were evil in all circumstances.

Two things stand out in Moneta's lengthy parading of Cathar statements and arguments on all these. First, there is a discrepancy. On the one hand the position would seem to be against sex and sexual distinction in an even-handed way. On the other hand, relentlessly and for thousands of words after thousands of words, it is female bodies and femaleness which bear the brunt.

nate – Moneta himself is the obvious choice, since with him no allowances need to be made for what shifts in a different setting or literary genre.
[99] *Descriptio fidei haereticorum*, in Moneta (p. 4).
[100] Moneta I.iv.1 (p. 52).
[101] Moneta II.vi.1 (p. 145).

Secondly, where we can compare Moneta with another source, introduced here as a control, we see him tending to understatement. Let us illustrate both of these, looking at Moneta's presentation of the first sin in mitigated dualism, the evil of the God of the Old Testament, the conceptions of John the Baptist and the Blessed Virgin Mary, pregnancy, and marriage.

The Cathars, write Moneta, maintain that the first sin was sexual intercourse:

> Semper [*recte* serpens] accessit ad mulierem, et cum cauda corrupit eam, et ex ejus coitu cum ipsa natum est Cain . . . mulier in luxuria assuefacta ad Adam ivit, et qualiter cum ipsa coiret, ostendit, et suasit.

> (The serpent got at the woman, and corrupted her with his tail, and from this sex with her Cain was born. . . . The woman, [thus] become accustomed to lust, went to Adam and showed him how to have sex with her, and persuaded [him]).[102]

In this moderate dualist Cathar account of the fall Eve's prior temptation by the devil may parallel her prior temptation in Genesis. However, the replacement of the sin of disobedience with the sin of sex pushes into the centre of the picture the woman's body – a body explicitly envisaged in a gross connection with the devil and also, implicitly, envisaged in sexual instruction. Tacky though this may be, the story is more lurid in the Cathar text known as the *Secretum* (*Secret*) or the *Interrogatio Iohannis* (*Questions of John*):

> Diabolus . . . de sputo suo fecit serpentem et precepit ei in arundine manere . . . diabolus . . . effudit super caput eius concupiscentiam peccati; et fuit concupiscentia Eve sicut fornax ardens. Statimque diabolus exiens de arundine in forma serpenti fecit concupisentiam suam cum Eva cum cauda serpentis.

> (The devil . . . made a serpent out of his spittle, and bade him remain [hidden] in some reeds . . . the devil . . . poured out upon her [the woman's] head a lust for sin, and Eve's lust was like a glowing oven. Forthwith the devil in the form of a serpent came out of the reeds and sated his lust on her with the serpent's tail.)[103]

Other Catholic theologians allow into their texts the lurid details of some Cathar creation myths, for example, the myth of a primordial struggle in heaven making women abort, with the aborted foetuses then providing the flesh of animals and birds in this evil material world.[104] The comparisons

---

[102] Moneta II.i.2 (p. 111).

[103] *Le livre secret des cathares: Interrogatio Iohannis, Apocryphe d'origine bogomile*, ed. E. Bozóky, p. 60.

[104] Cited by L. Paolini, 'Italian Catharism and written culture', in Biller and Hudson, *Heresy and Literacy*, pp. 83–103 (94).

suggest a general restraint in Moneta, who is more interested in carefulness in the scriptural exchanges which we continue to examine.

Fertile women's bodies are scattered in the series of oppositions that Cathars make between the Old Testament and the New as part of their proof of the evil nature of the God of the Old and the good of the God of the New. For example, the Cathars say, 'Aperiebat vulvas mulierum, ut habetur Genes. 29. Vide quanta turpitudo fuerit in Deo Veteris Testamenti' ('He used to open women's wombs, as is contained in Genesis 29 [Genesis 29.31]. See what great foulness there will have been in the God of the Old Testament!').[105]

The point is pressed home in several further approaches to pregnant bodies. The familiar detail of Luke's description of Elizabeth's pregnancy is evoked by Moneta and presented in his terms: her conception, the infant leaping in her womb, the good nature of the fruit of her womb, her being a holy and good woman whether pregnant or not. Then the Cathar's polar opposites are stated in relation to this case. 'Dicis gravidas spiritum malignum in se habere. . . . Asserunt etiam praedicti haeretici eum fuisse malum ab utero matris suae' ('You [the heretic] say that pregnant women have a malign spirit in them. . . . The aforesaid heretics assert that he [John the Baptist] was evil from the womb of his mother').[106] Obviously Mary attracted the greatest attention, though varying from different Cathar groups. She 'nec sexum habebat foemineum, nec foemina erat in veritate' ('did not have female sex, nor was in truth a female'). In sum, she was not, 'foemina materialis' ('a material woman'). Moneta includes one Cathar detail which reflects the shying away from the fertile female body, the notion that Christ 'per aurem Mariae intravit in eam, et per aurem ejus exivit' ('entered through Mary's ear into her, and exited through her ear').[107] Note the wording in a contemporary Italian account of Cathar belief on this point, in the treatise by the pseudo-James Capelli. Opposing the incarnation, he writes, 'Frivolum enim et ignominiosum dicunt credere quod filius dei in visceribus mulierculae sit involuntus [sic] et tandem per pundibunda [sic] genitalia natus' ('they say that it would be frivolous and ignominious to believe that the Son of God was bound up in the viscera of a woman and then born through [her] shameful genitals').[108] Where one Catholic author is content to reproduce the vivid vocabulary of Cathars' shuddering aversion, Moneta by contrast is reticent.

In Moneta's very long account of Cathars' views on marriage, which was utterly condemned along with all carnal union of any sort, the same drift is observable. An opposition, which is in principle directed against all human flesh, is in practice expressed almost entirely in terms of opposition to female flesh. What is opposed is wide. It includes physical contact, where this may be

105 Moneta II.vi.2 (p. 158).
106 Moneta III.i.2–3 (p. 227).
107 Moneta II.ii.1 (pp. 232–3).
108 Pseudo-James Capelli, *Disputationes nonnullae adversus haereticos*, ed. D. Bazocchi, *L'Eresia catara. Appendice* (Bologna, 1920), p. cxv.

literally contact (just touching) or may be sex, and also physically based affection. 'I. Cor. 7. V. I. Dicit Ap. "Bonum est homini mulierem non tangere"; ergo malum est eam tangere; Ut quid enim dicit istud esse malum?' ('I. Corinthians 7. Verse one', says the Cathar, 'the Apostle says, "it is good for a man not to touch a woman". Therefore to touch her is evil. Why does he say this, except to show that this is evil?'). Moneta flatly rejects this, arguing that there is a hierarchy of goods here, and touching a woman is not an evil, simply a lesser good.[109] Later, he uses woman's figuration of the Church and the Church as good to reflect on woman, without qualification: 'Bonum est ergo eam tangere' ('therefore it is good to touch her').[110]

Moneta's counter-statements continue to provide a long and detailed map of the opposed Catholic and Cathar trenches. 'Quare ergo dicis praegnantem doemoniacam esse, cum testetur Lucas istam plenam Spiritu Sancto?' ('Why therefore do you say that a pregnant woman is diabolical, when Luke testifies that she [Mary] was full of the Holy Spirit?').[111] 'Being with a wife, however, is not evil, but a lesser good'.[112] Loving a wife means loving a woman who is among other things materially a woman: 'Ap. loquitur de materiali uxore, quam debet vir diligere' ('the Apostle writes about a material wife, whom the man ought to love').[113] The prose momentarily loses restraint as Moneta moves from bodies towards his in part romantic view of relations between husbands and wives. Referring to the 'firmitas, et vehementia dilectionis inter conjugatos' ('strength and fervour of love between the married'), he rises to this: 'dico quod vir, si opus esset, deberet se tradere morti pro salvanda uxore' ('I say that, if the need were to arise, a man should give himself over to death to save his wife').[114]

There is one fundamental problem here, in the ubiquity of the male viewpoint in texts written by men, in Catholic and Cathar theologians who were all men. Does this diminish the significance of the predominance in Moneta's text of the female rather than male body? Ultimately the ubiquity of male minds is an intractable problem, but there remains a significant contrast between the minds of the different males which are on display. When we read Moneta and a Cathar expounding one of the New Testament texts where both sexes are present, Moneta tends to present both sexes from both sides if the text in question presents both sexes, but the Cathar tends only to represent one. Thus there are the two pairs in I Corinthians 14 – (1) infidel husband and believing wife, and (2) infidel wife and believing husband – where uncleanness of children or sanctifying of spouse may result. For Moneta there are two pairs, and possibilities of sanctifying or spreading uncleanness which can go in two

---

109 Moneta IV.vii.1 (pp. 321–2).
110 Moneta IV.vii.4 (p. 336).
111 Moneta IV.vii.3 (p. 335).
112 Moneta IV.vii.1 (p. 324).
113 Moneta IV.vii.5 (p. 343), referring to Ephesians 5. 25–33.
114 Moneta IV.vii.1 (p. 326).

directions: from infidel man *or* from infidel woman. Moneta concentrates on sanctifying, and he has a spiritual interpretation of uncleanness, which is the danger to faith of the believing partner. By contrast the Cathar concentrates on uncleanness rather than sanctifying. He ignores a man making a woman unclean and he only envisages a woman making a man unclean. And he makes this physical: the woman touches the man physically and the woman thus makes the man unclean.[115]

A Dominican theologian from a Church which rejected the ordination of women and forbade them to preach may raise these issues with a heresy which promoted their ministry or preaching. Thus we have seen Moneta attacking the Waldensians for the fact that Waldensian women preached. By the same token, there is no reason for him to raise the lack of such things in a heresy which he is attacking. So, Moneta is silent, and this silence is a defect in his treatise insofar as the treatise is used to represent *all* Cathar written theology. Women were formally and totally excluded from the four Cathar Orders of Bishop, Older Son, younger Son and Deacon. There was presumably Cathar theology which argued women's unfittedness, the Cathar theological equivalent of Catholic theological justification of women's exclusion from orders. However, we will never know this theology and can only conjecture that a role was played in it by the Cathar view of the female body.

ii. Depositions

We now move from one Italian representation of Cathar scripture and written theology to the world which is constructed by, and partly reconstructable from, depositions. Those used here were mainly taken down in Languedoc between the 1230s and 1320s, but, because of long memories, their coverage extends back into the late twelfth century. Most of the time the witnesses were the adherents of the Cathars, the believers. They talked, and what they said came through several grilles or screens. These grilles are the inquisitors' police-type interests and questions, as we saw in the deposition of Aimersent,[116] translation from Occitan to Latin,[117] translation from Cathar to

---

115 Moneta IV.vii.1 (p. 322).
116 The classic treatment of this problem is H. Grundmann's 'Ketzerverhöre des Spätmittelalters als quellenkritisches Problem', *Deutsches Archiv* 21 (1965), 519–75, and the most sophisticated general comment is in G. G. Merlo, *Eretici e inquisitori nella società piemontese del trecento* (Turin, 1977), pp. 11–15. On questions used in mid thirteenth century Languedoc, see L. Kolmer, *Ad capiendas vulpes. Die Ketzerbekämpfung in Südfrankreich in der ersten Hälfte des 13. Jahrhunderts und die Ausbildung des Inquisitionsverfahren*, Pariser Historische Studien 19 (Bonn, 1982), pp. 92–5, 97, 159, 171–5, 182–5 and 204, and Dossat, *Crises de l'inquisition*, pp. 239–40 – see also pp. 242–4 on inquisitors detecting falsity in confessions. On questions and the reliability of depositions made to Jacques Fournier, see M. Benad, *Domus und Religion in Montaillou*, Spätmittelalter und Reformation, new series 1 (Tübingen, 1990), pp. 9–15.
117 See Dossat, *Crises de l'inquisition*, pp. 73–8, Kolmer, *Ad capiendas*, pp. 124–5, and in

Catholic or inquisitors' vocabulary, and the accidents of survival or destruction of individual depositions. These problems are neither to be ignored nor exaggerated. Usually unremarked is the great contrast between depositions in front of inquisitors in Germany and in Languedoc. In the former leading-questions often clearly and crudely distort evidence, whereas in Languedoc there is less restriction of the deponent's voice and less obstruction by the grilles.

Several points need to be made about the openness to theology of the minds which are partly revealed in these depositions, the first of which concerns gender. None of the women is ever depicted as literate, and women's illiteracy is shared with the majority, but not all, of the men.[118] At most though not all times these women and men were exposed to an extraordinary amount of debate and talking about theology. There was preaching. The entry of mendicant friars into homes was paralleled by countless occasions of Cathar perfects also entering people's homes, and preaching in them. Public preaching by the clergy helped, for, in preaching against heretical errors, the clergy expounded them and thus became one of the sources of ordinary people's knowledge about them. There was debate. Alongside the famous public theological debates attended by Lords and Ladies from 1165 onwards were the many lesser theological debates which took place in houses in Quercy, densely attested in inquisitorial sentences of 1241. Typical is a deponent, the knight Sicart of Montgiscard, remembering the perfect Bernart Engelberti and two other perfects, coming around 1235 to the Church of Bruguières where they met some men 'and there disputed about marriage and talked together'.[119] The milieu or rank does not need to be high. A joiner's wife living among other joiners and their wives in the Ile-de-Tounis in Toulouse comments appraisingly on disputes in Toulouse about the Eucharist between a cleric and mendicant friars, effortlessly articulating the central theological point.[120] The setting does not need to be formal. Another woman stops what she had been doing inside her house in Ravat – cooking – and goes to sit down outside, at the entrance to her house. Men amble over, one sits down beside her, and as a group they start discussing whether we are resurrected in our flesh.[121] She and other women talk a great deal about theology, with knowledge and sophistication, often but not only with other women.[122]

As these women presented themselves in their depositions, they chose.

particular N. Z. Davis, 'Note critique. Les conteurs de Montaillou', *AESC* 34 (1979), 61–73 (pp. 68–9).

[118] Brenon, *Femmes Cathares*, p. 74; Biller, 'Women and Texts in Languedocian Catharism'.

[119] Toulouse MS 609, fol. 67r: 'ibi disputaverunt de matrimonio et confabulabantur ad invicem inter se'.

[120] Paris, Bibliothèque Nationale, MS Doat 25, fol. 42r.

[121] *Fournier*, II, 259.

[122] Notable examples are contained in MS Doat 25, fols. 6r–10r (Peironella of Castanet), 38v–54v (Fauressa of Toulouse), 55v–60v (Arnauda Adrasa).

They believed, or did not believe, particular doctrines. Thus a woman married to Raimon of Gourvielle, Sapdalena, had believed in perfects from about 1233–1238, but then she heard them saying two things, that the earth's fertility owed nothing to God 'and that marriage was not valid, in fact it was a sin – but she the witness did not believe the aforesaid errors'.[123] They occasionally presented themselves as believing or not believing heretics *because* of a doctrine – thus a Lady Hylarda, wife of Guilhem of Villèle, who had made a candle to burn in Church, and had been reproved by perfects for this said that 'on account of this she no longer wanted to believe the heretics'[124] – and the irruption of these testimonies through the barrier of inquisitors' relative lack of curiosity in 'why' makes their appearance even more significant. Finally, belief has a spectrum, which includes 'indifference', and a history: a deponent 'did not believe firmly . . . as many times believed . . . as many times did not believe'.[125] We are shown women, part of a world where ordinary people thought acutely about theology, women who saw themselves as having *voluntas* (will)[126] and making theologically informed choices.

In what follows there is, then, set alongside written Cathar theology and the female body, the living-out of this theology. This living of theology is described in two areas: in beliefs, as Cathar stories and tenets were held and re-expressed by individuals, and in the intersections of Cathar theology and successive stages in women's lives.

Under the heading of beliefs two themes are examined, the original fall of angels (or spirits) and Christ's incarnation in Mary. The story of the fall of angels which Moneta described reappears in adherents' memories of Cathar perfects' sermons, especially those coming from the late Cathar perfects, the Autier family, and their last representative, the famous Guilhem Belibaste. In these versions the duped angels become more than grammatically gendered, as does the trickery itself: the devil promises them women. While retaining a stable central core, the story takes on different shades and colouring depending upon, probably, both preacher and the person remembering. See the deepening shades, deepening gradations of women in these versions, beginning with the gentlest.

First, in one version a wife is at the centre of a picture of domestic happiness. The devil says to the spirits:

'. . . dabo etiam uxorem sociam, et tenebitis hospicia vestra, et habebitis vestros infantes, et plus gaudebitis de uno infante, quando habebitis ipsum, quam de tota ista requie quam hic habetis'

---

123 Toulouse MS 609, fol. 63v: 'et quod matrimonium non valebat, immo erat peccatum; sed ipsa testis non credidit predictis erroribus'.

124 Toulouse MS 609, fol. 108r: 'et propter hoc ulterius noluit credere hereticis'. I cannot find 'Hylarda' in Brenon's *Prénoms occitans*.

125 Toulouse MS 609, fol. 22r: 'non credidit firmiter . . . quotiens credebat . . . quotiens discredebat'.

126 See further on this Biller, 'Common Woman', p. 148 and note 88.

('. . . I will also give [you] a wife as your companion, and you will maintain your households, and you will have babies, and you will have more joy in one baby, when you have it, than in all the peace that you have here')[127]

There is no reference to special revenge by the good God who loses his angels. A second version mainly emphasises love between men and women.

Dyabolus . . . intravit paradisum et introduxit secum unam mulierem, et quando fuit in paradiso dixit existentibus ibi quod talem uxorem eis daret, et diligerent dictas uxores et ipse eos multum.

(The devil . . . entered paradise and brought a woman in with him, and when he was in paradise he said to those who were around there that he would give them such a wife, and they would love the said wives a lot, and they [the wives would love] them [a lot].)[128]

So they fell. There is still no mention of revenge.

In the next version emphasis switches from love to the woman's physical appearance of beauty. The devil had, 'intratus in specie pulcherimme mulieris, in cuius pulcritudine angeli fuerunt allecti, et sequuti fuerunt dictam mulierem usque ad terram' ('entered in the form of a very beautiful woman, [and] the angels were enslaved by her beauty, and they followed the said woman down to earth').[129] One person gave this story without any addition about women. Another preached the same things, and,

. . . ad predicta adiecit quod propterea mulieres nunquam intrant quando moriuntur in gloriam paradisi, set quando moriuntur anime earum subintrant corpora masculorum, et si mortis tempore recipiuntur per hereticum vestitum, convertuntur in homines masculos . . . et introducuntur ad gloriam paradisi.

(. . . added to the aforesaid things that on account of this when women die they never enter the glory of paradise, but when they die their souls go into the bodies of males and if at the time of death they are received by a vested heretic [Cathar perfect] they are turned into male men . . . and they are brought into the glory of paradise.)[130]

The most extreme version in the depositions places at the centre of the stage woman's flesh and ornamentation, and sex with her. It spells out re-

---

[127] *Fournier*, III, 130. Pèire Maury is recalling what the perfect Jacques Autier told him.
[128] *Fournier*, II, 472. Joan [Jean] Maury is recalling what he was told by his father, Raimon.
[129] *Fournier*, II, 442. An inquisitor's emissary is recalling a sermon by Joan [Jean] Maury.
[130] *Fournier*, II, 442–3. The emissary is recalling what Guilhem Belibaste added to Joan [Jean] Maury's version.

venge as that of the good God. The devil told the good spirits that he would give,

> . . . cuilibet ipsorum uxores. Et tunc incepit laudare uxores multum et delectaciones carnales que cum uxore habentur ipse [sic],[131] et tunc dicti spiritus quesiverunt ab eo cuiusmodi res erant uxores, et ipse respondit eis quod mulieres erant, et si ipsi vellent videre aliquam de dictis mulieribus quas ipse se promittebat eis daturum, ipse adduceret unam mulierem ad eos ut eam viderent.

> (. . . wives to each of them. And then he began to praise greatly wives and he [conjectural: told them] the fleshly pleasures that are had with a wife. And then the said spirits asked him what sort of things were wives, and he replied to them that they were women, and that if they wanted to see one of the said women, whom he was promising to give them, he would bring in one woman to them, so that they could see her.)

The devil goes off to get a woman to display to them. The account continues:

> . . . adduxit mulierem pulcherimmam et formosam, auro et argento et lapidibus preciosis ornatam, et introduxit eam in regnum Patris . . . Quam cum vidissent, inflammati concupiscencie eius, quilibet eorum eam habere voluit, quod videns Sathanas eduxit secum de regno Patris dictam mulierem,et spiritus, concupiscencia dicte mulieris illecti, sequti fuerunt dictum Sathanas et mulierem eius. Et tot eos sequti fuerunt quod per novem dies et noctes per quoddam foramen unde Sathanas egressus fuerat cum muliere non cessaverunt cadere spiritus, et magis minutatim et spisse ceciderunt spiritus de celo per dictas dies quam cadat pluvia super terram.

> (He led along a very beautiful and shapely woman, decked out with gold and silver and precious stones, and brought her into the kingdom of the Father . . . And he showed this woman to the good spirits of God the Father. When they saw her, they were inflamed with desire for her, [and] each of them wanted to have her. Seeing this, Satan took the said woman with him out of the kingdom of the Father, and the spirits, enslaved by desire for the said woman, followed the said Satan and his woman. And so many followed them that for seven days and nights the spirits did not cease from falling through an opening where Satan had gone out with the woman, and for the said days the spirits fell from heaven more minutely and densely than rain falls on earth.)[132]

When he saw what had happened the good God 'iuravit . . . quod quia per mulierem regnum suum ita fuerat turbatam et spiritibus suis spoliatum, quod de cetero nulla mulier regnum suum intraret' ('swore . . . that, because his kingdom had been thrown into such turmoil and despoiled of its spirits by a

131 The text in *Fournier*, II, 34 line 7, is emended in Duvernoy, *Corrections*, p. 18.
132 Some biblical sources are suggested by Duvernoy, *Fournier*, II, 34, note 222.

woman, henceforth no woman would enter his kingdom'). Here the good God's oath to exclude women for ever precedes and thus explains the final need, before salvation, for the conversion of women's bodies into men's bodies. Spirits go from body to body until they come into the body of a man or woman who both believes rightly and comes into the hands of a Cathar perfect, that is to say, receives the consolamentum from a perfect. Ending thus in the bodies of men, spirits would then revert without further complication to the heaven of the good God. 'Si tamen dicti spiritus in corpore mulieris habentis entendensa de be subintrassent, egressi de corpore mulieris convertebantur in viros, quia Pater sanctus iuraverat quod nulla mulier de cetero ingrederetur regnum suum' ('If however the said spirits entered the body of a woman who had understanding of good, having left the body of the woman they were converted into men, because the holy Father had sworn that henceforth no woman would enter his kingdom').[133] Noteworthy here is the way the gender of bodies flows into the gender of spirits. Spirits are returned to being male after their existence in female bodies.

What preceded these stories, which were told to Jacques Fournier in the 1320s? Moneta's version did not include the woman and God's oath, but there are some indications of antiquity. There is the evidence of a treatise against the Cathars – probably those of northern France – which was written about 1200. The Catholic author, Évrard de Béthune, writes one chapter to prove 'Quod mulieres in muliebri sexu salvabuntur' ('That women will be saved in the female sex').

> Foemineo etenim sexui coelorum beatitudinem nituntur surripere et a tanto munere suas ipsarum mulierculas non differunt viduare. Cuius erroris phantasiam corroborant ex eo quod dicitur, 'Venite benedicti patris mei' (Matthew 25.34); 'Venite benedicti' dixit, non 'benedicta'.

> (For they [the heretics] try to deprive the female sex of the blessedness of heaven, and do not hesitate to make their own women widows [= separated from] of such a great reward. They support the fantasy of this error from the fact that what is stated is, 'Come, ye blessed of my father'. He said, 'Come ye blessed [male gender]', not 'blessed [female gender]'.)

Évrard's presentation of the Cathar position continues with their exposition of Ephesians 4. 13, 'Until we all meet in the unity of faith, and of the knowledge of the Son of God, unto a perfect man, unto the measure of the age of the fullness of Christ'. He writes, 'Ex hoc enim affirmant quod in speciei viri perfecti et in aetati xxx annorum ad iudicium veniamus, et mulieres suum permutent sexum' ('For on the basis of] this text they claim that we are to come to judgement in the form of a perfect man and at the age of thirty years,

---

[133] *Fournier*, II, 34–5. Arnaut Cicre is recalling a sermon by Guilhem Belibaste.

and that women are to change their sex').[134] Here is very early testimony to Cathar belief in change of sex, but caution is needed. Évrard's chapter does not link the theme with the story of the fall of spirits and the good God's revenge on women, and different light might be thrown on Évrard's discussion whenever his treatise receives the modern study which it so badly needs.

Can the century gap between Évrard's Cathars and Jacques Fournier's be bridged? Perhaps it can – paradoxically, through the late depositions given in front of Fournier. First of all, Fournier put the question about change of sex, along with other Cathar tenets, to the Waldensian Raymond de la Côte. 'Interrogatus si credit quod mulieres in sexu mulie[b]ri resurgant vel quod omnes resurgentes resurgant in sexu viril, respondit quod quilibet resurget in sexu suo' ('asked if he believes that women are to resurrect in the female sex or whether all who resurrect are to resurrect in the male sex, he replied that each is to resurrect in their own sex').[135] The significance of this for our argument is not the Cathar/Waldensian contrast, which we would expect, but what the date of the question suggests about the source of Fournier's knowledge of this Cathar doctrine. Fournier was only to hear this point in depositions which were directly about Cathars (those quoted above) at late dates, 1321 and 1323, but here he was putting the point to a Waldensian *earlier*, in January 1320. How did he know it? Was it part of a common stock of knowledge among the clergy of Languedoc about Cathar beliefs? Secondly, in another hearing, when Fournier asked what Catharism was and what its followers believed, the deponent replied by reciting in Occitan what he remembered of a Cathar prayer; this was followed, without a break and still in Occitan, by what looks like a fragment of a Cathar creed or catechism. It contains the devil's promise to the spirits, and that the devil 'dys que dar lor hia molers que amarian trop . . . caseron e for peritz' ('he said that he would give to them women, whom they would love greatly . . . they fell and perished').[136] This is most likely to have been ancient: prayers and creeds do not spring up overnight. However, since a fuller version of this statement of Cathar belief does not survive, and because the depositions of the late 1230s and the 1240s, which are generally thin in reporting doctrine,[137] are silent, we can only say that Fournier's register contains hints of this earlier history, and then conjecture on their basis the presence and ramifications of this doctrine among Cathar followers in thirteenth-century Languedoc. When on firmer ground, with the stories told in the 1320s, we need, further, to be wary of overstating the presence of the most

134 Évrard de Béthune, *Liber antihaeresis* 18, ed. M. De La Bigne, *Bibliotheca Patrum et Veterorum Auctorum Ecclesiasticorum*, 9 vols. in 6 (Paris, 1624), IV, 1148.
135 *Fournier*, I, p. 88.
136 *Fournier*, II, 461–2 and note 392.
137 Before the depositions in front of Jacques Fournier in Pamiers, extensive reporting of conversations about doctrine is most marked in the depositions before the Dominicans Pons of Parnac and Renous of Plassac in Toulouse in the 1270s, which are contained in MS Doat 25.

extreme version. We have seen a spectrum, ranging from less to more gendered versions. And there was a variety of responses to the stories from both women and men, not necessarily ones which corresponded simply with gender. One woman who was questioned about this in 1323, Esperta Cervel, varied in her statements. At one point she remembered one of the more extreme elements very clearly, saying 'quod audivit dici ab eis . . . quod mulieres revertebantur in homines, alias non salvarentur' ('that she heard it said by them [the heretics] . . . that women reverted into men, otherwise they would not be saved'). This, which does not seem to be based on a leading question, is more convincing than her later denial.[138] Esperta at least knew the doctrine: and she persisted for long as a strong adherent of the Cathars.

Similarly chameleon-like is the presentation of the denial of incarnation and the role of Mary as fleshly mother. Here the chance survival of some of the denials or questions suggests a pattern, women displaying more curiosity, especially in conversations with other women, men more often grounding denial of incarnation in terms of physical abhorrence of female flesh. One woman from Cordes, called Arnauda Adrasa, surrounded her report of her theological conversation with another woman, Lady Beserza of Cestayrols, with details of physical intimacy, saying that she saw that Beserza 'portat cordulam cinctam ad carnem nudam subtus mamillas' ('wears a little cord wound round her bare flesh under her breasts'), and also that 'fuerunt se adinvicem osculatae' ('they kissed each other') to seal their promise of secrecy. Thus assured of confidentiality, Lady Beserza told Arnauda that 'Deus nunquam venit carnaliter in beatem virginem nec in aliam mulierem, nec beata virgo fuit mater Dei' ('God never came physically into the Blessed Virgin nor into any other woman, nor was the Blessed Virgin the mother of God').[139] Another woman, Raimonda of Mazerac, once a Cathar perfect, 'quaesivit a monialibus si Beata Virgo ita lactavit filium carnaliter, et ita doluit in partu, ut aliae mulieres' ('asked nuns whether Mary breast-fed her child physically or felt pain in childbirth, like other women'), presumably sarcastically.[140]

A wealthy man, however, Benazeit Molinier, moved among the urban elite of Cordes and in the society of Cathar perfects, and was thus closer to literacy and written Cathar theology. He put the denial in terms which are reminiscent of pseudo-Capelli's treatise when he confessed in 1301, stating that, 'dicebant etiam quod inpossibile erat Deum fuisse incarnatum, quia nunquam tantum

---

[138] *Fournier*, II, pp. 447 and 452. Cf. Koch's discussion of change of sex, *Frauenfrage*, pp. 102–5, and Bynum's discussion of early Church discussions of resurrection without sex-distinction, in her *Resurrection*, ch. 2, in particular on p. 90 her quotation of St Jerome misogynistically describing heretical women taking pleasure in this, and the further literature cited on p. 86 note 106.

[139] MS Doat 25, fol. 60r. See comment on the cord in Guiraud, *Questions*, p. 134, and *Inquisition*, I, pp. 133 and 145; against Guiraud, Duvernoy maintains this is not a vestige of a perfect's habit, *Religion des cathares*, p. 157.

[140] MS Doat 21, fol. 307r.

humiliavit se quod poneret se in utero mulieris' ('they [the Cathar perfects Raimon *del Boc* and his companion] used to say that it was impossible for God to have been made flesh, because he never humiliated himself so much as to place himself in the womb of a woman').[141] A literate man, the notary Alberto, upon whom a posthumous sentence was passed in Treviso in north-eastern Italy in 1297, had confessed that 'filius Dei non accepit corpus de uirgine Maria, quia non carnem assumpsisset de tam uilli creatura, sicut est femina' ('the son of God did not take [his] body from the Virgin Mary, because he would not have taken on flesh from such a vile creature as a female is').[142] Similar was the phrase used by the former notary and Cathar perfect, Pèire Autier, when preaching in Languedoc. Sebèlia of Arques heard him 'dicens quod non erat dignum cogitare vel credere quod Dei filius natus esset de muliere vel quod in re tam vili, sicut mulier est, Filius Dei se adumbraverit' ('saying that it was not worthy to think or believe that the Son of God was born of a woman or that the Son of God shadowed himself into such a vile thing as a woman is').[143] The repetition of 'as vile a thing/creature as a woman is' and its expression in geographically distant literate Cathar milieux suggests that it may have been a commonplace of Cathar sermons about the incarnation, which was once contained and transmitted in no longer extant Cathar books. The last example occurs through the memory of a woman. Sebèlia's lukewarmness about Catharism suggests further gender speculation. Our deponents seem to fall into three categories: firstly, fervent women discussing the theme with more understanding and curiosity and in milder form; secondly, fervent male Cathar adherents in literate milieux echoing extremism in textual theology; and, thirdly, a woman who was less keen on Catharism distancing herself by formulating the doctrine similarly, in its most rebarbative form. These are three possible positions, from an irrecoverable past reality which will have contained infinitely varying reactions to this extraordinary doctrine, including, possibly, different fervent women who proclaimed this in extreme form.[144]

We turn now to stages of life-cycle, adolescence, marriage and sex, pregnancy, childbirth, and breast-feeding, some of which are fitfully illuminated by the depositions. With the first, there is only the suggestion of a theme which needs further research. The depositions, especially relating to the nobility in early thirteenth-century Languedoc, seem to indicate a pattern where a rather young girl becomes a perfect and takes on the abstinences of a perfect

141 Limborch, *Liber sententiarum*, p. 201. Further references to Molinier and the people with whom he mixed appear in Davis, *Inquisition at Albi*, pp. 19, 178, 208 and 292.
142 G. B. Picotti, *I Caminesi e la loro signoria in Treviso del 1283 al 1312* (Livorno, 1905), p. 264.
143 *Fournier*, II, 409.
144 Compare the heretical women described by St Jerome, quoted in Bynum, *Resurrection*, pp. 90–1.

for a few months a few years, and then leaves.[145] Put in different and modern language, an aristocratic girl, aged about ten and just pre-adolescent,[146] goes onto a vegan diet, at the same time eating very little and renouncing all sex. She then drops all this at the age of thirteen or fourteen, reverting to more normal eating and, perhaps, going out with men. Examples of similar patterns in the lives of pre-adolescent boys seem more difficult to find in the depositions.[147] These are preliminary impressions of a theme, which further investigation might confirm or modify: a deep and complex inter-relation between pre-adolescent and adolescent girls' experience of their bodies and the living through of Catharism.

Where the vow of chastity, which is involved both in being a Cathar perfect and being a Catholic nun or monk, suggests a rough equivalence, is the modern observer being subtly misled? Would secular and religious Catholic lives have been envisaged with the starkness of the examples given below? The intersection of falling in love, marriage and sexual relations with Catharism or not-Catharism is often remembered by deponents in phrases of remarkable brevity. In about a dozen words lives are summarised. There are two elements. Becoming a heretic is coupled with leaving a husband. Stopping being a heretic is coupled with marrying, or returning to, a husband. Thus, 'recessit a viro et fecit se haereticam' ('she left her husband and became a heretic').[148] The other way round, 'fuit heretica per tres annos et amplius, sed postea accepit virum et habit inde infantes duos' ('she was a heretic for three years and more, but afterwards she took a husband and thereby had two babies').[149] 'She left being a perfect and took a husband', or, in a slightly

---

[145] Two examples in Toulouse MS 609, fol. 20r, given in depositions of 1245 and referring respectively to forty and forty-five years previously, c.1205 and c.1200: 'dixit quod quando erat puella circa .x. annos, fuit heretica induta, et stetit heretica bene per quinquennium, et postea exivit inde' ('she said that when she was a girl, about ten years old, she was a clothed heretic, and she remained a heretic for a good five-year period, and afterwards she left'); 'dixit quod non erat .x. annorum mater sua violenter fecit fieri ipsam testem hereticam, et fuit heretica induta per .ix. Menses' ('she said she was not yet ten-years old [when] her mother violently made her become a heretic, and she was a clothed heretic for nine months'). Many other reminiscences by women who say that they were heretics many decades before, without specifying their age or saying that they were then young girls, are likely to have been of similar patterns of experience. The phenomenon was noted by Douais, 'Hérétiques du comté de Toulouse', p. 158. See another example in Guiraud, *Questions*, pp. 112–13.

[146] On medieval girls' age of adolescence, see J. B. Post, 'Age at Menopause and Menarche: Some Medieval Authorities', *Population Studies* 25 (1971), 83–7. Further investigation would have to begin with consideration of Bynum's profound presentation of girls' and women's fasting in her *Holy Feast*.

[147] There are some instances, e.g. MS Toulouse 609, fol. 70r: 'cum esset puer . . . indutus per annum et duos menses' ('when he was a boy [he was] a clothed [heretic] for a year and two months').

[148] MS Doat 21, fol. 190r.

[149] MS Doat 21, fol. 1r. Cf. Guiraud, *Questions*, pp. 78–9.

different formulation, 'conversa fuit ad fidem Catholicam, et accepit virum' ('she was converted to the Catholic faith and took a husband').[150] In 1244 a knight's widow, Azalaïs, recalls the patterns in both her mother's life and hers. 'Forneria mater ipsius testis fuit haeretica, et recessit a viro suo' ('Her, the witness's, mother Fornèira was a heretic, and left her husband'), while she herself was a heretic for three and a half years, around 1208, and then 'ipsa testis deseruit sectam haereticam et duxit in virum Alzievum de Massabrac' ('she, the witness, deserted the heretical sect and took as husband Alzieu of Massabrac').[151] The alternatives were also envisaged as Catharism and love. A knight, Raimon Aiffre, recalled that, 'Veziada uxor quondam Petri Guillelmi Carratier tunc temporis haeretica, et ipse testis adamavit eam et extraxit eam inde' ('Véziada, formerly wife of Pèire Guilhem Carratier, was at that time [c.1224] a heretic, and he – the witness – loved her passionately, and dragged her out from that').[152] Direct and terse are these statements, and they frustrate us, denying us further detail. But this very terseness conveys something of the starkness and fundamental nature of the connection which a witness is recalling.

Direct glimpses of Catharism's obvious intrusion into sexual relations in marriage are, however, rare. A Toulouse citizen who believed in the Cathars and said that as a consequence he had not slept with his wife for two years is an exception.[153] Elsewhere we must conjecture Catharism introducing a dark shadow of sin and co-operation with the devil into the hearts and minds of those many married and Cathar-believing women and men who continued to sleep together and have children. Some, at least, must have been acutely aware of Cathar disgust of the sexual act itself, characteristically turned against woman in this late formulation by Guilhem Belibaste, that 'quando aliquis cognoscebat carnaliter mulierem, fetor illius peccati ascendebat usque ad capam celi, et dictus fetor se extendebat per totum mundum' ('when someone knew a woman physically, the stench of this sin ascended to the top of the sky, and the said stench spread through the whole world').[154] Certainly there could be pressure to leave one's spouse, for a marriage to break up: a perfect 'monuit ipsum testem quod dimitterent uxorem suam et fieret hereticus' ('advised him the witness to leave his wife and become a heretic').[155] This has dropped away by the early fourteenth century, when depositions show some Cathar interest in the formation of marriage.

---

[150] MS Doat 23, fol. 124r.
[151] MS Doat 24, fols. 204r, 205v.
[152] MS Doat 23, fol. 84v.
[153] MS Doat 22, fol. 97v: 'at Pentecost it will be two years that he had not slept with his wife' [non iacuerat carnaliter cum uxore sua duo anni erunt in pentacoste]; ed. C. Douais, *Documents pour servir à l'histoire de l'inquisition dans le Languedoc* (Paris, 1900), p. 99.
[154] *Fournier*, II, 500.
[155] Toulouse MS 609, fol. 70r.

The documentary trail becomes a little richer with pregnancy. The pregnant woman is a demoniac. She has the devil in her belly. This statement is attested in written theology, and it is generalised as an assumption about one group of Italian Cathars, the Albanenses, through its appearance in a list of questions to be put to suspects – where the assumption is that the *consolamentum* for the dying would be denied to a pregnant woman who was dying.[156] And it appears in the Languedoc depositions as a snatch of a sermon from Cathar perfects, or something passed around in conversation among Cathar adherents. The point is given both a ritual and doctrinal construction. Depositions are littered with believers recalling their participation in one rite, 'adoring' perfects when they met them on the road, or with other believers at the end of the sermon. The demoniac pregnant body was excluded from this rite. Guillelma *de Bono Loco* was taught by a female perfect how to adore, but 'non potuit adorare quia erat pregnans' ('she could not adore because she was pregnant').[157] There are hints at more than one meaning being given to the exclusion, or the exclusion *possibly* being presented as at least in part concern for the pregnant woman's condition. This can perhaps be seen in the experience of Esmengart, the wife of the knight Pèire of Mazerolles, who was riding along a road, escorted by a knight. Both were adherents of the Cathars, and would ordinarily engage in the rite of adoration if meeting them. The pair did bump into two male perfects, and the knight engaged in the ritual of adoration, while the woman did not. 'Quia ipsa testis erat tunc pregnans, non descendit, nec dimiserunt eam dicti heretici descendere de equitatura, et ideo non adoravit' ('Because she, the witness, was then pregnant, she did not get down, nor did the said heretics let her down from horseback, and so she did not adore').[158]

We cannot be certain – and there is still uncertainty in an example of

---

[156] 'Quare non faciunt manus impositionem dyacones vestri mulieri pregnanti et morienti sive cum moritur; si mulier impregnata a viro suo habet demonem in corpore; si aliquo modo possit salvari talis mulier si moreretur in partu' ('Why do not your deacons carry out the laying on of hands on a woman who is pregnant and dying or when she dies? Does a woman impregnated by her husband have the devil in [her] body? Can such a woman in any way be saved if she dies in childbirth?'), ed. by Molinier, 'Rapport', 295. See the opposition of the 'Catholic' to the 'Heretic' (Cathar) in the *Disputatio Catholici contra Haereticos* ii, ed. E. Martène and V. Durand, *Thesaurus novus anecdotorum*, 5 vols. (Paris, 1717), V, 1714–15: 'Quod autem praegnantes non damnentur, sicut mussitatis, quia irremediabiliter damnantur, si moriantur ante partum vel in partu, improbamus illa ratione' ('We prove by this argument that pregnant [women] are not to be damned as you have murmured that they are – [saying that they are] irrevocably damned if they die before childbirth or in childbirth'). See in general Borst, *Katharer*, p. 181 and note 5, Koch, *Frauenfrage*, pp. 112–13, and Duvernoy, *Religion des cathares*, p. 264. In her *Vrai visage*, pp. 168–9, Brenon argues that the doctrine was favourable to women, in running counter to Catholic emphasis on fertility.

[157] MS Doat 21, fol. 296r.

[158] Toulouse MS 609, fol. 196v; see also fol.124r.

exclusion from another rite, even though reasons seem to be spelled out. In 1245 a Lady Mabelia stated that when her (first?) husband, Huc de Villèle, was dying about thirty years beforehand, perfects came to administer the consolamentum to him. 'Nec interfuit dicte hereticatione, quia fecerunt eam removeri, quia erat pregnans, propter dolorem quam habebat ipsa testis' ('She was not present at the said heretication, because they had her removed, because she was pregnant, on account of the pain she the witness had'). Presumably the action was seen differently by the actors involved, and we can do no more than conjecture, with questions. Was she removed because the demoniac pregnant body had to be kept apart from the rite? Or because of compassion for her grief for her husband? Or because her grief would disturb her husband? Or for several reasons – that is to say, the perfects saw her body as demoniac, but presented to her a more palatable reason for her exclusion? While it seems that the pregnant female body, demoniac, had to be kept apart from Cathar rites, we must remember that we have only a handful of examples and only wisps of explanatory comment.

The existence and expression of the theological construction of the pregnant female body is much clearer. Perfects make a point of it to individual pregnant women, and they do not beat about the bush. 'The said heretics said to her the witness . . . who was pregnant . . . that she had the devil, in her belly'.[159] 'Dicti heretici dixerunt ei que loquitur que erat pregnans quod so decederet pregnans non posset salvari' ('The said heretics said to her who is speaking', a Peirona *de Claustra*, 'that if she died pregnant she could not be saved').[160] Cathar theology here gets through without diminution. It is quite different in tone from the ascetic statements about childbirth and pregnancy found in the fathers and used in texts like *Hali Meidenhad*, with their emphasis on women's experience of pain and danger in childbirth and exhaustion in bringing up children. These are nowhere evoked in Cathar presentation of the doctrine. The comforting gloss – that Peirona's soul would have to continue its transmigratory journey after the death of her body, and this soul could be saved in the next body it inhabited – is not added here or elsewhere. Whether the gloss was not added, or was added and forgotten, we cannot know. What remains is that deponents remembered there was damnation for pregnant bodies which died.

Clearly many women were caught in the middle, compromised between their faith and the fertility of their bodies. One such was the Lady Beserza, wife of the knight Peter Isarn of Cestayrols. He seems to have been an adherent, and she was certainly this and possibly even a perfect.[161] Despite this and despite her conviction that sex was sinful, she continued to conceive and give birth. Curious depositions survive concerning her, coming ultimately from the

159 See above and note 2.
160 MS Doat 22, fol. 57r. Peirona's case and two others were noted by Guiraud, *Questions*, pp. 92–3.
161 See her statements above and note 114.

five women, three of them married, who used to assist Lady Beserza when she was in labour. Women in labour were wont to call upon Jesus Christ or Mary – as those in northern Europe called upon St Margaret – but those assisting Beserza were shocked at her omission of this, remembering that she cried out, 'Holy Spirit of God, help me!'[162] There is perhaps more than a glimpse of Catholicism here, Catholic midwives maintaining and perpetuating a tradition of orthodox prayers.

In another deposition from the 1270s there is a young woman called Filipa, from several generations of staunch Cathar adherents, who takes care to say that a woman called Gordona and other women visited her when she was in labour – both Gordona and her husband were also staunch adherents.[163] Now, Filipa's mother used to spead the doctrine about demoniac pregnancy – 'You should pray God to free you from the demon you have in your belly'.[164] Here, in these Cathar women visiting Filipa while she was in labour and in her mother's instruction in prayer to another pregnant woman, we have a fleeting glimpse of a Cathar practice. With Cathar women beside the bed, there is a specific prayer which is to be uttered by the woman who has evilly conceived, who has a demon in her belly, and whose soul will be condemned – or condemned to more wandering? – if she dies.

Finally, we turn to milk. There is no extant example of a lactating body

---

[162] MS Doat 25, fol. 60v: 'cum in quodam puerperio ipsa testis fuerit obstetrix eiusdem Bezersae, nunquam audivit eam clamantem "Dominum" nec "Jesum Christum" nec "Beatam Virginem", sed tamen [*perhaps mistake for* tantum] "Sancte Spiritus Dei, vale mihi"; unde mulieres aliae obstetrices aborrent eam in puerperiis, quod nolunt ibi esse libenter quia non rogat Beatam Virginem' ('when she, the witness, was Bezersa's midwife in a particular childbirth, she never heard her crying out "Lord!", nor "Jesus Christ!", nor "Blessed Virgin!", but [only] "Holy Spirit of God, help me!". Whence the women [who were the] other midwives shrink back from in her childbirths – [to the extent] that they are unwilling to be present there – because she does not call upon the Blessed Virgin'). Fol. 62v: 'quando laborat in partu nunquam clamat "Jesum Christum", nec "Beatam Virginem", sed "Sancte Spiritus, adiuva me"' ('when she labours in childbirth she never cries out "Jesus Christ!", nor "Blessed Virgin!", but "Holy Spirit, help me!"'). The male deponent had heard this from five women, 'quae omnes simul et diversis temporibus interfuerunt quando dicta Beserza pariebat' ('who were all present together, and at various times, whenever Beserza gave birth'). In both depositions the final letter of 'Sancte' appears to be written over '-ae' (or '-oe'). The seventeenth-century scribe has presumably altered an '-e' to '-ae' [feminine plural], before correcting back to '-e' [masculine singular, vocative]; this comment is based on reading a microfilm of the manuscript. Cf. Guiraud, *Inquisition*, I, p. 164 and note 2.

[163] MS Doat 25, fol. 52v: 'Gordona uxor Pon. de Gomervilla visitavit ipsam testem in partu cum aliis mulieribus' ('Gordona, wife of Pons of Gameville, visited her in childbirth, together with other women').

[164] MS Doat 25, fol. 39v: 'quadam die dicta Fabrissa dixit ipsi testi praegnanti, quod rogaret Deum ut liberaret eam a demone quem habebat in ventre' ('one day the said Fauressa said to her the witness, [who was] pregnant, that she should pray God to free her from the demon she had in her belly'). Fauressa and her family are described by Brenon, *Femmes cathares*, pp. 285–93.

being barred, like a pregnant body, from Cathar rites, but a milk-producing breast was barred from the mouth of a baby who had received the *consolamentum*. There are several accounts of this after 1300, and women reacted to it very differently. Guillelma, confessing in 1311, recalled that she 'audivit a Blanca socru sua quod fecerat hereticari quandam filiam parvulam ipsius Guilelme tunc infirmum per Petrum Sancii hereticum, et inhibuerat sibi dicta Blanca ne daret lac ad bibendum dicte filie sue post dictam hereticationem, et mortua est dicta filia hereticata' ('heard from Blanca, her mother-in-law, that she had had her, Guillelma's, little baby girl, [who was] then ill, hereticated by the heretic Pèire Sans, and the said Blanca forbade her to give milk to her said daughter after the said heretication, and the said hereticated daughter died').[165] This mother did as instructed, and it posed no problem for her faith in the Cathars, which she stoutly affirmed.

Sebèlia of Arques, on the other hand, resisted pressure from several men. One was the perfect Andreas, who hereticated the baby daughter Jacmeta and told Sebèlia not to feed her, while the other was Sebèlia's husband Raimon, who was rejoicing in the imminent death and salvation of his daughter. However, when both men 'postquam exiverant de domo lactavit dictam filiam suam, quia non potuit videre, ut dixit, quod sic dicta filia eus moreretur' ('had left the house, she breast-fed her said daughter, because, as she said, she could not see her said daughter dying like this') Her husband was enraged when he learnt this, and another man, who calmed him down, addressed both the baby and Sebèlia, telling the baby, 'Malam matrem habuisti' ('You have had an evil mother!'), and to Sebèlia, 'quod mala mater erat' ('that she was an evil mother'), and 'quod mulieres erant demones' ('that women were devils').[166] Mengarda Buscalh, mother of a two or three-month old baby boy , was urged to have him hereticated. In this case she would have had to desist from breastfeeding not only because of the prohibition of milk after the reception of the *consolamentum*, but also because of the possibility of her female touch contaminating a male. When she learnt that she would have to give up breast-feeding if he was hereticated, 'dixit quod nullo modo dimitteret dare mamillam puero quamdiu viveret' ('she said that in no way would she leave off giving the breast to her boy while he lived').[167]

Are the attitudes to the pregnant and lactating body revealed in these vignettes to be regarded as typical or exceptional? Are they the tip of an iceberg, or isolated ice-floes? There is a moment in Moneta's dialogue with a Cathar about marriage which suggests one answer. The Cathar tries to associate the Catholic Church with the condemnation of marriage, saying 'quod Ecclesia Romana puerperam immundam judicat, et quasi paganam usque ad

---

[165] Limborch, *Liber sententiarum*, p. 104.
[166] *Fournier*, II, 415. In my 'Common Woman', p. 156, when citing this story I mistakenly made the husband the person who said, 'You women are devils!' – the speaker was the friend, Pèire Maury.
[167] *Fournier*, I, 499.

Missam diei ultimae suae purificationis' ('that the Roman Church regards a woman in childbirth as unclean and virtually a pagan until mass on the last day of her purification'). Moneta rejects the point, and proceeds to the answer which had been standard for centuries, some physical uncleanness but no spiritual uncleanness whatsoever in the post-childbirth woman, and a rite which can be praiseworthily followed but is not obligatory.[168] This is not as interesting as the implications of the Cathar's taunt. It is a rhetorical ploy in the course of debate – 'you Catholics are like us on this' – which then goes on to misrepresent by overstatement the Church's position: in all this it implies the Cathar position as a generality. That is, the pregnant, childbearing and lactating female body is not only materially unclean but also spiritually and in a much deeper sense unclean: diabolic in its operation, pagan, and to be kept utterly apart from the holy.

This abhorrence of the conceiving, pregnant and lactating female body must be put alongside wariness about the not necessarily generating female body. Male perfects should not touch women. This was not a euphemism for sex, which was obviously out of the question, rather it was intended literally: there should be no *touch* of any sort. St Francis forbade his followers even to touch a coin: Cathars were the Franciscans of this other area of revulsion. When conferring the consolamentum perfects held hands above the recipient's head, carefully not touching if it was a woman, while the interposition of a book enabled these male perfects to avoid touching a woman in the ritual of the kiss of peace, and opportunities for casual contact were minimised by the practical measure of male and female perfects eating at different tables.[169] The leading perfect in the last Cathar revival, Pèire Autier, told a follower 'that if he happened to touch a woman, he would have to abstain [and fast] on bread and water for nine days continuously'.[170] All of this *could* be seen as working in both directions, that is to say, this system *also* protected female perfects from contamination by contact with male flesh. But statements and anecdotes given by deponents – whatever their gender – present this only in one direction. Though male perfects were men who 'nullo modo tangerent in carne nuda mulierem' ('would in no way touch a woman on her bare flesh'),[171] female perfects are not defined in depositions as women who 'would in no way touch a man on his bare flesh'. Depositions make it clear that the point of a story is men who have received the *consolamentum* not being touched by

168 Moneta IV.vii.2 (p. 330). On the medieval church's ideas and treatment of impurity through childbirth, see P. Browe, *Beiträge zur Sexualethik des Mittelalters* (Breslau, 1932), chapter 3 'Die Geburt' (pp. 15–35).
169 Guiraud, *Questions*, pp. 83–4, and *Inquisition*, I, pp. 178 and 192–4, Koch, *Frauenfrage*, pp. 108–9 and 127, Duvernoy, *Religion des cathares*, p. 183, and Biller, 'Common Woman', pp. 151–2 and 155.
170 *Fournier*, III, 111. For the one instance – only one – of a comparable but less extreme Waldensian position, see *Fournier* I, 74, and note 24.
171 *Fournier*, II, 12.

women; it is difficult to find depositions where the point is the other way round.

One unexpected aspect of this problem concerned medical practice. The depositions provide many glimpses of two groups of medical religious, Waldensian Brothers and Cathar perfects, acting as doctors (*medici*). Where we are given details, the appear to use conventional medicine of the time, herbs, plasters and ointments, and conventional practice is also the inference from Cathar possession of a book of medicine (*liber medicine*).[172] Now, feeling the pulse through touch (*tactus*) was one key diagnostic method in medicine.[173] Surely, then, diagnosis of women, and perhaps their further treatment, would have posed a problem for a Cathar perfect who was also a *medicus*? On the other hand, there were the Waldensian *medici*, conventionally ascetic men whose theology was devoid of the abhorrence of female flesh, and in particular its touch. Presumably treatment of women would have been no *unusual* problem for them? Turning with these questions in mind to the depositions, we find the following. The specified consultations of Waldensian *medici* are numerous enough to provide statistics. Eighty-two witnesses reported consulting them, thirty-eight of them women, forty-four of them men. Although the high proportion of men consulting for their own illnesses skews the figures – men as ever the more hypochondriac sex – many of those treated were women. Nineteen women consulted on behalf of themselves, two for a daughter, and one for a maid, while four men obtained medical help for their wives, three for their daughters, and two for their sisters-in-law: thus we see thirty-one women being treated. The only additional comment we ever get, apart from specification of payment or ailment (two with eye-problems), is Waldensian care and assiduity. For example, 'the Waldensians came to the house of the said ill woman virtually every day'.[174] The scanty details preserve some interesting gender patterns in consultation, but not in the Brothers' treatment of women and men. When we turn to Cathars we find fewer examples, rendering statistics less useful. The best documented Cathar *medicus* is Guilhem Bernart d'Airoux.[175] Guilhem did treat both women and men. However, curiously, he is seen in two cases refusing to treat ill women. In the case of one, who had a facial ailment, no explanation was given, while the other, who had a fever, was not treated 'because it was the month of August'.[176] Given the intertwining of astrology and medical practice, a reference to August could

---

172 Cathar medical practice was surveyed by W. L. Wakefield, 'Heretics as Physicians in the Thirteenth Century', *Speculum* 57 (1982), 328–31, and Waldensian by P. Biller, '*Curate infirmos*: the medieval Waldensian practice of medicine', in *The Church and Healing*, ed. W. J. Sheils, SCH 19 (Oxford, 1982), 55–77 (61–6).
173 See for example Avicenna on the pulse, *Liber canonis medicinae* I.ii.2.1–19 (Venice, 1527), fols. 36r–39v.
174 Doat 21 fol. 269r: 'fere singulis diebus Valdenses veniebant ad domum dictae infirmae'.
175 Wakefield, 'Heretics as Physicians', pp. 330–1.
176 Wakefield, 'Physicians', p. 330.

have been Guilhem's allegation of astrology impeding medical treatment, designed to conceal from the ill woman the real reason for refusing. For Guilhem is never seen turning a man away, and, as we have seen, there is not the slightest hint of this with any Waldensian *medicus*. We are driven to the suggestion that the Cathar perfect Guilhem sometimes turned away women because their treatment would have entailed touching them.

Reactions? It is not easy to find explicit reactions to this avoidance of contamination by touch. Here are two instances of concern about touch in depositions. In one a seventeen-year-old girl, Grazida, and a girl who seems to have been a friend, Raimonda, saw a perfect and talked about him as they were leaving together. 'Raymunda dixit eidem Grazidae . . .quod erat multum bonus homo et quod pro toto mundo non tangat mulierem' ('Raimonda said to her Grazida . . . that he was a very good man, and not for the world does he touch a woman'). In another, Bona Cicre's father has received the *consolamentum* and is dying, and Bona 'audivit a dicto patre suo quod de cetero ipsa non tangeret eum quia nulla mulier debebat tangere eum . . .et ex tunc non tetigit eum' ('heard from her said father that henceforth she should not touch him, because no woman ought to touch him . . . and from then on she did not touch him').[177] 'Not for the world does he touch a woman' translates Latin which translated Occitan. Is it a fragment, transmitted opaquely, of a serious, awed conversation about the life and high claims of perfects? Or a curiosity swapped between two amused young girls? Is it only a modern sensibility which reacts so strongly to the story of a daughter not allowed to touch her father as he lay dying? It is Bona Cicre who remembered this, and told the story this way. We are left tantalisingly without answers, but not without a moral that can be drawn: depositions raise these questions and more, always suggesting extraordinary human variety and resisting reduction to simplicities for a modern debate about the gender appeal of Catharism.

In the first part of this paper, I argued that the history of external observation and comment upon Catharism shows women's special role coming into being, as a theme, *after* the middle ages, and that historians have imposed various masks upon this theme. What, finally, are the principal propositions of the second part, the main features of the latest mask which I am applying?

In Moneta of Cremona's extensive but perhaps too restrained account of and polemic against Cathar doctrines, there is a detailed mapping of one sector of the terrain – 'material' women – over which Catholicism and Catharism fought. Cathar written theology is consistently more hostile. How was this written theology lived out? Depositions provide glimpses. Variety is the first impression. Leaving aside formal theological differences between Cathar churches – which have not been discussed here – we see that within one area of Catharism a key doctrine could be articulated in many different ways, altering in transmission and according to the outlook of an individual.

177 Limborch, *Liber sententiarum*, pp. 111 and 115.

The female body could be highly charged, represented in beauty, ornament, power and as such arousing the lust of spirits (who in this context are male) and performing the central role in the story of the devil's seduction of the angels of the good God. But the female body could also be present in less sexual form. And it could also be virtually absent, as is the case in the milder, domestic version of the story of this fall. Cathar theology was not just transmitted from high to low. Here we concentrate on women, adherents as well as female perfects. The depositions contain thousands of women, many of whom knew what Catharism was about. Adherents, non-literate women, can be seen in depositions chatting about theology, evidently people who are comfortable and familiar with theological issues. This must have been true, to a greater degree, with most perfects. These women have their views, and they decide – changing and altering doctrines, perhaps creating. Statistics? On the basis of figures, historians discuss two possibilities, (i) women specially attracted to Catharism, (ii) a neutral middle picture, where gender is irrelevant. Abels and Harrison plump heavily for the second of these, Brenon for the first.

The suggestions here are, first, that these alternatives are insufficient. Where figures show proportions of women among Cathar followers which are less than the proportion of adult women in the population, historians should add a third *possibility* to discussion: more ordinary women than ordinary men being repelled by Catharism. Statistics flatten, however, and above all the second suggestion here is that these women should not be seen as a bloc, 'women', so that we are prevented from seeing, for example, a (smaller?) number of more ascetic and more spiritual women probably drawn into Catharism in part for the reasons that, in part, repelled other women. While Brenon does not see women as a bloc, her *Femmes cathares* does need the addition of women who were indifferent or hostile to Catharism.

Statements generalising about women's responses betray these thousands of individual human beings living in the past, some more spiritual and some more attached to pleasure, or men, or babies; some more conservative and some more rebellious in outlook; some more bothered and some more unquestioningly accepting their bodies. Four of these individuals can be seen more clearly than most, talking about demoniac pregnancy, and what shines out is the variety of their experience, personality and outlook. On the one hand, we find in Toulouse a joiner's wife, Fauressa, a woman who was part of a strong family tradition of Catharism, much of it female. Her mother died after receiving the *consolamentum*, while this mother's first husband and Fauressa's daughter were executed for heresy. Fauressa was not only a tough, intelligent and theologically very aware person but also a mother and grandmother, and it is she whom we see plugging the doctrine of demoniac pregnancy when talking to another pregnant woman. On the other hand there was Aimersent, who was young and pregnant, and though married to a brutal husband happy, at least, with her pregnancy. For she said that it was hearing this doctrine which made her stop liking the Cathars. And in front of her were two unnamed celibate women, who were expressing their ideas in a fairly public setting and being heeded with respect by the men and women of Auriac who had come together to listen to them. Two ascetic women, then, were enjoying the rare privilege in a medieval community of doing something forbidden to women, preaching. What they expounded was the doctrine of demoniac pregnancy, and they made this personal, applying it to the adolescent pregnant girl in their audience.[178]

I conclude with a distinguished Italian historian. 'Women occupied a privileged place in heretical communities.' Citing some of the evidence he goes on to say, 'one must not force these data too much'. He alludes to variety on a point which is sometimes 'couched in a gentle persuasive form' and sometimes in 'openly violently misogynistic language'. This point is expressed in the final line of a heretical Gospel, which he quotes. 'Simon Peter said to them, "Let Mary leave us, for women are not worthy of Life." Jesus said, "I myself shall lead her in order to make her male, so that she too may become a living spirit resembling you males. Every woman who will make herself male will enter the Kingdom of Heaven".' The Italian historian summarises the point thus. 'The female function is essentially generative . . . the cause, however indirect, of the creation of the world and of humankind. By itself, however, it is incapable of aspiring to the heights. The process of salvation, in this sense, is essentially male, a process, as it were, of masculinisation.' [179]

The Italian historian cited here is Giovanni Filoramo, and I have altered 'Gnostic' to 'heretical' in the first quotation to postpone revealing the identity of the heretics he was describing: the Gnostics of the first and second centuries AD. His delicate delineation of a paradox in Gnosticism suggests comparison with the paradox which is revealed when we look at the roles women played in Catharism and Catharism's view of 'material woman'.

---

[178] Cf. Brenon's reading of this deposition, *Femmes cathares*, pp. 107 and 190.
[179] G. Filoramo, *A History of Gnosticism*, trans. A. Alcock (Oxford, 1990), pp. 176–7.

De impedimento sexus:
Women's Bodies and Medieval Impediments to Female Ordination

A. J. Minnis

In 1391–3 an educated lay Lollard, Walter Brut, was tried for heresy before the bishop of Hereford, John Trefnant. One of the views with which he was credited was the belief that 'women have power and authority to preach and make the body of Christ, and they have the power of the keys of the church, of binding and loosing'.[1] Trefnant, who recruited a large number of university men to refute this and other opinions, wrote about the matter extensively in his register; moreover a set of *quaestiones* has survived, presumably the work of members of Trefnant's team, which consider some of the issues raised by Brut.[2] One of these questions, which asks 'Whether women are permitted to instruct men assembled in public', has enjoyed a great deal of attention lately.[3] It draws extensively on material from the *Summa theologiae* of St Thomas Aquinas and the *Summa quaestionum ordinariarum* of Henry of Ghent, works which had been written over a century previously. Those earlier discussions are part and parcel of a substantial body of scholastic materials relating to the ordination of women and the priestly functions which they may (or more accurately, may not) perform, which has not yet received the attention it deserves. Hence the purpose of this paper is to, as it were, get behind the Walter Brut controversy, and review the earlier history of that tradition of theological discussion within which at least certain aspects of it should be placed.

[1] *Registrum Johannis Trefnant*, ed. W. W. Capes, Canterbury and York Society 20 (London, 1916), p. 364, no. 30; trans. by M. Aston, 'Lollard Women Priests?', in her *Lollards and Reformers. Images and Literacy in Late Medieval Religion* (London, 1984), p. 52.

[2] On the trial and its implications see the summary account by K. B. McFarlane, *John Wycliffe and the Beginnings of English Nonconformity* (London, 1952), pp. 135–8, and especially Aston, 'Lollard Women Priests?', pp. 49–70; also A. Hudson, *The Premature Reformation. Wycliffite Texts and Lollard History* (Oxford, 1988), pp. 47–8, 281–2, 284n, 291, 295, 298–9, 326–7, 368, etc.

[3] See the edition by A. Blamires and C. W. Marx, 'Woman Not to Preach: A Disputation in British Library MS Harley 31', *The Journal of Medieval Latin* 3 (1993), 34–63, and the partial translation in Blamires, *Woman Defamed*, pp. 251–5.

1. A Sequence of *Sentences* Commentaries

During a period roughly spanning *c*.1240 until *c*.1337, a major *locus classicus* for discussion of the non-ordination of women was afforded by distinctions 24 and 25 of the fourth book of Peter Lombard's *Libri Sententiarum*, which around 1223/7 had been established as the dominant textbook in the Parisian faculty of theology. This was the point at which the Lombard had discussed the sacrament of Holy Orders, and whilst he himself made no mention of the unsuitability of women as candidates for ordination, several of his commentators did address the issue. Here I shall discuss the relevant disquisitions by eleven of them: Richard Fishacre, O.P. (d. 1248),[4] St Bonaventure, O.F.M. (*c*.1217–74),[5] St Thomas Aquinas, O.P. (*c*.1225–74),[6] Peter of Tarantasia, O.P. (1224–76; the future Pope Innocent V),[7] Richard of Middleton, O.F.M. (*c*.1249–*c*.1308),[8] John Duns Scotus, O.F.M. (*c*.1265–*c*.1308),[9] Durandus of St Pourçain, O.P. (*c*.1275–1334),[10] Peter of la Palud O.P. (*c*.1275/80–1342),[11] Fran-

---

4   Richard's *Sentences* commentary, produced during the period 1241–8, was the first to issue from Oxford. His discussion of the non-ordination of women has been edited from two manuscripts by Martin, 'Ordination of Women', pp. 144–5. Richard's account is followed by his Oxford successor, Simon of Hinton O.P., in the *Summa theologiae* which he wrote 1254/6. See Martin, 'Ordination of Women', p. 148, who also picks up a relevant statement in the *Sentences* commentary which William of Rothwell O.P. produced around 1255 (p.149).

5   Bonaventure's *Sentences* commentary was composed at Paris during the period 1250–52. For *In IV Sent.* dist. 25, art. 2, qu. 1 ('Utrum ad susceptionem ordinis requiratur sexus virilis') see his *Opera* IV, 649–51.

6   Aquinas lectured at Paris during 1252–8. For *In IV Sent.*, dist. 25, qu. 2, art. 1 ('Utrum femineus impediat ordinis susceptionem') see his *Opera omnia*, 25 vols. (Parma, 1852–72), VII, 907–8.

7   Peter wrote his *Sentences* commentary in Paris, 1259–64. For *In IV Sent.* dist. 25, qu. 3, art. 1 ('An sexus muliebris impediat susceptionem ordinis') see *Innocentii Quinti . . . in IV Libros Sententriarum commentaria* (Toulouse, 1649–52; repr. Ridgewood, NJ, 1964), IV, 278–9.

8   Batchelor of theology in 1283, regent master at Paris 1284–7; Richard composed his *Sentences* commentary *c*.1285–95. For *In IV Sent.* dist. 25, art. 4, qu. 1 ('Utrum sexus muliebris impedit ordinis susceptionem') see his *Super quatuor libros sententiarum* (Brescia, 1591), pp. 388–9.

9   For *In IV Sent.* dist. 25, qu. 2 ('Utrum sexus muliebris, vel aetas puerilis, impediat susceptionem ordinum') see *Opera omnia* (Lyon, 1639, repr. Hildesheim, 1969), XI.2, 783–5.

10 A master of theology at Paris in 1312, Durandus lectured on the *Sentences* during the period 1307–8, but extensively rewrote his work later. The third redaction of the fourth book (dating from 1325–7) is the text which subsequently was printed, as in the edition which I have used, *In Petri Lombardi Sententias theologicas commentariorum libri IIII* (Venice, 1571, repr. Ridgewood, NJ, 1964), fol. 364v.

11 Peter started to read the *Sentences* in Paris *c*.1310; he began lecturing on book iv (by far the most original part of this commentary) before 1314, though the extant version probably was not finalised before the beginning of 1315. Peter was appointed

cis of Meyronnes, O.F.M. (before 1288–*c*.1328),[12] John of Bassoles, O.F.M. (d. 1347),[13] and Thomas of Strasbourg, O.E.S.A. (*c*.1275–*c*.1357).[14] In addition I shall draw on related discussions, the most important of which are two *quaestiones* in the prologue to the *Summa* of the secular master Henry of Ghent (d. 1293), 'Utrum mulier possit esse doctor seu doctrix theologie' (art. 11, qu. 2) and 'Utrum mulier possit esse auditor seu auditrix theologie' (art. 12, qu. 1).[15] While Henry is not directly concerned with the issue of ordination here, his interests are akin to those of the commentators of book iv, distinction 25 of the *Sentences*. In particular, his discussion of whether or not a woman can be a *doctor theologiae* is one of a sequence in which he has taken the usual impediments which were discussed in respect of ordination and reformulated them in terms of teaching, to produce the questions: can a sinner be a doctor of theology? a boy? a woman? Finally, our discussion will include the brief but fascinating remarks found in two works by Thomas of Chobham, a sub-dean of Salisbury who died *c*.1233–6,[16] which antedate all the other texts here listed.[17]

In viewing these materials side by side it is crucial to realise that like is not

---

Patriarch of Jerusalem in 1329. For his account of the non-ordination of women, *In IV Sent*. dist. 25, qu. 3, see *In quartum Sententiarum*, ed. V. Haerlem (Paris, 1514), fols. 134r–v. This discussion is heavily dependent on the earlier treatment of the same issue by Durandus, a thinker whom Peter attacked on other fronts. For their intellectual relationship see Dunbabin, *Hound of God*, pp. 36–42.

12 Francis studied at Paris, probably under Duns Scotus; he became a master of theology in 1323. Francis's very brief comments on the female sex as an impediment to ordination form part of the question 'Utrum cuilibet fideli possit conferri sacramentum ordinis' (*In IV Sent*. dist. 25, qu. 3); *Scriptum luculentissimum in quartum sententiarum* (Venice, 1507), fol. 41v.

13 *Opera in quatuor sententiarum libros aurea*, 2 vols. (Paris, 1516–17), II, 105r–6v. The relevant comments (which are heavily dependent on Scotus's treatment) form part of a *quaestio unica* entitled 'Utrum pena canonica vel etas puerilis vel sex muliebris impediat ab executione vel ministratione seu receptione ordinum'.

14 A master of theology at Paris in 1337, Thomas composed his *Sentences* commentary there *c*.1335/7. For *In IV Sent*. dist. 25 see *Thomas ab Argentina, Commentaria in IIII libros Sententiarum* (Venice, 1564), fols. 142v–3r.

15 *Summa quaestionum ordinariarum* (Paris, 1520, repr. Louvain and Paderborn, 1953), fols. 77v–8r, 83v–4v. The first of these questions has been reprinted (after the two early printed editions) by Blamires and Marx, 'Woman Not to Preach', pp. 50–55.

16 Thomas's *Summa confessorum* indicates that he had spent part of his life at Paris and that he had read arts and theology; he may have been a pupil of Peter the Chanter. He went on a foreign mission for King John in 1213. Having been a member of the *curia* of the Bishop of London, he moved to Salisbury; his appointment as sub-dean must have been between October 1206 and around 1208. Thomas was still alive in 1233. These biographical details are from the Rev. F. Broomfield's introduction to his edition of the *Summa confessorum*.

17 To these texts may be added the relevant remarks found in the *De eruditione praedicatorum* of Humbert of Romans (who was elected Master-General of the Order of Preachers in 1254) and the *quaestio* 'Utrum mulier praedicando et docendo mereatur aureolam' which was produced around 1263–6 by the Franciscan Eustace of Arras.

being compared with like. Production of a commentary or lecture-course on the Lombard's *Sentences* became, after Alexander of Hales (generally credited with having established the practice), a required task for students who were working towards their master's degree in theology. Such commentaries, however, survive in different forms. Several of the great theologians thoroughly revised their commentaries, providing fuller and more thoughtful versions of what they had said in lectures (sometimes called *ordinationes* late in the period). Other commentaries, unfortunately, survive only in students' notes (the so-called *reportationes*). The *Sentences* commentary of Duns Scotus is a particularly interesting case in point. Duns managed to lecture on the Lombard in no less than three places, Cambridge (*c.*1297–1300), Oxford (*c.*1300–2 and again in 1303–4) and Paris (*c.*1302–3 and 1304). The first version of his work (which dates from his time in Cambridge and Oxford) and the second (produced in Paris) survive only in *reportationes*. The third and definitive version, his *ordinatio*, was never completed; hence we must be content with a *reportatio* of his questions on ordination, among many others.

Then again, there is the fact that not all of the *Sentences* commentators felt obliged to address the issue of the ordination of women. It is something of a puzzle – and perhaps explicable simply as a matter of personal choice and interest – as to why some theologians considered the matter while others did not; why (for example) Alexander of Hales and Albert the Great were silent on the issue while Albert's pupil Thomas Aquinas held forth on it, or why Richard Fishacre took it on whilst his distinguished successor in the Oxford Dominican house, Robert Kilwardby (d. 1279), ignored the opportunity. There are some real disappointments, particularly the absence of a relevant discussion in Albert the Great (in either his *Sentences* commentary or his later *Summa theologiae*), who elsewhere has a lot of important, and often quite distinctive, things to say about women's nature and bodies, as for instance in his discussions of the creation of Eve and the status and significance of the Virgin Mary. Moreover, while Thomas Aquinas produced a short but thoughtful discussion of female ordination in his *Sentences* commentary, we lack the mature formulation of his thinking on the issue, for he stopped working on his *Summa theologica* tantalisingly close to the point at which the discussion of ordination was due to appear. What we have in the *Supplementum* to the *Summa* (qu. 39, art. 1) is simply a recycling of what St Thomas had said in the *Sentences* commentary.

All these caveats having been entered, it may be said that, to judge by such evidence as is available to us, the broad outline of how the discussion developed seems clear enough.[18] It is indubitable that commentators on the *Sentences* took over materials and methods of analysis from the text and gloss of

Both are discussed by Blamires, 'Women and Preaching', pp. 135–52. For Humbert's account see note 91 below.

[18] Obviously, this picture may have to be modified as and when more medieval discussions of the relevant issues come to light.

that highly authoritative canon-law collection of the twelfth century, Gratian's *Decretum*. The treatments by Fishacre and Simon of Hinton are very heavily dependent on the canonists. Then comes a period of theological elaboration of the issues involved, when the schoolmen brought to bear expertise of a kind not found in the *Decretum* commentaries, the most sophisticated treatments being, to my mind, those of Bonaventure, Henry of Ghent, and Duns Scotus. What they had to say was never bettered – until, of course, Walter Brut's challenge focused the minds of members of the English clergy on the matter as never before. After the time of Duns, the terms of reference of the debate seem very fixed, with little of substance being added, and variation occurring mainly in terms of how the received ideas are organised and where the emphases are placed. In short, the debate seems to have run out of steam well before the exegesis of books iii and iv of the *Sentences* atrophied, as four-teenth-century commentaries concentrated on the first two books – or, more accurately, used the first two books as springboards for discussion of what they were really interested in, the Lombard's text being left some distance behind.

2. Sex, Sacrament and Symbol

Some of the most telling arguments put forward by the theologians rested on the premiss that ordination was a sacrament, and hence (among other things) carried a specific and crucial symbolism which in its enactment and imple-mentation demanded conformity of a most rigid kind. Sacraments, explains Thomas Aquinas, are assigned to the general category of signs;[19] specifically, the term 'sacrament' denotes 'that which is a sign of a sacred reality inasmuch as it has the property of sanctifying men'.[20] Not every sign of a sacred reality is a sacrament, of course; the term 'sacrament' is reserved 'solely for those things which signify the perfection of human sanctity'.[21] This is part and parcel of an elaborate semiotic system which God in his infinite wisdom and awareness of the weakness of human powers of reasoning has established. The divine wisdom provides for each thing according to its condition (*modus*); 'it is connatural to man to arrive at a knowledge of intelligible realities through sensible ones, and a sign is something through which a person ar-rives at knowledge of some further thing beyond itself'.[22] 'Moreover', he continues, 'the sacred realities signified by the sacraments are certain spiritual and intelligible goods by which man is sanctified. And the consequence of this fact is that the function of the sacrament as signifying is implemented by means of some sensible realities.' A comparison with holy Scripture is then

---

[19] *Summa theologiae*, 3a, qu. 60, art. 1; *ST* LVI, 5.
[20] *Summa theologiae*, 3a, qu. 60, art. 2; *ST* LVI, 9.
[21] *Summa theologiae*, 3a, qu. 60, art. 2, ad 3; *ST* LVI, 11.
[22] *Summa theologiae*, 3a, qu. 60, art. 4; *ST* LVI, 15.

introduced, in that in order that the Bible can 'describe spiritual realities to us, corresponding sensible realities are used to illustrate them. And it is because of this that sensible realities are needed for the sacraments.'

This theory of sacramental symbolism encompasses the notion of the special *character* or distinguishing mark which is bestowed by certain sacraments. 'It has been customary', Aquinas explains, 'that whenever anyone is deputed to some definite function he is marked off for it by means of some sign. Thus in ancient times it was usual for soldiers on enlistment for military service to be marked with some form of physical "character" in recognition of the fact that they were deputed for some function in the physical sphere. In the same way, therefore, when in the sacraments men are deputed for some function in the spiritual sphere pertaining to the worship of God, it naturally follows that as believers they are marked off by some form of spiritual character.' [23] Consequently the sacrament of ordination leaves a particular imprint, which indicates that those in holy orders are marked off to perform certain spiritual functions.

In those 'ancient times' evoked by Aquinas, the marks imposed by soldiers were of course selected and imposed by the military authorities. 'It is for him who institutes the signs to determine which particular sign is to be used to represent that thing', explains Aquinas elsewhere.[24] Who, then, instituted the sacred symbolism and the *character* associated with ordination? And how does this bear on the issue of female ordination?

The argument *ex institutione* was one of the most powerful weapons in the armoury of the theologians who refuted the notion that women may receive holy orders. Richard of Middleton sums up the consensus view well when he says that the sacraments derive their power from their institution, and when Christ instituted the sacrament of ordination he conferred it on men alone, and not on women; hence the female sex is an impediment to ordination.[25] Having noted that the Church and the Apostles agree in excluding women, Duns Scotus goes on to emphasise that they alone would not have excluded a single person, let alone an entire sex, from a status so conducive to salvation.[26] It was their head, Christ himself, who instructed them in this regard, he being the institutor of the sacrament. (Durandus of Saint Pourçain, whose refutation of the idea of female ordination is heavily indebted to Duns' account, reiterates this point succinctly in saying that the sacrament's institution by Christ is its principal cause (*causa principalis*), and this institution involved the sacrament's administrators as much as its recipients.[27])

Later in his commentary Duns Scotus restates what is essentially the same

---

23 *Summa theologiae*, 3a, qu. 63, art. 1; *ST* LVI, 79.
24 *Summa theologiae*, 3a, qu. 60, art. 5; *ST* LVI, 19.
25 *Sup. lib. IV Sent.*, p. 389.
26 *Opera* XI.2, 784. Repeated by Scotus's ardent follower John of Bassoles, *In quat. sent. libros aurea*, II, 106v.
27 *In Sent. comm.*, fol. 364v. Followed by Peter of la Palud, *In quart. Sent.*, fol. 134r.

point with the aid of the twelfth book of Aristotle's *Metaphysics* and a commentary thereon.[28] In the case in which there is an agent and a passive recipient within one and the same species, that agent will not produce a diversity of effect (assuming that the effect is not dependent on outside forces). Now, a Bishop conferring the sacrament of ordination on a woman is an agent working in relation to a receiver from the same species, because sex is not a principle of distinction at the level of species; therefore the effect of the Bishop's action is the same in a woman as in a man. In replying to this Duns draws on the distinction between a principal agent and an instrumental agent. An instrumental agent acts only in accordance with the power of the principal and superior agent, as a Bishop acts in respect of God, who placed an impediment in the case of one recipient but not of another. And if the rationale of this restriction depended on sex difference, it would *not* follow that the effect would be the same in a female recipient as in a male. If a Bishop were to confer holy orders on a woman, he himself would not be acting as the principal agent which confers the *character* of orders, but only as a secondary and instrumental agent. As such his powers would be limited to those allowed him by the principal agent, God, as is right and proper; he can confer orders only on that sex which has no impediment, that being the male of the human species.[29]

In short, if God decrees that women are not to be ordained, then as far as this sacrament is concerned the only instrumental power which a bishop has relates to the masculine sex. The institution of the sacrament, then, remains all-determining and all-important; in the hands of the schoolmen, Aristotelian metaphysics serves only to confirm this. It is for him who institutes certain signs to determine which particular sign is to be used to represent a particular thing; Christ's choice of signs and determination of their significance is not to be gainsaid. We may now proceed to discuss some of the theologians' ideas on the sacred semiotics of the sacrament of ordination in more detail.

i. Imaging God

Only those who bear the image of God can possibly receive holy orders, Bonaventure declares, because in this sacrament (in a certain manner of

---

[28] *Opera* XI.2, 785.

[29] A succinct and slightly different version of this argument is offered by Thomas of Strasbourg (*Comm. in Sent.*, fols. 142v–3r). When an agency produces by a certain rationale an effect in one member of a species it can produce it in another. But man and woman are of the same species; therefore by the rationale in accordance with which a Bishop can confer the sacrament of holy orders on a man he can, by the same rationale, confer it on a woman. In refuting this Thomas notes that the *ordinatio* of a principal agent can determine an instrumental agent in respect of one of the recipients but not of another. As far as the bestowing of the character, or power, in question is concerned, an ordained Bishop is the instrument of God, disposing extrinsically according to the divine plan the masculine sex, and not the feminine, for the reception of the aforesaid power.

speaking) a person becomes God and participates in the divine power.[30] I Corinthians 11. 7 is cited in support of this proposition. There it is stated that the man should not cover his head 'because he is the image and glory of God', whereas 'the woman is the glory of the man' (to be interpreted in the sense clarified by v. 9, where it is explained that the woman was created for the man rather than *vice-versa*). This text, of course, recalled the passage in Genesis (1. 27) in which it is said that 'God created man to his own image; to the image of God he created him'. And there was a canon law (*Mulier debet*) which declared – somewhat twisting the words of St Paul – that a woman should keep her head veiled because she does not present the image of God (*non est imago Dei*).[31] Bonaventure, however, does not mention that canon, and actually goes on to declare that woman bears God's image just as much as man. This is in the context of an argument in favour of female ordination, to the effect that holy orders relate to the soul and not to the body. Sex is a bodily matter, there being no sexual difference within the human soul; 'ita imago Dei est mulier, ut vir'. Therefore, why should a woman not be entitled to receive holy orders, every bit as much as a man? Bonaventure will refute that particular argument,[32] but he – like Aquinas after him – is perfectly happy to concede that as far as her soul is concerned, a woman bears the *imago Dei* just as a man does.[33]

However, the belief that 'the image of God is common to both sexes'[34] did little to strengthen the case for female ordination. In his *responsio* Bonaventure affirms the sacramental nature of ordination, whereby Christ as mediator is signified, and since in Christ God took on male rather than female form, as mediator he can be signified only in the male sex and by the male sex.[35] Therefore the possibility of receiving holy orders relates to men alone, since

---

[30] *Opera* IV, 649.

[31] *Decretum* C. 33 q. 8 c.19, in Friedberg, I, 1255–6.

[32] *Opera* IV, 650.

[33] Aquinas says that 'God's likeness in the manner of an image is to be found in man as regards his mind (*mens*), but as regards his other parts only in the manner of a trace (*vestigium*)'. Furthermore, Scripture, having stated that 'After God's image he created him' adds 'male and female he created them' (Genesis 1. 27), 'not to present the image of God in man in terms of sexual distinctions, but because the image of God is common to both sexes, being in the mind (*secundum mentem*) which has no distinction of sex'. Aquinas proceeds to quote Galatians 3. 28, which declares that in Christ there is neither male nor female. *Summa theologiae*, 1a, qu. 93, art. 6; *ST* XIII, 69 and 71. This, however, does not impact on what St Thomas and his contemporaries felt about the natural inferiority of woman. In discussing the creation of Eve he argues that her subject-status would have existed even before the Fall: 'this sort of subjection would have obtained even before sin . . . Such is the subjection in which woman is by nature subordinate to man, because the power of rational discernment is by nature stronger in man'. *Summa theologiae*, 1a, qu. 92, art. 1; *ST* XIII, 37–9. For Bonaventure's views on such issues see P. L. Reynolds, 'Bonaventure on Gender and Godlikeness', *DR* 364 (1988), 171–94.

[34] Here I borrow a phrase from Aquinas as quoted in the previous footnote.

[35] *Opera* IV, 650. This aspect of Bonaventure's argument is emphasised by J. Razette, 'Le sacerdoce et la femme chez Saint Bonaventure', *Antonianum* 51 (1976), 520–7.

only they can naturally represent Christ, and in accordance with the *character* (i.e. the special mark or imprint of ordination) which they receive, function as an actual sign (*signum*) thereof. This is the 'more probable' (*probabilior*) position, Bonaventure declares, and may be proved from many *auctoritates sanctorum*.

What then of the argument that sex is corporeal whereas orders are of the soul? The truth of the matter, he argues, is that orders do not relate to the soul alone, but to the soul as it is joined (*conjuncta*) to the flesh. This is so on two counts. One is because of signification (*ratio significationis*), the necessity of providing an appropriate visible sign. The other is because of the practical necessity of carrying out (*exsecutio*) those rites which ordination entails, in which bodily actions are essential. In this regard ordination is comparable with the other sacraments; as Martin puts it, 'Sacramental practice inevitably involved washings, meals, anointings and the like. Activities such as these could never be carried out by a "soul" at an impersonal or disembodied level.'[36] The fundamental point, then, is that holy orders 'required some visible sign which involved the body'. The sacramental *character* 'and the activity flowing from it could not escape bodily identification'. And therefore sexual difference did matter after all. The human body must be either masculine or feminine, and only the masculine body was perceived as capable of serving as an appropriate *signum* or of receiving the appropriate *character*.

A few years after Bonaventure, in commenting on the fourth book of the *Sentences* Thomas Aquinas also canvassed the argument that the power of ordination resides in the soul.[37] Since 'sexus non est in anima', sexual difference does not make for a distinction in the reception of holy orders. In tackling this problem Aquinas makes a distinction between the types of quality that are necessary for the reception of a sacrament. There are certain qualities which are so necessary that without them neither the sacrament itself nor the reality of which it is a sacrament is received. Moreover, there are others which concern certain precepts relating to what is appropriate to the sacrament, these being significant inasmuch as their absence will hinder not the reception of the sacrament but rather the reality which the sacrament promises, i.e. that state of grace which it brings. The *sexus virilis* is necessary for ordination not just in the second sense but also in the first, declares Aquinas, because since a sacrament is a sign (*signum*) the symbolism must support what is being symbolised. The recipient, to borrow yet another phrase from Martin, 'must be able to be seen as a living sign, a living symbol, of what the sacrament claims to be offering'.[38] Aquinas offers a comparison with the sacrament of Extreme Unction. Here the ill are anointed, thus symbolising their spiritual healing.

---

[36] Martin, 'Ordination of Women', p. 161. Cf. Razette, who explains that for Bonaventure 'les réalités sacrementelles ne sont pas purement spirituelles, mais qu'elles ont toujours un rapport avec le corps par le truchement du signe visible' (p. 526).

[37] *Opera* VII, 908.

[38] Martin, 'Ordination of Women', pp. 164–5.

But if someone who was not ill received this sacrament, then he would not be a proper symbol of this process. Similarly, since on account of her subject-position (*status subjectionis*) a woman cannot signify that high status (*eminentiae gradus*) which is associated with the ordained, she cannot receive the sacrament of ordination.

Turning specifically to the 'sex is not in the soul' argument, Aquinas emphasises that this is indeed true, wherefore a woman can be found who as far as the state of her soul is concerned is better than many men. This is why the gift of prophecy and many other spiritual gifts can be received by women – but not ordination, which (unlike prophecy) is a sacrament, and requires *significatio* as well as *res*.

A version of this same argument is found in Thomas of Strasbourg's *Sentences* commentary.[39] Thomas plays an interesting variation on the theme by emphasising that, in respect of those things which aim towards the meriting of eternal life, there is not a distinction as far as the soul is concerned. Every human being, whether male or female, to the extent that he or she greatly loves God and conducts himself or herself virtuously in this world, will have the greater reward in the afterlife. However, he continues, there *is* a distinction as far as the soul is concerned in respect of holy orders, especially if the office in question is one in the exercise of which the soul is accompanied by the body as mediator, and involves such mediation in carrying out its corporeal activities. And this is the case with the various offices relating to holy orders. Therefore, although ordination is a certain spiritual power, on account of those things which are related to its offices, that power is not communicable by women. In short, mediation (in Thomas's terms) requires a body, and women have the wrong type of body.

The notion of the *eminentiae gradus* requires some clarification, however, since neither Bonaventure nor Aquinas go into it in detail in the discussions which have been summarised above. Bonaventure's thinking may be clarified with reference to a passage from earlier in his *Sentences* commentary where he asks if it would have been appropriate for Christ to have assumed flesh in female form.[40] His answer is in the negative, since 'without any doubt' Christ had to take on the male form on account of its greater dignity ('muliebris sexus non est tantae dignitatis, sicut virilis'). In his *Summa theologiae* Aquinas makes exactly the same point: the male sex is more noble (*nobilior*) than the female, and so it was most appropriate that Christ should assume what is perfect in human nature.[41] In the very next sentence this statement is qualified somewhat with the remark that, 'So that people should not think little of the female sex, it was fitting that he should take flesh from a woman'. But the essential point (as far as we are concerned) is abundantly clear. Because of the

---

[39] *Comment. in Sent.*, fol. 143r.

[40] *III Sent.*, dist. 12, art. 3, qu. 1; *Opera* III, 270.

[41] *Summa theologiae*, 3a, qu. 31, art. 4; *ST* LII, 23.

inferior, subject-status of the female sex, a woman's body cannot appropriately image God, no matter how noble her soul may be.

This is made utterly clear by Duns Scotus.[42] *Ordo*, he explains, is a certain
grade of eminence (*gradus eminentiae*) over other people in the Church, which
in a certain manner should be signified by an appropriate condition and grade
of eminence in nature.[43] Women are in a state of natural subjection to men;
therefore they cannot possess any grade of eminence over a man, because in
nature as in condition and nobility women in general are more ignoble than
any man whatever.[44] Whence after the Fall God subjected them in dominion
and power to men.[45] Anyone who receives a certain order in the church must
be able to preside and have dominion over others, but this is against the
condition of women. Therefore a bishop who conferred orders on a woman
would not only behave badly (in acting contrary to the precept of Christ), but
would do nothing, and she would receive nothing, because she is not material
(*materia*) capable of receiving this sacrament, because in instituting this sacrament Christ confined it to certain individuals within the human species and to
the male sex.

But what, then, of St Paul's statement (in Galatians 3. 28) that in Jesus
Christ there is neither masculine nor feminine, neither bond nor free? Here is
an *auctoritas* which seems to put the *sexus non est in anima* argument in a way
that has major implications for the issue of female ordination. Duns Scotus
quotes it at the very beginning of his *quaestio*.[46] It would seem from this
passage, he says, that neither sex nor condition (*conditio*) impedes ordination.
And in the same place it is said that Christ principally ordains (apparently a
ref. to v. 29, 'And if you be Christ's, then are you the seed of Abraham, heirs
according to the promise'). Duns' reply that, although as far as salvation and
eternal life are concerned there is no difference between male and female,
bond and free, yet nevertheless there is a difference as far as office is concerned, and the possession of a grade of eminence in the Church, because in
this the male is set before the female.[47] Similarly, Richard of Middleton argues
that, when it is said that there is neither male nor female in Christ, the point is

---

42 *Opera* XI.2, 784–5.
43 The term *ordo* recurs throughout the treatments I am discussing here; I have generally rendered it as 'ordination' or 'holy orders'. However, its range and nuances of
meaning are much more complicated than that. For a good general discussion see P.
Michaud-Quantin, 'Ordo et ordines', in P. Michaud-Quantin with M. Lemoine, *Études
sur le vocabulaire philosophique du moyen âge* (Rome, 1970), pp. 85–101. See further F.
Cardman, 'The Medieval Question of Women and Orders', *The Thomist* 42 (1978),
582–99.
44 A similar argument, concerning the *gradus excellentiae* which ordination requires
and which women cannot have, is put forward by Peter of la Palud, *In quart. Sent.*,
fol. 134v.
45 This point is reiterated by John of Bassoles, *In quat. sent. libros aurea*, II, 106v.
46 *Opera* XI.2, 783.
47 *Opera* XI.2, 785. Followed by John of Bassoles, *In quat. sent. libros aurea*, II, 106v.

that while in terms of merit there is no difference, as far as office (*officium*) is concerned there is indeed a difference.[48] A definite *gradus eminentiae* is presupposed by ordination, which in a certain manner should be signified by the natural eminence of the ordained person. But woman is in a state of subjection to the male sex, which is consonant with nature, and this is an impediment to the ordination of women.

It is apparent then, that woman's alleged natural inferiority, as well as the nature of her body, serves to bar her from ordination on the grounds that along with the *res* this sacrament requires an appropriate *significatio*. The female sex cannot bear the sacred *character*, that distinctive stamp which holy orders brings, and therefore in this case at least the female body cannot function as a valid *signum* of a higher truth.

ii. Crowning glories

The conviction that only the male sex can effectively symbolise those spiritual realities relating to ordination sometimes manifests itself in forms which may seem somewhat bizarre nowadays. Occasionally the natural imagery drawn on by the *Sentences* commentators tends to obscure, or perhaps even subvert, the supernatural issues involved. An instance of this occurs when Bonaventure blurs together natural sex and symbolic sex, in arguing that a woman cannot marry the Church because the Church is female. To be specific, what he actually says is that by dint of his office the bishop is the bridegroom of the Church.[49] A woman cannot be a bishop, but only a man; otherwise we could not speak of the bridegroom of the Church. And, since all the lesser holy orders are a preparation for the episcopate, and lead up to it, therefore only men can hold them.

Even more complicated configurations of nature and grace, of *significatio* and *res*, occur when the *Sentences* commentators focus on the issue of the clerical tonsure. The origins of the practice of shaving or cutting the hair in a particular fashion as a sign of reception into certain orders are obscure. Doubtless one of the influential factors was the belief of certain Church Fathers that long hair in men was effeminate or worse. Jerome, for instance, inveighed against long-haired monks: 'avoid men . . . when you see them loaded with chains and wearing their hair long like women, contrary to the apostle's precept [i.e. I Corinthians 11. 14], not to speak of beards like those of goats . . . All these things are tokens of the devil'.[50] And immediately before this he had attacked hypocritical religious women, who dress like men, 'being ashamed of what they were born to be – women. They cut off their hair and are not

---

[48] *Super quat. lib. sent.*, p. 389.
[49] *Opera* IV, 649.
[50] *Epistola* xxii.28 (Ad Eustochium); *PL* 22, cols. 413–5; trans. W. H. Fremantle *et al.*, *The Principal Works of St Jerome*, Nicene and Post-Nicene Fathers, 2nd series, 6 (1892; repr. Grand Rapids, MN, 1979), p. 34.

ashamed to look like eunuchs'.[51] But whatever the specific sources and motivations behind the practice, it was of course firmly established in the period with which we are here concerned, and it had developed an elaborate symbolism. In his *Sentences* commentary Thomas Aquinas noted that a crown was a symbol of royalty and its circular form a sign of perfection.[52] Those who are initiated into the divine mysteries acquire a royal dignity and should be perfect in virtue; therefore their tonsures constitute outward and visible natural signs of spiritual realities.

However, such ideas do not appear in any of the *Sentences* commentators' rejections of female ordination which are known to me. What is of crucial importance there is the scriptural text which lies behind Jerome's attack on hairy men and shorn women, namely I Corinthians 11. For example, Richard of Middleton quotes the Apostle as saying that it is 'a shame to a woman to be shorn or made bald' (v. 6), and a little later (v. 15) adding, 'if a woman nourish her hair, it is a glory to her'.[53] From these passages Richard concludes that women cannot be ordained or become clerics. In similar vein, Duns Scotus picks up on the contrast between women who have their hair as their crowning glory and priests who are prevented from nourishing (i.e. allowing to grow) their hair: 'Doth not even nature itself teach you that a man indeed, if he nourish his hair, it is a shame unto him?' (v. 14). Duns interprets this as meaning that priests must be tonsured.[54]

Bonaventure's discussion of this issue, which is the fullest known to me, exploits the discourse of natural capability with which we have already become familiar.[55] By no means can an *ordo* be conferred on that which does not have the natural potential or aptitude to receive it.[56] Now, no-one has the potential to be ordained who does not have the aptitude to receive the clerical tonsure and crown. And no-one who should always appear in Church with the head veiled has such a natural aptitude. Thus women, who must have their heads veiled whilst at prayer in Church, as St Paul says (I Corinthians 11. 5), are barred from ordination because they lack this natural capacity.

In such discussions the materiality of the symbolism is, perhaps, all too pervasive. Only Thomas Aquinas (among the discussants known to me) strikes a note of caution in noting that the tonsure is not a necessity for ordination as far as the sacrament itself is concerned (*de necessitate sacra-*

---

51 *Epistola* xxii.27; cols. 412–13, trans. Fremantle, p. 34.
52 *In IV Sent.*, dist. 24, qu. 3, art. 1; *Opera* VII, 899–90.
53 *Super quat. lib. sent.*, p. 389.
54 Thomas of Strasbourg is more concerned with another verse of I Corinthians 11, where Paul says that women should pray with their heads covered (v. 5). Ordination, he declares, involves teaching in a church and certainly not the covering of one's head therein. This is, of course, not to be reduced to the risible notion that one could not teach with one's head covered: no doubt Thomas had in mind the traditional sacred symbolism with which we are here concerned.
55 *Opera* IV, 649.
56 For the term *ordo* see note 43 above.

menti).[57] However, it is evident that he believes on other grounds that those who are ordained should be tonsured. Accordingly, this can be used as yet another argument to bar women from the *ordo* in question. In sum, symbolism relating to the male body is functioning as at once an agency and expression of power, in valorising certain aspects of physical appearance which women cannot – or are not allowed to – emulate.

3. Female Frailties

i. A woman's touch

Fishacre is the first *Sentences* commentator who is known to have presented the view that women cannot perform priestly functions because they are not permitted to touch sacred vessels or garments.[58] Here he is drawing on Gratian's *Decretum*, specifically the canon *Sacratas* falsely attributed to Pope Soter (who reigned from 166 to 174) to the bishops of Italy.[59] This says that it has come to the papacy's attention that consecrated women and nuns have been handling sacred objects and offering incense at the altar, which practices must cease forthwith. The implications of this canon for female ordination were emphasised by Fishacre's successors. Bonaventure cites it at the very beginning of his refutation of the idea of female ordination.[60] If women are not permitted to handle or touch holy things, affirms Duns Scotus, how much more are they not permitted to be ordained?[61] If their sex impedes the first, so also the second. And Richard of Middleton states that whatever hinders contact with the sacraments hinders the reception of holy orders; therefore the female sex hinders the reception of holy orders.[62] Versions of this argument, prompted by *Sacratas*, are also found in the *Summa* of Simon of Hinton and the *Sentences* commentary of Peter of Tarantasia.[63]

Thomas of Chobham goes farther than anyone else in my selected corpus of texts, in declaring that women may not wear sacred vestments or read the Epistle or the Gospel at Mass, on account of the uncleanness of their menses ('which often befalls them') or because their presence would inflame priests and other clerics with lustful desires for them.[64] Here the natural bodily functions of women are taken as an indication of their lack of spiritual purity, while the (apparently inevitable!) sexual attractions which those same bodies

57 *Opera* VII, 907.
58 Martin, 'Ordination of Women', p. 144.
59 *Decretum* D. 23 c. 25; Friedberg, I, 86.
60 *Opera* IV, 650.
61 *Opera* XI.2, 783.
62 *Super quat. lib. sent.*, p. 388.
63 John of Bassoles cites *Sacratas* to support St Paul's prohibition of public teaching by women in church. Aquinas, Durandus and Thomas of Strasbourg ignore the canon.
64 *De arte praedicandi*, ed. F. Morenzoni, CCCM 82 (Turnhout, 1988), p. 58.

are supposed to exude serve to exclude them from participation in ecclesiastical rites and rituals that involve men.

ii. Weak minds in weak bodies

To make matters even worse, those alluring bodies were believed to be animated by weak minds. Therefore, according to the argument of Henry of Ghent, they may be taught only those things which are sufficient for their salvation.[65] Theological subtleties are quite beyond their mental capacity (*ingenium*), he declares. It is not possible for a woman to attend scholastic lectures on theology, on two grounds: because in a lecture difficult and secret things are expounded from Scripture which are not appropriate for a woman to hear, and because it is not permitted for a woman to be taught in public, in accordance with what St Paul says in I Timothy 2. 11 ('Let the woman learn in silence'). By contrast, in preaching, whether public or private, a woman *may* hear theological truths, for in preaching deep matters are not propounded but rather those things which are appropriate for the general run of mankind to know. If women wish to learn anything further they should not publicly question the preacher but ask their menfolk in the privacy of their own homes (following the recommendation of I Corinthians 14. 34–5). The Carmelite theologian Gerard of Bologna (d. 1317), whose *summa* in this regard – as in so many others – is dependent on Henry's,[66] hammers home the distinction between what is heard 'in scolis' and what is heard 'in publica predicacione', limiting women to the latter sphere. Moreover, when Gerard states that the instruction of women should be confined to those 'broad (*grossa*), not subtle and difficult things' which are provided 'uulgari predicacione', his language expresses a professional's detachment from the 'vulgar' common herd as well as designating the 'vernacular' language which preachers used in addressing the populace at large.[67]

Women, then, cannot be 'students' (*auditores*) of theology in the academic sense of the term. Likewise, they cannot be professional teachers of theology. In order for someone to teach *ex officio*, Henry of Ghent argues, four things are required: constancy of teaching, effectiveness of performance, authority, and strength and vigour of speech.[68] However, women can neither be constant in teaching nor effective in its communication because they are the weaker sex. Woman's inconstancy is proved by her role in the fall of mankind. Moreover,

---

[65] *Summa quaest. ord.*, I, fols. 83v–4v.

[66] Gerard's debt to Henry was pointed out by Beryl Smalley, 'Gerard of Bologna and Henry of Ghent', *Recherches de théologie ancienne et médiévale* 22 (1955), 125–9.

[67] *Summa*, qu. 7, art. 1 ('Utrum omnes teneatur audire hanc scienciam'), in Paul De Vooght, *Les sources de la doctrine chrétienne d'après les théologiens du XIVe siècle et du début du XVe avec le texte intégral des XII premières questions de la 'Summa' inédite de Gérard de Bologne* (Paris, 1954), pp. 382–7 (pp. 383 and 386). Gerard composed his *summa* between 1313 and 1317.

[68] *Summa quaest. ord.*, I, fols. 77v–8r; also included in Blamires and Marx, 'Woman Not to Preach', pp. 51–2.

women are unable to make the necessary physical effort; because of the fragility of their sex, they simply lack the strength to speak at length and labour in public. As far as authority is concerned, a woman cannot have this because of her subject-status (as attested by Genesis 3. 16). Concerning vigour and liveliness of speech, the speech of women does not lead to mortification but rather provokes sins, which is why the *Glossa ordinaria* on Paul's prohibition of women preachers at I Timothy 2. 12 says that a female teacher would sexually inflame the males in her audience. In sum, because of her deficiency in each of these four crucial areas, a woman cannot hold the office of teacher of theology. All four of Henry's requisites for preaching *ex officio* were reiterated in one of the *quaestiones* prompted by the Brut controversy, 'Utrum liceat mulieribus docere viros publice congregatos' ('Whether women are permitted to instruct men assembled in public').[69]

Henry is, as already noted, not concerned here with the issue of female ordination as such. But the question of whether a woman could or should preach was intimately connected with that issue, as is made abundantly clear by, for example, Duns Scotus's account of female frailties. He identifies the main sphere of competence which priests possess as preaching.[70] It is perfectly obvious, then, that if women cannot preach *de facto* or *de iure* then they cannot be priests.

Duns proceeds to disqualify them from preaching on both these counts, in terms similar to those used by Henry of Ghent.[71] St Paul's prohibition of women from preaching (I Timothy 2. 12), is cited, which Duns explains as being on account of weakness of intellect and emotional instability, which drawbacks women generally suffer from more than men. However, the teacher (*doctor*) should have a lively intellect in the understanding of truth, and stability of emotions in confirming it. Similarly, Richard of Middleton argues that holy orders involve the function (*officium*) of teaching inasmuch as they are related to the priesthood (priesthood being the principal office, while that of the deacon is a delegated one).[72] Now, preaching is evangelical teaching; the clear implication is that it requires the best presentation and transmission possible. It is not appropriate, Richard declares, for those who have weak intellects and changeable emotions to teach publicly. It is generally agreed (held *de communi lege*) that women are more notably deficient in these areas than men are. The teacher (*doctor*) should have a lively intellect for under-

---

69 Ed. Blamires and Marx, 'Woman Not to Preach', pp. 59–60; trans. Blamires, *Woman Defamed*, pp. 253–4. Previously, Henry's arguments had been reworked by Gerard of Bologna. He lists five reasons why women cannot have the *officium docendi*: their speech is sexually provocative, their sex is weak and inconstant, they are inferior to men, for them to speak in church would be shameful, and they lack prudence (as was noted by Aristotle). See De Vooght, *Sources de la doctrine chrétienne*, pp. 371–2.

70 *Opera* XI.2, 784.

71 See further Peter of la Palud's statement concerning the *infirmitas corporis* and *imperfectio rationis* of women; *In quart. Sent.*, fol. 134v.

72 *Super quat. lib. sent.*, p. 389.

standing the truth, and stable emotions so that he may persist in his promise of fidelity (*confessio*). The obvious conclusion is that women cannot be teachers of theology. In respect of the *officio docendi*, says Durandus, boys and women are not suitable as teachers, boys on account of their deficiency of reason and women on account of the Apostle's interdict.[73]

Durandus (like Aquinas, Duns Scotus, Francis of Meyronnes, John of Bassoles and Gerard of Bologna) considers together the impediments to ordination presented by a boy's age and a woman's sex;[74] in other *Sentences* commentaries the age issue is treated as a separate matter, as is also true of Henry of Ghent's *Summa*. But these two problems are clearly related, and the contrast in the solutions offered is highly revealing. For boys are able to leave their deficiencies behind; with age and maturity their reasoning powers increase and their emotional instabilities decrease (and of course their sex ensures that they have the potential to receive the special *character* of ordination and image the divine in the way that Christ wanted). Women, on the other hand, never grow out of their frailties. Trapped in bodies which are at once weak, impure and highly provocative sexually, hindered by weak minds and unstable emotions, and designed to live in subjection to men (even if the Fall had never occurred, to follow Aquinas),[75] they make highly unlikely candidates for ordination. Their sex presents impediments which may never be removed, in this life at least. Nothing can deliver women from their bodies of death.[76]

4. Power and Precedent:
Test-cases from Canon Law and the Bible

On the other hand, certain canons as collected in the *Decretum* seemed (on the face of it) to offer precedents for certain kinds of female ordination. Thus, the canon *Diaconissam* states that a deaconess should not be ordained before the age of forty.[77] And the canon *Presbyter* speaks of how, from the time when he was put in charge of a church, a certain *presbyter* loved his *presbytera* as a sister but treated her as he would an enemy in that he did not allow her to come near him.[78] Taken together they seem to indicate that female deacons and presbyters once existed and therefore can exist in the present.

---

73 *In Sent. comm.*, fol. 364v.
74 Indeed, Gerard of Bologna managed to consider the possible impediments of youth, sex and sin in a single *quaestio*, 'quis uel qualis possit esse doctor huius sciencie'; *Summa*, qu. 6, art. 2, ed. De Vooght, *Sources de la doctrine chrétienne*, pp. 369–75.
75 Cf. the statement quoted in note 33 above.
76 To echo Romans 7. 24, 'Who shall deliver me from this body of death?' (Revised Standard Version). Cf. p. 3 above.
77 *Decretum* C. 27, q. 1, c. 23; Friedberg, I, 1055.
78 *Decretum* D. 32, c. 18; Friedberg, I, 122.

The first of these canons, *Diaconissam*, was a product of the Council of Chalcedon. It held no fears for the *Sentences* commentators. Fishacre, Bonaventure, Aquinas, Peter of Tarantasia, Richard of Middleton, Duns Scotus, Durandus, Peter of la Palud, Francis of Meyronnes and Thomas of Strasbourg unite in the view that it refers to women (sometimes specifically identified as nuns) who are given, as a special privilege, the task of reading the homily at Matins. Richard of Middleton and Duns Scotus include a reference to a *Decretum* gloss in which it is explained that *diaconissa* means 'Abbess'. But such women cannot take part in the ministry of the Mass, Peter of Tarantasia and Peter of la Palud emphasise, or recite the Gospel. In short, the term means simply that they participate in one act, and one alone, which is proper to a deacon (as Aquinas succinctly puts it). Hence they are very far away from being ordained priests.

The second canon, *Presbyter*, derives from pseudo-Gregory the Great's *Dialogues*.[79] Pseudo-Gregory's anecdote is worth recounting in more detail. It tells of how, after his elevation, the *presbyter* in question avoided not only carnal relations with his wife (for such was her status) but all forms of contact, not even allowing her to render him the necessary domestic services. One day, when he was ill and on the point of death, this woman put her ear to his face, trying to hear if he was still breathing. Aware of her presence, he summoned all his strength and shouted, 'Go away from me, woman. The fire is still flickering. Take away the tinder.' As she stepped back, his strength seemed to return to him, and he exclaimed that he could see the Apostles in front of him. Saying 'I come, I come', he breathed his last. Even on the point of death, it would seem, the (apparently inevitable) sexual lures of a woman's body can threaten a holy man's sanctity; the tinder is still capable of bursting into flame, even in these quite improbable circumstances.

The *Decretum* and the *Sentences* commentaries listed above do not go into such detail, but there was never any chance that the canon *Presbyter* could seriously challenge the *status quo*, particularly in view of the fact that Gratian himself had provided an explanation which rendered it null and void as a precedent for female ordination. The term *presbytera* actually referred to a widow or some senior woman, he declares, and then presents a canon from the Council of Laodicea which says that women who in the Greek church were called *presbyterae* are nowadays ('apud nos') called widows, senior *univirae* (i.e. women who have had only one husband) or 'churchmothers' (*matricuriae*), but they cannot be ordained.[80] Versions of this argument are found in Bonaventure, Aquinas, Richard of Middleton, Durandus and Peter of la Palud. Others do echo it, but add the view that in the ancient church the word designated the *wife* of a presbyter. Hence Richard Fishacre glosses it as 'uxor presbyteri vel etiam vidua matricuria', explaining the latter in terms of a

---

[79] *Dialogi* iv.11; *PL* 77, 336–7.
[80] *Decretum* D. 32 c. 18; Friedberg, I, 122.

materfamilias of the church. Duns Scotus speaks of *uxores presbyterorum*,[81] Peter of Tarantasia of *coniugata sacerdoti*, and Peter of la Palud of *uxor sacerdotis*, while Thomas of Strasbourg states that in the Greek kingdom ('in regnos Graecorum') a *presbytera* was the wife of a presbyter, while in the Roman church the term means an abbess or some other honest matron who shows others the right path by good behaviour and examples.

What then of those holy women who often feature in the book which has the greatest authority of all, the Bible? Fishacre, Duns Scotus, Durandus, John of Bassoles and Thomas of Strasbourg all cite the case of the Virgin Mary, who was of the greatest dignity and sanctity, and yet Christ did not confer on her holy orders. Without a doubt, enthuses Thomas of Strasbourg, Christ's own mother was the most noble and most holy of creatures. But he did not ordain her, which proves that no woman is capable of receiving this particular sacrament. For Christ, as a good son, honoured his mother over all other creatures; consequently, if according to the divine plan any woman was capable of receiving this sacrament, Christ would certainly not have denied Mary this level of eminence.

Duns Scotus is unique among the *Sentences* commentators I have studied so far in introducing the case of Mary Magdalene, who was a female apostle (*apostola*) and preacher (*praedicatrix*), and a prefect over all sinful women. His response is somewhat feeble, in that he simply refuses to admit that she might have set a precedent for other women. In his view the Magdalene was a single woman (*singularis mulier*, meaning both numerically one and unique), and exceptionally acceptable to Christ; therefore her privilege was a personal matter relating to her own person, and remained with her alone. Mary Magdalene reappears in the anti-Brut *quaestio*, 'Utrum liceat mulieribus docere viros publice congregatos', and also in the attack on John Purvey's alleged views on women preachers which is included in the vast *Doctrinale antiquitatum fidei catholicae ecclesiae* of Thomas Netter (*c*.1377–1430), Carmelite theologian and confessor of King Henry IV of England.[82]

---

[81] Duns's interpretation of *Presbyter* is followed by Francis of Meyronnes, who cites him by name. *Script. luc. in quart. sent.*, fol. 41v.

[82] Blamires and Marx, 'Woman Not to Preach', pp. 56, 62 and 63; trans. Blamires, *Woman Defamed*, pp. 251–2 and 255. Here it is argued that the amount of spiritual work which needs to be done and the paucity of (male) teachers means that on very special occasions women have to lend a hand. This argument is derived from Henry of Ghent; cf. the summary of his relevant discussion on p. 132 below. On Mary Magdalene as mentioned in Henry's *Summa* and elsewhere see further Blamires, 'Women and Preaching', pp. 137–44 and 148–9, to which may be added Gerard of Bologna's reiteration of Henry's account, in De Vooght, *Sources de la doctrine chrétienne*, p. 374. For Netter's discussion of her see his *Doctrinale antiquitatum fidei catholicae ecclesiae*, 2 vols. (Venice, 1757–59), I, 639. This forms part of Book ii, art. 3, ch. lx[x]iii, 'Contra quendam Doctorem Wiclevistam [i.e. John Purvey] quod non licet singulis Christianis passim praedicare quiuslibet, sine authoritate antistitis'. Netter's specific target is a work of Purvey's, *De compendiis scripturarum, paternarum doctrinarum et canonum*, which he presents as having extended the *officium praedica-*

Two other women appear regularly in the *Sentences* commentators' discussions, namely Anna (Luke 2. 36) and Deborah (Judges 4). The former was taken as an example of the prophetess; the latter, of the woman who had the power of judgement over men. With reference to Anna, the question was raised: surely if women can prophesy they can also be ordained? By the gift of prophecy one is not given power over another, as is the case with the gift of holy orders, declares Peter of Tarantasia. Richard of Middleton makes a fuller response. The fact that a woman like Anna prophesied does not mean that women can be ordained, for we are not dealing with similar things. By her ability to prophesy the woman is not given power of the appropriate kind over the man. The man who is ordained enjoys a degree of eminence higher than that of men who are not ordained. Similarly, there is nothing repugnant in a woman being an abbess over other women, on account of the perils which would exist if women cohabited with male superiors. But it would be discordant if she were to be an abbess over men.

Thomas Aquinas takes Huldah (cf. IV Kings 22. 14) rather than Anna as his test-case of a prophetess, but his solution is the same, although his argument-line is somewhat different. The *officio prophetiae* is surely greater than the *officio sacerdotis*, and since the former is granted to women, why not the latter? Prophecy, he replies, is not a sacrament, but a gift of God, and therefore it may be given to women as much as men, since *secundum rem* as far as the affairs of the soul are concerned men and women do not differ. But women's bodies cannot bear that sacramental symbolism which the priesthood requires (cf. pp. 117–18 above).

Deborah is mentioned by Bonaventure, Aquinas and Thomas of Strasbourg. If the female sex was antithetical to holy orders, postulates Thomas of Strasbourg, this would appear most obviously in respect of the most important aspect of the activities which are involved, which would mean that women could not be capable of possessing the power of judgement (*potestas iudicandi*). But it would seem that this is not an obstacle, for as is clear from Judges 4. 5, Deborah judged the people of Israel, and had done so for many years. Thomas tackles the problem with a crucial distinction. The power of judgement is twofold (*duplex*); one is in temporal things, the other in spiritual matters. In the first case there is nothing to impede women, because many women have great temporal power, and such women exist in different parts of the world. And this was the type of power which Deborah had. But the power of spiritual judgement is not appropriate to women, and consequently neither are holy orders, the power of which is purely spiritual. Bonaventure says very much the same thing, though he adds the refinement that in the case of

toris very widely, allowing it to very many different kinds of layfolk, including women. Cf. Netter's earlier statement, col. 619. On this (now lost) Purvey work see Aston, 'Lollard Women Priests?', p. 65, and Anne Hudson, 'John Purvey: A Reconsideration of the Evidence for his Life and Writings', rpt. in her *Lollards and their Books* (London and Ronceverte, 1985), p. 94

spiritual dominion the person who possesses it has to be able to function as a type of Christ, but since woman cannot be the head of man (cf. I Corinthians 11. 3) therefore women cannot be ordained.

Bonaventure proceeds to tackle the issue of certain 'abbesses' who are seen in the New Testament (no examples being cited); such women do not hold the position of ordained prelates but rather a 'substituted' position, whereby they are placed in a position of authority because of the perils which would be involved if men cohabited with them. (This, of course, is the very argument which Richard of Middleton makes with reference to the prophetess Anna, as noted above). Aquinas has a remarkably similar discussion, though he speaks of such women as appearing in both the New and the Old Testaments (the only example cited being Deborah from the Old Testament), and terms the power which abbesses have over other women as delegated or 'commissioned', *ex commissione*. The case of Deborah fits a little awkwardly into this treatment, for Aquinas goes on to say that her precedence was in temporal rather than sacerdotal matters, just as nowadays women are able to rule temporally.

Turning finally to the matter of Biblical precedents for women preachers, it should first of all be noted that the ordination discussions tend to focus on the belief that women cannot preach, on account of their female frailties and St Paul's prohibition (cf. our previous section). Apart from Duns Scotus' reference to Mary Magdalene as a *praedicatrix* there is – at least, in the sample of *Sentences* commentaries identified at the beginning of this article – no reference to documented accounts of women actually having preached (or appearing to have preached). However, considerations of this matter may be found elsewhere. I shall review a few of them here, given their significance for the debate concerning female ordination.

Relevant material is included in the *Summa theologiae* of Thomas Aquinas, within a question on whether the gift of wise and 'scientific' speech ('gratia sermonis sapientiae et scientiae') pertains to woman; the term *praedicatio* is not actually used.[83] Here Deborah and Huldah are cited along with the four daughters of Philip 'who did prophesy' (Acts 21. 9); moreover, Aquinas adds, St Paul refers to women 'praying or prophesying' (I Corinthians 11. 5). Given that the gift of prophesy is a greater gift than the gift of speech, just as the contemplation of the truth is greater than its enunciation, it would seem that the gift of wise speech very much pertains to women. But Aquinas goes on to argue that the gift of prophesy involves a mind (*mens*) illuminated by God, and as far as the mind is concerned there is no sexual difference (here he quotes Colossians 3. 10–11 on there being neither male nor female in Christ). The gift of speech, however, relates to the instruction of persons, among

---

[83] *Summa theologiae*, 2a 2ae, qu. 177, art. 2; *ST* XLV, 132–5. This *quaestio* is one of the major influences on 'Utrum liceat mulieribus docere viros publice congregatos'; ed. Blamires and Marx, 'Woman Not to Preach', pp. 58–9; trans. Blamires, *Woman Defamed*, pp. 252–3.

whom sexual difference is found. Aquinas also considers the significance of
Proverbs 4. 3–4, in which Solomon says that he was taught by his mother; this,
he concludes, is private teaching, whereby a mother teaches her son.

Indeed, the distinction between public and private teaching is at the centre
of Aquinas's response to this question.[84] Speech of the kind under discussion,
he explains, can be used in two ways: privately, with one person speaking to a
few others, familiarly conversing (*familiariter colloquendo*), and publicly, in
Church. Women may speak in the first manner but not in the second. (In
passing, here one may recall one of the things which Margery Kempe said
when being examined in front of the Archbishop of York. St Paul's prohibition
of preaching by women having been quoted at her, she replied that she does
'not go into any pulpit' but uses only 'conversation (*comownycacyon*) and good
words'.[85] Clearly, this was the right answer – particularly in view of the
controversy which the Lollards had sparked off concerning female preachers.)
For teaching and persuasion in Church must be done by superiors, declares
Aquinas, and not by inferiors. Moreover, women's speech would lead men

[84] As it was to be at the centre of Henry's discussions of whether women could be
doctors or auditors of Scripture, and also of the anti-Brut *quaestio*, 'Utrum liceat
mulieribius docere viros publice congregatos'. For the former see Minnis, '*Accessus*
in Henry of Ghent', pp. 311–16; for the latter, see Blamires and Marx, 'Woman Not to
Preach', pp. 56 and 62, trans. Blamires, *Woman Defamed*, pp. 252 and 254–5. See
further the relevant discussion in Thomas Netter's *Doctrinale*, I, 639–40, where it is
emphasized that women should teach within the home. There they may educate
girls and boys (and in particular they should teach members of their own sex,
especially the virtues of prudence and chastity). Netter cites Saint Jerome's admir-
ing account of the exemplary behaviour of Marcella (*Epist.* cxxvii.7). Having been
instructed by Jerome, after his departure from Rome she was often called upon to
settle debates concerning the testimony of Scripture. On those occasions Marcella
made it abundantly clear that she was not responsible for the answers she provided:
'she gave her own opinion not as her own but as from me or someone else, thus
admitting that what she taught she had herself learned from others. For she knew
that the apostle had said, "I suffer not a woman to teach" (1 Tim. 2. 12), and she
would not seem to inflict a wrong upon the male sex many of whom (including
sometimes priests) sometimes questioned her concerning obscure and doubtful
points' (trans. Fremantle *et al.*, pp. 255–6). Behold, exclaims Netter, a devout and
prudent woman who wished to edify and scorned to usurp, behaving in a way
which is appropriate to her sex. She made it clear that she was a pupil (*discipulus*)
rather than a master (*magister*), for women cannot teach publicly.
[85] *BMK*, p. 126. See further Julian of Norwich's careful specification of her status. As a
woman, ignorant and frail, she is not setting herself up as a teacher, but rather
speaks as one who has received a special divine gift from the sovereign teacher:
'Botte god for bede that ȝe schulde saye or take it so that I am a techere, for I meene
nouȝt soo, no I mente nevere so; for I am a womann, leued, febille and freylle. Botte
I wate wele, that this I saye, I hafe it of the schewynge of hym that es souerayne
techare. . . . Botte for I am a womann, schulde I therfore leve that I schulde nouȝt
telle ȝowe the goodenes of god, syne that I sawe in that same tyme that is his wille,
that it be knawenn?' Short text, ch. 6; *A Book of Showings to the Anchoress Julian of
Norwich*, ed. E. Colledge and J. Walsh, 2 vols. (Toronto, 1978), I, 222

into lecherous thoughts, as Ecclesiasticus 9. 11 indicates when it warns that female 'conversation burneth (*exardescit*) as fire'.

Henry of Ghent's question, 'Whether a woman can be a teacher (*doctor, doctrix*) of theology?', proceeds in a similar manner; once again the distinction between public and private teaching is crucial.[86] Solomon's mother appears again – the reference might be to his father, Henry suggests – along with Deborah, Huldah and Anna, with Miriam (Exodus 15. 20) being added. Then again, at I Peter 4. 10 we read that everyone who has received a gift should employ or manage it to common benefit, and since women sometimes receive the gift of knowledge, therefore they should share it with others, which they cannot do unless they teach. Thus, Mary (Magdalene) and Martha received the gift of different tongues along with the Apostles, and were sent out to teach and preach publicly just as the menfolk were.

Henry freely admits that any knowledgeable person, whether male or female, old or young, religious or secular, cleric or lay, can teach what he or she knows, and then proceeds to make a distinction between teaching by office (*ex officio*)[87] and teaching by special privilege, promotion or benefit (*ex beneficio*). Women cannot teach *ex officio*, given St Paul's prohibition and their natural weaknesses (as noted above, pp. 123–4), but *ex beneficio* it is perfectly permissible for a woman to teach, providing she has sound doctrine and that this is done privately rather than publicly and in church.[88] However, their audience should consist chiefly of other women and girls, but not men, be-

---

[86] This distinction is also important in Henry's *quaestio* on whether or not women should be taught theology (on which see p. 123 above). Being an *auditor* of the science of theology (to the extent that one is gaining knowledge whereby one can help the pious and oppose the impious) entails being thoroughly instructed in its depths, and equipped to persuade others publicly about those truths and to defend them against adversaries. In those terms, a woman cannot learn theology, for women cannot teach publicly. See Minnis, '*Accessus* in Henry of Ghent', p. 314. There is, however, more to it than that. It may be speculated that when Henry rejects the idea that women may be taught speculative, scholastic theology he must have in mind the pedagogic conventions of his own day, wherein an education in theology at the highest level involved the pupil's delivering lectures and engaging in disputation – which were public affairs (in Henry's terms), and hence not open to women, no doubt for all the same reasons which were used in excluding women from preaching. For instance, one may imagine Henry worrying about the perils of a male audience being sexually inflamed by the provocative voice of a female disputant.

[87] Henry speaks of the *officio docendi* (as did Gerard of Bologna who, as already noted, is heavily dependent on Henry; cf. notes 66 and 69 above). On the more specific concepts of the *officium* and *magisterium praedicatoris* see J. Leclercq, 'Le Magistère du prédicateur au XIII siècle', *AHDLMA* 21 (1946), 105–47; also A. J. Minnis, 'Chaucer's Pardoner and the "Office of Preacher" ', in *Intellectuals and Writers in Fourteenth-Century Europe*, ed. P. Boitani and A. Torti (Cambridge and Tübingen, 1986), pp. 88–119.

[88] Reiterated in the anti-Brut *quaestio*, 'Woman Not to Preach', ed. Blamires and Marx, p. 61 (where Henry is explicitly cited). The *quaestio* (which is difficult to understand at this stage) seems to be saying that the issue of having sound doctrine is not

cause female speech would inflame men to lust (cf. yet again the idiom of Ecclesiasticus 9. 9 and 11); besides, men would regard it as unseemly and shameful to be taught by women. The female prophets referred to in the Bible were given their gift for private rather than public instruction, and if men were taught thereby this was by a special dispensation, wherein divine grace did not respect sexual difference.

The public preaching or teaching of women is acceptable only in special cases. For example, there were Old Testament women who did indeed prophesy, but this was a deliberate affront to men, because they had become effeminate; only in those special circumstances, and to make that particular point, were women set above men in a position of pedagogic superiority. (It would seem, on this occasion at least, that if men became like women, women had to become more like men.) Similarly, Henry continues, it was granted that Martha and Mary (Magdalene) should preach, and that Philip's daughters should publicly prophesy. But this, in Henry's view, was due to a shortage of skilled labour in those productive times: since there were many harvests (of converts) to be made and a small number of labourers (cf. Luke 10. 2), the aid of women was necessary. The clear implication is that, when there are enough men to do the job, the assistance of women should be dispensed with.[89]

A similar case for St Catherine (of Alexandria) is made by Thomas of Chobham in his *De arte praedicandi*.[90] When she heard that the Emperor was violently compelling faithful Christians to take part in pagan festivals and make wicked sacrifices to idols, of her own free will – she was neither called nor compelled – Catherine went to his palace to defend the faith. This is a specific example of a principle which Chobham had laid down a little earlier

relevant here – perhaps because it is dealing with the views of heretics who hold doctrines which are anything but sound?

[89] Hence Thomas Netter (*Doctrinale*, I, 639) remarks that even though the safety of a ship is entrusted to its captain, when a storm strikes every sailor does whatever he can to help. Thus, Judith instructed certain priests at a time of extreme peril (Judith 8. 9–31). This was done not *ex officio* but as one rendering assistance. In the same way Mary Magdalene preached in the time of the primitive Church. After the Ascension the Virgin Mary did teach the Apostles, but this was done in the manner in which a friend teaches a friend; as a friend of the faith Mary shared those secrets concerning the Incarnation which only she knew. Netter also mentions the cases of the women who at Jeremiah 9. 20 were told to receive the word of the Lord 'and teach your daughters wailing, and every one her neighbour mourning', the Samaritan woman who went into the city to proclaim Christ to the men there (John 4. 28–9), and Evodia and Syntyche (Philippians 4. 3). None of the women named above, Netter declares, possessed the *magisterium* of teacher, which is contrary to the sexual hierarchy. A woman would rule over a man if she exercised the *magisterium docendi* over him. The female sex cannot exercise such power, and cannot teach authoritatively.

[90] On St Catherine as preacher in hagiographic tradition and in the *quaestio* by Eustace of Arras (on whether a woman can merit the celestial crown by preaching and teaching), see Blamires, 'Women and Preaching', pp. 144–9. The text of Eustace's *quaestio* is printed by Leclercq, 'Le Magistère', pp. 119–20.

in his art of preaching: while it is perfectly true that in general no lay person or no women can preach publicly, that is to say in church, nonetheless in times of necessity (*in tempore necessitatis*), namely when the faith is threatened, anyone is able to preach, no matter what their condition, age or sex.[91] At one point in his *Summa confessorum* he tacitly pushes that principle even further, in suggesting that wives should be preachers (*praedicatrices*) to their husbands.[92] When priests are advising women after confession, they should advise them to teach their husbands to live better lives, given that no priest can soften a man's heart as effectively as his wife can. Chobham envisages a woman lying in bed, in her husband's arms, talking to him softly, doing everything in her power to improve his conduct. If he is hard, merciless and an oppressor of the poor, she should encourage him to be compassionate. If he is avaricious, she should arouse in him generosity, and secretly dispense alms from their common possessions – thus the gifts which he neglects to give she should provide. It is perfectly permissible for a wife to act in this way, Chobham declares, with her husband being ignorant of what she is doing. Though he does not say so in so many words, this cleric expects wives to at once 'preach' to their husbands and practise what they preach in their own lives.[93]

Here, of course, the term *praedicatio* is used in a very loose sense, and private rather than public instruction is assumed. It could be said that Chobham is indicating the breadth and scope of what Henry of Ghent was later to describe as teaching by special privilege, promotion or benefit (*ex beneficio*). Perhaps he is even widening it. At any rate, it is highly significant that Chobham was writing in the second decade of the thirteenth century. Had he lived around the end of the fourteenth, doubtless he would have been far more cautious about what he said concerning the preaching of layfolk. Things looked very different in 1393, the year in which Walter Brut subjected himself to the correction of Bishop Trefnant.[94]

---

91 Within the *artes praedicandi* genre there is wide variation in the attention given to the issue of women preaching. In his *Forma praedicandi* (1322) Robert of Basevorn limited himself to the statement that 'no woman, no matter how learned or saintly, ought to preach'; trans. L. Krul in *Three Medieval Rhetorical Arts*, ed. J. J. Murphy (Berkeley and Los Angeles, 1971), p. 124. Humbert of Romans (writing between 1263 and 1277 in his *De eruditione praedicatorum*) gave four reasons why the preacher had to be male: women lack understanding, are inferior in status, have a sexually provocative physical appearance, and would call to mind 'the foolishness of the first woman', Eve, who 'taught once and wrecked the whole world'. See *Early Dominicans: Selected Writings*, ed. and trans. S. Tugwell (Ramsey, NJ, and London, 1982), p. 223.

92 *Summa confessorum* VII.ii.15 (p. 375).

93 This account should be seen in the context of the medieval genre of recommendations that women should guide their husbands and help them to lead better lives, recommendations which anticipate the later 'woman as angel of the house' discourse. On these see especially S. Farmer, 'Persuasive Voices: Clerical Images of Medieval Wives', *Speculum* 61 (1986), 517–43.

94 Similarly (and unsurprisingly), unlicensed, 'unofficial' teaching is treated with great

5. A Contemporary Context?

Particularly in view of the furore which Brut's advocacy of women preachers and priests caused, it may be wondered if the relevant comments of the expositors of the *Sentences* are reflections of any immediate problem, if they envisage any real or potential threat to the established order. At first sight, it would seem that in discussing the issue of female ordination the theologians maintain a lofty detachment from the contemporary world. This is perfectly normal academic practice, it must be emphasised, in the great *Sentences* commentaries and *Summae*. The fact that such scholastic works do not explicitly cite some current *cause célèbre* need not mean that their authors were unaware of it or that it did not form some part of their motivation in formulating a particular *quaestio*. Moreover, on occasion a reference to a contemporary problem does indeed intrude. For example when Henry of Ghent is discussing what type and level of theology women should be taught, he attacks certain foolish people who instruct them in this science beyond what is decent and crucial for them to know – especially those who disclose the secrets of Scripture and translate them into the vernacular (*in vulgari sermone*) so that women may read them.[95] Could Henry be worrying about the then-current practice of translating certain parts of the Bible into French? Or had he specifically in mind Waldensian Bible translation, which he certainly was well-placed to have known something about?[96] This is not clear; what is clear is that he is concerned with something contemporary.

There is, however, no reference of this type in my sample of medieval discussions of the ordination of women dating from *c.*1240 until *c.*1337. When our theologians do identify a heretical sect which believed that women could receive holy orders of some kind, they are looking back as far as the second half of the second century, to heap opprobrium on a group of Montanist heretics known as the Cataphrygians. (The name derives from Phrygia, the home of the putative leader of the movement, one Montanus. His followers

---

suspicion in Netter's *Doctrinale*. He quotes with warm approval Jerome's strictures on those unqualified persons who think that they can understand holy writ (*Epist.* liii.6 and 7). 'The chatty old woman, the doting old man, and the wordy sophist, one and all take in hand the Scriptures, rend them in pieces and teach them before they have learned them. Some with brows knit and bombastic words, balanced one against the other philosophize concerning the sacred scriptures among weak women. Others – I blush to say it – learn of women what they are to teach men' (trans. Fremantle *et al.*, p. 99). Netter echoes Jerome's words: 'I blush to say it! Behold women teaching men the divine scriptures!' *Doctrinale*, I, 638.

95 See Minnis, '*Accessus* in Henry of Ghent', p. 315.

96 For a recent brief account of Waldensian Bible translation, and bibliography, see A. Patschovsky, 'The Literacy of Waldensianism', in Biller and Hudson, *Heresy and Literacy*, pp. 112–36 (pp. 113–17).

were also called Perpuzians, after Pepuza in Phrygia, believed to be the place to where the Heavenly Jerusalem would soon descend). The apocalyptic theology of this group valorised female as well as male prophets, and according to Bishop Epiphanius of Salamis (315–403) they gave thanks to Eve for eating of the tree of knowledge; moreover it was claimed that they had women for their bishops, in honour of Eve. Two prophetesses in particular were associated with Montanus, namely Prisca or Priscilla (alternatively called Quintilla) and Maximilla. Thus Saint Jerome, in his forty-first epistle (addressed to Marcella, whom the Montanists had tried to recruit) mocks their belief that God 'descended by the Holy Spirit upon Montanus and those demented women Prisca and Maximilla; and that thus the mutilated and emasculate[97] Montanus possessed a fullness of knowledge such as was never claimed by Paul', for Paul was content to say, 'We know in part, and we prophesy in part' and that now we see merely through a glass darkly (I Corinthians 13. 9 and 12).[98]

When the Cataphrygians appear in the *Sentences* commentaries – specifically, the commentaries of Fishacre, Bonaventure and Thomas of Strasbourg – all that is said about them is that they believed that women could be deaconesses or *presbyterae*.[99] But this claim was easily demolished with the argument (as already explained above) that in the ancient church the former term denoted those who were allowed to read a homily at Matins while the latter referred to presbyters' wives or certain widows (or senior, respectable women) who looked after churches.[100]

In the accounts of female ordination found in the *Sentences* commentaries (at least the ones I have read), there is no clear or explicit reference to any contemporary heresy or problem. However, the discussion of this issue in the University of Paris at that time may be taken as a reaction, however oblique, to the role which the Waldensian heretics were supposed to have granted

---

[97] Perhaps because he had been a priest of Cybele? But Jerome may simply have been slandering him.

[98] *Epist.* xli.4, *PL* 22, col. 476; trans. Fremantle *et al.*, p.56.

[99] Thomas of Strasbourg goes so far as to present the Cataphrygians as actually adducing authorities from both canons, namely canon law and holy Scripture, in disguising their error – which would seem to indicate that his knowledge of the sect was sketchy, to say the least. The Cataphrygians are not mentioned in the discussions of Aquinas, Peter of Tarantasia, Richard of Middleton, Duns Scotus, Durandus, Peter of la Palud, Francis of Meyronnes and John of Bassoles.

[100] This material seems to have entered the *Sentences* commentaries via the *Decretum* and its commentaries, glosses on the canon *Diaconissam* being the crucial source. In reinforcing the view that women cannot be ordained to the diaconate Huguccio of Pisa and John Teutonicus cite the authority of St Ambrose, who is supposed to have attacked the Cataphrygians for having twisted St Paul's words (at I Timothy 3. 11) to mean that women could indeed receive this *ordo*. In fact, they were following not Ambrose but 'Ambrosiaster', who in his commentary on the abovementioned passage from I Timothy says that the Cataphrygians falsely believed that Paul was talking about female as well as male deacons. See Martin, 'Ordination of Women', pp. 133–7.

136   *A. J. Minnis*

women within their sects.[101] Though it could be argued that by then the scare
had passed its peak, there were sufficient reiterations to keep it alive. Furthermore, it may be suggested that in the minds of at last some of the theologians
who spoke about the power of abbesses was the challenge to male authority
presented by certain high-ranking holy women who seemed to have spiritual
(rather than merely secular, which could easily be accommodated) power
over men. An obvious case in point was the Order of Fontevrault, as founded
by Robert Arbrissel, which had male and female members under the rule of a
woman, and of course the Camaldolese and the Gilbertines were open to
criticism for the high positions which they allowed to women, even though
their supreme leaders were male. The perils of cohabitation could easily be
raised in criticisms of such arrangements. The early thirteenth-century *Liber
Sancti Gileberti* duly emphasises the elaborate arrangements which Gilbert of
Sempringham had made for the segregation of his monks and nuns. For
instance, it explains that only the church where divine service was celebrated
was 'common to all, but then only for the solemn rite of the mass, once or
twice a day, and there is a wall which blocks it throughout so that the men
cannot be seen or the women heard'.[102]

It is, however, more likely that the medieval theologians with whom we are
dealing would have had in mind the case of the abbesses of Las Huelgas de
Burgos, mainly because a letter (of 1210) in which Pope Innocent III protests
that they seem to have usurped certain clerical functions had been included,
in part, in the *Decretals* of Pope Gregory IX.[103] But none of the theologians
whom I have read specifically refer to Las Huelgas, and only one of them
explicitly cites Innocent's letter, namely Peter of la Palud. Peter also echoes
Innocent's idioms –

> . . . abbatissae . . . moniales proprias benedicunt, ipsarum quoque
> confessiones in criminibus audiunt, et legentes evangelium
> praesumunt publice predicare[104]

> (. . . abbesses bless their own nuns, and indeed hear their confessions on
> things concerning which they have been accused, and in reading aloud
> the gospel they presume to preach publicly . . .)

– in spelling out what women are not permitted to do:

> Tenendum est igitur quod mulieres non possunt ordinari ex Christi
> institutione nec predicare nec confessiones audire . . .[105]

---

[101] For discussion and bibliography, see P. Biller's article above, especially pp. 65–7.
[102] *The Book of St Gilbert*, ed. R. Foreville and G. Keir (Oxford, 1987), p. 47.
[103] Given this inclusion, in theory after 1234 Innocent's statement could have become
widely known. At any rate, it was potentially available to all the *Sentences* commentators here discussed. Cf. P. Biller's account, on pp. 67–8 above.
[104] *Decretales* V.37.10; Friedberg, II, 886–7.
[105] *In quart. Sent.*, fol. 134v.

(It is to be held that women cannot be ordained through Christ's institution, neither can they preach nor hear confessions . . .)

This citation is the less surprising if it is recalled that in his commentary on the fourth book of the *Sentences* Peter had introduced 'his extensive knowledge of contemporary canon law into the corpus of theological speculation' (as Jean Dunbabin says),[106] this being the reason for that work's popularity. There are, however, a few other occasions on which one may wonder if some of the other *Sentences* commentators (in my sample) are drawing on the pope's language. Richard Fishacre points out that Christ denied the Virgin Mary the power of the keys (cf. Matthew 16. 18–19) –

Nec etiam beate Marie clavis dedit Christus, sed Petro licet ipsa fuerit apostolis excellentior[107]

(For Christ did not give the keys to the blessed Mary, but to Peter, although she was more excellent than the apostles.)

– in terms which are partly reminiscent of this statement by Innocent:

. . . licet beatissima virgo Maria dignior et excellentior fuerit Apostolis universis, non tamen illi, sed istis Dominus claves regni coelorum commisit.

(. . . although the most blessed virgin Mary was more worthy and more excellent than all the apostles, yet not to her but to them did the Lord commit the keys of the kingdom of heaven.)

Several of the *Sentences* commentators cite the case of Mary in discussing the non-ordination of women (as already noted), but Fishacre is the only one to mention the *claves*. There is no close verbal parallel in the texts of any of the others, namely Duns Scotus, Durandus, John of Bassoles and Thomas of Strasbourg. Furthermore, when commentators like Bonaventure and Aquinas discuss abbesses their idioms and their emphases seem rather far removed from Innocent's. Indeed, against this attempt to postulate some contemporary context it could be argued that the term 'abbess' was a regular modernising gloss for 'deaconess' (as found in the canon *Diaconissam* and elsewhere; cf. p. 126 above), and hence the late-medieval theologians were preserving the fossilised remains of crises from long ago.[108] And yet: given the frequent reiteration of the principle that holy women should not have power over men, it would be unwise to rule out the possibility that at least some of the theologians were responding, in their own abstract way, to concerns which were

---

[106] Dunbabin, *Hound of God*, p. 51.
[107] Ed. Martin, 'Ordination of Women', p. 144.
[108] This gloss on *Diaconissam* is explicitly cited as a proof-text by several schoolmen, as already noted (p. 126 above).

rather more pressing than the dubious practices of the long-dead Cataphrygians.

That, it would seem, is as far as we can go, in the present state of our knowledge, in postulating a contemporary context for at least some of the issues raised by the theologians who considered the ordination of women in their treatments of matters arising out of Peter Lombard's *sententiae* on ordination. In the England of the 1390s it was a very different story. Then the threat was immediate, and the contemporary targets of orthodox ire were clearly identified. Thomas Netter records with horror something which had occurred 'in the city of London' of his day: 'the most foolish of women, set up on stools, publicly read and taught the scriptures in a congregation of men'. . .[109] But how frequent were such events? 'The fact that we hear so little, even polemically' regarding actual incidents, avers Margaret Aston, 'suggests the extreme rarity of such proceedings as illicit ordinations or bowdlerised masses, conducted by male or female celebrants'. Had 'a nascent counter-church' existed it would have been impossible to conceal.[110] Besides, it would be utterly naïve to credit Lollardy with exceptionally enlightened views on the capabilities of women.[111] However, the thoroughness with which the case against Walter Brut was pursued is proof positive of the extent to which the church authorities were worried about the issues he had raised. His examination was something of a show trial, certainly, but the fact that this was deemed necessary would seem to indicate orthodox anxiety that many people apart from Brut could entertain a notion as absurd as the belief that women were able to

---

[109] '. . . in civitate Londinensi foeminae super sellas elevatas congregationi virorum stultissimae publice legerent et docerent Scripturas'; *Doctrinale*, I, 638; trans. and discussed by Aston, 'Lollard Women Priests', p. 65. However, Netter cites the *Pepuziani* as having held the same view as Purvey concerning women priests; here he draws on Augustine and Damascenus (*Doctrinale*, I, 638). And a little earlier, in attacking Purvey's compendium for its wide extension of the *officium praedicatoris* to layfolk (cf. note 82 above), he identifies the Waldensians as having held this same opinion; Alan of Lille is quoted on how those heretics presumed to preach, led by their own spirit and not sent by God, being without prelatical authority, knowledge or training (*Doctrinale*, I, 619). Clearly Netter is fully aware of the existence of earlier manifestations of erroneous views now held by the Lollards.

[110] Aston, 'Lollard Women Priests?', p. 66.

[111] Cf. S. McSheffrey, *Gender and Heresy: Women and Men in Lollard Communities, 1420–1530* (Philadelphia, 1995), p. 4. The status and dignity afforded to women within earlier heretical sects, particularly Catharism, has also been exaggerated: see the cogent remarks by P. Biller, pp. 63–81, 106–7 above; also R. Abels and E. Harrison, 'The Participation of Women in Languedocian Catharism', *MS* 41 (1979), 215–51.

[112] Alternatively, it could be argued that Brut's opinions on this matter were seen as something of a soft target, as an easy means of demonizing him: if Lollards could believe in something as absurd as that they were certainly not be to trusted!

perform priestly functions. The *theory* had great potency and challenge even if it was rarely put into practice.[112]

Whatever the truth of that specific matter may be, the fact remains that those who opposed Brut had a considerable body of doctrine to draw upon, from *Sentences* commentaries and elsewhere. When the authors of the *quaestiones* which Brut's views had prompted, and Thomas Netter in his *Doctrinale*, attacked the notion that women might usurp certain priestly functions, they were sharpening even more acutely certain arguments which had already been honed in the minds of some of the greatest schoolmen, for whom the threat posed by women priests may have seemed somewhat remote.

Acknowledgements

I am grateful to Dr Peter Biller, Dr Alcuin Blamires, Dr W. G. East and Prof. Anne Hudson for their valuable comments on earlier versions of this paper.

Against that, however, it may be pointed out that some of Brut's other views were equally absurd to the orthodox eye. Therefore the thought remains that the justification of women priests was held to be *particularly* subversive.

The Physiology of Rapture and Female Spirituality

Dyan Elliott

'Souls follow bodies' (Jean Gerson, *De mystica theologia practica*)

'The action of the soul greatly changes the body' (John Nider, *Formicarium*)

'My poor friend, my poor friend, the soul is nothing but blood' (Guillemette Benet of Montaillou)[1]

Body and soul: two constructs which are frequently pitted against one another as rivals in the race for salvation and yet, as these epigraphs – two orthodox, one heretical – acknowledge, the path that body and soul must traverse is not only identical, but must be traversed in tandem. Caroline Walker Bynum has done more than any other scholar to correct our misperception of body and soul as opposites, first in her exploration of the embodied nature of female spirituality and, more recently, in her analysis of the doctrine of the resurrection of the body.[2] Body and soul are married: and the marriage is indissoluble – if not in the short run, certainly in the long run. But it is impossible to argue that the marriage was always a happy one. In fact, from the perspective of patristic misogyny, the archetypical marriage of Adam and Eve presented an apt metaphor for describing some of the tensions between the flesh (the lower reaches of the body) and the spirit (the upper reaches of the soul). Thus, in the widely cited letter to Augustine of Canterbury that was attributed to Gregory the Great, it was the serpent who suggested the first sin, Eve representing the flesh was delighted by it and Adam representing the spirit consented to it.[3]

---

1 Gerson, *De mystica theologia practica*, c. 2, in *Oeuvres complètes*, ed. M. Glorieux, 10 vols. (Paris, 1960–73), III, 21; Nider, *Formicarium* iv.1 (Douai, 1602), p. 265 (citing Albertus Magnus); E. Le Roy Ladurie, *Montaillou: The Promised Land of Error*, trans. B. Bray (New York, 1979), p. 279 (as related by Alzaïs Munier to the inquisition). Cf. another heretical comment by a peasant of upper Ariège: 'the soul is bread' (p. 134). Note that the quotation from Gerson, which was something of a medieval commonplace, was loosely based on Galen (see Wack, *Lovesickness*, p. 299, note 11).

2 See Bynum, *Holy Feast*; also her 'The Female Body and Religious Practice in the Later Middle Ages' (in *Fragmentation*, pp. 222–35) and *Resurrection*.

3 Bede, *Ecclesiastical History of the English People* i.27, ed. B. Colgrave and R. A. B. Mynors, OMT (Oxford, 1967), p. 101. See Bynum's exploration of the female's

My present purpose is to continue the exploration of the relationship between body and soul by focusing on the phenomenon of rapture as it was articulated by medieval theologians between the thirteenth and fifteenth centuries. Though generally perceived as the quintessential out-of-body experience, rapture is here considered as a bodily production, with a focus on the enrapt body as a symptom of various abnormal states. I will begin by examining rapture as a physical response to divine alterity. Then I will turn to the various means by which rapture was perceived as compromised: the body's penetration of the soul through the senses, the imagination, the passions and physical illness – all of which give rise to the need for spiritual discernment. The latter part of the paper will emphasize the enrapt female body as a zone of increasing ambiguity, and the gradual criminalization of female mysticism in the later Middle Ages.

1. Mystical Rapture and the Presence of God

Rapture (*raptus*) comes from the verb *rapire*: to carry off by force, to seize, to ravish. It was the common legal term for rape or any violence against a woman in the Middle Ages. In a mystical context, it connotes the alienation from the senses that occurs during an encounter with a higher spirit.[4] This is not the word's only meaning: as the verb *rapire* would imply, *raptus* is also used to designate rape and abduction, which is doubtless one of the factors that led thinkers such as Alexander of Hales (d. 1245) and Thomas Aquinas (d. 1274) to insist that the action implies a certain amount of violence.[5] The term rapture is frequently, but not inevitably, used as a synonym for other mystically-charged words like ecstasy (from *ex stasis*: literally standing outside

---

identification of the flesh in relation to the male's identification with the soul in 'The Female Body and Religious Practice,' in *Fragmentation*, pp. 205–22.

[4] The standard definitions offered convey only that it is a crime perpetrated through physical force – especially against women. The mystical usage does not even figure in the various dictionaries. See, for example, D. du Cange, *Glossarium mediae et infimae latinitatis*, 10 vols. (Paris, 1937–8), VII, 17; Lewis and Short, pp. 1523–4; J. F. Niermeyer, *Mediae latinitatis lexicon minus* (Leiden, 1976), p. 881. For an introduction to mystical rapture, see the entries by T. Szabó, 'L'extase chez les théologiens du XIIIe siècle', and F. Jetté, 'L'extase: tradition spirituelle du XIIIe au XVIIe siècles,' in *DSP* IV. 2, 2120–31 and 2131–51.

[5] Alexander of Hales, *Quaestiones disputatae 'Antequam esset frater'*, qu. 68, mem. 1, c. 2, ed. College of St. Bonaventure, 3 vols. (Florence, 1960), III, 1348; Aquinas, *Summa theologiae*, 2a 2ae, qu. 175, art. 1, resp. and art. 2 resp. ad 1, in *ST* XLV, 94–5 and 100–1. Note, however, that Dionysius the Carthusian will disagree with this imputation of violence. See further *De contemplatione* iii.18, in *Doctoris ecstatici D. Dionysii Cartusiani opera omnia*, ed. Monachi sacri ordinis Cartusiensis, 42 vols. in 44 (Tournai, 1896–1935), XLI, 278.

one's senses), and alienation or departure of the mind (*alienatio mentis* or *excessus mentis*),[6] or to be in spirit (*in spiritu*).[7]
Many theological discussions of rapture take their starting point from Paul's description of an experience – presumably his own – in II Corinthians 12. 2–4.

> I know a man in Christ; above fourteen years ago (whether in the body, I know not, or out of the body, I know not; God knoweth), such a one caught up to the third heaven (*raptum huiusmodi usque tertium caelum*). And I know such a man (whether in the body, or out of the body, I know not; God knoweth); That was caught up into paradise and heard secret words which it is not granted to man to utter.[8]

The *Glossa ordinaria* glosses rapture as 'elevated against nature' (*contra naturam elevatum*): a meaning that was seldom contested since, in the normal course of things, the soul relies on the senses, and hence its link to the body, for knowledge.[9] But there was still some speculation about just what exactly was elevated. Was Paul actually raised up in both body and soul or was it only his soul that was seized? Though some commentators, such as William of Auxerre (d. 1231), argued that Paul was in no way implying that he might have endured physical transport, most insisted that we must take Paul's twice repeated uncertainty at face value: if he himself was unsure, we had best leave it there.[10] There was, however, a general consensus that Paul actually viewed the divine essence directly and without mediation. An unmediated experience of God enlisted the intellectual vision – a faculty that surpassed corporeal or even spiritual vision, the other two types of vision that were classified by Augustine. The superiority of intellectual vision was assured by the fact that it functioned independently of images. Rather than seeing mere similitudes of objects, intellectual vision perceived the things themselves. This rarefied vision places Paul's experience in a category that surpasses even John's mode of

---

6   Bonaventure, for example, distinguishes between ecstasy and rapture, placing rapture at the peak of an ascending hierarchy of six gradations in intellectual vision, corresponding to the six days of creation. See *Collationes in hexaemeron* iii.24 and iii.30, in *Opera* V, 347 and 348. See further, Vincent of Beauvais's less exacting definition in *Speculum naturale* xxvi.111 (I, 1916).

7   See William of Auvergne, *De universo*, pt 2, 3, c. 20, in *Opera*, 2 vols. (Paris, 1674), I, col. 1058. Henceforth referred to as William, *De universo*.

8   I am using the Douay translation of the Vulgate. Most theological discussions of Paul's rapture and visions generally are based on the twelfth book of Augustine's *De Genesi ad litteram*; cf. the translation by J. H. Taylor, 2 vols., Ancient Christian Writers, nos. 41–2 (New York, 1982), II, 178–231.

9   *Glossa ordinaria* on II Cor. 12. 2, ad *raptum*; *PL* 114, 568. See further Aquinas, *Summa theologiae*, 1a, qu. 84, arts. 6–8 (*ST* XII, 32–47).

10 William of Auxerre, *Summa aurea* iii.57, ed. J. Ribaillier, 4 vols. in 7, Spicilegium Bonaventurianum 16–20 (Paris and Rome, 1980–6), XVIII.B, 699–70. The following authors are representative of the more cautious majority: *Glossa ordinaria* on II Cor. 12. 2 ad *Sive in corpore, sive* (*PL* 114, 568); Alexander of Hales, *Quaestiones disputatae*, qu. 68, mem. 1, c. 3 (III, 1346); Vincent, *Speculum naturale* xxvi.109–10 (I, 1914–15).

perception in the Apocalypse, wherein the seer's spiritual vision was nevertheless reliant upon images.[11] Thus Paul saw as a *comprehensor* ('one who attains' or 'arrives') as opposed to a *viator* (or mere 'traveller'), his vision crudely approximating the way in which angels see God.[12] In fact, the third heaven, to which Paul was raptured, was considered the abode of the higher angels.

Though commentators did not categorically urge that Paul's body remained stationary during this experience, it was all the same believed that such privileged access to God would require alienation from the body. The suspension of the sensitive faculty of his soul (i.e. the senses), if not the actual vegetative faculty (i.e. the animating principle), was likened to death and taken as an illustration of Exodus 33. 20, 'no man may see God and live'.[13] No one doubted the necessity of this distancing of the body, yet it was not immediately clear why it should be so. After the resurrection, body and soul would be united and the blessed would enjoy an uninterrupted vision of God without rapture. Yet Aquinas marks the difference as follows: 'In the resurrection, the body will be entirely subject to the spirit to such an extent that the properties of glory will overflow from the spirit into the body. Hence, they will be called spiritual bodies.'[14] By the same token, Christ, enjoying perfection in body and soul, would at no time have been prone to rapture.[15]

2. Souls Follow Bodies

And so rapture revealed a dissonance between body and soul. Even William of Auvergne (d. 1249), one of the few theologians who contested received opinion by urging that rapture was not in any way against nature, based his rationale on this central disjunction. For William, the soul's propensity toward rapture in response to divine illuminations (*irradiationes*) is comparable to the natural attraction of iron to a magnet. The fact that even sinners respond to such illuminations with rapture attests to the normality of the experience. Rapture is also a reminder that the soul is positioned at the crossroads between the higher sublime world and the present state of wretchedness and

---

11 Alexander of Hales, *Quaestiones disputatae*, qu. 68, mem. 3, c. 54–5 (III, 1362–3); Vincent, *Speculum naturale* xxvi.90 (I, 1916).
12 Peter Lombard, *Collectanea in epistolis D. Pauli*, ad II Cor. 12.1–4 (*PL* 192, 80); Alexander of Hales, *Quaestiones disputatae* qu. 68, mem. 5, c. 32 (p. 1356); William of Auxerre, *Summa aurea* III.xxxvii.2 (II, 701).
13 Peter Lombard, *Collectanea in epistolis D. Pauli*, in Ep. II Cor. 12.1–4 (*PL* 192, 82); Alexander of Hales, *Quaestiones disputatae*, qu. 68, mem. 1, c. 9–10 (III, 1348); Aquinas, *Quaestiones de veritate*, qu. 13, art. 3, resp. ad 1, trans. J. V. McGlynn, 2 vols. (Chicago, 1953), II, 193; Vincent, *Speculum naturale* xxvi.108 (I, 1913–14).
14 Aquinas, *De veritate*, qu. 13, art. 3, resp. ad 1 (trans. McGlynn, II, 195). For thirteenth-century discussions of the resurrected body, see Bynum, *Resurrection*, pp. 229–78.
15 Vincent, *Speculum naturale* xxvi.105 (I, 1910–11).

corruption. Though in an eschatological context William is seemingly reluctant to do away with rapture entirely, he is nevertheless prepared to grant that, were bodies immortal, less raptures would occur. But in our present condition the soul would always be enrapt, were it not for various interferences staged by the body.[16] So on the one hand, rapture directly resulted from the frailty of the flesh; on the other hand the frailty of the flesh impeded rapture.

The ambiguities ensuing from efforts to theologize the role of the body in rapture were not unique to William. It was widely held that the inadequacies of the body both necessitated and forestalled rapture. Interestingly, the prohibitive force of the body was often owing to effects that were not particularly corporeal. The problem of the senses – ultimately a spiritual faculty – is a case in point. William, for example, thought that the soul literally leaked out of the various apertures required by the senses. He supported this observation by reference to the handicapped: if one of their senses is obstructed, the others are sharpened. Thus ancient philosophers allegedly blinded young boys in order to capitalize on the prophetic powers that lie latent in the soul.[17] In a similar vein, Aquinas supports the belief that the natural powers of divination inherent in the soul are blocked by the union with the body.[18]

Vision, arguably the most spiritual of the senses, presents particular challenges. In line with the three-fold Augustinian contours mentioned above, corporeal vision perceives a body through the senses, and spiritual vision abstracts images of bodies and stores such images in the memory. These images can be accessed by the imaginative power. Intellectual vision, however, by which the spirit contemplates abstract forms such as God or love, is entirely aloof from such images.[19] Though some theorists, such as Albert the Great (d. 1280) and Bonaventure (d. 1274), reserved the term rapture for intellectual vision alone and the perception of God's essence,[20] others applied it to the imaginary visions witnessed during a mystical elevation from the outer senses – as experienced by the apostles Peter (Acts 10. 10) or John (in the Apocalypse).

And yet any experience which enlists the imaginative faculty was already threatened by material corruption. Vincent of Beauvais, citing what he believes to be Hugh of St Victor, alleges that the imagination (in addition to the senses and sensuality) is as much a power of the body as of the mind.[21]

---

16 William of Auvergne, *De anima*, c. 133, in *Opera* II (supplement), p. 192; cf. his *De universo*, pt 2, 3, c. 19 (I, 1056) and also Peter Lombard's assertion that rapture anticipates the afterlife in *Collectanea in epistolis D. Pauli*, ad II Cor. 1–4 (*PL* 192, 82).

17 William, *De universo*, pt 2, 2, c. 18 (I, 1049–50).

18 Aquinas, *Summa theologiae*, 2a 2ae, qu. 172 art. 3 ad 3 and resp. ad 3 (*ST* XLV, 36–9).

19 Augustine, *De Genesi ad litteram* xii.26 (trans. Taylor, II, 216–7).

20 Albert the Great, *Quaestio de raptu*, art. 2. 1, *in Quaestiones*, ed. A. Fries, in *Opera omnia*, 37 vols. to date (Aschendorff, 1951–93), XXV, pt ii, 90. For Bonaventure, see note 6 above.

21 Vincent, *Speculum naturale* xxv.84 (I, 1828). Vincent's source, *De spiritu et anima*, is

Thomas of Cantimpré (d. after 1276) positions the imagination between the tip of the corporeal soul and the bottom of the rational soul. Because of its special debt of dependence on the senses, moreover, he perceives the imagination itself as a likeness of the body.[22] The images mobilized by the imagination are impressions of material things, linked by authorities like the pseudo-Dionysius and Hugh of St Victor with uncleanness and defilement.[23] Most importantly, as all would agree, the imaginative power was especially prone to demonic vitiation. In the words of Vincent of Beauvais,

> And so the malign spirit imprints images of delectable things on the soul, from which arise evil thoughts, and then the soul devotes itself to those images. Moreover [the devil] imprints these things in the imaginative virtue because it abounds in humours. But the devil does not enter the soul to shape images of this kind in it, but somehow he mixes himself or joins himself to the imaginative virtue and he shapes images for it. And these images end up in a person's imaginative virtue, just as if a mirror is moved in front of another mirror and the form impressed in it ends up in the other. And so when the soul apprehends a delectable thing and becomes preoccupied and devoted to its image, it is moved to concupiscence for the delectable thing that corresponds to the image. And thus a thought, which is a sin, arises with the delectation. And because the soul is delighted by those corporeal things through the five senses, on that account it is not only through the imagination, but also through the senses, that the devil incites souls to illicit and immoderate delectations and depraved thoughts, by moving corporeal shapes in the senses, or even mixing himself with the sensible spirit, and thus altering it.[24]

---

variously attributed to Hugh of St Victor, Augustine, and others. It is now believed to have been written by the twelfth-century author Alcher of Clairvaux. The text is printed in *PL* 40, 779–832.

[22] Thomas of Cantimpré, *Liber de natura rerum* ii.15, ed. H. Boese, 1 vol. to date (Berlin and New York, 1973), I, 95.

[23] Aquinas, *De veritate*, qu. 13, art. 3, ad 6 (trans. McGlynn, II, 194).

[24] 'Imprimit itaque malignus spiritus imagines rerum delectabilium in ipsa anima, ex quibus surgunt malae cogitationes dum ipsa anima operatur circa illas imagines, has autem imprimit in virtute imaginatiua, quoniam abundat humoribus. Nec ideo diabolus intrat animam, vt in ea formet huiusmodi imagines sed quodammodo miscet se vel coniungit virtuti imaginatiuae, et illae imagines quas in seipso format, resultant in imaginatiua hominis, sicut si speculum admoueatur speculo forma impressa in vno resultat in alio. Et ita per apprehensionem rei delectabilis, dum anima circa imaginem eius negociatur vel operatur, mouetur ad concupiscentiam illius rei delectabilis, cuius est imago. Et ita surgit cogitatio cum delectatione quae est peccatum. Et quoniam anima delectatur in ipsis rebus corporeis per quinque sensus, ideo non solum per imaginationem, sed etiam per sensum irritat animas ad illicitas et immoderatas delectationes et prauas cogitationes, species corporales sensibus admouendo, vel etiam miscendo se spiritui sensibili, et ipsum immutando' (Vincent, *Speculum naturale* xxvi.66; I, 1879. Cf. ii.119; I, 153).

Vincent grants that the devil is not permitted to enter the soul as can God or a good angel (who only enters by the special grace of God). Nor can the devil read all of the thoughts of our souls since, interestingly, the darkness surrounding the human body casts a shadow which seemingly protects the soul. He nevertheless can mix himself with the body. From this vantage point, the devil can set the soul aflame through the imagination in the same way that a baker lights an oven from the outside.[25]

If a legitimate mystical experience which enlists spiritual vision is already to some extent compromised by the body through its dependence on the senses and their ethereal client – the imagination (whether this faculty suffered demonic interference or not) – bodily interference can also take more insidious, but ultimately more aggressive forms. Jacquart and Thomasset have argued that 'the originality of the Middle Ages lay in their bringing together the facts provided by psychology and physiology, so as to constitute a model capable of accounting for the overlapping of physical and mental states'. Thus the passions, which in classical times were chiefly disturbances or accidents which raged through the soul, develop a 'hybrid status as both physical and mental states'.[26] The passions were especially susceptible to demonic influences: William of Auvergne gives a detailed description of how the devil, pressing himself on a certain organ, produces a passion so powerful that physical seizures can follow, and he excoriates certain medical experts who argue that such disorders have a simple physical origin. He then proceeds to relate how the devil applied sufficient pressure to one man's imaginative organ, with the result that the latter, while lying in a stupor, was convinced he was a wolf ravaging the countryside.[27] Now certain passions, such as fleshly concupiscence, were, as Alexander of Hales argued, opposed to the spirit and forestalled mystical rapture.[28] However, extreme carnal love was believed to induce a complete abstraction from the senses – symptomatic of the famous lovesickness of the Middle Ages. Moreover, a widely held

---

[25] Vincent, *Speculum naturale* xxvi.69–70 (I, 1881). Most authors agree that the devil cannot enter the soul, with the possible exception of William of Auvergne. When discussing the devil's temptation of holy men, for example, he asks 'Qualiter autem hoc possunt, si non est eis accessus ad animas eorum, et si non est eis facultas pingendi cogitatum hujusmodi in imaginationibus eorum, et forsitan virtute intellectiva ipsorum?' ('Moreover how can they [i.e. demons] do this if they do not have entrance into the souls [of holy men], and if they do not have the ability of painting [sordid] thoughts of this sort in their imaginations, and perhaps in their intellective virtue'). *De universo*, pt 2, 3, c. 23; I, 1061.

[26] Jacquart and Thomasset, pp. 83–4 and 82. See Galen's definition in *On the Passions and Errors of the Soul*, trans. P. W. Harkins (Columbus, Ohio, 1963), p. 32, and Augustine's discussion in *De civitate Dei* xix.4–6, trans. H. Bettenson (Harmondsworth, Middlesex, 1972), pp. 345–51.

[27] William, *De universo*, pt 2, 3, c. 13 (I, 1041 and 1043–4).

[28] Alexander of Hales, *Quaestiones disputatae*, qu. 68, mem. 7, c. 36–7 (III, 1358–9); cf. Aquinas on the question of prophecy, *Summa theologiae*, 2a 2ae, qu. 172 art. 2, resp. ad 3 (*ST* XLV, 38–9).

understanding of mystical rapture is that the soul is literally seized by divine love.[29] William of Auvergne would contest, however, that this reversion to bodily things is in fact the opposite to mystical rapture, while Jean Gerson (d. 1429) would similarly urge that such abstractions are not really raptures but a 'dragging downwards or drowning of the spirit'.[30] Yet these physical effects were nevertheless indistinguishable from those visited by a more noble abstraction. Thus Dionysius the Carthusian (d. 1471) capitalizes on the parallels between the two kinds of rapture by demonstrating how the celebrated symptoms of carnal lovesickness also correspond with their rarefied counterparts in spiritual love.[31]

Physical frailty was an equally potent source of possible deception. Raptures could result from the kind of physical malfunction associated with illness or madness.[32] In a state of abstraction from the body, the soul continues restlessly to manufacture images. The invalid is, in turn, incapable of discerning between the images apprehended by the corporeal or spiritual vision.[33] In other words, the imaginary is mistaken for the real and vice versa. Moreover, the recipient of these 'visions' may interpret them as direct communications from God. William of Auvergne further suggests the ways in which the devil may take advantage of illness to insinuate various diabolical suggestions, giving numerous examples of unfortunates who come to believe that they are Christ, the Holy Spirit, or Antichrist. Less loftily, Jean Gerson claims that he knew a learned man of science who thought he was a rooster, and even sang like one. He fled into the woods, not to be heard from again. Another individual believed he had grown a horn on his forehead; others thought they had feet of iron (and stomped around), while still others thought they had feet of glass (and were afraid to walk).[34] Often, such disturbances arise from a defect in the play of humours that determine an individual's complexion. For example, a person suffering from melancholia, an illness associated with an excess

---

[29] Aquinas, *De divinis nominibus*, lect. 10, in *Opuscula omnia*, ed. P. Mandonnet, 5 vols. (Paris, 1927), II, 396; Gerson, *De theologia mystica* c. 39 (*Oeuvres complètes*, III, 284); Dionysius the Carthusian, *De contemplatione* iii.18 (*Opera* XLI, 279).

[30] William, *De anima*, pt 33 (*Opera* II, 192); Gerson, *De theologia mystica*, c. 37 (*Oeuvres complètes* III, 284).

[31] Dionysius the Carthusian, *De contemplatione* iii.16 (*Opera* XLI, 274–6). Cf. Constantine the African's classic symptoms for lovesickness in his *Viaticum*, edited in Wack, *Lovesickness*, pp. 188–9, ll. 17–32. For a discussion of parallels between secular love and mystical rapture, see pp. 23–7 and 152–7.

[32] Aquinas, *Summa theologiae*, 2a 2ae, qu. 175, art. 1, resp. (*ST* XLV, 95–7); William, *De universo*, pt 2, 3, c. 13 (I, 1040); Vincent, *Speculum naturale* xxvi.2 (I, 1842–3).

[33] See Vincent of Beauvais, *Speculum naturale* xxvi.96–97 (I, 1903–4). Vincent's discussion consists mainly of citation of Augustine's *De Genesi ad litteram*, bk 12.

[34] William, *De universo*, pt 2, 2, c. 35 (I, 878–9); Gerson, *De passionibus animae*, c. 20 (*Oeuvres complètes*, IX, 20). See also Gerson's similar list of delusions, where the rooster again emerges, in *De distinctione verarum revelationum a falsis* (*Oeuvres complètes*, III, 44).

of black bile, is especially prone to these lower kinds of raptures.[35] Not surprisingly, melancholia was also linked with lovesickness.[36]

But complexions, sound or unsound, inform a person's spiritual aptitude. William of Auvergne believed that certain complexions engorge the soul, impeding their higher powers. He cites Galen as saying that the phlegmatic complexion was particularly unspiritual. Aristotle, on the other hand, is purported to have said that the most intelligent individuals tend to have a melancholic complexion, and they are also most prone to divine illuminations. Gerson also emphasizes the importance of complexion in determining an individual's spiritual disposition. For instance, the humours act as a conduit for the passions which, in turn, have a major impact on the imagination.[37]

3. Angelic or Demonic Rapture

Spiritual aptitude was something of an open invitation for the involvement of higher spirits, although the spirits who accept the invitation might be either good or bad. This is perhaps especially problematical for the spirit of prophecy – an inspiration that does not necessarily require alienation from the senses, but which, according to Aquinas, is always mediated by angels.[38] The highest form of rapture is, as we have seen, free of spiritual intermediaries, being effected directly by God. Yet lesser orders of mystical rapture do involve angelic interpolation. Unlike Aquinas, William of Auvergne tended to see contact with an angelic spirit as necessarily entailing alienation. He explains this response in terms of the angelic resemblance to God, evoking a similar response on behalf of the soul. When these sublime substances apply themselves to our souls, we leave our bodies in ecstasy like iron being attracted to a magnet.[39] Gerson, though maintaining that only God can enter our spirits, nevertheless uses the magnet analogy to describe the way in which angels affix themselves to our spirit by divine dispensation. In the process of urging that angels work on the passions of the soul in order to stimulate the higher 'spiritual passions', he tantalizingly points to the ways in which they alter the

---

[35] William of Auvergne, *De anima*, pt 33 (*Opera* II, 193); *De universo*, pt 2, 3, c. 13 and c. 21 (I, 1041 and 1058); Dionysius the Carthusian, *De contemplatione*, bk 3, art. 18 (XLI, 279). Also see Galen, *On the Affected Parts*, iii.9–10, trans. R. E. Siegel (Basel, 1968), pp. 88–94.

[36] See, however, Peter of Spain's bewilderment over the fact that young people are more prone to lovesickness, though less prone to melancholia than are the old, in his commentary on *Viaticum*; ed. Wack, *Lovesickness*, pp. 242–3.

[37] William, *De universo*, pt 2, 3, c. 20 (I, 1054); Gerson, *De passionibus animae*, c. 18 (*Oeuvres complètes*, IX, 17–18).

[38] Aquinas, *Summa theologiae*, 2a 2ae, qu. 172, art. 2 and 2a 2ae, qu. 173, art. 3 (*ST* XLV, 34–5 and 62–3); Vincent, *Speculum naturale* xxvi.88–91 (I, 1896–8).

[39] William of Auvergne, *De universo*, pt 2, 3, c. 152 (I, 1002–3).

corporeal senses to achieve this end. 'But these things ought not to be discussed in only a few words', he concludes.[40]

Thus angelic rapture was not only a possibility but, under certain circumstances, a necessity – at least according to some authorities. But what about
bad angels? Is there such a thing as demonic rapture? Gerson, while not
addressing the question of rapture directly, basically assigns bad angels the
same range as the good, provided that the bad are permitted to operate by
divine providence.[41] Others, such as Aquinas and Vincent of Beauvais, point
to demonic possession as proof of the evil spirits' ability to rapture.[42] Vincent
is careful to distinguish this state from more modest demonic besiegement in
which the devil enters the body through the senses or some such access point
to suggest evil to the soul. A possessing demon may similarly enter through
the senses. Some of the more graphic tales, for example, actually have someone ingesting a demon – a theme that goes back at least as far as Gregory the
Great.[43] With possession, however, the devil fully inhabits the individual's
body and suspends his or her free will.[44] Interestingly, although theologians
were timid in alleging Paul's bodily rapture into third heaven, some eagerly
attested to the physical raptures effected by demons. Thomas of Cantimpré
provides some especially vivid descriptions. Unabashedly incorporating aspects of folkloric tradition as proof of physical rapture, Thomas relates how
certain women are physically seized by demons at the moment of death. After
a demonic simulation of their body has been buried, they are later discovered
among the living.[45] An equally uncanny fate befell the daughter of a count,
raised in a cloister 'who was seized by demons for some hours in the night
and she proved to be invisible and untouchable in that rapture'. Her brother,
who happened to be a Franciscan friar, held her tightly in his arms so that this
rapture could not be repeated. But when the appropriate time came, she was
torn from his restraining grip.[46] Lest we dismiss such stories as the terrain of

---

40 Gerson, *De passionibus animae*, c. 15 (*Oeuvres complètes*, IX, 14).
41 Gerson, *De passionibus animae*, c. 17 (*Oeuvres complètes*, IX, 15).
42 Aquinas, *Summa theologiae*, 2a 2ae, qu. 175, art. 1, resp. (*ST* XLV, 97–8); cf. 2a 2ae, qu.
   72, art. 5 (*ST* XLV, 42–5); Vincent, *Speculum naturale* xxvi.97 (I, 1904).
43 Gregory the Great, *Dialogues* i.4; trans. O. J. Zimmerman, Fathers of the Church 39
   (Washington, DC, 1959), p. 18; cf. Nider, *Formicarium* v.105 (pp. 413–14).
44 See Vincent, *Speculum naturale* xxvi.69 (I, 1881).
45 Thomas of Cantimpré, *Bonum universale de proprietatibus apium* ii.56 (Cologne,
   c.1481), unpag., hereafter cited as *De apibus*. Cf. Walter Map, *De nugis curialium*
   ii.12–14 and iv.8, ed. and trans. M. R. James; revised C. N. L. Brooke and R. A. B.
   Mynors, OMT (Oxford, 1983), pp. 154–63 and 344–5, and the Middle English poem
   Sir Orfeo.
46 '. . . quae per aliquas horas a demonibus nocte rapitur et in ipso raptu inuisibilis et
   incontrectabilis conprobatur' (Thomas of Cantimpré, *De apibus* ii.56). Cf. Caesarius
   of Heisterbach's account of a certain Henry of Soest who was raptured into the air
   by a female succubus. She eventually put him down in a field, but he was enfeebled
   in body and mind and died within a year. See *Dialogue on Miracles* iii.11, trans. H. V.
   E. Scott and C. C. S. Bland, 2 vols. (New York, 1929), I, 138.

mere 'pop theologians', Thomas of Cantimpré informs us that his teacher, none other than Albert the Great, disputed this 'quaestio de raptu mulierum talium' ('question concerning the rapture of such women') in front of the bishop of Paris.[47]

4. Discernment and the Body[48]

Thomas of Cantimpré seeks to evade the potential crisis arising when similar effects are wrought through diametrically opposed agents by optimistically positing that intellectual vision transcends all possible error. Nor can the soul err when united to a good angel, as the revelation of John in the Apocalypse attests.[49] As comforting as such Augustinian-inflected assurances may be,[50] they provide amorphous and impracticable standards since a mystical rapture had so many carnally inspired analogues. The apostolic admonition that Lucifer could disguise himself as an angel of light was frequently invoked to put spiritual directors on their guard (II Corinthians 11. 14). On the other hand, though the father of lies (John 8. 44), Lucifer could and did speak truth as did those possessed by him.[51] Thus the thirteenth-century Caesarius of Heisterbach's rather simple anecdotes regarding demoniacs spitting out coarse truths about their neighbours were essentially corroborated by the ruminations of

---

[47] Albert was not always so forthcoming. Thomas tells another story of a soldier in Flanders who killed a demonic simulation of his sister and then restored his real sister. But when asked about this, Albert dissembled, not wishing to specify how such things might occur (Thomas of Cantimpré, *De apibus* ii.56). If there is any truth to this story, it is possible that Albert was nervous about the loose application of the word 'rapture', since he reserved this term to specify intellectual vision alone (see note 20, above). Moreover, Albert also argues that an individual cannot be raptured into evil (*Quaestio de raptu*, art. 2.3, in *Quaestiones*, XXV, pt ii, 93). Thomas also describes less dramatic moments of demonic rapture. For instance, an ailing boy simply experienced his soul being seized and tortured (*De apibus* ii.54). As Thomas explains elsewhere, souls, though incorporeal, carry within them a likeness of the body and it is this likeness which is rewarded or tortured after death and before the resurrection of the body (*Liber de natura rerum* ii.15; I, 94). On the nature of such spirit bodies in otherworld journeys, see Bynum, *Resurrection*, pp. 291–305.

[48] On the discernment of spirits, see F. Vandenbroucke, 'Discernement des esprits au moyen âge,' *DSP* III, cols. 1254–66; W. A. Christian, *Apparitions in Late Medieval and Renaissance Spain* (Princeton, NJ, 1981), pp. 188–203; K. Kerby-Fulton, ' "Who has Written this Book?": Visionary Autobiography in Langland's C Text', in *The Medieval Mystical Tradition in England*, ed. M. Glasscoe, Exeter Symposium 5, Papers read at the Devon Centre, Dartington Hall, July 1992 (Cambridge, 1992), pp. 101–16.

[49] Thomas of Cantimpré, *Liber de natura rerum* ii.13 (I, 93).

[50] Cf. Augustine, *De Genesi ad litteram*, xii.14; II, 196–7.

[51] Aquinas, *Summa theologiae*, 2a 2ae, qu. 172, art. 6 (*ST* XLV, 44–9); Vincent, *Speculum naturale* xxvi.99 (I, 1905); William, *De universo*, pt 2, 3 (I, 1003).

more sophisticated thinkers, like Aquinas.[52] To complicate matters, it was generally acknowledged that there was no necessary correlation between demonic assaults and an individual's sinful state. Indeed, many thought the devil more inclined to vex holy people – Christ himself, after all, was transported to a mountain by Lucifer.[53] Moreover, the recipient of a supernatural visitation was a totally unreliable assessor of its efficacy. Aquinas claimed, for instance, that a prophet cannot distinguish between his or her own voice and that of an illuminating spirit. The only people capable of discerning between good and evil spirits were, as Paul had intonated (I Corinthians 12.10), those who had received this ability as a special gift.[54]

By the end of the fourteenth century, an entire genre devoted to spiritual discernment had developed which adduced general principles for deciphering the source of mystical inspiration. But this task proved so arduous that one of the labourers in this field suggested that Aquinas's failure to discuss the gift of spiritual discernment in his treatise on the gifts of the Holy Spirit was owing to its difficulty.[55] How did these self-styled experts address the enigma of bodily raptures? Interestingly – in a time of intensely somatic spirituality when blessedness was so frequently enacted physically through raptures, stigmata and the like, and when hagiographers dwelt lovingly on these bodily manifestations as *ipso facto* proofs of sanctity – the writers of these treatises austerely downplay somatic changes, including raptures. This could be construed as a tacit recognition of how unreliable a witness the body was.

When aspects of somatic spirituality are introduced in treatises devoted to the subject of spiritual discernment, it is more often than not for the purpose of discrediting such physical indicators. Henry of Langenstein (d. 1397) is careful to enumerate the way in which the humours, passions, and melancholia can affect an individual's receptivity and perceptions. He cautions against excessive austerities which can lead to stupefaction and even madness. But he also introduces a new twist that could complicate the problem of discernment considerably. Out of misplaced spiritual pride, some individuals consider themselves worthy of raptures and other revelations and constantly beseech

---

52 Caesarius of Heisterbach, *Dialogue on Miracles* iii.2, iii.3, iii.5 (I, 125, 127 and 129); cf. iii. 6 (I, 132–3). For a discussion of the extent of demons' penetration into our minds, see Aquinas, *De malo* xvi.8, ad 3, which resolves that angels and devils, though they cannot actually read our thoughts, can read the various images in our minds. Cf. Aquinas, *Opera omnia*, ed. S. E. Fretté, 30 vols. (Paris, 1871–1876), XIII, 606; see also his *Summa theologiae*, 1a, qu. 57, art. 4, resp. ad 3 (*ST* IX, 138–9) and 1a, qu. 64, art. 1, resp. ad 5 (*ST* IX, 286–7).

53 William, *De universo*, pt 2, 3, c. 23 (I, 1061); Vincent, *Speculum naturale* xxvi.65 (I, 1878).

54 Aquinas, *Summa theologiae*, 2a 2ae, qu. 171, art. 5 (*ST* XLV, 20–3); also see Vincent, *Speculum naturale* xxvi.99 (I, 1905). On a very concrete level, Caesarius of Heisterbach gives examples of religious who are literally deceived by false angels: *Dialogue on Miracles* v.47 (I, 381–2).

55 Dionysius the Carthusian, *De discretione et examinatione spirituum*, art. 3 (*Opera* XL, 269).

God for such proofs of their holiness. Occasionally, God will retaliate out of annoyance, sending them delusory visions, which, in turn, induce delirium.[56] Jean Gerson, who produced several of the most influential treatises on this subject, including his famous attack on Bridget of Sweden (d. 1373), links visions and revelations – especially those received by women – with brain damage, melancholia and epilepsy.[57] He too suggests that such disorders are frequently brought on by excessive austerity. Moreover he goes to great lengths to differentiate 'true' inspiration from the misleading signs generated by a physical predisposition, arguing that John the Baptist was possessed of a sanguine complexion, not melancholic. Bernardino of Siena (d. 1444) warns against 'the deception of artificial transformation. For there are many who violate themselves for tears or fervours, and through certain outer acts they elaborate supernatural sentiments.'[58] He is especially concerned that one not be deceived by false raptures and visions. If they seem to corroborate Scripture and good morals, however, 'you should not despise them – because perhaps you will despise those things which are of God'.[59] As one would expect from someone called 'Doctor Ecstaticus', Dionysius the Carthusian is considerably more forthcoming on these matters. While citing Henry of Langenstein's cautionary remarks concerning the way in which physical imbalances can simulate spiritual privilege, he nevertheless recognizes certain raptures, inflammations, elevations and the like as important signals of divine favour. But his main preoccupation is to ensure that these experiences be adequately proven by a qualified judge – one who has also experienced similar mystical favours.[60] With regard to solid indications of efficacy, the best

56 Henry of Langenstein, *De discretione spirituum*, c. 2, 3–4, ed. and trans. into German, T. Hohman, *Heinrichs von Langenstein 'Unterscheidung der Geister' Lateinisch und Deutsch* (Munich, 1977), pp. 56–8 and 69–70.
57 Gerson, *De probatione spirituum*, c. 7 (*Oeuvres complètes*, IX, 180); *De distinctione verarum revelationum a falsis* (III, 45) and also his account of the pseudo–mystic from Arras who was starving herself to death (p. 43). On the clerical struggle to contain female spirituality culminating in Gerson, see J. A. McNamara, 'The Rhetoric of Orthodoxy: Clerical Authority and Female Innovation in the Struggle with Heresy', in *Maps of Flesh and Light: The Religious Experience of Medieval Women Mystics*, ed. U. Wiethaus (Syracuse, NY, 1993), pp. 9–27, esp. 24–7; R. Lerner, *The 'Heresy' of the 'Free Spirit' in the Later Middle Ages* (Berkeley and Los Angeles, 1972), pp. 164–8.
58 '. . . deceptionum est artificiosae transformationis. Sunt namque plerique qui seipsos violentant ad lacrimas et fervores, et per quosdam exteriores actus ad sentimenta supernaturalia elaborant': Bernardino of Siena, *De inspirationum discretione*, in *Opera omnia*, ed. by the Fathers of the College of St. Bonaventure, 7 vols. (Florence, 1950–59), VI, 270.
59 '. . . non despicias ea; quia forte despiceres ea quae Dei sunt': Bernardino, *Opera*, VI, 274. See further the wider context of the quoted remarks, as indicated on pp. 273–4.
60 Dionysius the Carthusian, *De discretione et examinatione spirituum*, arts. 2 and 5 (*Opera* VIII, 268 and 270–72); cf. this flowery (but vague) description of mystical experience to his more explicit examples of somatic experiences in rapture in a treatise clearly written with a different end in mind. Thus he cites Aquinas's and Francis's levitation, the latter's reception of the stigmata, the miraculous lights

he can do is to assure that when raptures or ecstatic movements 'begin spontaneously or are caused suddenly on the peak of the affective or the tip of the
intellectual power, so that the apex of affective and the tip of the intellectual
are touched, illuminated, set aflame and bound in a marvellous way, it is
certain that [the source] is not an evil spirit'.[61]

More concrete signs suggesting the source of inspiration can, however,
occasionally be gleaned from other theological fora. The theologian William of
Auvergne, bishop of Paris from 1228 to 1249, was remarkable for his intense
interest in magic or, to put it another way, in the effects of spirits on bodies.
His major work *De universo*, a massive and heterogenous endeavour, is especially preoccupied in its final chapters with subjects like divination, the
ambit of angelic influence (which includes the mechanics of rapture), and
maleficia.[62] Thomas of Cantimpré was a Dominican theologian present in Paris
during William's stint as bishop. He had equally broad and diverse interests.
In the context of his support of the Beguine movement and as companion of
Jacques de Vitry (d. 1240), he is remembered for his lives of holy women.[63] His
interest in natural science led him to write *De natura rerum*, which includes
sections on the human body and soul. Lynn Thorndike classifies Thomas as
'one of the most credulous of our authors'[64] and this credulity is especially in
evidence in his later work, the short title for which is *De apibus* ('Concerning
bees'), inspired by Thomas's admiration for these intensely industrious in-
sects. Seemingly modelled on the *Dialogues* of Gregory the Great, *De apibus* is a
similar miscellany of marvels.

Neither William of Auvergne nor Thomas of Cantimpré had much immediate theological impact, generally, or on questions regarding rapture in particular. It is our third writer, the Dominican theologian John Nider (d. 1438), who

around the enraptured Clare and Francis, Elisabeth of Spalbeek's rapture during
communion, Catherine of Siena's physical immoveability in rapture, and the miraculous lightening resulting from John Ruysbroeck's contemplation (*De contemplatione*, art. 19, in *Opera* XLI, 281).

61 '. . .improvise aut subito incipiunt et causantur in apice affectivae aut vertice intellectivae potentiae, ita quod apex affectivae vertexque intellectivae immediate, re-
pente miro modo tanguntur, irradiantur, accenduntur ac perstringuntur, certum est
a spiritu malo non esse': Dionysius the Carthusian, *De discretione et examinatione
spirituum*, art. 6 (*Opera* VIII, 274).

62 See L. Thorndike, *A History of Magic and Experimental Science*, 8 vols. (New York,
1923–58), II, 338–71. For William of Auvergne's influence in the development of
ideas relating to witchcraft, see J. B. Russell, *Witchcraft in the Middle Ages* (Ithaca, NY,
1972), pp. 145 and 146–7.

63 On Jacques de Vitry's and Thomas of Cantimpré's work with the Beguines, see D.
Devlin, 'Feminine Lay Piety in the High Middle Ages: the Beguines,' in *Distant
Echoes*, ed. J. A. Nichols and L. T. Shank, in *Medieval Religious Women*, 3 vols. in 4
(Kalamazoo, MN, 1984–95), I, 183–96. Thomas wrote four hagiographical works: the
lives of Lutgard of Aywières, Christine the Marvellous, Margaret of Ypres and the
supplement to Jacques de Vitry's life of Marie of Oignies.

64 Thorndike, *History of Magic*, II, 380.

would eventually secure their prominence. As the title *Formicarium* ('An Ant Colony') suggests, and the author explicitly confirms, Nider modelled his work on *De apibus*.[65] Moreover, his appetite for the marvellous encouraged him to rely heavily on William of Auvergne. Well-stocked with anecdotes about contemporary saints, demoniacs and witches, the *Formicarium* constitutes the first major work on witchcraft and an essential source for the notorious inquisitional manual, *Malleus maleficarum*. In short, William of Auvergne, Thomas of Cantimpré and John Nider all share in an intense appetite for supernatural marvels. Undeterred by mainstream theology's trepidation over the body's unreliable evidentiary status, these three writers confidently concern themselves with the physical indications of discernment.

William has much to say on this score. He claims that a demoniac is recognizable by his hoarse voice, since demons usurp the vocal chords through violence. They are sufficiently ill-adapted to the human form that he compares their appropriation of the voice with a person attempting to walk with feet of wood. This is not the case with angelic possession since angels are the friends of humanity, thus applying themselves softly to the vocal chords. Angels speak quietly and gently through their human host; demons through madness and raging.[66] The devil never enters a body without inflicting damage: at the very least, he will leave a horrible expression on the face of the individual from whom he has departed.[67] Thomas of Cantimpré reports similar physical vestiges. A nun was found in mystical rapture in the corner of a church. Beneath the veil which she wore, her face was shining not unlike Moses following his conversation with God (Exodus 34. 29). After a vision of Christ, one mystic's eyes began to shine like a mirror.[68] Demonic possession, on the other hand, causes irreparable harm. The faces of erstwhile demoniacs become pallid and emaciated; their eyes rove. Once liberated by human or even divine intervention, there is still a danger of recurrence – similar to the relapses common to mental illness.[69] Frequently an individual will lose his or her voice in the presence of a demon since fear makes the natural humours dry up as would occur in the presence of a natural danger like a wolf.[70]

Likewise for John Nider, angelic possession is in sympathy with human and divine ends, while demonic possession is essentially a hostile takeover:

It is not to be understood, however, that whoever is possessed by God's holy angels loses the use of his reason, the mediation of which is neces-

65 John Nider, *Formicarium* i.1 (pp. 1–2).
66 William, *De universo*, pt 1, 3, c. 36 (I, 881); cf. pt 2, 3, c. 13 (p. 1042).
67 William, *De universo*, pt 2, 3, c. 18 (I, 1050).
68 Thomas of Cantimpré, *De apibus* ii.53.
69 *De apibus* ii.56.
70 *De apibus* ii.56. Cf. William of Auvergne's discussion of a demoniac's instinctive terror of demons. William likens this to a natural repulsion – again using his magnet image (*De universo*, pt 2, 3, c. 13; I, 1043).

sary for a meritorious act, but inhabiting the body and soul, angels know how to direct discreetly. And thus according to Blessed Dionysius they are the most clean and lucid mirrors that rather perfect [and] illuminate the human mind and press it towards divine service, while the demon works the contrary in infested bodies . . . . Experience indeed indicates that just as we see that those possessed by or familiar with demons – as are witches and their disciples – develop deformities in their eyes, face, and gestures [which are] horrible for other men to look at, which effects doubtless [arise] from the most wicked presence of the devil, so with those who serve God entirely in their endeavours and virtues we experience an especially chaste body, pleasing face, benign gestures, and they display the most humane expressions even when looked upon by sinners.[71]

Thus when a novice of thirteen was demonically possessed, the symptoms of his possession were raptures and other external indications of devotion, including a miraculous knowledge of Latin. After exorcism, however, 'the boy was again a rustic as before but with a difference: his face took on an unwonted and horrible aspect and such a doltish expression that it was unclear that he could attain the degree of literacy required for the priesthood.'[72] Although most of the somatic evidence had seemingly collaborated in a simulation of sanctity, the body's 'truth' only emerged retrospectively in the doltish expression – vestiges of the departing spirit.

[71] 'Non tamen intelligendum est, a sanctis Dei Angelis quemquam possideri cum priuatione vsus rationis, qua mediante necesse est meritorium actum perficere, sed sua inhabitatione corpus et animam regere norunt discrete. Et cum secundum Beatum Dionysium sint specula mundissima, et lucidissima, potius mentem humanum perficiunt, illuminant, et promouent ad diuinum famulatum; quorum contraria daemon obsessis infert corporibus. . . . Experentia quidem, quia sicut videmus a daemone possessos, vel eisdem familiares, vt maleficos, et eorum discipulos, in vultu deformitates oculorum, faciei, vel gestuum contrahere horribiles ad inspiciendum alijs hominibus, quae nulli dubium effectus sunt maliciosissimae praesentie demonis: ita eos qui toto nisu Deo et virtutibus inseruiunt potissime castos corpore experimur, gratam faciem, benignos gestus, et intuitus humanissimos etiam peccatorum aspectibus preferre' (*Formicarium* ii.9; pp. 155–6). Cf. Gerson's allegation that magicians develop terrible twitches from their excessive fasting (*De distinctione verarum revelationum a falsis*, in *Oeuvres complètes*, III, 44). Note that here Nider is arguing that demonic possession necessitates loss of reason. Later, however, he relates an anecdote about a certain virgin who was possessed, 'nevertheless she always had the good use of her reason' ('semper tamen vsum rationis bonum habuit'): *Formicarium* v.11; p. 414.
[72] Nider, *Formicarium* iii.1 (pp. 183–4).

5. Women and Rapture

Woman, perceived as overly embodied, was insufficiently defended against the constant slippage between spirit and matter.[73] As such, she was alternately considered the potential site of particular celestial privilege and of demonic infestations. The female body as superior receptor of various inspirations was based on its unequivocal inferiority – familiar terrain that need not detain us long.[74] The negative assessment of woman's physiology, though constant throughout the Middle Ages, received new purchase in the late twelfth century with the reintroduction of Aristotle and the ensuing rhetoric of woman as a deformed male.[75] Though the conviction of women's inferiority was used to explain and justify any and all instances of female subordination in the temporal world, it could also be applied to more abstruse issues. Hence one theory advanced by William of Auvergne, bearing on spiritual discernment, was that when good angels were required to borrow a body or simulate a corporeal form (having none of their own), they invariably chose to appear as men. A female-seeming angel was a clear indication that the spirit in question was a demonic succubus.[76]

Female deficiency was agreed to have resulted from an absence of heat: the female complexion was cold and wet, compared with the more perfect masculine configuration of hot and dry.[77] Thus in a world of 'ideal types', with no intervening sickness to create an imbalance, a female's disposition would tend towards the phlegmatic as phlegm was associated with the element water (cold and wet). But another, and more promising, possibility for the female disposition was melancholic, as the dominant humour, black bile, was associated with earth (cold and dry).[78]

---

[73] On some of the potentially empowering ways that this blurring of spiritual and material boundaries develops in woman's somatic spirituality, see Bynum, 'Female Body,' in *Fragmentation*, pp. 186–94, and *Holy Feast*, pp. 245–76; Lochrie, *Margery Kempe*, esp. chs. 1 and 2; E. A. Petroff, *Body and Soul: Essays on Medieval Women and Mysticism* (New York and Oxford, 1994), pp. 204–24; E. Robertson, 'Medieval Medical Views of Women and Female Spirituality in the *Ancrene Wisse* and Julian of Norwich's *Showings*', in Lomperis and Stanbury, *Feminist Approaches*, pp. 143–67.

[74] For an overview, see C. Thomasset, 'The Nature of Woman', trans. A. Goldhammer in *Silences of the Middle Ages*, ed. C. Klapisch-Zuber, in *History of Women in the West*, ed. G. Duby, 5 vols. (Cambridge, Mass., 1992–4), II, 43–69.

[75] See Aquinas, *Summa theologiae*, 1a, qu. 92, art. 1, ad 1 (*ST* XIII, 36–7); I. Maclean, *The Renaissance Notion of Woman: A Study in the Fortunes of Scholasticism and Medical Science in European Intellectual Life* (Cambridge, 1980), pp. 8–9.

[76] William, *De universo*, pt 2, 3, c. 24 (I, 1066 and 1068). For Aquinas on the assumed bodies of angels and demons see *De potentia*, qu. 6, art. 5, in *Opera omnia*, ed. Fretté, XIII, 205–7.

[77] Maclean, *Renaissance Notion of Woman*, pp. 30–2 and 36–7; Cadden, *Meanings of Sex Difference*, pp. 170–86.

[78] Cadden, *Meanings of Sex Difference*, p. 184.

It is not difficult to deduce some of the spiritual ramifications of these physical 'facts'. Women were generally understood to be more concupiscent than men – a flaw that was often linked to their deficiencies of complexion.[79] Albert the Great does grant that since women are less prone to nocturnal emissions than men, a woman could conceivably remain physically and mentally chaste throughout her life. Often, however, such preternatural chastity is the result of some defect in the complexion.[80] Elsewhere, Albert explicitly links female humidity with moral failings, arguing that women's 'mobile' complexion fosters mutability and a desire for novelty.[81]

Women's greater humidity, and thus greater softness, made them literally and figuratively more impressionable. The benefits of this flexibility were exploited in views of conception, which were grounded in the belief in an intensely psychosomatic dynamic. Vincent of Beauvais, for example, cites Jerome's discussion of how Jacob placed speckled rods before drinking ewes at breeding time, trusting that they would be mounted while drinking and give birth to speckled offspring (Genesis 30. 37): 'Nor is it marvellous that this is the nature of the conception of women – namely that they should conceive offspring similar to the image seen in the agitation of extreme desire'. He goes on to cite Augustine's provocative suggestion that love or desire vehemently affects the entire being, likening the potential impact of these emotions to the changes which occur in the body of a chameleon. Augustine associates the chameleon's mind/body symbiosis with the mother and foetus – the latter will naturally absorb the mother's desires (*libidines*) and fancy (*phantasia*).[82] In the richly physical milieu of late medieval spirituality, this doctrine's potential for naturalizing the supernatural is immense. Pietro Pompanazzi (d. 1525), for example, will eventually raise the possibility of stigmata being imposed on a fetus by the meditation of the mother.[83]

Given the requirements of conception and the theological disesteem for the imagination (which is, as we have seen, the most corporeal part of the soul), it

---

79 Aquinas, *Summa theologiae*, 2a 2ae, qu. 156, resp. ad 1 (*ST* XLIV, 20–1); Aquinas, *Commentum in lib. IV sententiarum*, 4 dist. 35 qu. 1, art. 4, resp. ad 5 (*Opera* XI, 176).

80 Albert the Great, *De animalibus* IX.i.1, in *Opera omnia*, ed. A Borgnet, 38 vols. (Paris, 1890–99), XI, 498.

81 Albert the Great, *Quaestiones de animalibus*, bk xv, qu. 11, as cited in H. R. Lemay, *Women's Secrets: A Translation of Pseudo-Albertus Magnus's 'De Secretis Mulierum' with Commentaries* (Albany, NY, 1992), introd., p. 48. For the pejorative implications of the term 'mobility' in a spiritual context, see John Cassian, *Collatio VII: De animae mobilitate et spiritualibus negritiis*, in *Conférences*, ed. and trans., E. Pichery, *Sources chrétiennes*, no. 42 (Paris, 1955), I, 242–77.

82 Vincent, *Speculum naturale* ii.36 (I, 1629); cf. ii.43 (I, 1634). See Augustine, *De trinitate* xi.2, trans. A. W. Haddan, in *St. Augustin: On the Holy Trinity, Doctrinal Treatises, Moral Treatises*, NPNCF, vol. 3 (Grand Rapids, MN, 1887), p. 147.

83 Pietro Pompanazzi, *De naturalium effectuum admirandorum causis, seu de incantationibus liber*, c. 5, in *Opera* (Basel, 1567), pp. 67–8 and 81–4; cf. c. 3, p. 32. See further G. Zarri, *Le sante vive: Cultura e religiosità femminile nella prima età moderna* (Turin, 1990), p. 59.

is no surprise that women were deemed more imaginative. Thus, in an effort to debunk certain superstitions spread by old women, William of Auvergne argues:

> You ought, however, to know about these things which you heard, that many of these visions and phantastic apparitions are produced in many people by the illness of melancholia. This is especially true with women, just as is the case with true visions and revelations. And the reason is, in addition to what the doctors say, the nature of female souls – namely from the fact that they are far easier of impression than male souls.[84]

A woman who was naturally melancholic, as for instance Hildegard of Bingen implies she was, would have a physical predisposition to mystical rapture.[85] If, on the other hand, she developed melancholia, she might be prone to non-mystical raptures – either the kind associated with lovesickness or related ecstasies arising from humoural imbalance. William of Auvergne confuses the matter still more when he cites Galen as a witness to the way that certain individuals, from the vehemence of their devotions and their ardent desire to enjoy the beauty of God, will develop melancholia. The symptoms are, moreover, especially deceptive in that, at least initially, some one afflicted with melancholia will experience great illuminations. All too soon, however, that light is dramatically shut off as the corrupted vapours reach the mind, provoking alienation and delirium.[86] Finally, there is that peculiarly female disease – the suffocation of the womb wherein the absence of sex permits corrupted humours to build up so that the womb actually rises and presses against the heart. This, in turn, induces a kind of abstraction. The pseudo-Albert the Great's *De secretis mulierum* relates how Galen cured one woman who, judging from her total immoveability which seemed to include a loss of pulse, was given up for dead.[87] One of the commentators on this text draws explicit parallels with suspect spirituality:

---

[84] 'Debes autem scire cum his, quae audivisti, quia multae de visionibus istis, et apparitionibus fantasticis, ex morbo melancholico in multis fiunt, sed in mulieribus maxime, sicut vides etiam de visionibus veris, ac revelationibus. Et causa in hoc est praeter eam, quam medici dicunt, natura muliebrium animarum, ob hoc videlicet, quia longe facilioris impressionis sunt qua[m] anime viriles' (*De universo*, pt 2, 3, c. 24; I, 1066). See also Gerson, *De passionibus animae*, c. 20 (*Oeuvres complètes*, IX, 19–20).

[85] On Hildegard's self-diagnosed melancholic disposition, see P. Dronke, *Women Writers of the Middle Ages: A Critical Study of Texts from Perpetua (d. 203) to Marguerite Porete (d. 1310)* (Cambridge, 1984), pp. 182–3. For a discussion of Hildegard's treatment of humours in her writings, see B. Newman, *Sister of Wisdom: St. Hildegard's Theology of the Feminine* (Berkeley and Los Angeles, 1987), pp. 126–33; and J. Cadden, 'It Takes all Kinds: Sexuality and Gender Differences in Hildegard of Bingen's "Book of Compound Medicine" ', *Traditio* 40 (1984), 149–74.

[86] William, *De universo*, c. 20 and 21 (I, 1054 and 1058. Note that chs. 20 and 21 both appear as c. 20 in this edition).

[87] *Women's Secrets*, c. 11; trans. Lemay, p. 132.

Women who suffer this illness lie down as if they were dead. Old women who have recovered from it say that it was caused by an ecstasy during which they were snatched out of their bodies and borne to heaven or to hell, but this is ridiculous. The illness happens from natural causes, however they think that they have been snatched out of their bodies because vapors rise to the brain. If these vapors are very thick and cloudy, it appears to them that they are in hell and they see black demons; if the vapors are light, it seems to them that they are in heaven and that they see God and his angels shining brightly.[88]

Even Thomas of Cantimpré, no mean sceptic about the supernatural origin of trances or the efficacy of female mysticism, states that 'this disease especially occurs with widows and whenever this occurs they fall just as with heart disease'.[89]

Of course woman's very physical inferiority, inseparable from a derivative moral inferiority, also identified her as a potential celestial favourite. Thomas Aquinas argued that women's very defects made them more humble and devout, corresponding with 'the last shall be first' (Matthew 19. 30) ethos of the high Middle Ages that has recently been emphasized by André Vauchez and others.[90] The body could also facilitate rapture in a more direct way through its impingement on the soul. According to Gerson's analysis of the various powers of the soul, which were perceived as determining essential aspects of emotional responses, women were dominated by the concupiscible power. Thus women were reckoned as soft-hearted and easily drawn into contemplation through a consideration of Christ's passion.[91] Finally, if rapture actually resulted from physical frailty, the female body was clearly more susceptible. Moreover, female weakness and incumbent passivity played an

---

[88] Commentator B in *Women's Secrets*, p. 134.

[89] 'Hec maxime mulieribus viduis accidere solet passio; de hac quandoque cadunt sicut de cardiaca passione' (*Liber de natura rerum*, i.60; I, 66).

[90] Aquinas, *Summa theologiae*, 2a 2ae, qu. 82, art. 3, ad 2 (*ST* XXXIX, 42–3). See A. Vauchez, *Les laïcs au moyen âge: pratiques et expériences religieuses* (Paris, 1987), p. 254. For the humility topos as an instrument of empowerment in Hildegard's writings, see Newman, *Sister of Wisdom*, pp. 2–4 and 34–41. See also Bynum's argument that woman and her weakness in God's eyes began to be perceived as a liminal condition to which spiritually-ambitious men aspired (' ". . . And Woman his Humanity": Female Imagery in the Religious Writing of the Later Middle Ages', in *Fragmentation*, pp. 151–79).

[91] Gerson, *De mystica theologia practica*, c. 2 (*Oeuvres complètes*, VIII, 22–3). The dominance of the concupiscible power was not exclusive to women: Gerson designates Gregory the Great and Bernard of Clairvaux as concupiscible, Jerome as irascible, and Augustine and Thomas Aquinas as rational. Aquinas only speaks of two powers of the soul (the irascibile and concupiscible) – divisions of the sense appetite, which are controlled by reason (Thomas Aquinas, *Summa theologiae*, 1a, qu. 81, art. 2; *ST* XI, 206–11). Gerson's division is closer to Thomas of Cantimpré's (see *Liber de natura rerum* ii.9; I, 89).

essential part not only in the the the construction of gender roles but in the actual gendering of rapture. For instance, Isidore of Seville had argued:

The bodies of each [man and woman] are distinguished by strength and weakness. Therefore the greater strength of the man and the lesser strength of the woman is in order that she should submit to the man. Otherwise, with women resisting, libido would force men to seize another thing or to fall upon another sex.[92]

In other words, sexual violence was implicit in the medieval construction of gender. Rapture not only partook of this language of sexual violence, but theorists such as Aquinas insisted on its presence. Thus, rapture presupposes a heterosexual dynamic between a swooning female mystic and an over-powering male deity. The irregularity of the union is eventually ratified in mystical discourse by the more consensual mystical marriage, widespread amongst female mystics.[93]

These are some of the implicit premises behind the surge in the number of female saints in the high Middle Ages.[94] Moreover, the hagiography of the high Middle Ages staked out mysticism as a predominantly female domain, thus identifying the female body as a privileged zone of receptivity to divine infusions. We can see this pattern emerging in the twelfth century with the the supernatural experiences of Hildegard of Bingen (d. 1179), a visionary who experienced waking visions, and in the actual raptures of her younger con-temporary, Elisabeth of Schönau (d. 1164).[95] The identification of women and

---

[92] 'Utrique enim fortitudine et imbecillitate corporum separantur. Sed ideo virtus maxima viri, mulieris minor, ut patiens viro esset, scilicet, ne feminis repugnan-tibus, libido cogeret viros aliud appetere, aut in alium sexum proruere' (*Etymologiae* XI.ii.19; *PL* 82, 417). Note that Vincent of Beauvais's appropriation of this statement without even so much as a citation demonstrates the extent to which it was part of the intellectual infrastructure (*Speculum naturale* xxxi.114; I, 2384).

[93] See P. Adnès, 'Mariage spirituel', in *DSP* X, 387–408, esp. the section 'Les épousailles mystiques de hagiographie' (394–6), and Bynum, *Holy Feast*, pp. 246–50. See K. Gravdal's *Ravishing Maidens: Writing Rape in Medieval French Literature and Law* (Philadelphia, 1991), for an excellent discussion of the ambiguities implicit in terms denoting rape. Barbara Newman observes that Gérard of Liège actually describes God as the best rapist – thus pushing this nexus of associations to the limits; see *Virile Woman*, p. 286, note 20.

[94] See D. Weinstein and R. M. Bell, *Saints and Society: The Two Worlds of Western Christendom, 1000–1700* (Chicago and London, 1982), pp. 220–1; A. Vauchez, *La sainteté en occident aux derniers siècles du moyen âge d'après les procès de canonisation et les documents hagiographiques*, Bibliothèque des Écoles Françaises d'Athènes et de Rome 241 (Rome, 1981), pp. 316–18.

[95] On Hildegard's reception of visions, see Dronke's translation of her letter to Guibert of Gembloux in *Women Writers of the Middle Ages*, pp. 168–9. Also see K. Kerby-Ful-ton and D. Elliott, 'Self-Image and the Visionary Role in two Letters from the Correspondence of Elizabeth of Schönau and Hildegard of Bingen', *Vox Benedictina* 2 (1985), 204–23 (pp. 206–7).

rapture was well established by the early thirteenth century. Hence, in the famous prologue to the life of Marie of Oignies, the formative work in the rise of the female mysticism, the theologian Jacques de Vitry describes what sounds like colonies of women who are enraptured and literally wasting away in divine love as a result of bodily illness as well as self-mortifications.[96] Thomas of Cantimpré describes how the entire community of nuns looked on as Lutgard of Aywières (d. 1246) was 'elevated two cubits from the earth into the air'.[97] His life of the aptly named Christine the Marvellous (d. 1224) transgresses against the laws of physicality still further. It begins with her first death, from which she was resuscitated in the midst of her funeral mass only to fly to the ceiling and perch on the rafters.[98] After her return from the grave, she was never quite the same.[99] When she prayed 'and the divine grace of contemplation descended upon her, all her limbs were gathered together into a ball as if they were hot wax' and she curled up like a hedgehog; when in rapture Christine would 'roll and whirl like a hoop,' while a 'wonderous harmony sounded between her throat and breast.'[100]

In the thirteenth century and the first half of the fourteenth, rapture was frequently so effective a shorthand for denoting sanctity that it was essentially freestanding, requiring little, if any, theological commentary regarding its meaning or even its ultimate source. What was instead provided, as the above examples would suggest, were physical details that made the experience both more tangible and more individual. Thus the enrapt Vanna of Orvieto (d. 1306), burning with divine love, would sweat so profusely that she could not wear clothes; she was so still and deathlike that flies settled on her half-open eyes, but she did not blink. Sometimes she would be elevated many cubits above the ground.[101] Though she ate little, she was nevertheless fleshy – fed

96 Jacques de Vitry, *AA SS* (Paris and Rome, 1867), June, V, 548–9.
97 Thomas of Cantimpré, *AA SS*, June, IV, 192–3; trans. M. H. King, *The Life of Lutgard of Aywières* (Saskatoon, 1987), p. 12.
98 Thomas of Cantimpré, *AA SS*, July, V, 651.
99 Thomas narrates how after she died, angels led her soul to purgatory – where she witnessed individuals in torment, and then visited heaven. When given the option of remaining in heaven, she chose to return to the earth to do penance for the souls she had seen there (*AA SS*, July, V, 651–2). On visionary women as intercessors for the dead, see B. Newman, 'On the Threshold of the Dead: Purgatory, Hell, and Religious Women', in Newman, *Virile Woman*, pp. 108–36. For Thomas's explanation regarding how a likeness of souls can be tortured, see note 47 above.
100 *AA SS*, July, V, 653 and 656; trans. M. King, *The Life of Christina of Saint-Trond* (Saskatoon, 1986), pp. 10 and 21. See W. Simon's discussion of the body language of these women in 'Reading a Saint's Body: Rapture and Bodily Movement in the *Vitae* of Thirteenth-Century Beguines', in *Framing Medieval Bodies*, pp. 10–23; cf. J. Le Goff, 'Gestures in Purgatory', in *The Medieval Imagination*, trans. A. Goldhammer (Chicago and London, 1988), pp. 86–92.
101 Giacomo Scalza, OP, *Leggenda latina della B. Giovanna detta Vanna d'Orieto del Terz' Ordine di S. Domenico*, c. 5, ed. and trans. V. Marreddu (Orvieto, 1853), pp. 13–18.

by celestial honey. Once when she descended from the mountain of contemplation, her face was fiery red.[102]

These mystics were, of course, submitted to the taunts of the occasional sceptic, but the doubts they raised were frequently tautologically resolved by recourse to rapture. For instance, though Clare of Rimini (d. 1326) is denounced from the pulpit as a Patarene possessed of unclean spirits, such besmirchments are seemingly offset by accounts of ecstatic rapture.[103] During rapture, Margaret of Cortona (d. 1297) was permitted to experience the pain of Christ's passion. She began by wailing and gnashing her teeth as if she was being eaten by worms, and eventually lost colour, pulse and the power of her senses. This performance, which occurred in the church of St Francis, drew everyone in town.[104] But the local community of Franciscans were suspicious of the source of her inspiration. They took advantage of a rapture brought on by the reception of communion to shake and throw her body around – presumably testing the degree of alienation from her senses.[105] Similarly, a certain Father Albrandinus was disappointed and suspected fraud when the body of Christine of Stommeln (d. 1312) was insufficiently rigid in the early stages of her rapture. But he was chastened when he returned later and found her body hard, and totally contrite when she emerged from the rapture and he saw the stigmatic image of the cross on her palms. He did figurative penance for his earlier disbelief since his hand, holding hers, was trapped against the wall when she suddenly returned to her rapture.[106] Physical proofs, often cruel ones, were freely practised on a given saint's immobile body. The immobile Douceline was jabbed with nails, chisels, and even had molten lead poured over her feet.[107] Such tests need not arise from any particular doubts but were often engineered to exploit the spectacle value inherent in the enrapt female form.[108]

---

[102] Scalza, *Leggenda*, c. 6 (pp. 22–3).
[103] The life was written *c*.1350 – probably by a nun in Clare's order – and is included in her process in the Vatican Archives (Archivo Segreto Vaticano, Riti, Proc. 88). For the denunciation of Clare, see fols. 144r–5r; for discussions of her raptures, see fols. 141r–v, 147v–9r, 149v–50r.
[104] *AA SS*, February, III, 320. The *vita* is by her confessor Giunta Bevegnati.
[105] *AA SS*, February, III, 320.
[106] *AA SS*, June, V, 248. Christine's life was written by the theologian, Peter of Dacia. For a discussion of the peculiarities of Peter's account and a detailed analysis of their relationship, see A. M. Kleinberg, *Prophets in their Own Country: Living Saints and the Making of Sainthood in the Later Middle Ages* (Chicago and London, 1992), pp. 71–98.
[107] Kleinberg, *Prophets*, pp. 121–5; D. E. Bornstein, 'Violenza al corpo di una santa: fra agiografia e pornografia. A proposito di Douceline di Digne', *Quaderni medievali* 39 (1995), 31–46.
[108] See my discussion of John Matteotti's gratuitous proofs of Frances of Rome in ' "Dominae or Dominatae"? Female Mysticism and the Trauma of Textuality', forthcoming in *Women and Marriage in the Middle Ages: A Festschrift for Michael Sheehan*, ed. J. Rosenthal and C. Rousseau (Kalamazoo, MN).

And yet, as the emergence of the genre of spiritual discernment would suggest, by the end of the fourteenth century, suspicion surrounding rapture could no longer be resolved by reference to more rapture. The case of Bridget of Sweden, who became something of a rallying point for resistance to female mysticism, amply demonstrates hagiographers' need for a more theorized defense. As her process of canonization indicates, Bridget encountered a high degree of scepticism in her lifetime of a kind that anticipated Jean Gerson's critique; a monk in the monastery of Alvastra told her that she had brain damage and was thus given to phantasms, while a Swedish noble assured her that her 'dreams' would disappear if only she ate and drank more.[109]

The Briggitine *corpus* is seemingly framed with such considerations in mind. According to her revelations and *vita*, Bridget twice fled from her inaugural vision of Christ brought on by a rapture – fearing demonic illusion. After each occurence she confessed and took communion. When she eventually stopped running and listened, Christ told her to go and announce her role as 'sponsa mea et canale meum' ('my bride and my channel') to her confessor, the theologian Master Matthias, 'who had experience in discerning the two types of spirit'.[110] Matthias's prologue to the first book of revelations, moreover, tackles the question of spiritual discernment directly, arguing against those who wanted to disregard Bridget's visions as resulting from the devil or from the spirit of vain glory.[111] He also identifies the nature of the vision she experiences in the course of her raptures as spiritual, urging that this means of viewing Christ was more stupendous than if he had revealed himself in the flesh.[112] The prologue concludes with six proofs intended to vindicate Bridget's inspiration (two of which turn on the fact that a formula that she received in one of her visions of Christ was effective in casting out demons).[113]

---

[109] *Acta et processus canonizacionis beate Birgitte*, ed. I. Collijn, Samlingar utgivna av Svenska Fornskriftsällskapet, ser. 2, Latinska Skrifter, vol. 1 (Uppsala, 1924–34), art. 16 and 19, pp. 488 and 493. On Bridget's critics, see E. Colledge, '*Epistola solitarii ad reges*: Alphonse of Pecha as Organizer of Birgittine and Urbanist Propaganda', MS 18 (1956), 19–49; J. A. Schmidtke, ' "Saving" by Faint Praise: St. Birgitta of Sweden, Adam Easton and Medieval Antifeminism', *American Benedictine Review* 33 (1982), 149–61.

[110] 'The Life of Blessed Birgitta', c. 26, trans. A. R. Kezel, *Birgitta of Sweden: Life and Selected Revelations* (New York, 1990), pp. 77–9. This *vita* was written by two of her confessors – a Cistercian prior and a theologian, both named Peter Olaf. For an abbreviated relation of this incident, see Bridget of Sweden, *Revelaciones extravagantes*, c. 47, ed. L. Hollman, Samlingar utgivna av Svenska Fornskriftsällskapet, ser. 2, Latinska Skrifter, vol. 5 (Uppsala, 1956), pp. 162–3. Note that *canalis* ('channel') could also refer to the female cervix (Lewis and Short, p. 276).

[111] Bridget of Sweden, *Revelaciones, Bk I*, ed. C.-G. Undhagen, Samlingar utgivna av Svenska Fornskriftsällskapet, ser. 2, Latinska Skrifter, vol. 7.1 (Uppsala, 1978), Matthias's prologue, pp. 231–4.

[112] *Revelaciones, Bk I*, ed. Undhagen, pp. 234–5.

[113] *Revelaciones, Bk I*, ed. Undhagen, p. 239.

Similarly, a number of the revelations-proper explicitly turn on the question of spiritual discernment.[114] Bridget also practises discernment on a potential competitor: in one vision, Christ marks his disapproval of ecstatic spectacle by announcing that a certain woman who publicly makes outlandish and 'marvellous gestures' during prayer was sorely tempted by grievous sin.[115]

Finally, the preface for the entire set of revelations is the *Epistola solitarii ad reges* by Alphonse of Jaén (d. 1388) – an apology for Bridget's visions which essentially took the form of a treatise on discernment. Beginning with general principles of reception, Alphonse urges the need for careful distinctions. Do the visions occur while the individual is awake or asleep? Where does the vision fit in terms of the triune Augustinian schemata? Does the recipient of a rapture feel the sweetness of divine love? Does he or she hear someone expounding divine mysteries and, if so, in what shape does that supernatural commentator appear?[116] Alphonse then proceeds to apply these criteria to Bridget's experience. We thus learn that he frequently saw Bridget prostrated in prayer as if dead, insensible to the outside world. Her bodily powers would fail 'but her heart was inflamed and exulted in the ardour of charity'. The exultation of the heart seemed to carry over into waking moments as she felt it stirring, as if it were a child rolling around. Fearing demonic illusion, she called her confessors to testify, who likewise felt this movement in amazement. Her doubts were eventually clarified in rapture when Christ and Mary explained these stirrings as the divine workings of the Holy Spirit. Sometimes the shapes and forms that she witnessed in the course of her raptures remained unintelligible, but usually they were glossed by Christ, Mary, or an attendant angel.[117] Eventually, Bridget herself became an adept in the art of discernment, having herself been instructed by the Virgin Mary in seven differences between divine and diabolical visions.[118] Alphonse concludes with a series of seven signs that proved the divine inspiration of her visions: the second is that during a vision the soul feels itself inebriated by the fire of divine love which the devil, excluded from entering souls, cannot simulate. The sixth concerns her demise. Bridget, as a sign of celestial favour, was warned of her death – a matter especially open to demonic deception since the devil was anxious to trick people out of the last rites. On her deathbed itself,

---

[114] In his defense of Bridget, Alphonse of Jaén lists the following visions as bearing on discernment: 1.4; 1.54; 3.10; 4.23; 4.90; 6.52; 6.68 (*Epistola solitarii ad reges*, c. 2, in *Alfonso of Jaén: His Life and Works with Critical Editions of the 'Epistola solitarii', the 'Informaciones' and the 'Epistola servi Christi'*, ed. A. Jönsson, Studia Graeca et Latina Lundensia 1 (Lund, 1989), p. 126).

[115] Bridget of Sweden, *Revelaciones*, Bk VI, c. 122, ed. B. Bergh, Samlingar utgivna av Svenska Fornskriftsällskapet, ser. 2, Latinska Skrifter, vol. 7.6 (Uppsala, 1991), p. 280.

[116] Alphonse of Jaén, *Epistola solitarii*, c. 2; pp. 124–5.

[117] *Epistola solitarii*, c. 4; pp. 137–8.

[118] *Epistola solitarii*, c. 6; pp. 152–3.

moreover, she was permitted to see Christ with her corporeal eyes – a joy that presumably anticipates the bliss enjoyed by the blessed souls after the resurrection of the body.[119]

The care taken by Bridget's theological team set a standard for subsequent treatment of mystical phenomena. Thus, the theologian John of Marienwerder, confessor and hagiographer of Dorothea of Montau (d. 1394), incorporated a treatise in miniature into her *vita*, which offered twenty-four proofs of her divine inspiration.[120] This trend to vindicate mystical phenomena will accelerate. By the time we get to the life of Osanna of Mantua (d. 1505) – attributed to her confessor, the Dominican theologian Francis Silvestris who had a reputation for astuteness – we find that any discussion of rapture is prefaced and protected by the most substantial rearguard action:

> The most erudite men relate that a person can be deprived of the use of the senses by three causes: either by a sickness of the body preventing the vital spirits flowing to the organs; or by the the work of the demon filling the mind with phantastic illusions; or by a certain divine power, raising the soul to those things which are above human understanding. Corporeal illness certainly makes people perceive either nothing at all or certain things that are confused and disordered; the demon places images into our spirits that are fixed so that he may induce a certain appearance of things [which is] similar to what is [in fact] laid out [in the external world] for the senses. However, he is not able to presage divine things to a person. But when immortal God gives a person over to a rapture of this kind, the mind is able to be borne off to such a degree that it contemplates not some sort of human attribute, [present] in excess, but God himself.[121]

---

[119] *Leggenda Epistola solitarii*, c. 6; pp. 163–4. Cf. the experience of Vanna of Orvieto, who was warned by Christ of her approaching death. She alarmed her superior by saying 'Mater mortua sum' and, then, 'Mater, mortua sum omnino'. She took sick that day and died three days later (Scalza, *Leggenda*, c. 10; pp. 36–7). Regarding the devil's lies about the time of death, see Caesarius of Heisterbach, *Dialogue on Miracles*, iii.15 (I, 143–4); and Thomas of Cantimpré, *De apibus* ii.56. On the perfection incumbent on the reunification of body and soul and the beatific vision, see Bynum, *Resurrection*, pp. 267–8 and 283–9.

[120] John of Marienwerder, *Vita Dorotheae Montoviensis* i.5–6, ed. H. Westpfahl (Cologne and Graz, 1964), pp. 39–49.

[121] 'Tradunt eruditissimi viri, tribus ex causis posse hominem sensuum usu destitui: aut enim corporis morbo, vitales spiritus ne decurrant ad organa prohibente; aut opera [*perhaps a mistake for* opere] daemonis, phantasticis mentem illusionibus occupantis; aut divina quadam virtute, animum ad ea quae supra humanam intelligentiam sunt, extollente. Efficit sane corporalis morbus, ut aut nihil omnino; aut confusa quaedam et inordinata percipiant: daemon sic defixas in spiritibus imagines locat, ut quamdam profecto similem sensibus rerum apparentiam inducat, divina tamen homini praemonstrare non potest: at immortali Deo, hujuscemodi raptu hominem donante, usqueadeo mens efferri potest, ut Deum ipsum, nedum quamdam humanam superantia facultatem, inspectet' (*AA SS*, June, IV, p. 570).

Francis then proceeds to establish that Osanna's rapture could not be mistaken for illness on the basis of her immoveablity and the impossibility of disturbing her. He eliminates the suspicion of demonic rapture, arguing that the 'divine secrets were not expressed by phantastic images, but grasped with intellectual vision alone'.[122] And it is only after a further disquisition on the various types of vision that he proceeds to an actual discussion of her raptures.

The progressive caution of hagiographers reflects a dangerous collapse in the representation of the familiar polarities of female spirituality. As the famous example of Joan of Arc would suggest and as a number of scholars have recently argued, women as vessels of devotion and vessels of depravity were fast becoming virtually indistinguishable.[123] My contribution to this discussion will be to emphasize how the physicality of female spirituality not only faciliated but even required an eventual slippage into the diabolical.

Nowhere is the confusion greater than in Nider's *Formicarium* in which women are portrayed as subjects and objects of genuine and bogus spiritual devotion. Nider's contribution was not so much to generate any new theory about women's spiritual capacity as to provide a synthesis of different discourses. We have seen that this was already occurring in hagiography, wherein the hagiographer attempted to contain criticism by addressing it more fully in the *vita* itself – ultimately creating a hybrid genre of saint's life and treatise on spiritual discernment. Nider accelerates this trend, creating a discursive tower of Babel which places saints, pseudo-saints, heretics and witches in close proximity to one another. Moreover, this is achieved in an eminently accessible frame. Nider decants the subject-matter of William of Auvergne and Thomas of Cantimpré into the popular dialogue format – one that is well-suited to Nider's ambivalence toward women since the dull-witted interlocutor (appropriately named *Piger*) is permitted to attack women,

---

122 '. . . divinaque secreta non phantasticis expressa imaginibus, verum solo intellectus obtutu deprehensa. . .' (*AA SS*, June, IV, p. 570). For a fascinating discussion of the political uses to which which Osanna, and other fifteenth-century female saints, were put by secular princes in Italy, see Zarri, *Le sante vive*, pp. 51–85.

123 See M. Craveti, *Sante e streghe: Biografie e documenti dal XIV al XVII secolo* (Milan, 1980), introduction, pp. 7–62; P. Dinzelbacher, 'Sante o streghe. Alcuni casi de tardo medioevo', in *Finzione e santità tra medioevo ed età moderna*, ed. G. Zarri (Turin, 1991), pp. 52–7 and R. Kieckhefer, 'The Holy and the Unholy: Sainthood, Witchcraft and Magic', *JMRS* 24 (1994), 355–85. The first two authors perceive witchcraft and sanctity as two sides of the same coin. Kieckhefer, on the other hand, cautions against a reading based on the simple principle of inversion, arguing that 'if they mirrored each other, it was in nonsystematic ways' (p. 372). For studies of the difficulties ensuing from conflicting classifications of heretics and saints, see Barbara Newman's treatment of the Guglielmites of Milan (*Virile Woman*, pp. 182–223), Robert Lerner's discussion of Marguerite Porete ('*Heresy*' of the '*Free Spirit*', pp. 200–8), and Robert Brentano's treatment of the antinomian Paolo 'de Carcere' in his *A New World in a Small Place: Church and Religion in the Diocese of Rieti, 1188–1378* (Berkeley and Los Angeles, 1994), pp. 233–74.

while *Theologus* defends them.[124] More important still, Nider provides a key to his many exemplary women that lends a coherence to his view of female spirituality: the frailty of the female body.

This was innovative in a limited but important way. For – despite the advanced somatism of hagiography with its detailed descriptions of female stigmata, levitations or physical debilitations as evidence of sanctity – hagiographers had refrained from identifying these bodily changes with a quasi-medicalized discourse addressing female physiology. To do so would be to put the extraordinary physical changes of the female saint on an explicit continuum with the ordinary aptitudes of the female body. Prior to Nider, this circle that threatened to unite sanctity and depravity still remained open. Nider closed it. His arguments are familiar. Women are mobile in spirit (*mobiles animo*) and thus have more visions than men – who have stronger and more stable minds.[125] Drawing on William of Auvergne, he explains this mobility in terms of the tenderness of the female complexion and ultimately of the female mind.[126] This predisposition, in addition to woman's excessive moistness, makes her more prone to sexual incontinence. Nider offsets this undesirable trait with a citation of Albert the Great who comments on how certain women can remain chaste until old age, while exceptional female ascetics actually cease to menstruate not out of sickness of the body but from purity of the soul.[127] But this physiological optimism is undercut by a later reference to women who pretend to choose chastity just so that they will not need to submit to the rule of a husband, meanwhile corrupting themselves through masturbation.[128]

Despite the potential for negative reverberations, Nider supports the view that women are capable of superior levels of devotion. Moreover, this devotion is also more inclined to seek an external outlet. For instance, the dialogue's naïve interlocutor is very concerned about women who leap around and make yelps of exultation in church: what causes that? Can it be a truly spiritual experience? *Theologus* reassures as follows:

> The fire of devotion is more mobile in the heart of the weaker vessel and more apt for producing shouts: so that it can happen that there would be

---

[124] Nider explicitly acknowledges his indebtedness to these two authors for stories about incubuses and succubuses (*Formicarium* v.9; p. 393). For a sampling of the many antifeminist diatribes, see iv.1 (pp. 260–3), iii.4 (pp. 203–5), and v.8 (pp. 390–1).

[125] *Formicarium* ii.1; p. 97. Nider cites II Timothy 3 in support.

[126] Nider, *Formicarium* ii.1 and v.10 (pp. 47 and 406).

[127] *Formicarium* iv.1; pp. 263–5, cf. p. 262. Seemingly miraculous instances of fasting are explained in terms of complexion – thus certain women are likened to frigid men, frogs, serpents and hibernating bears (i.9; p. 66). See the amusing discussion of why, though women are the weaker vessel, men need to be warned against them more frequently than vice-versa (iii.4; pp. 205–6). The short answer is that men, who are close to God in nature, are more easily polluted. Moreover, since their complexions are hotter, they are more quickly inflamed.

[128] *Formicarium* v.10; p. 398.

a great fervour of compunction in the heart of the fragile sex, while there would be little in the virile spirit. Just as we see, in comparison, that the female feeling – when it is impassioned by some emotion – contains itself less within the cloister of the heart than does male [feeling].[129]

On the other hand, woman's weak moral nature causes her to be more susceptible to vices like vain glory. Hence, *Theologus* also notes that a nun once confessed to him that, after reading about the abstraction of saints, she began alternately leaping in jubilation in church, and collapsing in feigned rapture. He also tells of another female penitent who confessed to shouting out in church, prompted by vain glory.[130]
Moreover, because of women's deficient reason, they are constantly exploited by predatory men by means of the slippage between spiritual and carnal love. Thus in the province of Swabia in north eastern Germany, antinomian heretics are said to convince both virgins and widows that the 'highest contemplation and the most excellent rapture' can be achieved through sexual intercourse.[131] Similarly, when gullible women are debauched by men sometimes identified as Beghards or Lollards, during the sex act 'they are said to have rare revelations by the work of the devil, and many such women who are allured [by these revelations] cling to them obstinately as though to illuminations [which had come] from a good spirit.'[132]
But women also figure as deceivers – whether consciously or unconsciously. One incident in particular is worth recounting in depth as it reveals how these tensions could be played out in female spirituality in the later Middle Ages.[133] A certain Sister Magdalena, a Clarissan nun of Freiburg in the diocese of Constance, was prone to lengthy raptures. On one memorable occasion, she disappeared for three days, during which time it was alleged

---

[129] '. . . deuotionis ignis in corde infirmioris vasculi mobilior, et ad prodeundum in clamores aptior: vnde euenire potest, vt fortassis magnus compunctionis feruor foret in corde sexus fragilis, qui modicus esset in animo virili. Sicut videmus in simili, quod affectus femineus minus quam masculinus intra claustrum cordis se continet cum aliqua passionatur affectione' (*Formicarium* iii.1; p. 187).
[130] *Formicarium* iii.1; pp. 185–6.
[131] '. . . supremam contemplationem, et raptum excellentissimum' (*Formicarium* iii.5; pp. 214–15).
[132] '. . . dicuntur opere daemonis quasdam reuelationes raras habere, quibus illecti tales, velut boni spiritus illuminationibus multae impersuasibiliter adherent' (Nider, *Formicarium* iii.5, pp. 221–3; quoted extract is on p. 223).
[133] For instances of feigned sanctity, see the anthology edited by G. Zarri, *Finzione e santità*, esp. her introductory essay ' "Vera" santita, "simulata" santita: ipotesi e riscontri', pp. 5–36. Also see J. Brown's study of the nun Benedetta Carlini in *Immodest Acts: The Life of a Lesbian Nun in Renaissance Florence* (New York and Oxford, 1986). For a discussion concerning the ambivalence toward rapture in the sixteenth century, see A. Weber, 'Between Ecstasy and Exorcism: Religious Negotiation in Sixteenth-Century Spain', *JMRS* 23 (1993), 221–34; M. E. Perry, *Gender and Disorder in Early Modern Spain* (Princeton, NJ, 1990), pp. 82–3 and 109–17.

that she had been raptured not only in soul, but also in body. Nider adds that this was either the literal truth or she hid herself for the stipulated period, since she was not discovered during the ensuing search. In any event, she was eventually returned with a celestial page detailing how the nuns should re-form themselves to avert divine vengeance. The nuns gave up their illicit personal affects, vengeance was averted, and her reputation for prophecy spread throughout the country. And then on Christmas she received a new and startling message which she took pains to broadcast: on a certain date (which Magdalena specified) around the feast of the Epiphany, she would die corporeally and migrate from the world. The devoted nuns believed her and followed her directions for the funeral to the letter. A newly painted sarcopha-gus was prepared, a great many candles were ordered and the news of the event flew not only around Constance, but through several adjacent dioceses. Some believed, others doubted, but a huge multitude assembled of every class, both clergy and laity. Nider, whose monastery in Basel was only a day's journey from Freiburg, thought the occasion potentially important enough to send the monastery's proctor to testify to the events. The men of the city council, moreover, prudently sent suitable witnesses and their own physician:

> Therefore with all the sisters standing around in the choir that morning and the said men, and many other mature ecclesiastics and regulars, and with the people outside the choir in [the main body of] the church, awaiting a great marvel, Sister Magdalena came and inclined her head on the breast of a certain sister, immediately showed that she was rapt in ecstasy whether truly or feigned, and thus lay for sometime sufficiently immobile. And when certain women doubted whether she was dead or alive, the doctor publicly touching her pulse announced that life was present. Nevertheless she sent forth a certain voice, no longer virginal as earlier, but somewhat coarse saying: To the sarcophagus.[134]

After a seemly period of repose, Magdalena got up from her sarcophagus and asked for food. A few believed that she had died, but the majority remained unconvinced. While some of the sceptics were prepared to laugh at their own credulity, most were angry and created a disturbance in the monastery.

The hoarse (demonic?) voice that spoke through the raptured Magdalena and the fact that Nider implied that Magdalena retained her pulse throughout

---

[134] 'Astantibus igitur sororibus omnibus mane in choro, et dictis viris, et multis alijs maturis ecclesiasticis et regularibus, plebeis vero extra in ecclesia tantum prodigium expectantibus, venit soror Magdalena, caput suum in gremium cuius-dam sororis inclinauit, extemplo satis se raptam in extasi vere vel ficte ostendit, et ita satis immobilis aliquandiu iacuit. Cumque quaedam ambigerent an mortua foret, vel viua, medicus publice pulsum eius tangens vitam adesse dixit. Tandem vocem quandam nullatenus, vt antea virgineam, sed grossam satis, emisit dicens. Ad sarcophagum' (Nider, *Formicarium* iii.8; p. 231).

her rapture would suggest that John perceived this as an example of 'phantastica luminaria' – phantasy illuminations, something he describes as more dangerous than demonic possession.[135] That Magdalena was still alive eight years after the event further undermines her credibility, at least according to Nider.[136] I might add that her revivification need not undermine the miracle if she was attempting the kind of death and resuscitation experienced by Christine the Marvellous – though it seems that she may have adopted this as a strategy mid-way in her trance. Nider concludes his account by alluding to a parallel predicted death, this time by a Beguine in Poland, which created a similar disturbance.[137]

Despite his apparent incredulity, *Theologus* still resists absolutely satisfying his interlocutor's query as to whether Magdalena was motivated by God, a demon, nature, or guile. Instead, he responds that she had been well brought up by her mother, an exceptionally devout woman, and it was doubtless from her mother that she received the natural knack of abstracting herself from her body, since her mother also had this ability.[138] He adds that, unlike Magdalena, however, the mother was never spiritually deceived – except possibly late in life when she was plagued by the illusion that she should leave her monastery and found a new hospital.

Nider's reluctance to pronounce absolutely on the source of Magdalena's inspiration is perhaps the most effective strategy of all in undermining female spirituality. For this ostensibly detached narrator reveals his implicit scepticism with his gentle dig at her mother's obsession about founding a hospital. *Formicarium* is, in fact, replete with unarticulated judgements. Magdalena's potentially inherited traits brings to mind Pomponazzi's speculations about a meditating mother imposing the stigmata on an unborn child. Heredity in a body inherently predisposed to rapture by gender doubles the extent of her liability.

The physiological bases of woman's mercurial spiritual potential – epitomized by saintly mother and pseudo-saint daughter – were always present in Christian tradition. Yet they do, as we have suggested, only manage to coalesce and achieve full visibility over the course of the high and later Middle Ages. Moreover, John's treatment of Magdalena's case is typical not only in the way it blurs the boundaries between true and false inspiration, but also in

---

135 *Formicarium* iii.1; pp. 181 and 184.
136 *Formicarium* iii.8; p. 234. Also see his parallel account of a woman in the diocese of Constance, celebrated for her raptures, who prophesied that she would receive the stigmata on a fixed day (iii.11; pp. 349–50). Cf. Newman's account of the heterodox Beguine treatise *Schwester Katrei* in which a three-day mystical death is described as a stage toward a permanent union with God (*Virile Woman*, pp. 173–4).
137 *Formicarium* iii.8; p. 235.
138 *Formicarium* iii.8; p. 232. Nider goes on to cite Augustine's amazing list of unusual, but voluntary, abilities – ranging from ear wiggling to a rapture accompanied by total insensibility (see *De civitate Dei* xiv.24; pp. 588–9).

its confusion between inadvertant error and the will to deceive. Women, by virtue of their more active imagination and innately weak judgement, are susceptible to the realm of the demonic in incalculable ways. Thus some would-be holy women may mistake the source of their inspiration and are too proud or too foolish to submit their visions to proper clerical authority; others, either from impressionability or over-scrupulosity, believe themselves to be possessed by demons when they are not.[139] Finally there are those who are deeply complicit with the realm of the demonic and these women, of course, are the ones who participate in witchcraft.[140]

In defense of Nider, it should be added that he refrained from absolutely associating witchcraft with women – a connection that would be consolidated soon after as the female gendering of witch in the title *Malleus maleficarum* implies.[141] But Nider did bequeath a useable frame. As the first significant writer on witchcraft, he described an arc or trajectory between the witch and the saint. It was natural enough for the authors of *Malleus*, inquisitors and clerics both, to efface the positive extremity in favour of the negative, and additionally erase the interim positions connecting the two poles. Thus in *Malleus maleficarum*, while positive female spirituality is suppressed altogether, many of its markers have an eery continuance. A supernatural insensibility is certainly one of them.

> [A judge] must not be too quick to subject a witch to examination, but must pay attention to certain signs which will follow. And he must not be too quick for this reason: unless God, through a holy Angel, compels the devil to withhold his help from the witch, she will be so insensible to

---

[139] Nider explains that many women imagine themselves vexed by or pregnant by an incubus (*Formicarium* v.10; p. 406). He also tells of a pious matron who, through some defect in the complexion, became convinced she was possessed (v.11; pp. 427–8). Cf. the account of a sister in Nuremburg whose exaggerated sense of her own sinfulness almost led to her demise. This too is blamed on a defect in complexion, which Nider describes as a common failing in the fragile sex (ii.12; p. 174).

[140] See *Formicarium* v.3 (pp. 351–2) for classic accounts of witches of both sexes who cook and eat infants.

[141] For the contemporary theological context of *Malleus maleficarum* see J. C. Baroja, 'Witchcraft and Catholic Theology', in *Early Modern European Witchcraft: Centres and Peripheries*, ed. B. Ankarloo and G. Henningsen (Oxford, 1990), pp. 19–43, esp. 30–1; R. Kieckhefer, *European Witch Trials: Their Foundations in Popular and Learned Culture* (Berkeley and Los Angeles, 1976), pp. 73–92 and Russell, *Witchcraft*, pp. 230–3. For the impact of the pseudo-Albert the Great's demonization of women's bodies on the authors of the *Malleus maleficarum*, see Lemay's introduction to her translation of *Women's Secrets*, pp. 49–58. For the influence of the *Malleus maleficarum* on Renaissance thought, see G. S. Williams, 'The Woman/the Witch: Variations on a Sixteenth-Century Theme (Paracelsus, Wier, Bodin)', in *The Crannied Wall: Woman, Religion and the Arts in Early Modern Europe*, ed. C. A. Monson (Ann Arbor, MN, 1992), 119–37.

the pains of torture that she will sooner be torn limb from limb than confess any of the truth.[142]

Here is the terminus of a previously auspicious and vindicatory current in the assessment of female spirituality.

---

[142] Heinrich Institoris and Jakob Sprenger, *Malleus maleficarum*, pt 3, qu. 13, trans. M. Summers (New York, 1971), p. 223. Elsewhere, the authors claim that a witch's power of silence was maintained through charms secreted somewhere on her body – thus she had to be stripped and shaved (pt 3, qu. 15; pp. 227–30). Though, as Russell, points out, this strip search was not in order to find any distinguishing marks (*Witchcraft*, p. 232), it seems to me that there may be some relationship between this capacity for silence or resistance to pain and the emergence of the alleged area of insensibility known as the 'devil's mark' – still a rarity in the fifteenth century. According to J. Tedeschi's account of the procedures of the Congregation of the Holy Office (the reorganized papal inquisition of the early modern period), however, the search for the devil's mark was foreign to later inquisitorial practice ('Inquisitorial Law and the Witch', in *Early Modern European Witchcraft*, ed. Ankarloo and Henningsen, pp. 84 and 93). Similarly, Russell notes that the devil's mark was rarely addressed by theorists (*Witchcraft*, p. 242). Cf. Zarri's observations on the parallel abilities of saint and witch ('Le sante vive', p. 118). Her comments are framed within the assumption of the oppositional relationship of saint and witch – a position similar to Craveti's or Dinzelbacher's (see note 123 above). I am attempting to argue for the essential sameness of these two representations of female spirituality.

Beholding Men's Members:
The Sexualizing of Transgression
in *The Book of Margery Kempe*

Rosalynn Voaden

For a work which set out to be 'a schort tretyse and a comfortabyl for synful wrecchys, wher-in þei may have gret solas and comfort to hem and vndyr-stondyn þe hy & vnspecabyl mercy of ower souereyn Sauyowr Cryst Ihesu',[1] *The Book of Margery Kempe* imparts a considerable amount of information about Margery Kempe's sexual life – her fantasies, her fears and her frustra-tions. We learn, for example, that she was tempted, and consented, to an adulterous liaison, and then was humiliatingly rejected.[2] We know that her husband John, who, like Augustine, agreed with the virtue of living chastely 'but he mgth not ȝett',[3] insisted on his marital rights, and that Margery 'in hir ȝong age had ful many delectabyl thowtys, fleschly lustys, & inordinat louys to hys persone'.[4] We know that Margery wore a hair-shirt to bed and that John never noticed, which does make one wonder about the range of his lovemak-ing.[5] Moreover, even though the couple eventually lived apart to establish their chastity, people still thought that they sneaked off 'to woodys, grouys, er valeys to vsyn þe lust of her bodijs'.[6] We are privy to Margery's enormous fear of sexual assault, to her conviction that all men wanted to defile her, and to the unsavoury image of the steward of Leicester struggling with a middle-aged Margery, showing her 'vn-clene tokenys & vngodly cuntenawns', and threat-ening to rape her.[7] We are told that she was accused of having had a child while ostensibly on pilgrimage to Jerusalem,[8] and that the mayor of Leicester accused her of being a strumpet as well as a Lollard.[9] And finally, we know that for Margery, hell is beholding men's members.

> And, as sche beforn had many gloryows visyonys & hy contemplacyon
> in þe manhod of owr Lord, in owr Lady & in many oþer holy seyntys,
> ryth euyn so had sche now horybyl syghtys & abominabyl, for

---

1 *BMK*, p. 1.
2 *BMK*, pp. 14–15.
3 *BMK*, p. 12.
4 *BMK*, p. 181.
5 *BMK*, p. 12.
6 *BMK*, p. 180.
7 *BMK*, p. 113.
8 *BMK*, p. 103.
9 *BMK*, p. 112.

anythyng þat sche cowde do, of beheldyng of mennys membrys & swech oþer abhominacyons.[10]

Why this inordinate emphasis on sexuality? What was the purpose, and what was the effect of the text's constructing Margery in such overtly sexual terms? Did it just reflect the unhealthy obsession of an attention seeker, or was it rather the result of the inability of Margery and the scribe to discriminate in their recording? How did Margery's self-fashioning as a sexual being – or, as she might have it, as an ex-sexual being – reflect the Christian traditions of the time and prevailing views of women?

Considerable scholarly attention has already been focused on the relationship between Margery's spirituality and her sexuality.[11] However, in this essay I will argue that it was specifically and exclusively that aspect of her spirituality comprising her sense of sin which was mapped onto her sexuality. In Margery's perception sin was always sexual, therefore her identification of herself as a sinner, albeit a reformed sinner, meant identifying herself as sexual. In addition, just as transgression was sexualized, so too was punishment. I will also consider the historical context of *The Book of Margery Kempe*, and argue that two of the models on which Margery shaped her spirituality intensified the emphasis on her sexuality. These are the model of Mary Magdalene and Margery's quest to invite scorn and abuse in *imitatio Christi*.

The roots of Margery's association of sin and sexuality were in her body. She was profoundly and consistently aware of herself as a physical, fleshly being, an amalgamation of appetites and sensations.[12] Throughout *The Book* Margery demonstrates this awareness of her physical self in numerous ways. In her youth, her pride found its expression in fine clothes; pride, and awareness of the effect of physical presentation, is also manifested in her later obsession with white clothing. She wrote of food – of cakes and beer and good red herring. She was concerned with her safety on pilgrimage, especially on sea voyages. She was afraid of storms. At one point she prayed that she might

---

[10] *BMK*, p. 145.
[11] This issue has been examined from a number of different perspectives. See, for example: D. Aers, 'The Making of Margery Kempe', in his *Community, Gender and Individual Identity* (London, 1988), pp. 73–116; S. Beckwith, 'A Very Material Mysticism: The Medieval Mysticism of Margery Kempe', in *Medieval Literature: Criticism, Ideology and History*, ed. D. Aers (Brighton, 1986), pp. 34–47; J. Dillon, 'The Making of Desire in The Book of Margery Kempe', *Leeds Studies in English* n.s. 26 (1995), 113–44; L. Higgs, 'Margery Kempe: "Whete-Breed or Barly-Breed?" ', *Mystics Quarterly* 13 (1987), 57–64; Lochrie, *Margery Kempe*; N. Partner, ' "And Most of All for Inordinate Love": Desire and Denial in *The Book of Margery Kempe*', *Thought: Fordham University Quarterly* 54 (1989), 254–67.
[12] Lochrie makes a valid and significant distinction between flesh and body in *Margery Kempe*, pp. 13–47. However, this distinction, while it is useful and does go some way to support my contention about Margery's bodiliness, is not directly relevant to my discussion of her sexuality.

not become seasick, at another Christ advised her not to look at the waves, a classic remedy for avoiding seasickness.[13] She was upset, naturally enough, about catching 'vermyn' from the poor folk with whom she travelled.[14] She was physically timid; although she felt she should welcome martyrdom, she confessed to fear of dying, and admitted choosing the least painful form of death she could think of: 'sche ymagyned hyr-self þe most soft deth . . . þat was to be bowndyn hyr hed & hir fet to a stokke & hir hed to be smet of wyth a scharp ex for Goddys lofe'.[15] When she was fettered at Cawood, she tucked her hands under her mantle to hide their trembling.[16] She said that she would rather suffer cruel words than the pain of her chronic illness.[17] As all these examples indicate, not only was Margery aware of her body, she was also protective of it. In this she presents an interesting contrast to the majority of late-medieval holy women, who actively sought physical suffering, in order to imitate Christ and to subdue the unruly flesh.[18]

Because Margery was so rooted in her body it was inevitable that her sense of both sin and redemption would be located there. What is significant, however, is that it was not her body as a whole which generated her sense of sin, or presented a locus of expiation. It was her sexual self, located specifically in her genitals, which performed this function. It was not so much that she sinned sexually, as that for her sin was sexual; the consequence was that, as I stated above, for Margery transgression was inevitably sexualized, as was punishment.

This can be observed in Margery's struggle for salvation, a struggle played out in her virtual obsession with chastity. Her sense of herself as a sinner was rooted overwhelmingly in her sense of herself as not-virgin. Her first vision of Christ occurred after her post-natal breakdown, when the consequences of her sexual activity would have made her acutely aware of her fissured, female body. His appearance at this time, sitting on the side of her bed, locus of that same sexual activity, helped to valorize her sexuality in its association with motherhood.[19] When Christ himself informed her of a later pregnancy, her

---

13 *BMK*, pp. 232–3.
14 *BMK*, p. 237.
15 *BMK*, p. 30.
16 *BMK*, p. 124.
17 *BMK*, pp. 137–8.
18 Julian of Norwich, for example, prayed for illness, and for three wounds: *Julian of Norwich: A Revelation of Love*, ed. M. Glasscoe (Exeter, 1976), p. 2. Bridget of Sweden dropped burning wax on her hands every Friday, and wore knotted cords tied tightly around her waist and knees: B. Gregersson and T. Gascoigne, *The Life of Saint Birgitta*, trans. J. B. Holloway (Toronto, 1991), pp. 21–2. Such practices were *de rigueur* for medieval holy women; many more examples can be found in Bynum, *Holy Feast*. For a more general study of mortification of the flesh, see P. Camporesi, *The Incorruptible Flesh: Bodily Mutilation and Mortification in Religion and Folklore*, trans. T. Croft-Murray (Cambridge, 1988).
19 N. Partner points out the centrality of the image of the marriage bed to the organisa-

equation of sin with sex was evident in her distress. 'Lord, I am not worthy to heryn þe spekyn & þus to comown [have sexual intercourse] wyth myn husbond.'[20] Christ replied that it was no sin but rather 'mede & meryte', and promised to 'ordeyn for an kepar' for the child – the practical kind of divine assistance for which many a harried mother prays. As in her first vision, Christ valorized Margery's procreative sexuality. The most significant part of this episode, though, is Christ's comment, '3a, dowtyr, trow þow rygth wel þat I lofe wyfes also, *and specyal þo wyfys whech woldyn levyn chast, 3yf þei mygtyn haue her wyl . . .*'.[21] This equating of the will to live chastely with the act of doing so was a vital component in Margery's re-construction of her chastity, the sealing up of her fissured body which influenced much of her self-fashioning.

Her first impulse to chastity came when she heard an unearthly melody while lying beside her husband. 'Alas, þat euyr I dede synne, it is ful mery in Hevyn', she exclaimed.[22] The careful location of this experience – lying beside her husband in bed – with the immediate conjunction of her desire to live chastely, leaves the reader in little doubt that she had probably not just been holding hands with her husband. Her awareness of her own recent sexual activity accounts for the poignancy of her exclamation, with its implication that she would be excluded from the merriment of heaven. From that point on, she attempted to minimize her status as a married women. In effect, she tried to retrieve her virginity, to seal up her body, to become inviolate – and unviolated.[23] She recounts Christ telling her 'þu art a mayden in þi sowle . . .

tion of *The Book*, and argues that 'the narrative structure is governed by Margery's entry into the bed, and her leap out of it. . .' ('Inordinate Love', p. 257).
[20] *BMK*, p. 48.
[21] *BMK*, p. 49. My emphasis.
[22] *BMK*, p. 11.
[23] Margery would not be the first woman to have her virginity restored, either literally or figuratively. Medieval sources document several incidents in which the fissured body of a transgressive female is miraculously restored, generally after parturition. Accounts of two such incidents are translated in J. Boswell, *The Kindness of Strangers: The Abandonment of Children in Western Europe from Late Antiquity to the Renaissance* (London, 1988). One account is Aelred of Rievaulx' mid twelfth-century letter about the nun of Watton (pp. 452–8). When the nun was discovered in her cell, no longer pregnant but with no sign of a baby, the other sisters examined her thoroughly, not to say brutally. 'They squeezed her breasts, but elicited no liquid from them. Not sparing her, they pressed harder, but expressed nothing. They ran their fingers over every joint, exploring everything, but found no sign of childbirth, no indication even of pregnancy . . . they all found the same thing: everything restored, everything proper, everything beautiful' (p. 457). The other text (pp. 459–60) is from a mid twelfth-century Anglo-Norman collection of miracles of the Virgin. It concerns an unpopular abbess in England, whose pregnancy becomes known by the entire convent; the bishop is then informed. When the time for the birth arrives, the Virgin Mary intervenes: angels convey the child to a hermit for raising. The abbess's enemies raise a great tumult. Eventually 'the bishop ordered representatives to examine her uterus. They, marvelling, reported finding no sign whatever of what

& so xalt þu dawnsyn in Hevyn wyth oþer holy maydens & virgynes'.[24] The use of 'oþer' implies that as far as Christ is concerned she is no different from the rest.

One symbolic attempt to retrieve her virginity can be seen in Margery's determination to wear white clothes, a determination in which she stubbornly persisted despite the disapproval of numerous clerics. Indeed, one of her confessors accused her of causing the world to wonder at her by wearing white clothing,[25] and this is, surely, exactly what she intended. White clothes, traditionally worn by virgins or widows, would signal her chastity to the world.[26] Christ specifically promised her protection against 'ony velany [shame] of þi body' if she wore white clothes,[27] a promise which endowed the clothing with even greater significance in Margery's opposition of chastity and sin. In her perception, it seems, wearing white clothes guaranteed her chastity, and so her sinlessness.

For Margery sin was sexualized. Therefore, avoiding sin meant keeping herself inviolate. The rocky road to redemption was edged with briars, and all the thorns looked like penises. Once having achieved a chaste marriage, having established herself as a reformed sinner, Margery perceived threats to her chastity on all sides. On numerous occasions, she appeared to fear defilement more than any other punishment. In Hessle, when she was under arrest for Lollardy by the Duke of Bedford's men and being taken to Beverley, the townspeople said she should be burnt as a heretic.[28] This prospect did not seem to alarm her, yet she begged not to be put in prison with men. 'The sayd creatur preyde hym of hys lordschip þat sche xulde not be putte a-mongs men, for sche was a mannys wyfe.'[29] It is true that affirming her marital status in this way does have the effect of distinguishing her from vagrant women who were seen as threats to public order and in need of containment.[30] However, it is also true that there is an undoubted emphasis on the preservation of her chastity in the wording of Margery's plea. Ironically, her main weapon in

had been alleged' (p. 460). It is not unlikely that Margery would have heard of these, or other, similar accounts.

[24] *BMK*, p. 52.
[25] *BMK*, p. 77.
[26] G. Cleve suggests that Margery's struggle over her white clothes actually does have the effect of chastening and purifying her. See 'Semantic Dimensions in Margery Kempe's "Whyght Clothys" ', *Mystics Quarterly* 12 (1986), 162–70.
[27] *BMK*, p. 76.
[28] *BMK*, p. 129.
[29] *BMK*, pp. 132–2. See also p. 112 for a similar incident, in which Margery was arrested as a suspected Lollard in Leicester and pleaded not to be put in prison with men 'þat I may kepyn my chastite & my bond of wedlak'.
[30] F. Riddy suggests that the problem of ungoverned women in English towns was of sufficient concern to have influenced some late-medieval conduct books and poems. See 'Mother Knows Best: Reading Social Change in a Courtesy Text', *Speculum* 71 (1996), 66–86 (p. 74).

defence of her chastity is her status as a wife, that is, as a sexually active woman under the authority of her husband.

That sexual violation was a materialization of the entry of sin into her body is made explicit in Margery's account of her pilgrimage to Germany, when she was a widow in her sixties. Throughout the pilgrimage she could not sleep for fear of defilement, even when she had women or girls to sleep in the same bed with her.[31]

> And on nyghtys had sche most dreed oftyn-tymes, & perauentur it was of hir gostly enmy, for sche was euyr a-ferd to a be rauischyd er defilyd. Sche durst trustyn on no man; whedir sche had cawse er non, sche was euyr a-ferd. Sche durst ful euyl slepyn any nyth, for sche wend men wolde a defylyd hir.[32]

It seems abundantly clear that Margery feared a real-life reenactment of her experience of spiritual dryness, when God withdrew his presence from her, replacing it with visions of men's members and her own damnation, in which the torment was located in the genitals and the punishment specifically identified as sexual.

> Sche sey as hir thowt veryly dyuers men of religyon, prestys, & many oþer, bothyn hethyn & Cristen comyn be-for hir syght þat sche myth not enchewen hem ne puttyn hem owt of hir syght, schewyng her bar membrys vn-to hir. & þerwyth þe Deuyl bad hir in hir mende chesyn whom sche wolde han fyrst of hem alle & sche must be comown to [have sexual intercourse with] hem alle. . . . & hir thowt þat þes horrybyl syghtys & cursyd mendys wer delectabyl to hir a-geyn hir wille.[33]

Men's members were the tools of the devil, and Margery's vagina the point where sin entered her body and her soul. To be violated meant to be without God, that is, to be damned.

Having argued that it was specifically and exclusively her sense of sin which was mapped onto Margery's sexuality, I would like now to consider her mystical marriage.[34] Although the fact of a mystical marriage suggests that Margery also experienced a positive form of eroticized spirituality in her relationship with Christ, in fact her mystical marriage was decidedly asexual. This is especially apparent when it is compared to the overt eroticism of depictions of mystical union by other late-medieval women visionaries, or to the graphic sexuality of Margery's vision of damnation described above.[35]

---

31 *BMK*, pp. 236–7 and 240. Of course, neither age nor marital status protect a woman from rape. Margery's fears, however, persisted even when she had taken every possible precaution, and could, I think, be judged excessive.

32 *BMK*, p. 241.

33 *BMK*, p. 145.

34 *BMK*, pp. 86–91.

35 There are numerous instances of erotic descriptions of mystical union by late medieval women visionaries. Among the most vivid are those by the mid thirteenth-

Despite her devotion to the manhood of Christ, her marriage was to the Godhead, that is, to the unincarnated person of the Trinity.[36] The description of the wedding ceremony reads like a column in the society pages – it was public, not private.[37] Her marriage was specifically located in her soul,[38] and identified as the union of her soul: 'þi sowle xal partyn fro þi body, but God xal neuyr partyn fro þi sowle, for þei ben onyd to-gedyr wyth-owtyn ende'.[39] The consummation of the marriage was conditional, not actual; God telling her what she could do, rather than Margery describing what she did do. The description of the union was not erotic. It was domestic, with the bond between them described in terms of a whole amalgam of family relationships: husband-wife, father-daughter and mother-son. God tells her:

> . . . whan þu art in þi bed, take me to þe as for þi weddyd husbond, as thy derworthy derlyng, & as for thy swete sone, for I wyl be louyd as a sone schuld be louyd wyth þe modyr & wil þat þu loue me, dowtyr, as a good wife owyth to loue hir hosbonde.[40]

The bodily contact was specifically non-genital – a kind of cosmic cuddle: 'þu mayst boldly take me in þe armys of þi sowle & kyssen my mowth, myn hed, & my fete as swetly as thow wylt.'[41] For Margery, the fissured body, the sexual body, was a sinner's body, and her marriage to the Godhead would, of necessity and desire, be as chaste as that which she eventually achieved with John.

Although the principal evidence for the sexualizing of transgression in *The Book of Margery Kempe* comes from Margery's depiction of her own sexuality and sinfulness, transgression was also sexualized in her dealing with other

---

century beguine Hadewijch of Brabant, on whom see E. Petroff, *Medieval Women's Visionary Literature* (Oxford, 1986), pp. 196–7; Mechtild of Magdeburg (d. 1282), discussed by Petroff, *Visionary Literature*, p. 215; and Mechtild of Hackeborn (d. 1298), on whom see Gertrude the Great, *Revelationes Gertrudianae ac Mechtildianae*, 2 vols. (Paris, 1875), II, 312–14. For the Middle English text of another description of mystical marriage by Mechtild of Hackeborn, see A. Barratt, *Women's Writing in Middle English* (London, 1992), pp. 55–8. I consider medieval erotic visions and mystical marriages in the context of modern romance fiction in my article, 'The Language of Love: Medieval Erotic Vision and Modern Romance Fiction', in *Romance Revisited*, ed. L. Pearce and J. Stacey (London, 1995), pp. 78–89.

36 *BMK*, p. 86, ll. 15–23.
37 *BMK*, p. 87, ll. 13–31. A similar description of a public mystical marriage which also uses the language of the marriage service and lists the heavenly guests in attendance is found in the prose legend of St Katherine of Alexandria. Her mystical marriage is pointedly not consummated – the divine spouse departs right after the ceremony. See *St. Katherine of Alexandria: The Late Middle English Prose Legend in Southwell Minster MS 7*, ed. S. Nevanlinna and I. Taavitsainen (Cambridge, 1993), pp. 81–3. I am grateful to Katherine Lewis for bringing this to my attention.
38 *BMK*, p. 87, ll. 14, 18 and 25.
39 *BMK*, p. 89, ll. 12–14.
40 *BMK*, p. 90.
41 *BMK*, p. 90.

people. For example, she castigated a monk for his lechery with married women.[42] Christ thanked her for her charity to 'alle lecherows men & women', and for her prayers that they be delivered from sin.[43] She made a point of warning her dissolute son 'kepe þi body klene at þe lest fro womanys feleschep', and urged God to punish him if he did not.[44] The punishment came in the form of leprosy – or at least, something that looked like leprosy. 'Sone after [falling into lechery] hys colowr chawngyd, hys face wexe ful of whelys & bloberys as it had ben a lepyr.'[45] Thus the link between her son's transgression and his sexual activity was made explicit. It was a common medieval belief that leprosy was highly contagious, and that one of the principal methods of transmission was venereal.[46] Fear of contagion led to lepers being outcast from society, and having a variety of vices ascribed to them.[47] From as early as the second century, doctors associated leprosy with heightened sexuality and satyriasis,[48] and this belief persisted into the late Middle Ages.[49]

---

[42] *BMK*, pp. 26–7.

[43] *BMK*, p. 204.

[44] *BMK*, p. 222.

[45] *BMK*, p. 222.

[46] Leprosy was also believed to be transmitted through other forms of physical contact, and through breath. There are numerous medieval medical, theological and scientific treatises which deal with leprosy. A useful example is Book 7, *de lepra*, of Bartholomaeus Anglicus, *On the Properties of Things: John Trevisa's translation of Bartholomaeus Anglicus, De proprietatibus rerum*, ed. M. C. Seymour, 3 vols. (Oxford, 1975–88), I, 423–6. For a survey of medieval attitudes and writing on leprosy see Jacquart and Thomasset, pp. 183–93; see further L. Demaitre, 'The Description and Diagnosis of Leprosy by Fourteenth-Century Physicians', *Bulletin of the History of Medicine* 59 (1985), 327–44.

[47] In many ways leprosy functioned much as AIDS does in our own time. Both diseases have powerful sexual associations, provoke great fear in society, are seen as somehow uncontrollable and the sufferers are marginalized. Both diseases are articulated within a variety of discourses – medical, scientific and theological. In the latter discourse, both AIDS and leprosy are often constructed as divine punishments.

[48] Jacquart and Thomasset, pp. 185–6, cite Rufus of Ephesus describing the stages of leprosy: 'when the eyebrows swell, when the cheekbones go red, and patients are seized by ardour for coitus, these doctors give the name satyriasis to the disease . . .'.

[49] For further examples of the association of leprosy with sexuality see S. N. Brody, *The Disease of the Soul: Leprosy in Medieval Literature* (Ithaca, 1974), and S. R. Ell, 'Blood and Sexuality in Medieval Leprosy', *Janus: Revue internationale de l'histoire des sciences, de la médecine, de la pharmacie, et de la technique* 71 (1984), 153–64. A common belief was that the blood of pure virgins was a cure for leprosy (Brody, p. 147). Interestingly, Hildegard of Bingen used menstrual blood as an ingredient in her cure for leprosy. Given that it was generally thought that intercourse with a menstruating woman was one of the causes of leprosy, Hildegard may have been applying the principles of homeopathic medicine here. See Cadden, *Meanings of Sex Difference*, p. 72.

In literature, lepers were frequently represented as utterly depraved. For example,

Leprosy was also frequently seen as a disease of the soul, a punishment for various kinds of immorality, but especially for lust.[50] Margery's son, a sinner whose principal vices seem to have been those to which she herself had been prone – vainglory, pride, vanity, and lust – was thus specifically identified as a sexual sinner through seeming to be stricken with leprosy. His transgression and his punishment were sexualized just as Margery's were.

It is within this context that it is important to understand Margery's choice of lepers as a special object of her pious devotion.[51] Margery restricted her good works to female lepers – her extreme sensitivity to sexual implications prevented her from kissing male lepers, but allowed her to embrace female ones.[52] One of these women was tormented by the devil. 'And sche was labowryd wyth many fowle & horybyl thowtys, many mo þan sche cowde tellyn. &, as sche seyd, sche was a mayde.' [53] There can be little doubt about the nature of the 'foul and horrible thoughts'; in this case the punishment was sexualized even if it did not fit the crime. The fact that Margery saw fit to assert the woman's virgin state suggests that she was aware of the usual association of lepers with sexual activity. It also suggests once again the pervasive association in Margery's mind of sexuality and sin.

Having explored the sexualizing of transgression and punishment in *The Book of Margery Kempe*, I would like now to return to one of the questions with which I started this essay: why is there this inordinate emphasis on sexuality? To answer this I will examine two of the informing structures for Margery's spirituality: the model of Mary Magdalene, and Margery's desire to be slandered and abused in *imitatio Christi*.

---

in the mid twelfth-century *Roman de Tristan*, King Mark hands Yseut over to the lepers as a fitting punishment for her fornication with Tristan. Ivain, the leader of the lepers, urges the king: 'Give Yseut to us and we will possess her in common. No woman ever had a worse end. Sire, there is such lust in us that no woman on earth could tolerate intercourse with us for a single day' (Beroul, *The Romance of Tristan*, trans. A. S. Fedrick (London, 1970), pp. 73–4). Later versions of the prose *Tristan* also include giving Yseut to the lepers, although Beroul's version is probably the most graphic. Although we do not know whether Margery had any knowledge of this romance, there is an interesting resemblance between this description and her vision of men's members. In Henryson's late fifteenth-century 'Testament of Cresseid,' Cresseid is punished with leprosy : Robert Henryson, 'The Testament of Cresseid', in *The Poems of Robert Henryson*, ed. D. Fox (Oxford, 1981), pp. 111–31.

50 Jacquart and Thomasset, p. 185; Ell, 'Blood', p. 154; Brody, *Disease*, p. 147. But see also Bartholomaeus Anglicus, who, despite the fact that this is a preachers' encyclopedia, does not include punishment for immorality in his list of the causes of leprosy (*Properties of Things*, vii.64, ed. Seymour, I, 426).

51 *BMK*, pp. 176–7. Lepers were the object of good works and devotional exercises for many medieval holy women. It is possible that Margery modelled her behaviour on stories she heard of such figures as Angela of Foligno, who drank the bathwater of lepers. See Lochrie, *Margery Kempe*, p. 43. For the possibility that Margery may have known of Angela, see *BMK*, pp. lv and 295 (note on p. 73, l. 28).

52 *BMK*, p. 177.

53 *BMK*, p. 177.

Margery had a special devotion to Mary Magdalene.[54] Considerable scholarship has been devoted to her knowledge of the legend of the Magdalene and her exposure to various depictions of the Magdalene in plays and devotional reading.[55] It would appear that Mary Magdalene presented Margery with a model of the reformed sinner and non-virgin with which she could readily identify. In one of her visions, when she deplored her own unworthiness, Christ told her: 'Haue mend, dowtyr, what Mary Mawdelen was, Mary Eypcyan, Sent Powyl . . . for of vnworthy I make worthy, & of synful I make rytful.'[56] It may seem strange that she did not construct herself to a greater extent according to the models offered by married women saints and holy women such as Elizabeth of Hungary or Bridget of Sweden, whose work she definitely knew.[57] They, after all, presented lives closer to the reality of Margery's than did Mary Magdalene. They were widows, having been respectably married and having mothered children, just like Margery, whereas the Magdalene was a reformed prostitute. The reasons for Margery's devotion to Mary Magdalene can be suggested. I believe they lie, first, in the intensity of Margery's perception of herself as a sinner, which, as I have argued, meant as a sexual being, and, second, in Margery's competitiveness.

First, her perception of herself as sexual. Few other medieval holy women – or would-be holy women – demonstrate Margery's preoccupation with sex. Bridget of Sweden, Elizabeth of Hungary, and the majority of married holy women constructed themselves as naturally and preeminently chaste.[58] Their

---

54 Mary Magdalene was, after the Virgin Mary, possibly the most popular saint in the Middle Ages; cf. R. M. Karras, 'Holy Harlots: Prostitute Saints in Medieval Legend', *Journal of the History of Sexuality* 1 (1990), 3–33 (p. 17). Margery's parish church had a dual dedication, to St. Margaret and St. Mary Magdalene: see S. Eberly, 'Margery Kempe, St. Mary Magdalene and Patterns of Contemplation', *DR* 107 (1989), 209–23 (p. 210). However, familiarity alone cannot account for Margery's devotion to the Magdalene; she was also very familiar with the works and life of St Bridget, to the extent of visiting Bridget's one-time maid in Rome (*BMK*, p. 95). Although she did model herself to some extent on Bridget, the identification is not as ardent as it is with Mary Magdalene.

55 For example: S. Craymer, 'Margery Kempe's Imitation of Mary Magdalene and the "Digby Plays" ', *Mystics Quarterly* 19 (1993), 173–81; S. Eberley, 'Margery Kempe, St. Mary Magdalene, and Patterns of Contemplation'; C. Atkinson, *Mystic and Pilgrim: the Book and the World of Margery Kempe* (Ithaca, NY, 1983).

56 *BMK*, p. 49.

57 Margery's scribe had read the treatise of Elizabeth of Hungary, and compared her crying with Margery's (*BMK*, p. 154). R. Ellis considers the influence of Elizabeth's treatise on the writing of Margery's book in considerable depth in 'Margery Kempe's Scribe and the Miraculous Books', in *Langland, the Mystics and the Medieval English Religious Tradition*, ed. H. Phillips (Cambridge, 1990), pp. 161–75 (pp. 164–8). Margery mentions St Bridget many times, and states that she has read (or heard read) 'Bridis boke' (*BMK*, p. 39).

58 D. Elliott considers the manner in which the institution of chaste marriage influenced the hagiographical construction of late-medieval holy women in *Spiritual Marriage*, pp. 195–265.

motherhood is made to appear almost accidental, its association with sexual activity remote if not non-existent. Chastity was portrayed as their natural state, a state to which marriage and motherhood were interruptions.[59] Most holy women did not represent themselves as having to struggle, internally, to achieve chastity, though they may have undergone harrowing external struggles. Moreover, once achieved, chastity was solid, a given of their lives, not something which had to be vigilantly and continuously preserved.

Mary Magdalene, on the other hand, was identified preeminently as sexual and corporeal. Jacobus de Voragine (Jacob of Varazze) wrote of her in the *Legenda aurea*: 'As rich as Mary was, she was no less beautiful; and so entirely had she abandoned her body to pleasure that she was no longer called by any other name than "the sinner".'[60] She was a prostitute – for the pleasure of it, not the money. In some of the mystery play cycles it was as much her passion for luxury and sensuality as her overt sexual behaviour which condemned her.[61] She knew about precious ointment. She loved fine clothes; she was depicted in stained-glass windows and church paintings wearing a luxurious red robe, and having long flowing hair.[62] But, and this was the point, Mary Magdalene reformed. She sealed up her body, she reconstructed herself as chaste, she restored her virtue through her devotion to Christ, just as Margery wanted to. The Magdalene wept, she contemplated, she cared for Christ physically, she travelled, in some legends she preached, and she even resurrected a young mother who died in childbirth.[63] The parallels with Margery are obvious. She too loved clothes and was vain; she had achieved chastity through her devotion to Christ; she certainly wept, and she contemplated; she travelled, she almost preached,[64] and while she did not raise a young mother from the dead, she did restore one to her wits.[65] Mary Magdalene offered Margery a model of an actively sexual being, at least as sinful as she saw herself, who reformed, lived chastely and loved Christ. This was far more

---

[59] As an example of this, after her husband's death, Bridget of Sweden removed the ring he had given her, saying that it reminded her of carnal pleasures (Elliott, *Spiritual Marriage*, p. 226).

[60] Jacobus de Voragine, *The Golden Legend*, trans. and ed. G. Ryan and H. Ripperger, 2 vols. (London, 1941), II, 356.

[61] R. M. Karras briefly surveys representations of the Magdalene in late-medieval literature ('Holy Harlots', pp. 19–20). See also M. Malvern, *Venus in Sackcloth: The Magdalen's Origins and Metamorphoses* (Carbondale, 1975).

[62] Eberly, 'Margery Kempe, St. Mary Magdalene and Patterns of Contemplation', p. 212. See also S. Haskins, *Mary Magdalen: Myth and Metaphor* (London, 1994), pp. 134–227, for an illuminating examination of the development and various representations of Mary Magdalene in the late Middle Ages.

[63] Jacobus de Voragine, *Golden Legend*, pp. 358–60. See also Haskins, *Mary Magdalen*, pp. 222–8.

[64] Margery was several times accused of preaching. On one such occasion she replied: 'I preche not, ser, I come in no pulpytt. I vse but comownycacyon & good wordys, & þat wil I do whil I leue' (*BMK*, p. 126). Cf. A. J. Minnis's article, p. 130 above.

[65] *BMK*, pp. 177–8.

engaging than the model presented by her closer contemporaries, asexual holy women such as Bridget of Sweden or Elizabeth of Hungary.

Margery's competitiveness provided the second reason for her devotion to Mary Magdalene. She found the Magdalene additionally compelling because of her closeness to Christ. She was the woman Christ loved and allowed to be near him. Margery too yearned to be exclusive to Christ, and highest in holiness. There is a sense of triumph in the ways in which she demonstrated Christ's esteem for her. In one vision, for example, Christ told her that, although she was a wife, he loved her as well as any virgin in the world.[66] At another point, after Margery had experienced a eucharistic miracle, Christ told her that 'My dowtyr Bryde [Bridget of Sweden], say me neuyr in þis wyse'.[67] In yet another incident, with a widow of Lynn who had pretensions to visionary status, Margery reports being bidden by Christ to have a letter written to the widow stating that she would never have the grace that Margery had.[68] Margery knew that Mary Magdalene was the woman closest to Christ after his mother, she was the woman whom Christ praised and protected. Margery also aspired to be Christ's 'trewe louer', the position that Mary Magdalene occupied. Eventually, it would seem that she achieved it.

'A, blysful Lord,' seyd sche, 'I wolde I wer as worthy to ben sekyr of thy lofe as Mary Mawdelyn was.' Þan seyd owr Lord, 'Trewly, dowtyr, I loue þe as wel & þe same þes þat I ȝaf to hir þe same pes I ȝeue to þe.'[69]

However, to identify with Mary Magdalene meant identifying herself as sexual as well as reformed. It was this re-inscription of sexuality on the body she had sealed with chastity which facilitated Margery's quest for slander and scorn in *imitatio Christi*. The text fashions Margery in conflicting discourses, a conflict which encompasses her paradoxical presentation as simultaneously chaste and sexual. On the one hand she is constructed as holy woman, as visionary, intimate of Christ and channel for the divine word. Traditionally, this discourse ignores the body and privileges the voice of the visionary.[70] The troublesome female body is erased from the narrative, leaving a disembodied voice uttering the word of God. On the other hand, in the particular enactment of a holy life to which Margery felt herself called, she is to be the despised and rejected of men as well as the intimate and instrument of the divine. Offering herself as an object of scorn and abuse, however, undermines her construction as a holy woman and a visionary. To be credible as a visionary she must conform, she must be beyond suspicion, she must be obedient to

[66] *BMK*, p. 48.
[67] *BMK*, p. 47.
[68] *BMK*, p. 44.
[69] *BMK*, p. 176.
[70] This issue is explored in depth in my dissertation, 'God's Words, Women's Voices: *Discretio spirituum* in the Writing of Late Medieval Women Visionaries' (unpublished D.Phil. dissertation, York, 1994).

the power of the church. Conversely, in order to elicit abuse she has to be nonconforming, she has to be suspect, ultimately, indeed, she has to be out-cast.[71] These conflicting discourses resulted in an inherently unstable interpre-tation of her calling, condemning Margery to a life on the mystical margins.

At the beginning of this essay I commented on Margery's physical timidity and disinclination for bodily suffering. Further evidence of this is offered by the fact that sooner or later in her devotional praxis, bodily chastisement – fasting, the hair shirt, even, eventually, her 'krying & roryng' – was relin-quished in favour of the spiritual chastisement of harsh words and verbal attacks which that relinquishing helped to provoke.

> 'Dowtyr, I badde þe fyrst þat þu xuldist leeuyn flesch mete & non etyn, & þu hast obeyd my wyl many ȝerys & absteyned þe aftyr my cownsel. Þerfor now I bydde þe þat þu resort a-geyn to flesch mete.' . . .Than had sche many a scorne & meche reprefe for sche eete flesch a-geyn.[72]

Christ always assured her that this kind of suffering was the most pleasing to him.

> 'Dowtyr, it is mor plesyng vn-to me þat þu suffyr despitys & scornys, schamys & repreuys, wrongys & disesys þan if þin hed wer smet of thre tymes on þe day euery day in sevyn ȝer.'[73]

The mocking of Margery, the forms of her chastisement, fell into two prin-cipal categories: she was denounced for hypocrisy, as in the example just given, or she was charged with sexual misconduct. Sometimes she was ac-cused of both together.[74] Certainly, for a woman deliberately courting abuse, the easiest, most certain route was to write herself in a way which allowed her to be read as not only sexual, but deviantly sexual. Traditional Christian views of women as essentially lustful and inferior to men meant that a woman's place was under the control of men: father, husband, priest. A woman out of her place was a woman out of control, liable to the prompting of her nature. Margery flouted convention, and was insistently out of place: she travelled without her husband, she dressed in white like a maiden or a widow, she spoke in public and she continually drew attention to herself. Her unconven-tional behaviour reinscribed sexual activity on to her construction of herself as chaste. The result is that the reader is constantly reminded of Margery as sexual while being presented with Margery as chaste. This paradoxical con-

---

71 The impetus for this paradoxical self-fashioning is found in one of Margery's earli-est visions, in which Christ both promises to send her revelations and tells her that he wants her to be 'etyn & knawen of þe pepul of þe world' (*BMK*, pp. 16–18).

72 *BMK*, pp. 161–2.

73 *BMK*, p. 131.

74 An example of this is when Margery and her husband are accused of pretending to live chastely when in fact 'þei vsyd her lust & her likyng as þei dedyn be-forn her vow makyng' (*BMK*, pp. 179–80).

struction is explicit in the incident when Margery complained to her Dominican anchorite confessor that 'He þat is my confessowr in ȝowr absens is rygth
scharp vn-to me'. The anchorite replied: 'He knowyth wel ȝe han ben a synful
woman, & þerfor he wenyth þat God wold not ben homly wyth ȝow in so
schort tyme.'[75]

One of the most telling examples of this reinscription of sexuality occurred
when Margery had just returned from pilgrimage to Jerusalem and Rome, a
time when her odour of sanctity should have been at its highest. Almost
immediately upon landing, she went to visit an anchorite who had previously
loved her well. He accused her of having conceived and borne a child – and,
seemingly, of abandoning it – while she was away. Her response to such an
outrageous allegation was curiously feeble, and, in fact, colluded in the anchorite's re-presentation of her sexuality.

> 'Ser, þe same childe þat God hath sent me I haue browt hom, for God
> knowyth I dede neuyr *sithyn I went owte* wher-thorw I xulde haue a
> childe.'[76]

The oblique phrasing of her reply does nothing to assert her habitual chastity;
moreover, it should be noted that this incident occurred two years after she
and John took their vow of chastity. While righteous indignation would seem
a more fitting response, and certainly one not beyond Margery's capabilities,
instead she chose 'lowly & mekely' to try to persuade the anchorite that God
wished her to wear the controversial white clothes. The juxtaposition here of
Margery as adulterous woman and unnatural mother with Margery as icon of
chastity is a telling example of the text's continual negotiation between chastity and transgressive sexuality.

Further instances of this reinscription of sexuality occur whenever Margery
felt her chastity threatened. At these times she would assert that she was a
man's wife, thereby raising the spectre of her legally sanctioned sexual activity as a defence against defilement.

> 'I neuyr had part of mannys body in þis worlde in actual dede be wey of
> synne, but of myn husbondys body, whom I am bowndyn to be þe lawe
> of matrimony, & be whom I haue born xiiij childeryn.'[77]

---

[75] *BMK*, p. 44. In the presentation of this incident there are, of course, echoes of the
hostility and disbelief which greeted Christ's intimacy with Mary Magdalene (Jacobus de Voragine, *Golden Legend*, p. 356).

[76] *BMK*, p. 103. My emphasis.

[77] *BMK*, p. 115. This is the only place in the text where Margery gives a tally of her
children, and one of the very few places where her children are mentioned at all.
Although it seems to have been fairly standard for married holy women not to
dwell on their progeny, few write them out of the narrative to the extent that
Margery does. With some, for example, Dorothy of Montau, children – or the deaths
of children – became instruments of suffering: see R. Kieckhefer, *Unquiet Souls:*

Although her chastity may be thereby defended, she is yet again simultaneously defined as a sexual women.

This same tension is reflected in Margery's account of the difficulties she and her husband encountered in persuading others of their chastity. Although she gave this account as evidence of the hostility she experienced in her community, it had the effect, nevertheless, of rewriting sexuality onto her sealed body. She recounts how they finally decided to live apart, in order to convince people of their chastity. Nevertheless, the blameless husband and chaste wife were still accused of doing it like rabbits, in the fields and ditches.[78] However, it might be remarked that her subsequent reminiscence of the fleshly delights of their youth together does leave the reader wondering whether the spark was truly dead.[79]

Traditional Christian views of women and their sexuality certainly influenced not only responses to Margery's behaviour, but also accounted for her need to reconstruct herself as chaste in order to claim her place in the heavenly dance. Yet she, and her scribes, did have available to them models of holy women such as Bridget of Sweden and Elizabeth of Hungary whose sense of transgression was not sexualized. Far from being rooted in their bodies as Margery was, these women wrote their fissured, fleshly bodies out of their narratives. The sexualizing of transgression in *The Book of Margery Kempe* reflected Margery's acute awareness of herself as a sexually active 'creatur',

Fourteenth-Century Saints and their Religious Milieu (Chicago, 1984), pp. 22–8. For others, like Angela of Foligno, the death of children cleared the way for complete and utter devotion to Christ : see Angela of Foligno, *Complete Works*, ed. P. Lachance (New York, 1993), p. 126. For Bridget of Sweden, some of her children became extensions of her own sanctity, aiding in her construction of her own virtue; see *The Liber Celestis of St. Bridget of Sweden*, ed. R. Ellis, EETS OS 291 (Oxford, 1987), pp. 315–16. I would argue that the fact that Margery does not adopt one of these models is still further evidence of her identification of sex, even procreative sex, with sin. A similar argument applies to Margery's complete lack of emphasis on her eventual status as widow. It is evident that for Margery this kind of second class virginity is not enough. She wants to be a maid in Heaven.

Newman explores the maternal attitudes of medieval holy women in *Virile Woman*, pp. 76–107.

78 *BMK*, p. 180.
79 This and other similar incidents have some parallels with the portrayal of Mary and Joseph in mystery cycle plays of Joseph's Troubles, which deal with perceptions of Joseph as a cuckold and Mary as an adulterous wife. The underlying concern of such treatments was, of course, the presentation of Mary as at once virgin and mother, as both sealed and fissured – which is how Margery was struggling to construct herself. For an analysis of Joseph's Troubles in mystery cycle plays, see T. Coletti, 'The Paradox of Mary's Body', in Lomperis and Stanbury, *Feminist Approaches*, pp. 65–95. For a survey of the medieval theological debate occasioned by Mary's simultaneous virginity and maternity, see C. Wood, 'The Doctors' Dilemma; Sin, Salvation and the Menstrual Cycle in Medieval Thought', *Speculum* 56 (1981), 710–27.

always capable of being tempted by the joys of the flesh while desperately yearning for the harmony of heaven.

Margery's mapping of both sin and punishment onto her sexuality is neatly encapsulated in her meditation, towards the end of her life, while caring for her aged and incontinent husband: 'sche bethowt hir how sche in hir ȝong age had ful many delectabyl thowtys, fleschly lustys, & inordinat louys to hys persone. & þerfor sche was glad to be ponischyd wyth þe same persone . . .'.[80] In this episode can be found all the elements which constituted Margery's idiosyncratic devotion: her preoccupation with the things of the body, her yearning for union with Christ, her transmutation of sexual pleasure into awareness of sin. The body with which she transgressed – her own as well as John's – has become the instrument and site of her punishment.

The theme of the York conference in which this volume of essays originated was 'This Body of Death', a phrase from Romans 7. 22–5, in which St Paul struggles with his desire for good and his inclination towards evil. It is worth citing the whole passage.

> For I delight in the law of God, in my inmost self, but I see in my members another law at war with the law of my mind and making me captive to the law of sin which dwells in my members. Wretched man that I am! Who will deliver me from this body of death? Thanks be to God through Jesus Christ our Lord! So then, I of myself serve the law of God with my mind, but with my flesh I serve the law of sin.[81]

Paul's struggle is Margery's, and his despairing words could as well be hers.

[80] *BMK*, p. 181.
[81] Here the Revised Standard Version is followed.

The 1995 Quodlibet Lecture

Finding St Francis:
Early Images, Early Lives

Eamon Duffy

1. Inventing Francis: The Early Lives

St Francis of Assisi is at one and the same time the most attractive, the best
known and the most carefully constructed of all the saints of Christendom.
More than any other figure of the Middle Ages his early biographers attempted to capture not only his teachings, acts and miracles, but his personality. The character of the little poor man who transformed the Christian
imagination in the early thirteenth century by taking absolutely literally the
hardest sayings of the Gospels shines through even the stiffest of the early
writings about him. Where the other great founder of that age, St Dominic, left
almost no personal cult and few memorials, the Franciscan order and the
Franciscan way (which is and always has been wider than the order) has
consistently focussed on the person, and the personality, of its founder.[1]

This preoccupation with the personality of the saint was to have momen-
tous consequences for the order: as is well known, within a few years of his
death Francis himself had become the centre of a life and death struggle for
the soul of the movement he had founded. Already in his life-time some of his
followers, powerfully aided by the protector of the order, Francis's friend
Cardinal Ugolino, sought to soften and ease the rigour of Francis's vision. In
his last years Francis handed direction of the order to a much loved disciple,
Elias of Cortona, but was deeply grieved by the falling away from the rule of
absolute poverty which Elias and others then promoted. As soon as Francis
died, Elias and Ugolino, now pope Gregory IX, with bitter irony hijacked the
body of the saint into the service of the new and softer mood. Gregory, though
genuinely devoted to Francis, was to rule that the *Testament*, in which the saint
had made a final attempt to recall the brothers to the spirit of the early
movement and the absolute renunciation of property, had no legal status. But
he also came to Assisi and canonised Francis within two years of his death.
Over the saint's hidden bones Elias raised a grandiose basilica, a fortress to

---

[1] J. R. H. Moorman, *The Sources for the Life of St Francis of Assisi* (Manchester, 1940); R.
Brooke, 'The Lives of St Francis of Assisi', in *Latin Biography*, ed. T. A. Dorey (London, 1967), pp. 177–98.

guard the relics of the Poverello which within a few generations would become the living embodiment of extravagant ecclesiastical display. Gradually
crusted over with complex and sumptuous imagery glorifying the saint, the
Papacy and the order, the basilica at Assisi was a powerful weapon in estab-
lishing values and priorities which the saint had repeatedly questioned.
Above all, its grandeur and conspicuous display represented everything Francis most deplored: he had once climbed onto the roof of a newly erected
though much humbler Franciscan building at Assisi and with his own hands
pulled the tiles off the roof in an attempt to demolish it.[2]

All this was reflected in the earliest formal biographies. The first of these
was written in the immediate aftermath of the canonisation proceedings, by
Thomas of Celano in 1228, at the express command of Gregory IX: it was,
therefore, an official document designed to promote devotion and pilgrimage
to the new saint. Celano had been converted to religious life and received into
the order by Francis, and was probably at Assisi during Francis's last days,
but he certainly did not know the saint well, and he was far removed from the
simple, unlearned spirit of the early movement, a fact reflected by his ornate
and self-conscious Latin. Nevertheless, in some ways this first biography
remains the fundamental source for the life of Francis. For all their self-
conscious latinity and relentless tendency to sermonise and moralise (a characteristic of all Celano's work), the early chapters of *I Celano* do convey a vivid
sense of the contradictions and struggles of the youthful Francis, and the
emergence in his own painful experience of the distinctive Franciscan vocation.[3] This *Vita prima* contains many of the most treasured incidents in the
story of Francis: his dandified good-nature and popularity as the smartest of
young men-about-Assisi; his gradual awakening to the needs of the poor and
especially of the lepers whose disease at first had especially repelled him; his
spectacular renunciation of family and possessions in a scene at the episcopal
palace at Assisi where he stripped himself naked in the snow and threw his
clothing aside at his father's feet; the genesis of the Franciscan rule and his
conversion to a life of unshod poverty during Mass at the Portiuncula chapel

---

2 For the early history of the order and in particular the role of Elias, see J. H. R.
   Moorman, *A History of the Franciscan Order* (Oxford, 1968), pp. 75–104; R. B. Brooke,
   Early Franciscan Government (Cambridge, 1959); P. Gratien, *Histoire de la fondation et
   de l'evolution de l'ordre des frères mineurs au XIIIe siècle* (Paris, 1928). For Francis's
   onslaught on the roof at Assisi, see Thomas of Celano, *The Second Life of St Francis*
   (*Vita secunda*, hereafter also referred to as *2 Celano*), no. 57, in *St Francis of Assisi,
   Writings and Early Biographies: English Omnibus of the Sources for the Life of St Francis*,
   ed. M. Habig (Chicago, 1973), p. 412. Hereafter this collection is cited as *Omnibus*.
   Wherever possible, citations from the writings of St Francis or the early biographies
   are quoted from this edition, giving abbreviated title and paragraph number, followed by page number. Where the Latin text is used it is cited from the editions of
   the early lives printed as 'Legendae S. Francisci Assisiensis Saeculis XIII et XIV
   Conscriptae' in *AF* 10 (1927); hereafter referred to as 'Legendae S. Francisci'.
3 For Celano's *First Life*, (hereafter = *1 Celano*) see Brooke, 'Early Lives', and Moorman, *Sources*, pp. 55–81.

on St Mathias' day 1209; his preaching before the Sultan; his sermon to the birds; his invention of the Christmas crib at Greccio; his miraculous reception of the marks of the Crucifixion in his hands and feet and side during a long fast on La Verna in the late summer of 1224; and finally his death, naked on the floor of a hut at the Portiuncula chapel outside Assisi, on 3 October 1226, and his canonisation on 16 July 1228. But Celano is largely silent about the astonishing growth of the order in Francis's lifetime, and the crisis of identity and discipline which large numbers brought to a movement which had begun with the impulsive gesture of an idiosyncratic individual.

By the mid-1240s that growing crisis of identity, and the emergence within the order, if not of two parties, at least of two policies,[4] made a new life of Francis highly desirable. By now, also, those who had known the saint were ageing, and it was realised that many memories would be lost forever unless they were soon collected. In 1244 Crescentius of Iesi, the newly-appointed Minister General, invited all who had information about the life or miracles of Francis to write them down and send them to Assisi. It was this invitation which produced, among other irreplaceable testimonies, the most precious of all Franciscan documents, the so-called *Scripta Leonis*. This was a collection of stories gathered by some of the closest companions of Francis's last two years, the terrible and wonderful period after the stigmatisation on La Verna, when the saint's body was ravaged by barbaric 'treatment' for his growing blindness, crippled by kidney-failure and the effects of the stigmata, and when his spirit was even more wounded by the falling away from his original vision which he believed he saw within the order. The Francis of the *Scripta Leonis* is in part the joyous tramp who was depressed if he met anyone shabbier than himself, the mystic so much at one with natural forces that he would not quench 'brother fire' even when it had set light to his clothing, and who insisted that every Franciscan vegetable garden must have a patch for flowers.[5] But he was also the agonised witness of a growing worldliness among his sons, conscious of fighting a rearguard action to defend the stark austerity of the early days, and personally distressed by the lack of regard for his ideals displayed by some of the younger brethren.[6] One story from these writings

---

4 The distinction is Moorman's, 'Early Franciscan Art and Literature', *Bulletin of the John Rylands Library* 27 (1943), 338–58 (p. 339).

5 The writings of Leo and his companions have been edited by Rosalind Brooke, *Scripta Leonis, Rufini et Angeli sociorum S. Francisci*, OMT (Oxford, 1970). Another translation of substantially the same writings will be found as the 'Legend of Perugia' in *Omnibus*, pp. 977–1091. There is a fascinating exploration of the Leonine writings, focussed on those sections which explicitly claim to be written by 'nos cui cum eo fuimus' ('us who were with him'), in R. Manselli, *Nos qui cum eo fuimus: Contributo alla questione Francescana* (Rome, 1980). Manselli is particularly shrewd in characterising and interpreting the use made of the Leonine writings by Celano and (at a second remove) Bonaventure. For the divisions of the order in this period see Moorman, *History*, pp. 105–22 and Brooke, *Scripta Leonis*, pp. 176–9.

6 On this see Manselli, *Nos qui cum eo fuimus*, pp. 83–113.

will help to illustrate the tug of different views within the order. A novice
longed to have a Psalter of his own, to recite the office. The minister general
gave him permission to have one, but the young man wanted Francis's approval, and relentlessly badgered him on the subject. Beset by the novice once
again as he sat by the fire warming himself, Francis's patience snapped:

> 'After you have a psalter, you will want and hanker for a breviary: after
> you have a breviary, you will sit in an armchair like a great prelate,
> saying to your brother: "Bring me the breviary!" ' Thus saying, with
> great fervour of spirit he took some ashes in his hand and put them on
> his head, drawing the hand round his head as if he were washing it,
> saying to himself: 'I and my breviary, I and my breviary'. And he went
> on saying this again and again, dragging his hand round his head. And
> that friar was dumbfounded and ashamed.[7]

When, at the command of the Chapter General of the Order, Thomas produced in 1246 a *Vita secunda*, he did not attempt another chronological biography, but a character-sketch which amplified but did not replace the *Vita prima*.
The Leonine writings were his main new source, and though he softened the
sharper edges of the Leonine Francis, he clearly shared the rigorist convic-
tions of Francis's companions: the result at times reads like a sustained polemic in favour of strict observance.[8]

The passage of time and the circulation of these new writings did nothing
to ease the tensions within the order, and in 1260 an attempt was made to
restore harmony by recreating the image of the founder. St Bonaventure, the
new Minster General, was commissioned to produce a new official biography,
which duly appeared in 1263. It contained very little new material, and was
essentially a systematic reworking of Celano's first and second *Vitae* and his
Tractatus de miraculis. The Leonine writings appear to have been used only
through the medium of Celano's *Vita secunda*. Bonaventure's work reveals the
systematic approach and the theological preoccupations of a professional academic, but it nevertheless stands squarely in the mainstream of thirteenth-
century Franciscan reflection on the life of Francis. His Francis is a careful
theological construct whose whole life is presented with authorial hindsight
as mystically woven into a sevenfold pattern, based on seven visions of the
cross and the passion of Christ.[9] Bonaventure retained most of Celano's incidents, though it is true that he smoothed over some of the more awkward and
divisive traits of St Francis's character and deeds, especially those given special prominence in Celano's *Vita secunda*. In 1266 this more emollient version
of the saint's life, known as the *Legenda maior*, was declared to be the sole
authoritative life of Francis, and all others were ordered to be called in and

---

7 Brooke, *Scripta Leonis*, p. 215 (translation modified); the same story is rendered less
   vividly in *Omnibus*, p. 1049.
8 On 2 *Celano* see Moorman, *Sources*, pp. 112–27.
9 Bonaventure summarises these in *Legenda maior* xiii.10; in *Omnibus*, pp. 735–6.

destroyed. It is impossible now to be sure just what was lost as a result of this decree, but certainly many of the early testimonies disappeared for centuries, and in some cases for ever.[10]

Modern Franciscan studies can fairly be dated from the year 1894, when a Swiss protestant, Paul Sabatier, published his superb *Vie de S. François*, still, after a century, the best modern life. Sabatier's book produced an extraordinary revival of interest in Francis, and was to trigger a flood of work on the saint which has grown to oceanic proportions as the years have gone by. It quickly ran to over thirty editions, and was translated into English, German, Italian, Dutch, Swedish, Polish and Russian – Tolstoi oversaw the production of the Russian edition. But Sabatier's life of Francis was no neutral history. Sabatier was an ardent disciple of Ernest Renan, whose *Vie de Jesus* had portrayed Christ as a nature-mystic, the divine simplicity of whose message of the love of God and the brotherhood of mankind had been overlayed even in the New Testament by miracle, dogma and ecclesiastical politics. It was at Renan's personal command that his young Swiss disciple set out on a life-long search for the real St Francis, buried, as Jesus had been buried, under the dogmatic constructs of the Church and of the Franciscan Order, which sought to found its fortunes on the bones of the *poverello*. And so Sabatier's recovery of St Francis reworked the old struggles between the Spiritual and the Conventual Franciscans, the parties which emerged in the fourteenth century out of the tensions which, as we have seen, had existed within the order since the last years of the saint. Sabatier's Francis is a radiant nature-poet, a simple soul calling his contemporaries away from institutional entanglements to evangelical simplicity. The miraculous elements in Francis's story, as prominent in Celano's *Vita prima* as in Bonaventure's *Legenda maior*, were systematically played down, Francis's passionate devotion to the priesthood and the Blessed Sacrament lightly passed over, his relationship with the hierarchy and especially the papacy interpreted as part of the reworking of his image after his death. Sabatier thought the process of tidying up the image of Francis was already well-advanced in Celano's *Vita prima*, which he saw as at least in part a tract in defence of Elias and Pope Gregory IX.[11] Nevertheless, he recognised in it, whatever its faults, 'the large lines of a soul-history, a sketch of the affecting drama of a man who attains to the conquest of himself'. In Bonaventure's *Legenda maior*, however, Sabatier saw a disastrous supernaturalising and trivialising of the real saint, in which the 'loveliest incidents' of the earliest legends are 'ornamented and materialised'. In Bonaventure's work the

---

[10] Bonaventure was himself seen as a conciliating choice to heal and lead the order, nominated by his predecessor, John of Parma, an ardent supporter of strict and literal observance of the rule of poverty, who had been deposed by the Pope for his 'heretical' Joachite millenial beliefs. For the objectives and character of Bonaventure's *Legenda maior* see Moorman, *Sources*, pp. 136–51.

[11] A point of view certainly lent support by such passages as *I Celano* 73–5, in *Omnibus*, pp. 289–91.

nature-mystic of Assisi, a living, feeling, struggling man for all seasons, but especially, it seemed, for the liberal protestant *fin de siècle*, becomes a vague, impersonal figure, 'a great thaumaturgist'. The 'interior action' which is the true story of Francis and the stuff of his 'soul-drama' disappears 'before divine interventions'.[12]

Sabatier's biography of Francis has never been surpassed as an imaginative recreation of the saint, and although his distinctive presuppositions have been widely recognised, acknowledged, and allowed for, they have in fact continued to shape much writing and thinking about Franciscan history and Franciscan sources. This is true not least of the way in which historians have written about the early iconography of Francis. The crowning glory of the great pilgrimage Upper Church at Assisi is its extraordinary series of twenty-eight frescoes depicting the life and miracles of the saint. Painted sometime between 1290 and the 1330s, the series has provoked endless debate as to whether or to what extent it is by Giotto. However that may be, it is by general agreement 'one of the supremely important events in the history . . . of European art'.[13] It has also been read as a triumphant manifesto for an 'establishmentarian' understanding of the saint and his mission. The Francis of the frescoes in the Upper Church is emphatically a wonder-worker whose credentials are doubly attested by papal approval – the popes appear in six of the twenty-eight scenes – and by no fewer than twenty dreams, visions, healings or other 'miraculous interventions'. There is little overt emphasis on poverty, and the frescoes, profoundly moving as they are, do not quite offset the spectator's sense of the acute contrast between the 'wonders of the upper church' and the stark simplicities of St Francis's first rule, with its insistence that 'when the brothers go through the world they shall carry nothing for the journey, neither purse, nor bag, nor bread, nor money, nor staff . . .'.[14]

We need to avoid anachronism here. Francis's closest companions were certainly bitterly opposed to the slackening of standards and the falling away from the ideal of absolute poverty within the order in the years during which

---

[12] I have used the English version: Paul Sabatier, *Life of St Francis of Assisi* (London, 1901), pp. 365–9, 391–8.

[13] There is an immense literature on the 'Assisi problem' and the St Francis frescoes: a start can be made with A. Smart, *The Assisi problem and the Art of Giotto* (Oxford, 1971); L. Tintori and M. Meiss, *The Painting of the Life of St Francis in Assisi* (New York, 1962); H. Belting, *Die Oberkirche von San Francesco in Assisi* (Berlin, 1977); J. Poeschke, *Die Kirche San Francesco in Assisi und ihre Wandmalereien* (Munich, 1985); J. White, *Art and Architecture in Italy 1250–1400* (New Haven and London, 1993), pp. 199–244 and 344–8 (quotation in text at p. 207). J. H. Stubblebine has argued for a very late date, in the 1330s, for the Assisi cycle in *Assisi and the Rise of Vernacular Art* (New York, 1985).

[14] The Primitive Rule of 1209 is lost, but probably embedded in the Rule of 1221, for which see *Omnibus*, pp. 31–53. For two attempts to reconstruct the primitive Rule see Father Cuthbert, *The Life of St Francis of Assisi* (London, 1916), pp. 465–76 and Moorman, *Sources*, pp. 38–54.

the basilica was being built. But there is no real reason to believe that any of Francis's immediate circle protested at the honour done to the saint, and in due course his companions were to be buried close to him within Brother Elias's basilica. Francis himself had a particular reverence for the relics of saints, and was grieved when they were neglected or dishonoured. Moreover, Francis probably appreciated well enough the likely fate of his own relics. He understood perfectly well why the citizens of Assisi had sent an armed guard to escort him in his last illness back to his home town, lest another community should seize the precious body along the way. And as he lay dying in the closely maintained security of the episcopal palace at Assisi one of the brethren teased him: ' "For how much will you sell all your sackcloth to the Lord? Many rich brocades and silken cloths will be put on to cover this little body of yours which is now dressed in sackcloth".' Francis, within sight now of the end, was not disturbed, and replied 'with great fervour of spirit and gladness, "You say true, for so it will be".' Yet he can hardly have imagined the splendour of the structure which Elias was to raise over him, and it is hard to avoid the conviction that he would have hated it.[15]

All this has helped endorse Sabatier's general picture of the overlaying of the primitive simplicity of Francis's ideals, and it has had its effect on perceptions of the nature of the early lives themselves. Each scene in the Assisi frescoes is derived from the *Legenda maior*, and the whole cycle, with a few readily explicable exceptions, follows the sequence of events in Bonaventure's text. It is therefore often assumed that the wonder-working papal saint of the Upper Church is straightforwardly St Bonaventure's Francis. A recent study of Giotto's frescoes of St Francis in the church of Santa Croce at Florence associates the late thirteenth-century transformation of the image of Francis into a 'papal servant par excellence and a great miracle worker' with the establishment of the *Legenda maior* as the only official life of the saint. The author contrasts Giotto's Francis with earlier panel paintings of the saint, in the process setting 'Bonaventure's Francis', found in the Giotto paintings (and the Assisi frescoes), over against 'Celano's Francis', found in the early panels, and she sees this earlier Francis as perceptibly more human, more compassionate, and more overtly dedicated to poverty and the poor.[16]

This contrast has some truth in it, but it has been overdone. It exaggerates or at any rate misdescribes the differences between Celano's and Bonaventure's picture of Francis. Celano's biography, it should be remembered, was commissioned by Pope Gregory IX, and Celano was just as keen as Bonaventure to emphasise Francis's orthodoxy, to harp on the endorsement of his movement and of him personally by successive Popes, and to illustrate his

---

[15] Brooke, *Scripta Leonis*, pp. 190–3 and 260–3; White, *Art and Architecture in Italy*, p. 223.

[16] R. Goffen, *Spirituality in Conflict: St Francis and Giotto's Bardi Chapel* (University Park, PA, and London, 1988). See below, pp. 214–15.

prowess as a wonder-worker and healer.[17] Nor is it fair to see in Bonaventure's portrait of Francis a partisan triumph for the views associated with brother Elias. Bonaventure's aim in compiling the *Legenda maior* was to provide an image of the founder which both the advocates of strict observance and their opponents could join in approving, and in this on the whole he succeeded. He certainly included a great deal of material on the rigour of Francis's insistence on poverty and simplicity, though that material undergoes a sea-change in his conciliatory handling of it.

The general character of Bonaventure's work in the *Legenda maior* can be gathered from one example, the story of the brother at Rivo Torto who said he was dying of hunger.[18] The episode was one of those set down in the *Scripta Leonis* by Francis's companions in 1244, and in their version was a story about the startling austerities of the original Franciscans, 'Quodam tempore in primordio'. It tells of their extraordinary penances – fasting, vigils, and the wearing of hairshirts and metal fetters next to the skin. In his inexperience, one of the brethren pushed these austerities beyond endurance, and one night at Rivo Torto woke Francis with his cries of desperation. Francis summoned all the brethren, and with characteristic delicacy insisted that all should join the starving brother in a meal. He then lectured the brethren on the need for prudence in not pushing their bodies beyond tolerable limits, 'since the Lord will have mercy and not sacrifice'. But this prudence, he emphasised, was not to be an excuse to 'deviate at any time from the order's standard of poverty and conduct which the early brethren practised'.[19] The passage concludes with an insistence on the standard of poverty and austerity which Francis himself, despite his poor health, maintained: 'Do not the brothers think that a little indulgence is necessary to my body? It is because I need to be a model and an example to all the brothers that I want to use and be content with poor food and things that are not dainty.' [20]

In adapting this story for his *Vita secunda* Celano modifies it and its moral substantially, but retains the essential elements – the emphasis on the great austerity of the life-style practiced by the first brethren, with its implicit reproach of the slackness of the 1240s, the saint's insistence on prudence, and his sensitive dealing with the shame of the starving brother. Celano moves the final reference to Francis's own extreme asceticism to a more emphatic place

[17] See, for example, *I Celano* 28, 32–3, 47, 58–61, 62–70, 94–6, 114–15, 119–50; in *Omnibus*, pp. 251–2, 254–5, 268–9, 277–80, 280–7, 308–10, 327–30, 333–54.
[18] For the successive recensions of the story, see Brooke, *Scripta Leonis*, pp. 88–91 (another translation in *Omnibus*, pp. 977–8); *2 Celano* 21–2 (*Omnibus*, pp. 380–1); *Legenda maior* v.7 (*Omnibus*, pp. 667–8). There is an illuminating discussion of the episode in Manselli, *Nos qui cum eo fuimus*, pp. 83–94.
[19] The version of this sentence in *the Omnibus* translation of Leo's text, 'which are traditional among the senior brothers' (pp. 380–1), misses the emphasis in the Latin on the primitive observance of the early days.
[20] Brooke, *Scripta Leonis*, p. 91.

at the beginning of his account and ends the passage with the saint's warning that his example in eating with the brother was to be taken as a model only of charity, not an excuse for relaxing the rule.[21]

Bonaventure bases his account of this incident on Celano's version, but softens and redirects it. He opens the story not with an account of Francis's austerities, but with a resounding condemnation of excessive asceticism:

> Francis did his utmost to encourage the friars to lead austere lives, but he had no time for exaggerated self-denial which excluded tender compassion or was not tempered with discretion.

He also drastically modifies the details of the story, editing out the references to the austerities of the early brethren, Francis and the starving brother becoming the only people involved. According to Bonaventure Francis's homily on prudence, originally delivered at the end of the impromptu midnight meal, is in fact delivered the next morning, after the saint has told the brethren who had slept through the whole incident what had happened during the night. Yet it should be noted that although Bonaventure was concerned to remove the potentially divisive elements of the story – in particular its insistence on the superior asceticism of the early days at Rivo Torto – he has no desire to legitimate a general retreat from strict observance, or from the ideal of poverty itself. As in Celano, Bonaventure ends the incident with Francis's warning to the brethren to imitate his charity, but not to deduce from it that they might freely break their fasts. And Bonaventure adds a significant qualification of the injunction to prudence, in order to underline the continuing need for the strenuous pursuit of a life of perfection:

> He [Francis] taught them to practise prudence, not the prudence recommended by our fallen nature, but that practised by Christ, whose life is the model of all perfection.[22]

As this nuanced handling of his sources suggests, Bonaventure's *Legenda maior*, for all its undoubted diplomacy, is a richer and more complex document than the beguiling polarities of Sabatier's interpretation allows. There is more to his Francis than a mere papal miracle-worker or a spokesman for a lax view of the Franciscan vocation. The Francis of the Assisi frescoes, too, is a complex figure, and is certainly not so much 'Bonaventure's Francis' as a further construct made at a later time, representing different priorities and choices, though drawing its material from Bonaventure's *Legenda*.

---

[21] *Omnibus*, pp. 380–1.
[22] *Omnibus*, pp. 667–8.

2. Miracle and Image: The Earliest Pictures

All the same, the early paintings of St Francis do constitute a distinctive and revealing type of historical evidence, and provide a fascinating insight into shifting perceptions of the saint and his significance. Francis himself was intensely aware of visual images, and they played a prominent role in his own story. From Celano's *Vita secunda* onwards, Francis's conversion was linked to the Romanesque crucifix at San Damiano (now in the relic chapel at Santa Chiara's in Assisi), which Francis heard tell him, 'Go, and repair my house, which, as you see, is falling into ruins'.[23] Franciscan piety laid considerable stress on the visual evocation of the sacred, a pattern set in the story of Francis's invention of the crib at Greccio, and an emphasis endlessly recurring in Franciscan preaching and writing, from the detailed scene-setting of Franciscan devotional texts such as the *Meditationes vitae Christi* to the controversial employment of visual aids by preachers such as St Bernardino, and the allegations of idolatry which these brought.[24] But above all, Francis himself was understood and presented by his followers as the living image of Christ. The miracle of the stigmata by which, two years before his death, Francis was marked with the wounds of Christ in hands and feet and side, transformed him into a living crucifix. As Bonaventure wrote in the *Legenda major*,

> True love of Christ had now transformed his lover into his image . . . he bore a representation of Christ Crucified which was not the work of an artist in wood or stone, but had been reproduced in the members of his body by the hand of the living God.[25]

Thomas of Celano's *Tractatus de miraculis B. Francisci*, produced in the early 1250s to supplement the *Vita secunda*, contains a story which perfectly illustrates the centrality of the image in the early cult of the saint, and in particular the centrality of the representation of the stigmata. Thomas tells how a Roman matron devoted to Francis had a painting of him in her private oratory before which she prayed. The image was evidently painted soon after the saint's death, before a conventional iconography had developed, for, like what is perhaps the earliest known picture of Francis in Gregory IX's chapel at Subiaco (and therefore, interestingly, also of Roman provenance), it showed the saint without the stigmata. The stigmata rapidly established themselves as the distinctive emblem of St Francis, however, and Celano's story turns on the discrepancy between the woman's icon, and the stigmatised images of the saint which had now become the norm. While praying one day the woman

---

[23] *2 Celano* 10, in *Omnibus*, p. 370.

[24] On the *Meditationes* see M. Deanesly, 'The Gospel Harmony of John de Caulibus or S. Bonaventure', in *Collectanea Franciscana*, II, *British Society for Franciscan Studies* 10 (1922), 10–20.

[25] *Legenda maior* xiii.5, in *Omnibus*, p. 732.

turned an intense devotional gaze on the picture, and for the first time noticed the absence of the stigmata. She became confused and agitated, although, comments Celano, 'it was no great wonder they were not there, because the painter had left them out'. Happily, however, St Francis was more sympathetic to the pious woman's confusion than his biographer, for the stigmata duly appeared miraculously on the picture, only to disappear again when the woman began to wonder whether, after all, they had not always been there. Another story in the same collection tells of a canon of Potenza in Apulia stricken with doubts about the stigmata while praying before an icon of Francis on which they were portrayed. He was himself immediately stigmatised with a wound like an arrow-blow in the palm of his hand, though the glove he was wearing remained unharmed. This miracle found its way in due course onto a panel painting of the early 1280s, depicting scenes from the life of the saint and now at Orte.[26] The interest of the two stories for us lies in the evidence they provide for the establishment of a firm convention in the representations of Francis by the mid-1240s, and of corresponding lay expectations about what an icon of the saint must include.

In what follows, I want to explore that issue more fully by considering the iconography of some of the earliest surviving pictures of Francis, and to try to relate that iconography to the shifts in the canon of hagiographic texts by which the cult of Francis was shaped and promoted. I shall focus on the historiated panels, which group a series of scenes from the saint's life or miracles round a central figure of the saint himself. Such images were by no means restricted to Francis in thirteenth-century Italy – there are well-known examples at Florence devoted to the story of St Mary Magdalene and St Humilitas, and at Siena devoted to the legends of St Peter and St John the Baptist, as well as a panel devoted to the life of St Clare at Assisi.[27] But the

26 Celano, *Tractatus de miraculis B. Francisci*, 8 and 9, in 'Legendae S. Francisci', pp. 275–6. There is no English translation of the *Tractatus de miraculis*, but the same stories are repeated by Bonaventure, *Legenda maior*, 'De Miraculis . . . post mortem' 4 and 6, in *Omnibus*, pp. 749–50 and 752. The Orte panel is illustrated in P. Scarpellini, 'Iconografia francescana nei secoli XIII e XIV', in *Francesco d'Assisi, Storia e Arte*, ed. F. Prozio (Milan, 1982), pp. 91–126 with illustrations at pp. 104 and 120; and also in C. Frugoni, *Francesco e l'invenzione delle stimmate* (Turin, 1993), plate 180.

27 The standard listing of all such altarpieces is E. B. Garrison, *Italian Romanesque Panel Painting: An Illustrated Index* (Florence, 1949), especially sections xxi–xxii. For a comment on the relative abundance of panels dealing with the story of Francis, see W. B. Miller, 'The Franciscan Legend in Italian Painting in the Thirteenth Century' (unpublished Ph.D. dissertation, Columbia, 1961), p. 354. The St Peter and St John altarpieces are illustrated in E. Carli, *Siennese Painting* (London, 1983), pp. 8–9, and the St Peter painting only in P. Torriti, *La Pinacoteca Nazionale di Siena: i dipinti dal xii al xv secolo* (Genoa, 1977), no. 15, plates 4–6. For the St Mary Magdalene altarpiece see G. Bonsanti, *The Galleria della Accademia, Florence* (London, 1992), p. 54. There is a useful discussion of the Mary Magdalene panel in G. Sinibaldi and G. Brunetti, *Pittura Italiana del Duecento e Trecento. Catalogo della Mostra Giottesca di Firenze del 1937* (Florence, 1943), no. 70, pp. 228–31; for other similar panels see nos. 19, 22, 28 (the Siena St Peter) and 32 (the Siena St John the Baptist) in the same catalogue.

Plate 1: Bonaventure Berlinghieri, *St Francis and Six Miracles* (1234);
Church of San Francesco, Pescia

earliest known panel telling the story of Francis predates any of these, and it seems certain that Francis was the first saint, in the West at any rate, to have his life and miracles painted in this way. A larger number of such panels survive illustrating his story than for any other saint in the thirteenth century, a testimony to the importance and ubiquity of his cult, the vigour with which the Franciscan order promoted it, and hence its special attraction to painters.

In considering the earliest paintings of St Francis we are at a distinct disadvantage, for with the single possible exception of the image at Subiaco, perhaps commissioned sometime in the late 1220s by Gregory IX, we do not know and can barely guess at the circumstances in which they were produced.[28] Only one early image can be dated with certainty, the altar-piece now in the church of San Francesco in Pescia, thirty-eight kilometres north-west of Florence. Signed and dated by Bonaventure Berlinghieri in 1235, it was therefore painted within nine years of Francis's death.[29] Francis was a small man without much physical presence, particularly in his later years when his self-denying life-style had taken its toll and made him an emaciated and unkempt figure. The austere and looming solemnity of the central figure in this and indeed all the other thirteenth-century panel-paintings of the saint probably reflects the influence of Byzantine painting: it can hardly be an attempt at a realistic portrait, at any rate. Francis is portrayed between two angels. His stigmata are depicted, though not the wound in the side. He holds a closed and clasped book in his left hand, while his right is held up and outwards in a gesture of greeting and display which simultaneously shows the wound and echoes the gesture of the angels on either side. There is more than decorative symmetry at work here. The Franciscan order in the early thirteenth century was a rampant breeding-ground for apocalyptic speculation. Many sober men were persuaded that they lived in the last days, and Francis was widely identified with the angel of the sixth seal in the Apocalypse, who bears 'the sign of the living God'. Bonaventure is quite explicit about this identification in the prologue to the *Legenda maior*:

> He was filled with the spirit of prophecy and charged with the ministry
> of angels, as he burned with the flame of love worthy of the seraphim.

[28] The Subiaco image is illustrated and discussed in Scarpellini, 'Iconografia Francescana', p. 107.

[29] See our Plate 1. Reproduced in colour as plate 1 in A. Smart, *The Dawn of Italian Painting 1250–1400* (Oxford, 1978), and in black and white in G. Sinibaldi and G. Brunetti, *Pittura Italiana del duecento e trecento. Catalogo della Mostra Giottesca di Firenze del 1937* (Florence, 1943), no. 5, pp. 14–19, also in Scarpellini, 'Iconografia Francescana', p. 92 and in F. Hartt, *History of Italian Renaissance Art* (London, 1987), p. 32, fig. 24. This and all the earliest panels containing scenes from Francis's life and miracles are reproduced and perceptively discussed in B. Bughetti, 'Vita e miracoli di San Francesco nelle tavole istoriate dei secoli XIII e XIV', *Archivum Franciscanum Historicum* 19 (1926), 636–732. See also the discussions in Sinibaldi and Brunetti, *Catalogo della Mostra Giottesca*, nos. 18 and 55; it has been discussed most recently in C. Frugoni, *Francesco e l'Invenzione delle Stimmate* (Turin, 1993), pp. 321–45.

Like a man who has joined the ranks of the angels, he was taken up in a chariot of fire, so that there can be no doubt whatever that he came 'in the spirit and power of an Elijah', as we shall see in the course of his life. Therefore there is every reason to believe that it is he who is referred to under the image of an angel coming up from the East, with the seal of the living God. . . . When the sixth seal was broken, St John tells us in the Apocalypse, 'I saw a second angel coming up from the east, with the seal of the living God' (Apocalypse 7. 2) . . . we have an unimpeachable testimony, the seal of truth itself which was impressed on his body and which made him like the living God, Christ Crucified.[30]

Bonaventure did not write that, of course, till the early 1260s, but speculation about the meaning of the stigmata, and identification of Francis with the Angels of the Apocalypse, began immediately after the Saint's death, the latter indeed probably before, for from an early point in his ministry Francis's companions believed that he was destined to occupy the throne in heaven vacated by Lucifer's fall.[31] However, the fact that the stigmata were given in a vision of a crucified seraph provided the main stimulus to the development of this line of thought. So also did the miracle of the preaching to the birds, in itself a picturesque godsend to artists, and which prompted the further symbolic identification of Francis with the angel standing in the sun in Revelation 19. 17, who said to all the birds of the air, 'Come, gather yourselves together to the great supper of God'.[32] Together, the miracles of the stigmata and the preaching to the birds became instantly recognisable shorthand for the dignity and mission of Francis and the Franciscans, the stigmata as a unique sign of divine favour, the preaching to the birds as a symbol of Francis's and the order's mandate and right to carry the Gospel through the whole world: both scenes encapsulating the aura of apolcalyptic expectation which surrounded the expansion of the movement in the thirteenth and early fourteenth centuries. The two scenes are sometimes grouped together in thirteenth and early fourteenth-century Franciscan iconography, and both scenes were likely to feature in any sequence, however short, illustrating the glories of the saint, as

30 *Legenda maior,* Prologue 1 and 2, in *Omnibus,* p. 632. On Francis as the Angel of the Sixth Seal, see J. V. Fleming, *From Bonaventure to Bellini, an Essay in Franciscan Exegesis* (Princeton, 1982), especially pp. 129–57, and S. da Campagnola, *L'Angelo del Sesto Sigillo e l'Alter Christus* (Rome, 1971).
31 Brooke, *Scripta Leonis,* pp. 128–9, in *Omnibus,* pp. 999–1001. This belief, rooted in the vision of Brother Pacifico, is the subject of fresco 19 in the Upper Church at Assisi, though Bonaventure's account, on which the Assisi picture is based, does not name the fallen angel as Lucifer.
32 This dimension of the miracle of the birds was apparently particularly keenly explored in early English Franciscan iconography: see F. D. Klingender, 'St Francis and the Birds of the Apocalypse', *Journal of the Warburg and Courtauld Institute* 16 (1953), 13–23. But see Miller, 'Franciscan Legend', p. 126, for scepticism about Klingender's arguments.

they do in the famous panel from Giotto's workshop now in the Louvre.[33] It is no surprise, therefore, to find that these are the two scenes chosen to represent the life of St Francis on the Pescia altarpiece.

The four remaining scenes illustrate post-mortem miracles of St Francis, taken directly from the appendix of miracles in Celano's *Vita prima*, and which was itself derived from the list read out by the Pope's subdeacon during the canonisation ceremony at St Giorgio's, Assisi, in 1228. At the bottom left of the panel is a portrayal of the first of these stories given by Celano. It tells how on the day of Francis's funeral a little girl with a neck so deformed that her head was twisted down on to her shoulder was laid against the tomb, and healed. In the picture we see the contorted child leaning against the saint's temporary shrine, here represented by an altar on which are laid missal, chalice and ampule of wine. Her mother kneels in supplication before the altar. At the extreme left we see the aftermath of the miracle, as the rejoicing mother carries away the child, now able to sit upright on her shoulder. The scene does not exactly reproduce the details of Celano's text, in which the child herself runs away after the healing. We shall have occasion to refer again to the altar shrine in this picture.[34]

Scene four shows a group of kneeling cripples before St Francis's altar. The saint himself stands behind the altar, extending a hand to one of the supplicants, a beardless boy. Behind them stands a figure in the garb of a pilgrim, identifiable as a leper because of the castanets or clappers he carries prominently in his right hand, and which were used to warn people of the leper's approach. Behind him, the healed cripples leave the sanctuary. This scene ingeniously encapsulates nine separate miracles which took place at St Francis's first burial place in San Giorgio, Assisi. Immediately after the account of the girl with the twisted neck, Celano gives eight stories of cripples healed. There are eight kneeling figures in the picture, and one of them can be firmly identified from Celano's text, where St Francis heals a young boy from Montenero by appearing to him and offering him some pears. The boy reaches out to take them and finds he can move freely. The leper pilgrim standing behind the eight cripples is also identifiable from Celano's text: he is a boy named Acto, from San Severino in the Marches of Ancona, who was both a leper and a paralytic, and who was healed on vowing pilgrimage to St Francis.[35]

[33] For example, in the illuminated page from a thirteenth-century Franciscan antiphonal now in the capitular Archives of St Peter's in Rome (MS B27), showing both miracles, discussed and reproduced in F. Todini, 'I codici duecenteschi del Duomo di Assisi', in *Francesco d'Assisi, documenti e archive, codici e biblioteche, miniature* (Milan, 1982), pp. 171–2. It is reproduced in colour in G. Atanassiu, S. Gieben, R. Manselli *et al.*, *Francesco, in Italia, nel mondo* (Milan, 1990), p. 391. The Giotto panel is illustrated in L. Bellosi, *Giotto* (Florence, 1981), p. 27.

[34] *I Celano* 127, in *Omnibus*, pp. 341–2

[35] *I Celano* 128–34 and 146, in *Omnibus*, pp. 342–5 and 351.

Scene 5 depicts the healing of Bartholomew of Narni, a man paralysed while sleeping under a walnut tree, and whose limbs withered during the consequent illness of six years. Told in a dream by Francis to bathe in a particular place, he eventually does so and feels the hands of the saint straightening and healing his limbs in the bath. This story directly follows those of the other eight cripples in Celano's text, but was evidently sufficiently picturesque to warrant separate treatment. It certainly makes a striking and instantly recognisable image. The final scene depicts the exorcism of Peter of Foligno and other demoniacs at the saint's tomb: in Celano's texts these stories once again follow on directly from the miracles in the earlier panels, and the painter is clearly following the order and detail in the text closely.[36]

This panel by Berlinghieri is one of a series in which the same scenes recur in stereotyped form. The same four miracles appear on the rectangular panels now in the Tesoro of the Basilica at Assisi and in the Vatican Pinacoteca. The Roman panel is definitely the later and less skilled of the two, but the Assisi painting is almost certainly the product of a workshop associated with the basilica and supplying the devotional market created by the cult: the panel was probably intended for display to pilgrims near the shrine in the lower church.[37] The saint stands, holding a cross in his right hand, while in his left is an open book. The portrayal of the saint with a cross and open book may be particularly associated with Assisi, for the image of the saint painted on the wood of his bed-pallet now kept in the Basilica Museum at Assisi holds both.[38] On the Tesoro panel the pages of the book are painted with the words 'SI VIS PERFECTU / S ESSE VADE ET VE / NDE OMNIA QUE HABE / ES ET DA PAUPERIBUS' ('if you would be perfect, go, sell all that you have and give to the poor'). The emphasis on giving to the poor in this panel, painted for Brother Elias's basilica at Assisi, raises intriguing questions, and is yet another indication that we would be unwise to read the later confrontations of spirituals and conventuals over the poverty question into these early pictorial sources – unless, indeed, the *pauperes* to whom the panel urges us to give all be interpreted as the Order itself! But however that may be, the depiction of Francis here, bearing the words which Jesus spoke to the rich young man, inevitably carries a Christological weight.[39] Francis here calls to the imitation of Christ which is the basis of his rule, and he is himself the rich young man who has given away all he had and followed Christ. But in his hands the text is a call also to the imitation of Francis himself, as *Alter Christus*, and founder of the Order

---

[36] *I Celano* 135 and 137–8, in *Omnibus*, pp. 344–6.

[37] See Plate 2. Illustrated in Scarpellini, 'Iconografia Francescana', pp. 101 and 103. Scarpellini provides a very full discussion of the panel in *Il Tesoro della Basilica di San Francesco ad Assisi, saggi e catologo* (Assisi, 1980), pp. 34–8.

[38] J. H. Stubblebine, *Guido da Siena* (Princeton, 1964), pp. 107–9. The image on the bed-pallet is illustrated in colour in P. P. Magro, *Assisi: History, Art, Spirituality* (Assisi, n.d.), p. 138.

[39] Matthew 19. 21: 'Ait illi Jesus: Si vis perfectus esse vade vende quae habes et da pauperibus et habebis thesaurum in coelo et veni sequere me' (Vulgate).

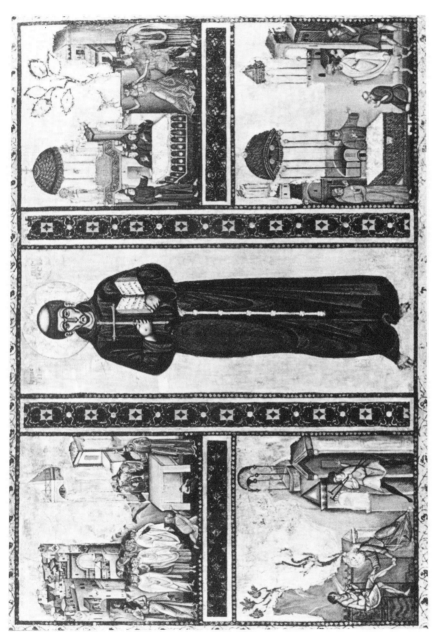

Plate 2: Anonymous, *St Francis with Four Post-Mortem Miracles* (c.1260); Assisi, Museo del Tesoro del Sacro Convento

whose mother church the Basilica at Assisi claimed to be. We shall return shortly to this *Alter Christus* theme in Franciscan art.

In this Assisi panel, two of the standard post-mortem miracles have been modified, in one case in the interests of pictorial simplicity, in the other to take account of newly available texts. In the scene of the healing of the cripples the figure of St Francis has been removed, and the crowd of eight suppliants has been reduced to one. He is no longer the boy from Montenero to whom Francis gave pears, but another of the eight cripples whose stories are given in Celano's *Vita prima*, a bearded man, identifiable as Nicholas of Foligno, healed after making a pilgrimage to Assisi and spending a night in prayer at the tomb. The figure of Nicholas the pilgrim relates more satisfactorily to the other pilgrim, the leper behind him, and the revised picture is simpler and more easily read than its prototype.[40] In the exorcism scene immediately above, the painter once again simplifies the prototype: only one demoniac, the girl of Norcia, is depicted, whose story comes not from Celano's *Vita prima*, but from his *Tractatus de miraculis*, formally approved by the Chapter General of the order in 1253. It is easy to see why this particular story of exorcism has replaced the earlier composite exorcism scene. The girl concerned was distracted, tearing herself with her teeth and deprived of rational speech. Brought bound by her parents to Francis's shrine on the feast of Candlemas, she vomits out the demon during mass, and is fully restored on kissing the altar: she begins to praise God and his saints in words from Psalm 150. Once again the new story makes a far more dramatic and pictorially satisfying exorcism scene, in which the anguished parents, the girl's disordered clothing and violent gestures, and the demon being expelled before the altar combine in a memorable and easily read image. In both these scenes the painter has quite recognisably set the scene in the lower Church at Assisi, for he has depicted the very distinctive high altar of the Lower Church, with its rows of lamps set within pointed arches.[41]

The Assisi and Rome panels show us the overall iconographic schema of Berlinghieri's altarpiece being retained, while individual scenes are adjusted and modified to take account of the wider range of miracle-stories available after 1253. The unmistakable basilican provenance of the Assisi panel makes explicit what we may take to be the principal aim of all these panels, the deliberate promotion of the cult of Francis and of pilgrimage to his shrine. Lay clients of the Franciscans worshipping at any of their great urban churches would be likely to encounter such pictures on the altar of St Francis, and might thereby be prompted to take their own needs to the saint at his shrine.

Some other gabled panels similarly modify or add to the Berlinghieri schema. The one from the Church of San Francesco at Pisa (now in the Museo di San Matteo there) allows us to see this policy of the promotion of the cult by

---

[40] *I Celano* 129, in *Omnibus*, p. 342.
[41] *Tractatus de miraculis* 153, in 'Legendae S. Francisci', p. 318.

the transmission of accounts of Francis's miracles of healing actually in process. The panel resembles the Assisi and Rome altarpieces in omitting any incidents from the life of St Francis, and portraying only post-mortem miracles, but it has six miracles instead of four. These include the four familiar to us from the Assisi panel, with the demoniac scene in its post-1253 form. Two entirely new scenes are portrayed, both similarly derived from the *Tractatus de miraculis*. One of these is the revenge miracle of the woman of Piglio, who refuses to honour St Francis by keeping his feast-day holy, and whose daughter is afflicted in retaliation by having her eyes squeezed up into her head till they pop out: she is restored on her mother's promise to observe the feast with devotion and alms to the poor in future.[42] The other new scene is altogether more edifying, the healing of the noblewoman with a fistula between her breasts. She had gone to pray in a Franciscan church in 'Galeta', and there encounters word of Francis's power to heal, not through a picture but through the written word. Celano tells us that there was a book in the church containing the life and miracles of Francis – presumably Celano's *Vita prima* or perhaps a liturgical legendary. The woman eagerly enquired about the contents of the book, and on having them explained to her, tearfully appealed to the saint to deliver her as he has delivered others. As her tears flow, her wound is healed. In the picture she is shown displaying her wound to the friars, and then departing cured. The story throws a fascinating light on the order's deliberate promotion of Francis's reputation as a wonder-worker, and the use of a hagiographic text to disseminate the saint's cult. In the process it offers an excellent example of the absorbtion of the miracles thus produced back into the textual and iconographic tradition which had triggered them in the first place.[43]

Another gabled panel now in the Museo Civico at Pistoia shows the further elaboration of the same basic schema.[44] This picture was 'modernised' in the early seventeenth century: it presents some difficulties of interpretation, and may not be in its original state. It has four scenes from the life of the saint, and four post-mortem miracles with which we are by now familiar – the girl with the twisted neck, the healing of the cripple Nicholas of Foligno, the miracle of Bartholomew of Narni in the bath, the demoniac girl from Norcia. The presence of miracles first recorded in Celano's *Tractatus de miraculis* indicates that this panel too was almost certainly painted after 1253. The four scenes from the life of Francis are the approval of the Rule by Innocent III, the stigmata, the preaching of the saint, and the death and ascension of the saint. Here the issues implicit in the depiction of the miracle of the birds on the Berlinghieri altarpiece – Francis's mission to preach to all creation – are spelled out in

---

[42] *Tractatus de miraculis* 103, in 'Legendae S. Francisci', p. 307. The panel is illustrated in colour in Frugoni, *Stimmate*, plate 34.

[43] *Tractatus de miraculis* 193, in 'Legendae S. Francisci', p. 328.

[44] Illustrated in Scarpellini, 'Iconografia Francescana', p. 97, and discussed on p. 117. It is reproduced in colour in *Francesco, in Italia, nel mondo*, p. 81.

institutional terms. The approval of the Rule by the Pope emphasises papal endorsement of Franciscan activities and privileges, and the particular right of the order to preach to all is emphasised by the scene in which the saint preaches from a raised pulpit. It is hard to place this scene in Celano's or indeed Bonaventure's biographies of Francis, and it may have been changed by clumsy restoration, but the listening figures on the left appear to be wearing turbans or veils, and this is perhaps a depiction of or at any rate a reference to Francis's preaching before the Sultan.[45] The scene of Francis's death and exaltation, with its visual reminiscence of Byzantine paintings and mosaics of the dormition of the Virgin, underlines the saint's privilege and dignity, and hence that of his order. By the mid-century when this picture was painted the order was in conflict both with the secular clergy, jealous of Franciscan invasion of the parishes, and with the Dominicans, their mendicant rivals for the favour of the laity. It is hard to avoid the feeling that this altarpiece is consciously designed to bolster lay support for the Franciscan order and its activities against such attacks. The depiction of the story of the saint is no longer intended merely to promote his cult, but also to foster loyalty and attachment to his children.

It is obvious that the Pescia altarpiece by Berlinghieri represents an early stage in the evolution of iconographic conventions in the depiction of Francis's story. Its essential pictorial scheme is developed directly from the section on miracles at the end of Celano's *Vita prima*, and the miracles selected for portrayal follow very closely Celano's sequence. But he in turn was using the miracles promulgated at the canonisation proceedings, so that all these programmatic panels perhaps should be understood, like Celano's biography itself, as officially commissioned instruments of the new cult. The basic scheme was not rigidly fixed, as we have seen, and could be subsequently modified in a search for simpler and clearer images, in response to new and more vivid texts, or to meet new challenges to the order.

But the Berlinghieri panel, early as it is, cannot I think be the prototype from which all the other images developed, since it betrays signs of being itself derived from an earlier image. If we look closely at this panel's version of the miracle of the girl with the twisted neck, we will find that there is something amiss with the altar. It certainly is an altar, for it has the conventional vessels and mass-book arranged along its top. But it is oddly draped, with a dark frontal raised in the centre and reaching the ground at the corners, and with an odd rectangular ornament in the centre just below the upper fringe. Comparison with other versions of the same picture solves the mystery. In the Assisi panel, for example, as in the same scene in the Rome and Pistoia altarpieces, the crippled girl is quite unmistakeably leaning against a wooden chest on four short legs, with a prominently displayed lock. The miracle took place on the day of St Francis's first funeral, and the wooden box

45 *I Celano* 57, in *Omnibus*, pp. 276–7.

in the pictures is almost certainly a stylised representation of the casket in which the saint's remains were kept in the church of San Giorgio, before their removal in 1230 to brother Elias's new basilica. It seems likely therefore that Berlinghieri was working from a pictorial pattern in which the sick girl leans against this shrine, as she does in Celano's text, but that he has misinterpreted his pattern, and turned the coffin into an oddly-draped altar. Berlinghieri, therefore, while certainly indebted to Celano's text, was also using a pictorial prototype dating from before 1235, which like Celano's biography itself, looks as if it was part of an official programme designed to publicise Francis's merits and miracles in the wake of the canonisation proceedings of 1228.[46]

All these panels could fairly be represented, I think, as offering us in some sense 'Celano's Francis', since they draw on Celano's writings for their incidental detail. But the Francis who emerges from them has no personality, and apart from that implicit in the compressed images of the stigmata or the preaching to the birds, no story. They are programmatic pieces designed to promote within Franciscan churches the cult of Francis as wonder-worker and healer, as Celano himself had emphasised at the end of the *Vita prima*:

> At his tomb new miracles are constantly occurring, and . . . great benefits for body and soul are sought at that same place. Sight is given to the blind, hearing is restored to the deaf, the ability to walk is given to the lame, the mute speak, he who has gout leaps, the leper is healed, he who has a swelling has it reduced . . . so that his dead body heals living bodies just as his living body had raised up dead souls.[47]

To this promotion of the cult and shrine at Assisi may have been added the desire, in panels like that from Pistoia, to draw attention to Francis's role as patron of an order whose mission and activities had provoked opposition and needed endorsement. But all of them reveal a greater interest in Francis's heavenly status and present role as intercessor and healer than in any effort to portray incidents from the saint's biography. We should not look to these early images for a 'primitive' or historical Francis.

---

[46] The same pictorial confusion is evident in the Pisa panel version of this miracle, and in that at Rome, which suggests that for this scene at any rate both depend on the Berlinghieri painting of 1235, or on a common prototype. In the scenes of the demoniac girl of Norcia and the healing of the cripples, however, the Pisa and Roman panels follow the simplified iconography found in the Assisi and Pistoian panels. Bughetti, 'Vita e miracoli', fig. xxiii, reproduces an eighteenth-century copy of a drawing of another panel, formerly at San Miniato, allegedly dating from 1228, and Scarpellini sees no reason to challenge this date. It is also accepted by Frugoni, who attributes the painting to Berlinghieri: *Stimmate*, pp. 321–5, and plate 129. But one of the six scenes portrayed (bottom left: cf. Frugoni, *Stimmate*, plate 175) appears to me to be the miracle of the woman of Piglio, whose first literary appearance is in the *Tractatus de miraculis*, making a date before 1253 problematic. I have therefore omitted the San Miniato panel from this discussion.

[47] *I Celano* 121, in *Omnibus*, p. 335.

3. Picture and Story: The Bardi Dossal

The most elaborate and impressive of the historical altar-pieces depicting the
life and miracles of St Francis is the dossal in the Bardi chapel of the Franciscan church of Santa Croce in Florence.[48] Here are represented no fewer than
twenty scenes from Francis's life and miracles, while the figure of the saint
himself differs in intriguing and significant ways from the other representations we have been considering. Santa Croce is one of the greatest of
Franciscan churches, and housed a community which harboured leading
'Spiritual' activists like Ubertino of Casale. The panel's location here, in the
same chapel as Giotto's superb set of seven frescoes from the story of Francis,
together with the fact that the twenty scenes represent the most extensive
treatment of the story of Francis (or indeed of any other saint) before the
Assisi frescoes, has meant that it has received more attention than any other
thirteenth-century image of the saint.[49] Most recent commentators on the
Bardi dossal have abandoned the earlier view that it depends on Bonaventure's *Legenda maior*, and must have therefore been painted after 1263, and
have wanted to give it an earlier date. It is now widely accepted that the panel
was painted before the completion of the *Legenda maior*, and that the painter
'relies solely on the writings of Thomas of Celano as the source for his narrative'.[50] J. H. R. Moorman believed that the Bardi dossal was an attempt to
translate into pictorial terms the spirit of Celano's second *vita* of Francis, and
Rona Goffen has contrasted 'Celano's Francis', as depicted on this panel, with
'Bonaventure's Francis', as portrayed by Giotto, and believes that the dossal
was painted before the end of John of Parma's Minister-Generalship, that is,
before 1257. She believes that the dossal was commissioned for the Church of
Santa Croce, and that it represents the views of a 'Spiritual' or observant party,
strongly represented in the Santa Croce community before the departure of
Ubertino of Casale and his supporters in 1289. For her, the Francis of the Bardi
dossal is 'a compassionate human being whose progress towards holiness is
depicted in scenes emphasizing his human character'. By contrast, once
Bonaventure's Francis became the norm, as it was for the Assisi frescoes,
Francis was perceived as 'the papal servant par excellence . . . and a great

---

48 See Plate 3. Reproduced and discussed in Sinibaldi and Brunetti, *Catalogo della
    Mostra Giottesca*, no. 55, pp. 176–80; and in Scarpellini, 'Iconografia Francescana', pp.
    95 and 117. It is reproduced in colour in *Francesco, in Italia, nel mondo*, p. 80.
49 Especially in Goffen's full-length study, *Spirituality in Conflict* (cf. note 16 above),
    which contains an extensive bibliography of earlier studies, and in Frugoni, *Stim-
    mate*, pp. 357–98 and illustrated in plate 31 with details in plates 32, 70, 86, 146, 152,
    160–2, 164–6 and 168–74.
50 J. E. Stein, 'Dating the Bardi St Francis Master Dossal: Text and Image', *FS* 36 (1976),
    271–95. Her conclusions substantially agree with those of Miller, 'Franciscan Legend
    in Italian Painting'. Frugoni relies heavily on Stein's work for her discussion of the
    Bardi dossal, but does not accept Stein's proposed date in the 1250s.

miracle worker'.[51] Richard Trexler, in a highly speculative book on Francis's renunciation of his father, has even suggested that the Bardi Dossal may predate Berlinghieri's Pescia altarpiece of 1235.[52] And most recently of all, in a major study of the development of Franciscan thinking about and representation of the Stigmata, Chiara Frugoni has argued that the Bardi dossal is derived exclusively from Celano's first biography, showing no acquaintance with 2 *Celano*, and that it was painted not later than 1243. Frugoni sees the Bardi panel, indeed, as a manifesto for the *zelanti*, the close companions of Francis who shared his dismay at the decline of the order from its first ideals.[53]

It seems to me that these recent opinions on the Bardi dossal are mistaken, and that the older view is correct. In the individual scenes depicted and in the overall emphasis of the panel the painter, or at any rate the deviser of the panel's programme, can be shown to have drawn heavily though not exclusively on the *Legenda maior*. It is also apparent that the painter used but significantly modified the inherited pictorial canon which we have considered in the Pescia, Assisi and other panels. Furthermore, no treatment of the panel to date seems to me to have come to terms satisfactorily with the overall programme of the dossal, which can be largely if not completely reconstructed. When we make the attempt to do so, we find in the Bardi dossal evidence of an independent and imaginative handling of both Bonaventure's and Celano's texts, and perhaps of others not now known to us. The supposed party polarities derived from an anachronistic projection on to the mid-thirteenth century Order of the hardened divisions of the early fourteenth are nowhere in evidence in the dossal. Instead, like Bonaventure's text, the panel represents an attempt to present a balanced and comprehensive picture of the saint which all Franciscans could relate to and accept. Its organisation of the story of Francis as found in Bonaventure's *Legenda* has at least as much in common as in contrast with the more elaborate cycle of frescoes in the Upper Church at Assisi. And the dossal is a salutary reminder that the presentation of a religious message in pictorial terms may be an independent theological exercise, and is by no means always the simple translation of text or texts into pictures.

We may begin by considering the central figure of St Francis. He stands, as

[51] Moorman, 'Early Franciscan Art and Literature', pp. 350–1; Goffen, *Spirituality in Conflict*, pp. 7, 29–30 and 59. This is the dating favoured by Scarpellini also, 'Iconografia Francescana', pp. 97–8 and 117, and by H. W. Van Os, 'St Francis of Assisi as a second Christ in Early Italian Painting', *Simiolus* 7 (1974), 115–32 (p. 117, note 9).

[52] R. C. Trexler, *Naked Before the Father: The Renunciation of Francis of Assisi*, Humana Civitas 9, Center for Medieval and Renaissance Studies (Los Angeles, 1989) p . 74.

[53] Frugoni, *Stimmate*, pp. 357–98. This paper was written before I had seen Frugoni's book, and I have not here attempted to address all the issues she raises. But if the case for a late date for the Bardi panel set out in what follows is sound, then her overall reading of the panel becomes untenable.

in all the other panels we have considered, facing us and portrayed at full length. In his right hand, as in the other gabled panels from Pescia, Pisa, and Pistoia, is a closed and clasped book: in the rectangular panels in Assisi and the Vatican the book is open. His right hand, however, is raised in a unique gesture derived from Byzantine paintings of *Christos Pantocrator*, with his thumb, index and forefinger raised in blessing, and the fourth and little fingers crooked. This Christ-like gesture is found in no other surviving thirteenth-century panel-painting of any other saint, though in the icon of the miracle of the canon of Potenza, depicted in the panel-painting of Francis and his miracles now at Orte, Francis raises his right hand in the same gesture.[54] His hands and feet are stigmatised, and his left foot points downwards to display the wound, in the process emerging from the pictorial space in which the saint stands and impinging on the border which surrounds the scene below. Inevitably, that scene portrays the bestowal of the stigmata on La Verna. In the borders round the saint seventeen small half-figures of Franciscan friars venerate him, raising their hands in a gesture which invites the spectator to attend to the central figure. The dossal has been slightly trimmed at some time in the past, and there were probably more than seventeen of these roundels originally, so no particular significance can be attached to the number. In the gable above the saint's head two angels flank a scroll which hangs from the hand of God, appearing out of an aureole symbolising the heavens. On the scroll are written the words, 'Hunc exaudite perhibentem dogmata vite' ('listen to this man, showing forth the teaching of life').

There can be little doubt that this central image presents us with an enormously high doctrine about Francis as *Alter Christus*, a second Christ. Chiara Frugoni has commented perceptively on the prophetic and evangelistic overtones of the phrase 'dogmata vite', but the Bardi presentation of Francis goes well beyond suggesting that the saint is a 'new evangelist'.[55] The scroll above his head held in the hand of God immediately recalls the voice from heaven at Christ's baptism, 'This is my beloved Son, in whom I am well pleased, listen to him'. Here we touch one of the most important themes in thirteenth-century Franciscan reflection on the meaning of Francis's life. His identification with Christ, central to the Joachite and other millenarian ideas which were so potent within the Order and which had undone John of Parma,[56] was of course implicit in the miracle of the Stigmata. It may have been implicit in the very development of the gabled dossal in which the central figure was surrounded by scenes from his life and miracles, for it seems likely that these were developed from the storiated Romanesque crucifixes on which the figure of Christ is flanked by scenes from the Passion, common in twelfth- and

---

54 As can be seen from the detail illustrated in Scarpellini, *Storia e Arte*, p. 120; also in Frugoni, *Stimmate*, plates 178–80. For the miracle of the Canon of Potenza see above, note 13.

55 Frugoni, *Stimmate*, p. 358.

56 Moorman, *History*, pp. 112–16, 145–6 and 258–9.

thirteenth-century Tuscan churches: both the Bardi dossal and the gabled dossal of Francis's life and miracles now at Pistoia have been attributed to the painter of one such historiated crucifix now in the Uffizi.[57] The parallelism was being given tentative pictorial expression by about 1260 in crucifixes which associated the stigmatised Francis with the wounds in the feet of Christ, and in the frescoes of the lower church at Assisi, where the Master of St Francis paired five scenes from the life of Francis with five from the passion of Christ. This pictorial pairing received its most elaborate and successful expression in the mid fourteenth-century series, painted by Taddeo Gaddi for the sacristy at Santa Croce and now in the Accademia in Florence, matching thirteen scenes from the life of Christ to thirteen episodes in the story of Francis.[58] The implications of such an association were already being explored in Celano's *Vita prima*,[59] were eagerly drawn out by countless Franciscan commentators, and would achieve an extraordinary apotheosis in Bartholomew of Pisa's immense treatise *De conformitate vitae Beati Francisci ad vitam Domini Iesu* of 1388, which scoured every surviving source for the life of Francis to elaborate comparisons with Christ.[60] But the presentation of Francis as *Alter Christus* is also one of the governing preoccupations of Bonaventure in the *Legenda maior*. From the very first words of his prologue, Bonaventure adapts the Christological language of the New Testament to present Francis as the morning star, the light which 'in these last days' has dawned on the human race, to enlighten those in darkness and the shadow of death. In his own body he bears the marks of a new covenant, and he is the scroll of Ezekiel and the Apocalypse, written within and without, inwardly and outwardly conformed to Christ, his body written on by the hand of God himself. Like Ezekiel's 'man clothed in linen' he is called to 'summon all men to mourn and lament, to shave their heads and wear sackcloth', and to 'mark the brows of those who weep and wail with a cross'. This cross is 'his own habit which was shaped like a cross', but it is also the stigmata, 'the seal of truth itself'. Francis hangs 'body and soul, upon the Cross with Christ'. Because of the seal of the stigmata, Francis's words and example 'must be regarded by everyone as

---

57 A. Smart, *The Dawn of Italian Painting 1250–1400* (Oxford, 1978), pp. 7–9; R. Oertel, *Early Italian Painting to 1400* (London, 1968), p. 39; Sinibaldi and Brunetti, *Mostra Giottesca*, nos 7, 13, 14, 20, 49, 50, 57 and 59. The storiated Crucifix no. 434 in the Uffizi is usually attributed to the painter of the Bardi Dossal: see Sinibaldi and Brunetti, *Mostra Giottesca*, no. 6, p. 22, and E. T. de Wald, *Italian Painting 1200–1600* (New York, 1978), pp. 53–4. But for a contrary view, see E. T. Prehn, *A Thirteenth-Century Crucifix in the Uffizi and the 'Maestro del San Francesco, Bardi'* (Edinburgh, 1958). For the attribution of the Pistoia panel to the painter of Uffizi 434, see Scarpellini, 'Iconografia Francescana', p. 117.

58 L. Marcucci, *I Dipinti Toscani sel secolo XIV* (Rome, 1965), pp. 56–62; A. Lodis, *Taddeo Gaddi: Critical Reappraisal and Catalogue Raisonné* (New York and London, 1982), pp. 114–26. For crucifixes with a figure of St Francis, see Sinibaldi and Brunetti, *Mostra Giottesca*, nos. 42, 43, 44, 46 and 48.

59 *I Celano* 114–15, in *Omnibus*, pp. 327–9.

60 Edited in *AF*, vols. 4 (1906) and 5 (1912).

genuine and sound beyond all cavil. . . . God's witness in [Francis's] favour is beyond all doubt'.[61] Here then in Bonaventure's pages is the stigmatised Francis we find also in the Bardi dossal, one pierced hand raised to bless, like the Christ to whom he has been conformed, the other holding a book representing 'the teaching of life' guaranteed by 'the seal of truth' on the hand that holds it.

When we turn from the central figure to the twenty scenes from Francis's life and miracles which surround him, we at once become aware that, unlike any of the other panels we have been considering, here something approaching a narrative sequence is in evidence. 'Narrative sequence' is perhaps a misleading phrase: the first four scenes do follow a clear narrative line, taken directly from Bonaventure, but the panel as a whole is in fact divided up into five sets of four scenes, thematically rather than chronologically arranged. The fivefold arrangement is almost certainly another reference to Francis's stigmata, a re-emphasis of the *Alter Christus* theme of the central figure. The themes of the five groups are, in order: **(A)** renunciation of the world and of property **(B)** mission to preach **(C)** passion **(D)** Francis's loving care for his own and **(E)** canonisation and cult.[62] Failure to note the existence of these five clusters has led to a misreading of the 'message' of the panel, and has contributed to the mistaken impression that it relies exclusively on Celano and was therefore painted before the composition of Bonaventure's *Legenda maiora*.

(A) The first cluster of four scenes deal with Francis's renunciation of secular life, his abandonment of family and property, and his embracing of apostolic poverty. The four scenes are all drawn directly from chapters two and three of the *Legenda maior*, and are set out in the order and with the detail found there, which differ widely from those in Celano. In the first scene Francis, having been locked up by his father for using his money to repair churches and for the poor, is released by his mother, to the fury of the father

---

61 *Legenda maior*, prologue, xiii.1–9 and xiv.1, in *Omnibus*, pp. 631–2 and 729–37; Fleming, *Bonaventure to Bellini*, pp. 133–42; van Os, 'St Francis as Second Christ', pp. 115–32; da Campagnola, *L'Angelo*.
62 See Plate 3. I suggest the following listing:
  (A) Renunciation: A1 Francis released by Pica, leaves home A2 Francis renounces his father A3 Francis takes the habit A4 Francis embraces apostolic poverty during Mass at the Portiuncula.
  (B) Mission: B5 Francis commissioned to preach by Innocent III B6 Francis preaches at Greccio B7 Preaching to the birds B8 Preaching to the Muslims.
  (C) The Passion of St Francis: C9 The sheep among the goats C10 The ransom of the lamb C11 Francis mocked at the pillar C12 The gift of the stigmata.
  (D) The Compassion of St Francis: D13 The Chapter of Arles D14 St Francis and the Lepers D15 The deathbed of St Francis D16 St Francis heals the cripples and the possessed.
  (E) The Cult of St Francis: E17 The canonization of St Francis E18 St Francis invoked by sailors in a storm E19 The sailors fulfil their vow at the shrine E20 The healing of Bartholomew of Narni.

A 1

A 2

A 3

A 4

B 5

B 6

B 7

B 8

E20

E19

E18

E17

D16

D15

D14

D13

| C 9 | C12 |
| C10 | C11 |

Plate 3: Anonymous, *St Francis with Twenty Scenes from his Life and Miracles* (post 1263); Capella Bardi, Santa Croce, Florence

when he returns home. In the picture Francis is being released from his bonds
by Pica, his mother, while on the left of the picture Pietro Bernardone is seen
returning and remonstrating with his wife. In both Celano and Bonaventure
this scene marks Francis's decisive break with the past. Having earlier tempo-
rised and hidden from his father, he now fearlessly declares his willingness to
suffer for Christ's sake.[63]

Scene 2 is Francis's dramatic renunciation of his father and his father's
property before the bishop of Assisi. Francis, dressed only in his drawers,
casts his clothing in a gesture of dismissal before his father's feet, while the
seated bishop folds his mantle around Francis to conceal his nakedness. Francis and his parents stand at opposite ends of the picture separated by the
background building, and this stark spatial separation seems to establish the
paradigm which is such a striking feature of the Assisi fresco of this scene.
However, the painter in all four scenes in this first grouping seems fond of
placing his key figures at the margins of his space, so we should not perhaps
make too much of the positioning here. Unusually, in the light of the subsequent development of the iconography of the scene, Pica is portrayed standing with her husband. This may represent a simple continuity with the
preceding scene, or an underlining of the theme of the renunciation of home
and the abandonment of father and mother which the Gospel calls for and the
Franciscan Rule reiterated.[64] But the scene may also be designed to recall the
viewer to the finding of Christ in the Temple (Luke 2. 48–9), where the Mother
asks Jesus, 'Son, why hast thou done so to us? Behold, thy father and I have
sought thee sorrowing', and where Jesus' reply, 'Did you not know that I must
be about my father's business?', recalls Francis's words to Pietro Bernardone,
'Until now I have called you father, but from now on I can say without
reserve, "Our father who art in heaven".' [65]

The third scene depicts Francis's creation of the habit, and has puzzled
some commentators. He stands before the bishop, a wand in his hand tracing
a line on the habit which is spread out, cross-wise, between them. At first sight
the scene matches perfectly neither Celano's nor Bonaventure's text. In
Celano Francis is said to 'design for himself a tunic that bore a likeness to a
cross', as in the picture, but there is no connection with the bishop, and the
incident takes place after, not before, the Mass at the Portiuncula, the subject
of the next scene. In Bonaventure's account, however, the incident follows
directly upon Francis's renunciation of his father, as it does here. Having
stripped himself of his clothes, Francis needs covering. The bishop, who has
sheltered him in his mantle, tells his servants to bring something for Francis to
wear, and he is given 'an old tunic which belonged to one of the bishop's
farmhands'. Francis gratefully accepts it 'and drew a cross on it with his own

[63] The first four scenes are all found within a few paragraphs of each other in
     Bonaventure, *Legenda maior* ii.3 – iii.1, in *Omnibus*, pp. 642–6.
[64] See the Rule of 1221, in *Omnibus*, p. 31.
[65] *Legenda maior* ii.4, in *Omnibus*, pp. 642–3.

hand with a piece of chalk making it a worthy garment for a man who was crucified and a beggar'.[66] The arrangement of the tunic in the shape of a cross in the picture has led some commentators to insist nevertheless that it is Celano's account, not Bonaventure's, which is here portrayed: but this is to ignore the presence of the bishop, explicable only if this scene is, as in Bonaventure, a continuation of the previous one, and Francis is still before the bishop. It also fails to account for the rod in Francis's hand, with which he is 'marking' the tunic, and it fails to explain why the painter should use Celano's text (while inserting circumstances found only in Bonaventure) and yet rearrange the four scenes in the order in which Bonaventure gives them, and not that of Celano. And in any case, it is not true that only Celano describes the tunic as shaped like a cross. In his prologue Bonaventure too talks of Francis's 'signing [his followers] with the cross of penance *and clothing them in his own habit which was shaped like a cross'*. Those who reject the painter's dependence on Bonaventure at this point are forced to argue that, while following Celano, the painter 'telescopes, reorders and indeed reinvents events for the sake of visual clarity'. In fact, we need suppose nothing of the sort. Every element in this and the other pictures in this first block, including their placing in the sequence, can be accounted for from Bonaventure's text, and only from there. This is Bonaventure's Francis, not Celano's.[67]

The fourth and final scene in this section on renunciation depicts the Mass at the Portiuncula chapel, where in February 1209 Francis heard the priest read the gospel for the day, in which the disciples are told that they should provide neither 'gold nor silver to fill their purses, that they were not to have a wallet nor a second coat, no shoes or staff'. This passage from the Gospels became for Francis the basis of his new way of life and one of the foundation-stones of the Rule. In the picture the priest stands at the altar, holding an open book which is on his left side. To his right stand the sub-deacon and other ministers, to his left the congregation, whom he appears to be addressing. Francis kneels to tear off his shoes in obedience. On the open pages of the book can be read the sentence 'Sequentia sancti evangelii secundum Lucam' ('The continuation of the holy gospel according to Luke'), which means that the painter thought the gospel passage which Francis heard was Luke 9. 1–6. On this, Professor Goffen comments that 'Celano's audience would have understood . . . that the text that inspired Francis was Luke 9. 1–5: the Master of the Bardi Dossal makes this explicit'. In fact Luke's version of this saying of Jesus cannot have been the one Francis heard, for Luke not only omits mention of a staff, but even of shoes, thereby depriving the whole incident of its central dramatic moment. The passage Francis heard must have been Matthew 10. 5–15, read as the Gospel for the day on the feast of St Matthias (24

---

[66] *I Celano* 22, in *Omnibus*, p. 247; *Legenda maior* ii.4, in *Omnibus*, p. 643.
[67] Goffen, *Spirituality in Conflict*, pp. 34–6; Stein, 'Dating the Bardi Dossal', p. 278.

February). And Bonaventure explicitly tells us that it was 'the feast of one of the Apostles'.[68]

Why did the painter insert this mistaken reference to Luke's gospel? I think the attribution to Luke is just a gaffe, for it is compatible with none of the surviving accounts of the incident, but the sentence is nevertheless crucial for identifying *which* account of the incident the painter is drawing on. The words serve to identify not so much which gospel is being read, but the precise point in the service at which it is being read. The reading of the gospel at low mass began with the placing of the book on the priest's left hand, his signing the book crosswise with his thumb, and his announcing 'Sequentia sancti evangelii secundum . . .'. It is these preparatory words which the painter has deliberately copied. So what we see in the picture is this precise moment of the beginning of the reading of the gospel, while Mass is in progress. And this makes it quite certain that it is Bonaventure's version of the story which is depicted. In Celano's account, Francis hears the gospel read, is uncertain of its meaning, and seeks the priest out after Mass is over, for a further explanation. Only then does he take off his shoes and set out on the path of total renunciation. In Bonaventure's version, by contrast, the story is simplified: there is no conversation with the priest after Mass, and Francis reacts joyfully and spontaneously to the passage as it is read in its normal place in the service.[69] And this is what we see in the picture.

(B) After renunciation, mission. Scene 5 inaugurates a new set of four incidents which pick up the message of the scroll above Francis's head by focussing on his preaching of the 'doctrine of life'. This scene is normally called the 'Approbation of the Rule', and so it appears to be, for it portrays Francis kneeling before Innocent III, who raises his right hand in blessing and with his left hands Francis a closed and clasped book, like the one he carries in the central panel. But although the scene depicting the approbation of the rule on the restored Pistoia panel also shows the Pope handing over a book, this is not a very likely representation of what actually happened. The Primitive Rule of 1209 was very brief, and would have been written on a single scroll. This is how it is depicted in the Assisi fresco of the scene, and it seems clear that here on the Bardi dossal this book stands for more than the Rule. It recurs in each of the following three scenes, and from it Francis will be seen singing the Gospel and preaching. It is in fact a gospel book, the 'doctrine of life'. This fits exactly with Bonaventure's account of the scene (which concludes the chapter which opens with the Mass at the Portiuncula, in the previous scene) in which Innocent says 'By his work and teaching, [this man] will uphold Christ's Church.' He then approved the rule, 'and gave them a mission to preach repentance, conferring the clerical tonsure on the laymen among Fran-

---

68 *Omnibus*, p. 646.
69 *I Celano* 22, *Omnibus*, pp. 246–7; *Legenda maior* iii.1, in *Omnibus*, p. 646.

cis's companions, so that they could preach the word of God without interference'.[70]

The next three scenes show Francis and his brethren carrying out that commission to 'preach the word of God without interference'. Scene six depicts the incident of the Crib at Greccio, when Francis constructed a crib scene with a doll to represent the bambino, and with a live ox and ass, in the hill village of Greccio: 'Mass was sung there and Francis, who was a deacon, sang the gospel. Then he preached to the people about the birth of the poor king, whom he called the babe of Bethlehem in his tender love.' Both Celano and Bonaventure add the story of how a knight of Greccio saw the babe in the manger come to life when Francis took it in his arms, and it is this aspect of the scene which is portrayed in the corresponding fresco in the upper Church at Assisi. Here, however, the painter keeps the spectator's attention on the theme of the four connected scenes to which this picture belongs. The priest stands at the altar with the book in the gospel position: Francis, vested as deacon, incenses the gospel book on the lectern, marking the moment in the Mass when, as deacon, he sings the gospel and then preaches on it.[71]

The crib at Greccio illustrates Francis's distinctive, affective, proclamation of the gospel of the humanity of God to the Christian people. Scenes 7 and 8 show him reaching out beyond Christendom to preach to the brute creation, and to the infidel, represented here by the Sultan. Once more the gospel book is well to the fore. The fact that in the scene of preaching before the Sultan the artist does not depict the 'trial by fire', painted both by Giotto in the Bardi Chapel and by the Assisi master in the upper Church there when they handled this incident, has been used to support the view that it is Celano's not Bonaventure's version which is being used, since only Bonaventure mentions it. This, however, is to miss the point of this series of scenes on preaching, for to depict the 'trial by fire' would be to suggest, as painters from the Assisi frescoes onwards would do, that the message of the scene was Francis's superiority to Muslim holy men. This would hinder the impact of the painter's real message, just as the miracle of the bambino would have done in the Greccio scene. As Professor Vincent Moleta, one of the most theologically sensitive commentators on the Bardi panel, has written,

> There is no place here for the trial by fire. This scene is a proof of Francis's preaching powers, his 'doctrine of life', as effective as at home, and the rows of Moslems face him spellbound like the birds in the scene above.[72]

---

[70] *Legenda maior* iii.10, in *Omnibus*, p. 653.

[71] *Legenda maior* x.7, in *Omnibus*, p. 711.

[72] V. Moleta, *From St Francis to Giotto: The Influence of St Francis on Early Italian Art and Literature* (Chicago, 1983), p. 22. For the two incidents, see *Legenda maior* xii.3 and ix.7–8, in *Omnibus*, pp. 723 and 702–3.

(C) The next four scenes form a solid block, on which the central figure of the saint stands, and to which his wounded foot points. The clear grouping of the first eight scenes into two clusters of four, each with their own theme, renunciation and preaching, naturally leads us to expect a common theme in this strategically placed block of four pictures, but at first sight that theme is elusive. Scenes 9 and 10 depict two rather odd incidents in which Francis rescues sheep or lambs from slaughter, scene 11 depicts an occasion at Assisi when Francis, having eaten some chicken during an illness, has himself denounced as a glutton and dragged naked through the streets of the town, and scene 12, the scene touched by the stigmatised foot of the central figure, depicts the vision of the Seraph and the giving of the stigmata on La Verna.

The two scenes in which the saint rescues sheep have not brought out the best in commentators: Professor Goffen suggests that they depict 'another theme of the Sermon to the Birds, namely, the saint's compassion not only towards men in need, but even towards animals'.[73] But this seems a bit feeble – St Francis as patron of bunny-rabbits and the children's corner – and would separate these scenes from the Assisi penance and the stigmatisation scene, which are clearly not about being compassionate to animals or human beings. It would also mean that these scenes relate to nothing else we have so far encountered on the panel, for the preaching to the birds is, as we have seen, about preaching, rather than about birds.

It is the stigmatisation which provides us with the key to the theme of the cluster as a whole, which, as we should expect in the scenes gathered underneath the central figure of the saint, is that of *Alter Christus*: these scenes represent the passion of St Francis. Neither of the scenes with sheep occur in St Bonaventure, and they are found only in Celano. Since, as we have seen, the painter routinely follows Bonaventure's text, this reversion to the earlier life demands particular explanation. Bonaventure provides it. In chapter eight of the *Legenda maior* he tells us that Francis 'reserved his most tender compassion for those creatures which are a natural reflection of Christ's gentleness and are used in sacred Scripture as figures of him. He often rescued lambs, which were being led off to be slaughtered, in memory of the Lamb of God who willed to be put to death to save sinners.' [74] The painter has followed up this clue, and in these four scenes explores a theme deeply embedded in Franciscan reflection on the saint's role as *Alter Christus*. Celano's reflections on the stigmata in the *Vita prima* explicitly link the wounds with the typology of the Lamb: 'O miracle worthy of everlasting memory, and memorable sacrament worthy of unceasing reverence, which represents to the eyes of faith that

---

73 Goffen, *Spirituality in Conflict*, p. 40.
74 *Legenda maior* viii.6, in *Omnibus*, p. 692. Bonaventure is using *I Celano* 77–9 here, but, unlike Celano, emphasises the significance of the atoning *death* of the Lamb. Celano simply emphasises the simplicity and humility of the lamb, 'because in the sacred scriptures the humility of our Lord Jesus Christ is . . . frequently likened to that of a lamb'.

mystery in which the blood of the lamb without blemish flowed from five outlets to wash away the sins of the world'.[75] As we have seen, the painter normally draws on Bonaventure for the details of his scenes, but he finds richer material for this particular theme in Celano, though, as we shall see, even here he does not hesitate to modify the details he finds in Celano to include material and emphases taken from Bonaventure. It is worth noting, and strengthens the argument for the use of the *Legenda maior* at this point, that in Bonaventure's account of the previous scene, the preaching before the Sultan, and in this alone, Francis and his companion set out 'like two lambs' for the Muslim camp, and are arrested by troops who fall on them like 'wolves upon sheep', phrases which provide a natural link to the next two scenes in which sheep and lambs feature, and which may have influenced the organisa-tion of the scenes by the painter or his adviser.[76]

Scene 9 depicts the story of the sheep among the goats. One day, while travelling in the hill region of Ancona, Francis encountered a goatherd with a flock of goats. In their midst was 'one little lamb going along and feeding humbly and quietly. The saint was deeply disturbed, and said to the friar with him, "Do you not see this sheep that walks so meekly among the goats? I tell you that our Lord Jesus Christ walked in the same way meekly and humbly among the pharisees and chief priests. Therefore I ask you, my son, for love of him, to have pity with me on this little sheep. Let us pay the price and lead her away from among these goats".' In Celano this story has an elaborate sequel in which the lamb is given to some nuns who send Francis a tunic made from its wool, but the painter is interested only in the moment of ransom. He has however significantly modified the details of the story. In the foreground of the picture there are pigs, which are nowhere mentioned in Celano's version of the incident.

This is not just rustic whimsy, for these pigs have wandered in from the pages of the *Legenda maior*. In the passage in which he deals with the symbol-ism of sheep for Francis, Bonaventure tells the story of a new-born lamb devoured by a pig at the monastery of San Verecondo near Gubbio, where Francis was staying, and the saint's lament for it, as he 'remembered the immaculate Lamb of God' and cried 'Brother lamb, innocent creature, you represent Christ in the eyes of men. A curse on the wicked beast which killed you.' The sow dies, and not even the dogs will eat it.[77] This story was first recorded by one of Francis's companions in the mid-1240s, copied into Celano's *Vita secunda*, and from there absorbed into Bonaventure's *Legenda maior*.[78] In this process of transmission it is fascinatingly theologised. In its earliest version Francis's companion tells it straightforwardly as an example of the saint's love for gentle creatures, and of the great power of his curse. The

[75] *I Celano* 114, in *Omnibus*, p. 327.
[76] *Omnibus*, p. 703.
[77] *I Celano* 77–8, in *Omnibus*, pp. 293–4; *Legenda maior* viii.6, in *Omnibus*, pp. 692–3.
[78] Brooke, *Scripta Leonis*, p. 301: 2 *Celano* 111, in *Omnibus*, p. 454.

lamb is not linked to Christ, Francis saying only that 'My brother the lamb is an innocent animal and extremely useful to mankind . . . always bleating and announcing good news'. Celano retains the reference to the lamb's usefulness, omits the fanciful reference to the bleating, but prefaces his account of Francis's words with the phrase 'Agni cuiusdam alterius recordatus' ('thinking of another Lamb').[79] It is on this hint from Celano that Bonaventure builds his interpretation of the incident, putting into Francis's mouth a more elaborate form of words making explicit the connection with the Lamb of God. The painter, in placing the pigs in the foreground, therefore, emphasises the typological meaning of the ransom scene, and its reference to the slaughter of Christ, the Lamb of God, in a way which strongly suggests that he has approached the material from Celano's *Vita secunda* through the more fully developed account in the *Legenda maiora*, and that he shared Bonaventure's more insistent theological preoccupations.

Scene 10 extends this Passion typology, in the story of how Francis used a cloak he had been loaned to ransom two lambs being carried to slaughter. He restores the lambs to the owner from whom he has bought them, with the instruction to do them no harm, but to keep and feed them. The parallel with the risen Christ's command to Peter to 'feed my lambs, feed my sheep' would certainly have struck the medieval audience of this story. It may or not may be significant that the cloak in the picture has no sleeves, and so is a single seamless robe.[80]

Scene 11 depicts the story, found in varying forms in *I Celano*, in the writings of brother Leo and in Bonaventure, of Francis's penance in the streets of Assisi for eating chicken when he was ill. But the painter is unmistakably using Bonaventure's version of the story, which differs in several important respects from either of the earlier versions. In Celano, Francis has himself dragged through the streets and denounced for gluttony to the citizens: he himself says nothing and there is no mention of any stripping. The account compiled by Francis's companions in the 1240s is far more circumstantial. The friar ordered to humiliate Francis is named as Peter Catanii, the first Minister General appointed by Francis, and the whole episode is set in the context of a sermon to which the entire population of Assisi is summoned. Francis has himself stripped of his habit before being dragged to the preaching-place, and he himself preaches the sermon denouncing his own gluttony.[81] Bonaventure's version is far closer to the account of the companions of Francis than it is to Celano's, but is both more and less detailed than their version. Bonaventure omits some circumstantial detail, such as Peter Catanii's name and rank, but significantly expands the incident in ways which are directly reflected in the Bardi panel. According to Bonaventure, Francis does not simply go to the

79 'Legendae S. Francisci', p. 196.
80 *I Celano* 79, in *Omnibus*, p. 295.
81 *I Celano* 52, in *Omnibus*, pp. 272–3; Brooke, *Scripta Leonis*, pp. 156–9, in *Omnibus*, pp. 1016–18.

'place where he preached', but to the stone in the square at Assisi 'where malefactors are punished', and there he denounces his own hypocrisy. It is this ritual of humiliation, where Francis is stripped like a malefactor and bound at the place of public punishment, which the Bardi dossal presents to us. Francis is depicted stripped, with his habit prominently in front of him. He is tied to a pillar, the 'stone where criminals are punished', and he is clearly addressing the spectators. In contrast to the four scenes on either side, no other member of the order is depicted. Quite clearly the painter here is dependent neither on the account in *I Celano* nor on that compiled by Francis's companions. It is Bonaventure's heavily typological version of the story, in which Francis, like Christ, is numbered among the malefactors in the place of public punishment, which he paints. And the point of the story is clear enough. Francis here reenacts the mocking of Christ and the scourging at the pillar. Like Christ, he is counted among the thieves, a sheep led out to slaughter.[82] Scene 12 completes this short passion sequence with the stigmatisation scene itself, in which Francis is decisively identified with Christ, and is marked as *Alter Christus* with 'the seals of truth'.[83]

(D) The next four scenes are harder to categorise, and the programme harder to discern. Scenes 13 and 14 deal with Francis's solicitude for the poor, both the members of his own order, and the most underprivileged members of society, the lepers. The miracle of his appearance in a vision at the Chapter of Arles, which he was unable to attend physically, demonstrated according to Bonaventure Francis's 'anxious care for his subjects'. Francis here is portrayed in a roundel, one hand raised in blessing. The fact that he is not portrayed as Bonaventure describes him, and as he is depicted by Giotto in the Bardi Chapel frescoes, 'with his arms stretched out in the form of a cross', has been taken to indicate the dossal painter's dependence at this point on Celano, rather than Bonaventure. It is hard to see why this should be thought to be so, since in fact Celano is just as clear as Bonaventure that Francis appeared 'raised up into the air, his arms extended as though upon a cross'. The point is not that the painter does not know of this detail, but that, as in the case of the trial by fire before the Sultan, he chooses not to depict it. Once again the painter focusses singlemindedly on making one point, Francis's Christ-like care for 'those who were his own in the world'. It is worth emphasising that it is only in Bonaventure's account that the dimension of care for the brethren is stressed: for Celano the miracle of Arles reveals rather that Francis knew the secrets of all hearts, even when absent.[84] Scene 14 portrays Francis's 'anxious care' for the poorest of all, the lepers, and the painter is unmistakably using Bonaventure's text at this point. There is nothing in Celano to correspond with the details of this picture, though of course Francis's love of the lepers is

---

82 *Legenda maior* vi.2, in *Omnibus*, p. 672.
83 *Legenda maior* xiii.1–3, in *Omnibus*, pp. 729–31.
84 Van Os, 'St Francis as Second Christ', p. 117, note 9; *I Celano* 48, in *Omnibus*, p. 270; *Legenda maior* iv.10 in *Omnibus*, p. 661.

often mentioned by him. Those who believe the painter does not know the
Legenda maior but relies on Celano are therefore obliged to surmise that the
painter 'seems to have invented the scene of the saint and the lepers . . . by
collating different events . . . '. But in fact there is no need for any such
invention, for Bonaventure tells us that Francis 'devoted himself to the lepers
and lived with them . . . he washed their feet and bound up their sores . . . He
was extraordinarily devoted to them and kissed their wounds.' [85] In the picture, accordingly, Francis, on the right, washes their feet, and on the left,
embraces a leper – a fair representation of the kissing of the wounds. The
foot-washing is particularly important here, for it is mentioned only in the
Legenda maior, and so helps to pinpoint the source: in addition, it offers, as we
shall see, an important clue to the meaning of this whole cluster of four
scenes.

Scenes 15 and 16 are composite pictures, in which the painter has unmistakably drawn from the existing canon of representations of the saint. Four
scenes – the death of the saint, the healing of the cripples, the girl with the
twisted neck and the possessed girl of Norcia, are all depicted in two frames.
The crippled suppliants kneel at the death-bed of the saint in scene 15, while
the girl of Norcia and the girl with the twisted neck share frame 16. It is the
linking of the healing of the cripples with the death-bed scene which gives us
our clue to the theme of these four scenes. Bonaventure tells us that as the
saint lay dying he asked to have the thirteenth chapter of St John's gospel read
to him: in the picture the friar at the saint's feet holds the open gospel book.
The thirteenth chapter of St John's Gospel tells how Jesus 'when he knew that
his hour had come to depart out of this world to the father, having loved his
own who were in the world, he loved them to the end': it goes on to describe
how Jesus washed the feet of his disciples at the Last Supper, and enjoined on
his followers the command to imitate his example of love. The picture of
Francis washing the feet of the lepers is unmistakeably modelled on Byzantine representations of the foot-washing at the Last Supper.[86] This evocation of
the Last Supper certainly goes back to Francis himself: one of our most reliable accounts of his death-bed tells us that he also enacted a 'para-liturgy' in
which he blessed and distributed bread to the brethren around him, and that
he told those around him that he thought it was Thursday, the day of the Last
Supper (though Francis actually died on a Saturday evening).[87]

This cluster of scenes therefore derives its theme from a Johannine understanding of the Last Supper as a manifestation of Christ's self-giving love for
his own. In all four scenes, even on his own death-bed, Francis reveals his love
for *his* own, to the end – the members of his order, the poor, sick and outcast
with whom he identified himself: signalling his identity with the Christ of the

[85] Goffen, *Spirituality in Conflict*, p. 43; Stein, 'Dating the Bardi Dossal', p. 289; *Legenda maior* xiv.5, in *Omnibus*, p. 740:
[86] Miller, 'Franciscan Legend in Italian Art', pp. 70–1.
[87] *Legenda* of Perugia 117, in *Omnibus*, pp. 1090–1.

Johannine Last Supper, he washes the leper's feet. The post-mortem miracles of scene 16 represent the continuation of this love beyond the grave, literally 'to the end', and make an appropriate prelude to the last group, in which the canonisation and cult of Francis are portrayed. It is worth noticing here that the painter, in combining these scenes, is clearly drawing on an existing iconography. The girl with the twisted neck and the demoniac scene occur in one form or another on all the early panels depicting the miracles of St Francis, and the uniting of these originally separate scenes was only possible because they had an established iconography and so were likely to be instantly recognisable to the spectator. The painter here is drawing not on Bonaventure, who does not give these miracles, and not necessarily on the texts in *I Celano* which describe the miracles, but directly on earlier pictures and what had clearly become an established iconographical tradition. The healing of the demoniac, it should be noted, is depicted not in its early form of a group of male demoniacs, but as the healing of the demoniac girl of Norcia, who first appears in a text in Celano's *Tractatus de miraculis*, and who, as we have already seen, is first incorporated into a modified canon of post-mortem miracles in panels like the Assisi Tesoro picture which everyone agrees date from the mid-1250s or later: this fact alone disposes of Trexler and Frugoni's suggestion of a very early date for the Bardi panel.

(E) The final cluster of four scenes deal with the canonisation and cult of Francis. None of them exactly matches anything in Bonaventure. The canonisation scene in picture 17 is compatible with the very brief account in the *Legenda maior*, but probably reflects the much more extensive account in Celano, just as the fresco of the canonisation in the Upper Church at Assisi does. The figure in a dalmatic holding a book facing the pope has been identified with Octavian, the pope's subdeacon who, according to Celano, read the list of Francis's miracles at the canonisation, but he appears to me to be a deacon with a gospel book, and there is nothing in the scene which a conventional representation of a papal mass might not include. Scenes 18 and 19, however, clearly move away from Bonaventure. In scene 18, Francis appears in a storm-tossed boat to a crowd of frightened sailors: in 19 the sailors appear, carrying candles and in penitential undress, at the saint's altar. These two scenes are usually called the rescue of the sailors of Ancona, but this identification is problematic. The story is told very briefly both by Celano (in the *Tractatus de miraculis*) and by Bonaventure. Sailors from Ancona are in danger of sinking in a storm: they invoke Francis, and a great light appears over the boat and the sea becomes calm. Celano, but not Bonaventure, adds that they subsequently gave a fine cloak as a votive offering, and 'to their rescuer offered countless acts of thanksgiving'. There is no mention in the story of an appearance of the saint himself, as in scene 18, and the penitential procession in scene 19, in which the leader seems to be handing over a candle, not a cloak, does not seem a very precise realisation of Celano's hint. I have found no sea-rescue story which exactly fits these pictures in any of the early sources. Bartholomew of Pisa, however, tells of a Venetian ship in danger of perishing: the sailors invoke St Francis 'with a vow to visit his shrine', and at once a Franciscan friar appears, carrying a candle which lights up the whole boat, and they complete their journey safely. Apart from the detail of the candle, this story fits all the details on the Bardi dossal, the vow of the visit *ad limina* providing a fuller cue for scene 19 than the problematic cloak in the Ancona story. Bartholomew is a late source, but he must have got his version of the incident from somewhere, and it is worth keeping an open mind as to whether the Bardi painter knew this story.[88]

The final scene is once again borrowed from the established iconography of the post-mortem miracles, and is an entirely conventional depiction of the miracle of the bath. The departing figure of Bartholomew of Narni with his crutches jauntily slung over his shoulder makes a fitting final image to this group of scenes which tell of the healing power of the canonised saint and, like the procession of mariners, would have reminded the spectator of the shrine with its abandoned crutches and other *ex votos*. No particular significance should be attached, I think, to the fact that the story of Bartholomew of Narni is not found in Bonaventure. This miracle is found on every one of the early panel-paintings we have been considering, and in visual terms is easily the most striking and memorable of the post-mortem miracles. As we have already seen, the Bardi painter was familiar with and quotes from the 'canon' of paintings of post-mortem miracles, as modified in the 1250s: he includes all four, and the retention of the miracle of the bath represents not a choice among texts, but adherence to an established pictorial canon.

The Bardi dossal, then, represents the culmination of the pictorial tradition which grew up in the years immediately following the canonisation of St Francis. To a far greater extent than any of the earlier panels it is a considered theological construct, and one can see the painter or his adviser making imaginative choices from the available repertoire of stories about Francis to present a sophisticated teaching about the saint and his order. The panel does not seem to me to be a manifesto for the *zelanti*, for Francis's early companions, or an incipient 'Spiritual' party. It is true that the themes of renunciation, love of the poor and the outcast, identification with Christ, are all prominent in the panel, but they are equally prominent in the panel's main source, the *Legenda maior* of Bonaventure, and any self-respecting Franciscan of whatever party would have understood them as fundamental to his or her vocation. The scenes of the ransom of the sheep in Celano's text do highlight the saint's dislike and distrust of money, but that dimension of the stories is not represented, as indeed it could not easily be represented, in the pictures.

---

88 *Legenda maior*, Book ii (*De miraculis*), iv.5, in *Omnibus*, p. 765; Celano, *Tractatus de miraculis*, in 'Legendae S. Francisci', p. 301; Bartholomew of Pisa, *De conformitate vitae Beati Francisci*, in *AF* 5 (1912), p. 482. Miller also suggests that this passage in Bartholomew of Pisa is a source for the picture, but appears to identify it with the sailors of Ancona; 'Franciscan Legend in Italian Painting', p. 74, note 63.

They are there to point to Francis's compassionate identification with the Lamb of God, an identification completed in the bestowal of the stigmata, to which, in the panel, they are the prelude. There is nothing here which a literally observant Franciscan would have found alien, but it is a mistake to force this panel into a speculative interpretative straightjacket which makes too much of the conflict within the order in the mid-thirteenth century. Chiara Frugoni, who sees Bonaventure as the chief villain in a conspiracy to suppress and tame the dangerous anarchy of the real Francis, believes that the Bardi dossal, and indeed all these early panels, preserve a 'primitive' witness to the real spirit of Francis which escaped the censorship that eclipsed all the lives written before the *Legenda maior*. She concludes her study of the Bardi dossal with the resounding claim that it contains 'the voice of the first companions of Francis, continuing to transmit its echo down to us: an image breaking the silence which Bonaventure tried ineffectually to impose'.[89]

On the contrary, I hope I have shown that the voice of Bonaventure himself, though not his alone, resonates from the Bardi panel. Like the *Legenda maior* itself, the dossal represents a rich and eclectic reading of Francis and his legend, drawing on the writings of Celano, Bonaventure and perhaps others, as well as on the pictorial tradition whose stereotyping is evident in the other panels we have examined, most of them conventionally dated around 1250–60. The Bardi dossal must be later than that, and later than the publication of Bonaventure's *Legenda* in 1263. It seems to me that the work of synthesis evident in the panel is the product of fairly sophisticated reflection, and so is unlikely to have been done while the ink was still wet on Bonaventure's pages. Just how much later than 1263 one places the panel, therefore, must depend on the extent to which one thinks Celano's writings were available and respectable after the decree of suppression of 1266. If one believes that the suppression of Celano's texts took immediate effect, and that after 1266 no Franciscan commision could have used texts other than Bonaventure, then the dossal would have to be dated between 1263 and 1266. It would be unwise, however, to rule out altogether a later date. The panel with four scenes from the life and miracles of Francis now at the cathedral of Orte, and datable fairly precisely to 1282, incorporates one incident which is found only in 2 *Celano*. The Assisi frescoes, while based on Bonaventure, likewise made use of other texts about Francis, including the writings of Celano and the early *Legenda trium sociorum*.[90] Assisi had the advantage of possessing file-copies of most of the suppressed writings, but elsewhere the memory of often-told stories about the saint will not have disappeared as soon as the texts which contained them were withdrawn from official circulation. The deviser of the programme of the Bardi picture may have drawn on memory, or on notes made at some earlier

---

89 Frugoni, *Stimmate*, p. 388.
90 The best edition of this 'Legend of the Three Companions' is by G. Abate in *Miscellanea Francescana*, 39 (1939), 375–432.

time. Nor does it seem to me to be inconceivable that a great Franciscan community like that at Santa Croce, with a strongly observant presence among the brethren, might have retained knowledge and perhaps an actual text of Celano's *Vitae* for some years after the official suppression. If one accepts that the picture was painted in Florence for veneration at Santa Croce, it is at least possible that it could have been painted in the early 1270s or even later.[91]

4. Scepticism and Defence: From the Bardi Dossal to the Assisi Frescoes

Scenes 15, 16 and 20 of the Bardi dossal incorporate or quote from the iconographic conventions of the earliest cult-pictures of Francis, but the panel as a whole embodies a richer and more sophisticated presentation of the saint than anything previously devised, in which the post-mortem miracles which dominated the earlier iconography play a comparatively minor role. The replacement of those miracles by other events from the life of the saint is a feature of the handful of surviving narrative pictures of the saint painted between the Bardi dossal and the fresco cycle at Assisi. The Orte cathedral panel has four scenes placed round a central figure of the saint who carries a closed book in his left hand, while extending the right hand in the open gesture of greeting found on the Pescia, Pisa and Pistoia panels. The stigmata are displayed. The four historical scenes consist of the preaching to the birds, the stigmatisation, the miracle of the wounding of the hand of the sceptical canon of Potenza, and an odd little miracle recounted only by Celano, in which Francis, pressed to eat chicken by his host while on a preaching trip, charitably accepts the meat but immediately gives it away to a poor man. Out of ill-will, however, the poor man publicly denounces Francis the next day as a hypocritical meat-eater. He produces the chicken to prove it, only to find it has been transformed into a piece of fish. Conversion and penitence follow.[92] None of the post-mortem miracles which had featured on all the earlier panels appear on the Orte altarpiece, which instead seems concerned to warn against scepticism about the saint's unique status. The stigmatisation and the preaching to the birds were, as we have seen, conventional emblems of Francis's sanctity and mission, while both the other scenes on the panel depict miracle-stories which tell of the punishment and conversion of men who cast doubt on Francis's holiness and privileges. The panel's overall scheme therefore perhaps suggests a

---

[91] Garrison dates the less sophisticated and less elaborate Pistoia dossal, which some commentators think to be by the same painter, to 1265–1275. See Garrison, *Italian Romanesque Panel Painting*, no. 409; also Scarpellini, 'Iconografia Francescana', p. 117.

[92] Scarpellini, 'Iconografia Francescana', pp. 120–1; 2 *Celano* 78–9, in *Omnibus*, pp. 427–9.

religious environment in which Franciscan claims were meeting with some resistance.

The gabled panel by a follower of Guido da Siena, formerly in the Franciscan church at Colle Val d'Elsa but now in the Siena Pinacoteca, probably reflects something of the same atmosphere of conflict. The painter draws on Bonaventure's *Legenda maior*, though all of the eight scenes depicted on it are also to be found in one or other of Celano's *Vitae*.[93] The central figure holds a cross and a closed book, and displays the wound in his side as well as the wounds in hands and feet. The scenes are arranged clockwise, starting in the bottom left-hand corner of the panel, and consist of the renunciation of family and possesions before the bishop of Assisi, the miracle of the Crucifix at San Damiano which told Francis to 'go and repair my church, which as you see is falling into ruins', the dream of Pope Innocent III, in which Francis supports the tottering structure of the Lateran basilica, the preaching to the birds, the chariot of fire in which the spirit of the absent Francis appeared to the sleeping brethren at Rivo-Torto, the stigmatisation, the crib at Greccio, and the funeral of Francis.

The principles of selection at work in this panel are not very obvious. All the scenes, apart from the first and last, are miraculous, and even the death-bed scene, in which a red-robed bishop bends to scrutinise the Stigmata, refers to the central miracle. The dream of Innocent III follows naturally from the miracle of the crucifix at San Damiano, for it drives home the point that the church which Francis is bidden by the crucifix to rebuild is not the ruined building at Assisi, but the 'Holy Roman Church' itself: to the private calling in the miracle of San Damiano is added the public endorsement of papal approval. There is another dimension to this grouping, however. In 1215 the Lateran Council had passed a decree forbidding the establishment of any new *religio* or order, and ruling that anyone seeking to enter religious life must enter one of the established orders. Both Francis and St Dominic were in Rome during the Council, and this decree represented a crisis for both of them, threatening the very existence of their new movements. The Dominicans were obliged to adopt the Augustinian rule, but Francis's position was different. He had already approached Innocent III for approval in 1210, and although the Order had not been formally established, the Pope had given his verbal blessing to their work, and promised further recognition in due course. Verbal promises are, notoriously, not worth the paper they are written on, but Innocent III stood by this endorsement, and announced to the Council that the Friars Minor were to be regarded as one of the established Orders.[94] Francis's encounter with Innocent III and the verbal approval of the primitive Rule then granted was therefore crucial for the very existence of the order: hence the

---

93 Discussed and illustrated as plate 61 in Stubblebine, *Guido da Siena*, pp. 107–9, and in P. Torriti, *La Pinacoteca Nazionale di Siena: i dipinti dal xii al xv secolo* (Genoa, 1977), no. 313, pp. 39–40.

94 Moorman, *History*, pp. 29–30.

appearance of the scene of the approval of the Rule on the Pistoia and Bardi dossals. The new scene of the dream of Innocent III was designed to emphasise that the Pope's approval was the result of heavenly inspiration. It was also designed to beat off Dominican encroachments, however, for by the later thirteenth-century Dominicans were claiming that the little poor man who sustained the Lateran basilica in the Pope's dream was not Francis, but Dominic, and round about the year 1267 the scene was carved on Dominic's tomb at Bologna.[95] The portrayal of the dream and the approbation scenes on the Siena panel, therefore, represents an emphatic reiteration of the Franciscan claim to uniquely privileged status as a movement raised up by God and recognised by God's Vicar on earth in response to divine inspiration. The scene of Francis's funeral may continue this theme of scepticism or rivalry rebutted, for the stooping figure of the bishop suggests the verification of the stigmata.

The other scenes on this panel cannot easily be pressed into a single overarching theme. As we have seen, the inclusion of the preaching to the birds and the stigmatisation was more or less mandatory. The chariot of fire at Rivo-Torto[96] illustrates Francis's loving care for his brethren even when absent, and so is perhaps a reference to the saint's patronage of his earthly clients, but it is also a reference to his role as a second Elijah, emphasised in Bonaventure's account of the incident. The placing of the scene of the crib at Greccio is a puzzle, since it occurs here out of order, after the stigmatisation. Its emphases, moreover, are quite different from those in the comparable scene in the Bardi dossal, for Francis here is portrayed not in his liturgical role as a deacon vested for mass and standing to sing the gospel, but, quite unhistorically, in Franciscan habit. He is kneeling to pick up the image of the Christ-child, a reference to the miracle in which the bambino comes to life in his hands. Like most of the other scenes, therefore, the emphasis appears to be on divine endorsement of the status and privileges of the saint and his order, and literal historical detail is sacrificed in the interests of bringing out this point. This theme is continued, as we have already noted, in the final scene of the death-bed of the saint and the attestation of the stigmata.

The Siena panel draws on the *Legenda maior*, but the painter was certainly not attempting a balanced summary of Bonaventure's presentation of Francis. Four of the eight scenes occur out of his narrative sequence, and the apparent emphasis on miraculous endorsement of the saint's status deprives the panel of the comprehensiveness of the Bardi dossal. Yet the Siena panel was in some ways as much an anticipation of the future of Franciscan iconography as the Santa Croce picture. All the scenes represented in it were to recur in the Assisi frescoes, and it parts company decisively with the choice of themes set by the cult-panels, dominated by a fixed canon of of post-mortem miracles, pro-

---

[95] Miller, 'Franciscan Legend', pp. 140–1.
[96] *Legenda maior* iv.4 and *I Celano* 47, in *Omnibus*, pp. 655–6 and 268–9.

duced before the composition of the *Legenda maior*. It has even been suggested that the altarpiece was painted after the completion of the Assisi frescoes, or at least with knowledge of the programme devised for the Upper Church there. On stylistic grounds alone this is unlikely: the iconographic conventions used in the scene at San Damiano, the preaching to the birds, the chariot at Rivo Torto, the stigmatisation, and the crib at Greccio are so markedly different from the corresponding pictures at Assisi that any dependence in either direction is extremely improbable. Instead, what the overlap of themes in these two cycles suggests is the emergence in Franciscan preaching and reflection of a new canon of 'central' stories and themes derived from Bonaventure's official account of the life of Francis. That canon would receive its definitive shaping in the Upper Church in Assisi: both the Bardi dossal and the Assisi frescoes, therefore, represent distinctive and very different readings of Bonaventure's account of Francis, which are very far from being merely illustrations of an establishmentarian text.[97] Both the dossal and the frescoes, like the earlier and less sophisticated altarpieces, are components of the cult of the saint, designed to be standing 'texts' for an unending stream of sermons preached on their subject-matter.

None of the pictures we have considered supports the notion of a 'primitive' phase of Franciscan history, overlaid later by miracle and churchliness, just as none simply 'translates' story into image. From the start, the painters of Francis's legend work within the framework of his cult, and portray him as miracle-worker before and after death. If anything, the Bardi dossal introduces for the first time a biographical interest absent from the primitive images, with their focus on the post-mortem miracles of the saint at his shrine, and the Bardi panel, by compressing three of the traditional post-mortem miracles into composite scenes marks a turning away from the earlier conventions and their constraints.

The advent of Bonaventure's *Legenda maior* broadened, not narrowed, the handling of the life of Francis: experiment, variety and range are a feature of the later pictorial tradition, not of its first programmatic expressions, tied as they were to a small fixed body of post-mortem miracles. And the sequences based on Bonaventure allow us to see the painters themselves as theologians. Each sequence of images represents a set of choices within and between texts, a new reading of a story which was, in any case, already textually complex.

97 The suggestion of the precedence of the Assisi pictures is by Stubblebine, *Guido da Siena*, pp. 21–3 and 107–9. The suggestion that the painter knew the Assisi programme but had never seen the frescoes is Miller's, 'Franciscan Legend', pp. 162–72. The likeliest date for the Siena panel is *c.*1280, a date supported both by the evident links of the picture with the circle of Guido da Siena, and the close stylistic similarities of the depiction of the stigmatisation in this panel and that on the Franciscan reliquary shutters displayed in the same room at the Siena Pinacoteca. See Marco Torriti, *Pinacoteca Nazionale di Siena* (Genoa, 1988), nos. 4 and 313; also Piero Torriti, *La Pinacoteca Nazionale di Siena* [cf. note 92 above], nos. 4 and 5, pp. 35–8.

The imposition in 1266 of a single text containing the authorised version of that story somewhat simplified the choices available to the deviser of these pictorial programmes, but only up to a point. No-one could or wanted to paint everything in Bonaventure, and to select was to rewrite. The Bardi dossal, painted after the *Legenda maior* had begun to circulate, blends Bonaventure's Francis with that of Celano, though the controlling theological ideas at work in the panel are all to be found in Bonaventure. Even the Assisi cycle, painted at least a generation after the withdrawal of Celano's and other early lives, draws on those sources, and in several cases patently 'reads' Bonaventure in the light of earlier versions of the same stories. The painters were thus the authors, and not merely the illustrators, of the stories they chose to retell.

Acknowledgement

I am grateful to Dr Rosalind Brooke for helpful comments on an earlier draft of part of this paper.

INDEX OF NAMES AND TITLES

The following index lists names and works of medieval writers and painters, and names only of post-medieval writers. Medieval names and titles of works have not been standardised to one language: Guillaume is found as well as William, *Epistolae* as well as *Letters*. The status of Saint (St) or Blessed (Bd) has been listed according to The Benedictines of Ramsgate, *Dix Mille Saints. Dictionnaire hagiographique*, French translation (Turnhout, 1991).